Jihadist Insurgent Movements

This path-breaking collection of papers examines the phenomenon of jihadist insurgent movements in the Middle East and North, East, and West Africa. It argues that military and strategic analysts have paid insufficient attention to the phenomenon of jihadism in insurgent movements, partly due to a failure to take the role of religion sufficiently seriously in the ideological mobilisation of recruits by guerrilla movements stretching back to the era of "national liberation" after World War Two. Several essays in the collection examine Al Qaeda and ISIL as military as well as political movements while others assess Boko Haram in West Africa, Al Shabaab in Somalia, and jihadist movements in Libya. Additionally, some authors discuss the recruitment of foreign fighters and the longer-term terrorist threat posed by the existence of jihadist movements to security and ethnic relations in Europe.

Overall, this volume fills an important niche between studies that look at Islamic fundamentalism and "global jihad" at the international level and micro studies that look at movements locally. It poses the question whether jihadist insurgencies are serious revolutionary threats to global political stability or whether, like Soviet Russia after its initial revolutionary phase of the 1920s, they can be ultimately contained by the global political order. The volume sees these movements as continuing to evolve dynamically over the next few years suggesting that, even if ISIL is defeated, the movement that brought it into being will still exist and very probably morph into new movements.

Jihadist Insurgent Movements was originally published as a special issue of *Small Wars & Insurgencies*.

Paul B. Rich is co-editor of *Small Wars & Insurgencies* and the author of several books and articles on insurgency, counter-insurgency, terrorism, and warlords. He has taught at the universities of Bristol, Warwick and Melbourne, and is currently completing a book entitled *Cinema and Unconventional War: Insurgency, Terrorism and Special Operations on Screen, 1930–2015*.

Richard Burchill is the Director of Research and Engagement for TRENDS: Research & Advisory. Previously he was with the Law School at the University of Hull, UK, where he was also Director of the McCoubrey Centre for International Law. He engages in teaching and consultancy work with international organisations and national governments.

Jihadist Insurgent Movements

Edited by
Paul B. Rich and Richard Burchill

LONDON AND NEW YORK

First published 2018
by Routledge
2 Park Square, Milton Park, Abingdon, Oxon, OX14 4RN, UK

and by Routledge
711 Third Avenue, New York, NY 10017, USA

Routledge is an imprint of the Taylor & Francis Group, an informa business

© 2018 Taylor & Francis

All rights reserved. No part of this book may be reprinted or reproduced or utilised in any form or by any electronic, mechanical, or other means, now known or hereafter invented, including photocopying and recording, or in any information storage or retrieval system, without permission in writing from the publishers.

Trademark notice: Product or corporate names may be trademarks or registered trademarks, and are used only for identification and explanation without intent to infringe.

British Library Cataloguing in Publication Data
A catalogue record for this book is available from the British Library

ISBN 13: 978-1-138-04036-6

Typeset in Myriad Pro
by RefineCatch Limited, Bungay, Suffolk

Publisher's Note
The publisher accepts responsibility for any inconsistencies that may have arisen during the conversion of this book from journal articles to book chapters, namely the possible inclusion of journal terminology.

Disclaimer
Every effort has been made to contact copyright holders for their permission to reprint material in this book. The publishers would be grateful to hear from any copyright holder who is not here acknowledged and will undertake to rectify any errors or omissions in future editions of this book.

Contents

Citation Information vii
Notes on Contributors ix

Preface 1
Ahmed Al-Hamli

Introduction 5
Paul B. Rich

1. The Islamic State and the Return of Revolutionary Warfare 15
   Craig Whiteside

2. How revolutionary are Jihadist insurgencies? The case of ISIL 49
   Paul B. Rich

3. Global Jihad and Foreign Fighters 72
   George Joffé

4. A Fratricidal Libya: Making Sense of a Conflict Complex 89
   Mikael Eriksson

5. Belgian and Dutch Jihadist Foreign Fighters (2012–2015): Characteristics, Motivations, and Roles in the War in Syria and Iraq 109
   Edwin Bakker and Roel de Bont

6. Who Goes, Why, and With What Effects: The Problem of Foreign Fighters from Europe 130
   Lasse Lindekilde, Preben Bertelsen and Michael Stohl

7. A Sectarian Jihad in Nigeria: The Case of Boko Haram 150
   Marc-Antoine Pérouse de Montclos

8. Operation Barkhane and Boko Haram: French Counterterrorism and Military Cooperation in the Sahel 168
   Christopher Griffin

9. Al Qaeda in the Islamic Maghreb: Terrorism, insurgency, or organized crime? 186
   Sergei Boeke

CONTENTS

10. Shapeshifter of Somalia: Evolution of the Political Territoriality of Al-Shabaab   209
    Bohumil Doboš

11. Jihadist insurgency and the prospects for peace and security   230
    Richard Burchill

    Afterword   240
    Paul B. Rich

    Index   249

Citation Information

The following chapters were originally published in *Small Wars & Insurgencies*, volume 27, issue 5 (2016). When citing this material, please use the original page numbering for each article, as follows:

Preface
Preface
Ahmed Al-Hamli
Small Wars & Insurgencies, volume 27, issue 5 (2016), pp. 729–732

Introduction
Introduction
Paul B. Rich
Small Wars & Insurgencies, volume 27, issue 5 (2016), pp. 733–742

Chapter 1
The Islamic State and the Return of Revolutionary Warfare
Craig Whiteside
Small Wars & Insurgencies, volume 27, issue 5 (2016), pp. 743–776

Chapter 2
How revolutionary are Jihadist insurgencies? The case of ISIL
Paul B. Rich
Small Wars & Insurgencies, volume 27, issue 5 (2016), pp. 777–799

Chapter 3
Global Jihad and Foreign Fighters
George Joffé
Small Wars & Insurgencies, volume 27, issue 5 (2016), pp. 800–816

Chapter 4
A Fratricidal Libya: Making Sense of a Conflict Complex
Mikael Eriksson
Small Wars & Insurgencies, volume 27, issue 5 (2016), pp. 817–836

CITATION INFORMATION

Chapter 5
Belgian and Dutch Jihadist Foreign Fighters (2012–2015): Characteristics, Motivations, and Roles in the War in Syria and Iraq
Edwin Bakker and Roel de Bont
Small Wars & Insurgencies, volume 27, issue 5 (2016), pp. 837–857

Chapter 6
Who Goes, Why, and With What Effects: The Problem of Foreign Fighters from Europe
Lasse Lindekilde, Preben Bertelsen and Michael Stohl
Small Wars & Insurgencies, volume 27, issue 5 (2016), pp. 858–877

Chapter 7
A Sectarian Jihad in Nigeria: The Case of Boko Haram
Marc-Antoine Pérouse de Montclos
Small Wars & Insurgencies, volume 27, issue 5 (2016), pp. 878–895

Chapter 8
Operation Barkhane and Boko Haram: French Counterterrorism and Military Cooperation in the Sahel
Christopher Griffin
Small Wars & Insurgencies, volume 27, issue 5 (2016), pp. 896–913

Chapter 9
Al Qaeda in the Islamic Maghreb: Terrorism, insurgency, or organized crime?
Sergei Boeke
Small Wars & Insurgencies, volume 27, issue 5 (2016), pp. 914–936

Chapter 10
Shapeshifter of Somalia: Evolution of the Political Territoriality of Al-Shabaab
Bohumil Doboš
Small Wars & Insurgencies, volume 27, issue 5 (2016), pp. 937–957

Chapter 11
Jihadist insurgency and the prospects for peace and security
Richard Burchill
Small Wars & Insurgencies, volume 27, issue 5 (2016), pp. 958–967

For any permission-related enquiries please visit:
http://www.tandfonline.com/page/help/permissions

Notes on Contributors

Ahmed Al-Hamli is the founder and President of TRENDS: Research & Advisory, Abu Dhabi, UAE. He is an expert in matters of security and human rights.

Edwin Bakker is Professor of (Counter) Terrorism Studies and Director of the Institute of Security and Global Affairs (ISGA) of Leiden University, the Netherlands, and Fellow of the International Centre for Counter-Terrorism (ICCT), the Hague, the Netherlands.

Preben Bertelsen is a Professor in the Department of Psychology and Behavioural Sciences, Aarhus University, Denmark.

Sergei Boeke is a Researcher at the Institute for Security and Global Affairs at Leiden University, the Netherlands. He conducts research on terrorism in the Sahel and the topic of cyber security governance.

Roel de Bont graduated Cum Laude from Leiden University, the Netherlands. He works as a Researcher at the Institute of Governance and Global Affairs. His research mainly covers jihadism and terrorism-related issues.

Richard Burchill is the Director of Research and Engagement for TRENDS: Research & Advisory, Abu Dhabi, UAE. Previously he was with the Law School at the University of Hull, UK, where he was also Director of the McCoubrey Centre for International Law.

Bohumil Doboš is a PhD student at the Institute of Political Studies, Faculty of Social Sciences, Charles University, Prague, Czech Republic. He also serves as a coordinator of the Geopolitical Studies Research Centre.

Mikael Eriksson is a Deputy Research Director at the Security Policy Unit at the Swedish Defence Research Agency. His main field of research is security studies, currently with a particular focus on international and regional organisations and power politics in the Middle East and North Africa.

Christopher Griffin is a Non-Resident Fellow at TRENDS: Research & Advisory, Abu Dhabi, UAE.

George Joffé currently teaches a postgraduate course at the University of Cambridge, UK, on the international relations and geopolitics of the Middle East and North Africa.

NOTES ON CONTRIBUTORS

Lasse Lindekilde is an Associate Professor in the Department of Political Science, Aarhus University, Denmark.

Marc-Antoine Pérouse de Montclos is a Senior Researcher at the Institut de recherché pour le développement, Paris, France.

Paul B. Rich is co-editor of *Small Wars & Insurgencies*. He has taught at the universities of Bristol, Warwick and Melbourne, and has written extensively on insurgency, terrorism, counterinsurgency, and warlordism.

Michael Stohl is a Director at the Orfalea Center for Global and International Studies, and Professor of Communication, Political Science and Global and International Studies, University of California Santa Barbara, USA.

Craig Whiteside is an Associate Professor at the Naval War College Monterey, USA, where he teaches national security affairs to military officers as part of their professional military education.

Preface

Jihadist insurgency is a phenomenon in today's world where armed groups are using violent tactics to challenge existing power structures locally, nationally, and globally. The primary justification for these challenges and the use of violence being used are derived from interpretations based upon beliefs, doctrines, and practices derived from Islam. At the outset, it is important to note that the violence is based on interpretations the insurgent group sees as authoritative; they are far from consistent or widely accepted.

The term *jihad* is particular to Islam and it has a wide range of meanings and applications within the faith. At its core, jihad is about striving to apply our efforts to the maintenance of the faith – *al-jihad fi sabil Allah* ('striving in the way of God'). This is most commonly understood as an individual's striving to ensure adherence to the faith. Jihad is also used to describe outward-facing action against those, whom it is believed, are threatening the Islamic faith. In this respect, jihad has been used to describe holy wars, such as confronting the Crusaders, or to describe violent action against fellow Muslims when one self-selecting group determines that they are the only true believers and all others are transgressors. In the first meaning, jihad is about struggle and striving in a personal way for the believer to better connect with their faith. In the latter version, jihad is explicitly about the use of violence in a manner that is justified as upholding and protecting the faith against any challengers. It is this violent version of jihad that we hear about most often today. A wide number of violent organisations and individuals claim that their actions are justified by beliefs in Islam. Despite efforts to explain how jihad is not inherently about violence, we remain in a situation where jihad, as a foundational element of the Islamic faith, and violence have become synonymous.

The complexities and challenges of jihadist insurgency are immense, and responses require new forms of thinking both in operational aspects of the insurgents and in the debate and discussion about justifications for the use of violence. To this end TRENDS Research & Advisory of Abu Dhabi, UAE came together with the International Centre for the Study of Radicalisation and Political Violence of King's College, London, UK for a two-day conference in 2015 to explore the complexities and challenges of modern jihadist insurgency. A number of the papers presented at that event are included in this special issue, along with further contributions. What the conference and subsequent papers show is that we can use our existing understandings of insurgency to categorise and discuss jihadist insurgency and plan operational responses. At the same time, how we respond to jihadist insurgency is a complex issue where security, politics, and beliefs in particular worldviews overlap and often conflict. Military and security responses are not enough when addressing the threats from jihadist insurgency. The key matter for understanding jihadist insurgency is that the violence and objectives being pursued are about more than achieving a particular political goal. At the core of jihadist insurgency is the view, albeit distorted, that there exists a divinely inspired obligation to implement a version of Islamic law and practice around the world.

Modern jihadist insurgencies are similar to other insurgent movements in that the group is seeking a form of political power and control over a territorial space. The insurgent movement will argue that they are somehow marginalised or excluded from power and therefore remedial action through the use of violent means must be taken to achieve their objective. In this respect, it is possible to identify the desired outcome of the insurgent movement: the object of political power or inclusion being sought. Insurgent movements will also be driven by some sort of ideological stance that may or may not be directly connected to the political objectives, but the violence of insurgency is directed at achieving political power. With jihadist insurgencies, the desire for some form of political power is a recognisable objective as well. However, there is also the ideological claim that there exists the higher obligation of implementing their version of Islamic law. Furthermore, a common characteristic of the modern jihadist insurgency is that the implementation of Islamic law is not limited to a particular political or geographical space, but must encompass the entire world. We also have the added dimension that jihadist insurgent movements are based on a worldview in which it is believed that God/Allah is sanctioning and supporting their actions. Within this there is the belief that death in the conduct of a jihadist insurgency guarantees the highest possible level of salvation. These psychological elements make the motivation underpinning jihadist insurgency very difficult to address. Regardless of any political or military achievements, the jihadist insurgency will continue to argue that the violence must be continued against anyone, Muslim or non-Muslim, who does not agree with their views until a strict, and misguided, interpretation of Islamic law has been imposed on all aspects of society.

There is a range of jihadist insurgent approaches seeking to force a version of Islam upon all others. We see the extensive violence and war being carried out by Daesh/Islamic State based on their argument that most Muslims are not true adherents to the faith and that non-Muslims must be forced to comply. Daesh attempts to use Islamic doctrine to justify their actions, and their programme has received support from extremists around the world, primarily due to the understanding of the world that Daesh presents. We also see jihad as an integral part of *athnā'ashariyyah*, an Iranian doctrine that has been translated into a political and foreign policy objective by Iran. This belief makes jihad, primarily understood in the violent manner, an obligation upon Muslims where all non-believers must be brought into conformity. Athnā'ashariyyah itself is not directed solely at violent activity, but Iran has made it part of its foreign policy efforts in supporting violent organisations around the Middle East to challenge anyone who does not comply with their version of Islam. We can also look to organisations, such as the Muslim Brotherhood, which are not typical insurgent movements as their primary objective is working within the existing political system, but whose ultimate objective is a return to what they see as the only true version of Islam based on highly conservative and restrictive understandings of the faith. In the US case of *Holder v. Humanitarian Law Project*, evidence was placed before the court showing the Muslim Brotherhood clearly calling for 'eliminating and destroying the Western civilization'. The evidence showed that political mechanisms were to be used where possible, but that recourse to the sword always remained an option.

This then is the crux of the issue in dealing with jihadist insurgency. It appears that these movements will not be satisfied until there is a complete reorganisation of the entire world on their terms and understanding of Islamic law – an understanding that is not shared widely among the entire Islamic community. This is not to reject the relevance of Islamic law. We, as Muslims, follow sharia in our day-to-day lives, but in the modern world we have to follow a wide range of laws, regulations, and practices that govern our societies, our states, and our interactions with others, which may or may not be obtained from a religious doctrine. While a faith can hope that new adherents wish to join, and Islam is currently the fastest growing religion in the world, a true sign of its success, we cannot use violence to force people to adopt a belief system and worldview. In response to the current challenges and threats posed by jihadist insurgency, politicians and commentators have attempted to conclude that the Islamic faith is the core cause of the violence. Yes, we can find statements, beliefs, and doctrines in Islam that can be used to support acts of violence, but this does not represent the entirety of the faith, and it is imperative to articulate understandings that not only challenge the beliefs of the jihadist insurgent movements but also discredit their actions. Individuals and political leaders may feel uncomfortable criticising the ideology of jihadist insurgencies as this may appear to be a challenge to Islam itself. Where we have to be clear is that the tactics of jihadist insurgency are very much against the spirit and practice of Islam.

In response to jihadist insurgency, we must redouble our security-based efforts, but we must also directly address the worldview and justifications that are being used to support their violence. We need to give attention to the different meanings of jihad because this helps to distance the term from any exclusive connection with violence. The core meaning of jihad relates to striving, taking extraordinary measures, and exerting oneself in the faith. For the individual, this act of striving can be in relation to a number of activities, most pertinently for jihad is the striving for an individual to become closer to their faith. The striving of jihad is about overcoming challenges and temptations that may weaken an individual's faith. Historically, these challenges came from outsiders seeking to use jihadist theology in order to defend, as they say it, the Islamic faith through force. In today's world many Muslims reject the idea that violence is an acceptable way to uphold their faith. Daesh has attempted to portray the use of violence as a religious obligation upon all Muslims grounded in doctrine and history; we have to reject this.

As with any belief system we can find elements within Islam that support peace and violence, understanding and intolerance. The true struggle today is to convince all extremists that violence, however justified, is unacceptable. The evidence is on our side as violence and extremism represent only a small percentage of human society. It is a very small group within Islam who say that the modern world is to be rejected through violence alone; we cannot let their understandings of our faith dominate global security. Today we live in a world where there are rules, processes, and norms that govern relations between peoples, societies, nations, and religions. These rules, processes, and norms are not wholly Islamic, but Islam is recognised and respected. The world is a highly diverse place in which all belief systems can contribute. We have to reject the claims of jihadist insurgency that the world must comply with their distorted understanding of Islam. Instead we have to strive to ensure that Islam is part of the global efforts to make the world a more secure place. Looking at the world today, it is clear this will be a substantial struggle. The research presented in this special issue is an important contribution to these efforts.

Ahmed Al-Hamli

Introduction

Paul B. Rich

This special issue of *Small Wars and Insurgencies* examines the phenomenon of jihadist insurgencies. It explores the strategic, political, and ideological significance of some of these movements operating in the Middle East and North and West Africa. These movements have become an increasingly important part of modern irregular warfare though they are by no means new on the international political landscape. They are termed 'jihadist' insurgent movements though not all are attached solely to waging guerrilla warfare. Some have evolved quite a larger military repertoire encompassing terrorism, suicide bombing, and assassination; in some parts of the Middle East and Libya, the huge supply of weaponry has led to conflict escalating almost to the level of a conventional small war, involving artillery, air strikes, trench warfare, and bitter urban battles.

The two key dimensions of this insurgency are terrorism and guerrilla warfare. As some articles in this issue point out, the two tactics are employed in different ways by different jihadist movements. Sergei Boeke, for instance (in an analysis that employs the analytical framework of Duyvesteyn and Fumerton) points out that terrorism and guerrilla warfare are essentially two different military strategies: terrorism is pivoted around generating a response in order to achieve a political effect, while guerrilla warfare is orientated towards the control of territory, population, and resources in order to wage a longer term war that might, in Maoist terms, escalate eventually to the conventional level.[1] What looks strategic at one level, though, might be viewed as tactical at another. Terrorism and guerrilla warfare may be less strategic than tactical when seen in terms of a longer term strategy of winning political power or establishing control over a state that will necessitate the development of other strategies including the development of a shadow state ready to take over power at the centre.

Leaving aside the issue of tactics versus strategy, it is clear that these essential differences between terrorism and guerrilla warfare impact on the way the movements are formed. Movements that are essentially terrorist in nature tend to be small and secretive conspiracies operating through underground networks; guerrilla movements, on the other hand, tend to evolve into more formal political entities, such as political parties and bureaucracies, that emulate the state structure they seek to defeat. For guerrillas, the support of the population is critical as a base of support and for potential new recruits; for terrorist organisations this is less the case, especially if enough new recruits can be found from outside the territory where the organisation functions.

These differences are never really absolute and jihadist insurgencies, like other insurgencies before them, have adopted a mix of tactics. Adapting to differing regional and political situations has been crucial in enabling many of these movements to become increasingly important actors in conflicts throughout the Islamic world. Even before the emergence of ISIL, for instance, many of the movements that were associated with al Qaeda referred to themselves as operating within a particular 'field of jihad' or *fi sahat al-jihad*. This meant that they were anchored in a particular region such as Somalia, Pakistan, or Iraq and were orientated towards a more specific set of short- to medium-term goals in that region. This would also be the case with *Jabhat al-Nusra* in Syria, which started out as being a rather secretive underground-type terrorist organisation but would evolve over time into becoming an important guerrilla movement in the Syrian civil war.

While only a few years ago, it is quite likely that future historians will look at the period between 2011 and the proclamation of a caliphate by ISIL in Mosul in June 2014 as a defining watershed in global politics. In the years before 2011 there had certainly been a variety of insurgencies proclaiming jihad: numerous movements of varying size and scale surfaced in terrains ranging from Kashmir and Afghanistan to Somalia and Yemen, exhibiting different lifespans and capacities to attract international attention. Some, like the movement led by Mohammed Farah Aideed in Mogadishu, briefly gained global interest following the confrontation with US peacekeepers in 1993 before lapsing into an obscurity alleviated only by continued interest in the film *Black Hawk Down*.

On the whole, jihadist movements have tended, until recently at least, to be quite localised even if the conflicts in which they were engaged (such as Jammu Kashmir) spanned several decades. It was 'global terrorism' rather than jihadist insurgencies per se which dominated much strategic debate in the decade after 9/11, though some analysts have suggested that this new type of terrorism had the capacity to turn itself into a 'global insurgency'. Al Qaeda (AQ), under its leaders Osama Bin Laden and Ayman Zawahiri, appeared to be the main radicalising force among disaffected Islamic youth across the globe rather than any specific guerrilla movement, even though AQ fostered a number of regional insurgent affiliates such as al Qaeda in Iraq (AQI), al Qaeda in the Arabian Peninsula (AQIP), and al Qaeda in the Islamic Maghreb (AQIM) over which it tried to maintain some form of central control.

All this changed substantially with the outbreak of the Arab Spring in 2011, a year in which Bina Laden himself was also killed in a raid on his Abbottabad compound in Pakistan by US Navy Seals. For the first time the whole pattern of the American-dominated order in the Middle East came under serious challenge at a time when the administration in Washington displayed a strong commitment to withdraw, as far as circumstances allowed, from future military engagements.[2] The challenge thrown up to traditionally authoritarian Arab regimes by the youthful and media-savvy democratic movements of the Arab Spring proved, though, to be short-lived, beyond the one surviving example of a multi-party regime in Tunisia. The Arab regimes mobilised, in several cases, a brutal response and crackdown, exemplifying what Jean Pierre Filiu has termed the power of a widespread 'deep state' in the Arab world, rooted in a long tradition of the ruthless exertion of power by loyal Mamelukes in the Ottoman empire.[3] The thesis, while compelling, has only limited explanatory for certain regimes, such as Kemalist Turkey, Egypt, and perhaps the Baathist regimes of Iraq and Syria.[4] The Libyan regime of Qaddafi proved only too fissiparous and it is hard to find there much evidence for a 'deep state', a concept which is also prone to the charge that it largely reduces history to being dominated by hidden conspiracies. The same applies to other states on the periphery of the Arab world, such as the relatively weak post-colonial state of Yemen, and the concept needs to be developed into a far more focused attention on the inner workings of particular states and their respective military and intelligence organisations.

In any case, in both Iraq and Syria the workings of the 'deep state' need to be seen alongside regional and global factors that have led local civil wars escalating into wider proxy wars and an increasingly permissive regional environment for violent forms of jihadist insurgency to flourish. What Filiu has termed the 'Arab Counter Revolution' was by no means united and monolithic, reminiscent of the 'Holy Alliance' of reactionary states organised by Russia in the wake of the Treaty of Vienna in 1815. Rival regimes in the Middle East ended up supporting and funding either the state or oppositional insurgent movements in both the Iraqi and Syrian conflicts, illustrating all too clearly that the region has become, as Alex Marshall recently pointed out in an introduction to a special issue on proxy wars in *Small Wars and Insurgencies*, 'the most obvious current cauldron of proxy conflict'.[5] Indeed, the integration of rival insurgent movements as well as the state itself in both the Iraq and Syrian conflicts have hampered the chances for any easy diplomatic resolution to a conflict that, in the Syrian case, has destroyed large parts of civil society and created a huge exodus of refugees to Europe.

These issues will be explored in some of the articles in this issue. At this stage, it is important to examine what is exactly meant by the term 'jihadist insurgency' and its links to Islamic religious belief before we locate the term in the wider literature on guerrilla warfare and small wars.

What do we mean by a jihadist insurgency?

The jihadist ideology that drives 'jihadist insurgent' movements is a heavily contested one. As a concept 'jihad' has its foundations in the Quran and a long history in the Arab world and Islamic societies generally. This history has provided a series of sacred concepts, personages, lessons, and images that amounts to nothing less than a providential history that contemporary jihadist ideologists draw on to justify current political agendas. There is thus an interesting dialogue between the present and the past in the Islamic world, though we would be loath to describe this as amounting to anything resembling a 'reformation' comparable to that in European Christendom. This idea, fondly held by some Western liberals, is pivoted around the idea that there needs to be a clean separation between Church and state in the Islamic world as occurred in Europe. However, this rather overlooks the break between religion and politics in most of the Islamic world outside Shi'ite interpretations of Islamic belief. Islam never had, in the Sunni world at least, any formal religious hierarchy, and the caliph, who has been opportunistically resurrected by ISIL, was first and foremost a prince rather than a pope, capable of building mosques but never acting as any source of religious authority.[6]

Generally speaking, jihadist insurgents seek to displace the established political power in a certain space and, to this degree at least, share at some of the features of former of guerrilla insurgencies that emerged after 1945 in colonial territories seeking 'national liberation' from European colonial rule. The national liberationist guerrillas in such former colonies as Vietnam, Algeria, Mozambique, and Zimbabwe were usually more nationalist than liberationist. Most, too, in the decades following their attainment of political power, adjusted quite rapidly to the international system. Mozambique, for instance, under its FRELIMO regime, ended up receiving loans from the International Monetary Fund within a few years of liberation. Others have tilted towards the West in the context of new patterns of regional power politics or maintained an uneasy independence such as Zimbabwe, though even here the currency eventually adopted was the US dollar.

Jihadist insurgent movements seem rather more ideologically zealous compared to the earlier secular national liberation models. They tend to be organised and led by figures who have, in many instances, learned a puritanical and Salafist interpretation of Islam through a variety of means including prison, the mosque, the university, the madrassa, and modern social media. This is, though, not true of all their leaders, who may, in some cases, come from a more conventional military background such as the Iraqi army of Saddam Hussein in the case of ISIL. Modern jihadist insurgencies are typically fighting to bring about a single, global system based on particular interpretations of Islam. They are heavily shaped by 'religious' ideology in the form of a highly politicised set of readings of Islamic sacred texts. This 'Islamic' ideology has become the key glue that binds these insurgent movements together, providing as it does the essential moral and ethical base for the movement's long-term aims, even if many of their recruits might have little actual knowledge of either Islam or the Quran, exemplified all too well by the apocryphal story of one group of British volunteer recruits to ISIL travelling to Syria equipped with *Islam For Dummies*.[7]

Jihadist insurgencies are characterised by a struggle over claims of political legitimacy. The primary objective is the overthrow of more secularly inclined states and the imposition of Islamic law in all elements of human society. In cases where the state already is guided by Islamic belief, such as Wahhabism in Saudi Arabia, the aim is to overthrow the royal elite that runs the state and replace it by a revolutionary regime. The degree of commitment to sharia law depends, to some degree, upon the wider networks to which the movement is attached and the degree of ideological zealotry of its leaders. This is not an issue confined solely to Islamic insurgent movements since similar patterns of terror and the enforcement of barbaric codes of law enforcement can be observed among drug gangs in Mexico and Central and South America.[8]

Jihadist insurgent movements, nevertheless, represent a new and distinctive phase of guerrilla insurgencies that have caught analysts rather by surprise. By the end of the Cold War in 1990–1991 it seemed as though the era of guerrilla insurgencies might be coming to an end, given that the main post-war insurgent movements of national liberation had all largely achieved their aims or, as in the case of the South African transition to an ANC-led government in 1994, been bypassed by a politically negotiated transfer of power. In the immediate post-Cold War period of the 1990s the main issues seemed to be collapsing or 'failed' states such as Somalia, Sierra Leone, and Liberia with the emergence of warlord-type militias that seemed very debased forms of guerrilla insurgency given the way they were led by violent macho godfather figures employing child soldiers and girls as sex slaves. Such 'movements' seemed to be little more than extended criminal gangs focused on drug dealing and the trade in valuable commodities such as hardwoods and diamonds.

What we can now see as the first main impetus for the emergence of modern jihadist insurgent movements was external military intervention by great powers into the Middle East and Asia, beginning with the Soviet invasion of Afghanistan in 1979 as well as the revolution in Iran the same year. The latter stages of the Cold War were not characterised by a simple retreat by the superpowers from imperial-type involvement but a fillip for a new type of military and political engagement in regions that had formerly escaped major external military involvement in the years after World War II. The Soviet invasion of Afghanistan led to the first real global awareness of jihadi guerrillas that were increasingly aided and supported by the CIA. But, in contrast to later jihadist insurgent formations in the 1990s, these were the 'good guys' as far as the Western media were concerned as well in feature films such as *Rambo III* and *Charlie Wilson's War*. Only with the departure of the Soviet Union in 1989 did a new image of the insurgencies start to emerge. By the 1990s a more militant pattern of jihadist insurgencies began to emerge characterised by an increasing resort to terrorist activities as well as an increasingly strident anti-Western rhetoric. The disaster for US forces in Mogadishu in 1993 also suggested a new form of menacing jihadist insurgency, located in disintegrating cities in addition to remote rural terrains like Afghanistan, that would be hard to control and defeat.

Religion and guerrilla insurgencies

The centrality of religious ideology in contemporary jihadist insurgent movements suggests that far more attention needs to be paid to the role of religion in the historical understanding of guerrilla warfare and the establishment of movements that Metz has termed 'spiritual insurgencies'.[9] Given that a guerrilla insurgency requires the active involvement of groups of ordinary people not normally linked to formal army or military structures, it would not be surprising to find that religion and religious symbolism play a major role. The study of guerrilla insurgencies since the nineteenth century suggests that religion has frequently been a crucial force in popular mobilisation though one that it is still rather poorly understood by military analysts; religion, for instance, clearly played among the conservative Spanish peasantry drawn into the guerrilla resistance to the Napoleonic invasion of Spain between 1808 and 1814.[10]

Religion, after all, has traditionally provided important iconic symbols for local and communal identities in rural societies: the church, the synagogue, the mosque, or the Buddhist or Hindu temple has frequently served as a centre of local identity along with festivals, feast days, and periods of fasting. Any insurgent leadership moving into a rural area would be ill-advised to ignore the religious beliefs of peasant and farming communities living there; while in urban areas, local religious centres continue to serve as major points of community identity as well as locations for the storage of weapons and propaganda and the recruitment of new members of insurgent cells. Likewise, the language used by religious communities and groups of believers can be adapted for the formation of ideologies of revolutionary insurgency in situations of crisis and political repression; this is a dimension that has been frequently underplayed by secular, Western analysts of insurgencies, who have often preferred to focus on the frequently self-justifying writings of insurgent leaders such as Mao Zedong, Ho Chi Minh, or Che Guevara. Religion, or a form of spiritual belief, it can be argued, has often formed a moral centre of gravity (COG) of a guerrilla movement and one that in turn will help define the critical capabilities essential for the COG to function. This is an observation that some political anthropologists have been making for years; as far back as 1970, for instance, the French anthropologist

Georges Balandier pointed out that 'religious conflicts are a clear expression of political struggle – which they provide with a language and means of action – in situations caused by the weakness of central power.'[11]

It is surprising how many analysts have neglected this religious dimension of insurgency, preferring to focus on the apparently more compelling appeals of nationalism, socialism, and Marxism. General surveys of guerrilla insurgencies by Walter Laqueur, John Ellis, Max Boot, Ian Beckett, and Douglas Porch have all rather underplayed the role of religion in insurgencies.[12] This general indifference to religion is partly due to the way many guerrilla insurgencies became harnessed to Marxist movements of 'national liberation' in the years after 1945. The three decades from 1945 to 1975 might be said to form a sort of Procrustean bed for much subsequent analysis, acting as a historical yardstick through which to understand how most guerrilla insurgencies operate in the modern world.

The Western left also tended to see many modern guerrilla insurgencies as largely secular in orientation; they more or less accepted at face value the language of the insurgents themselves in their desire to secure a revolutionary transformation of their societies to remove the power not only of traditional landlords and capitalists but of organised religion.[13] For the 'new left' in Europe and the United States it was the example of the Castroite revolution in Cuba, as much as any, that fostered a myth of guerrilla war in the late 1960s and 1970s – linked as this was for a period to the celebrity-like image of Che Guevara. Indeed, it was Cuba that especially helped to sustain the 'guerrilla myth' of the Western new left until it was overtaken by the harsh crackdown by a series of military regimes in Latin America in the 1970s and 1980s.[14]

In parts of the Islamic world, especially the Middle East and North Africa, jihadist insurgencies have developed in the last decade in a context of a growing crisis of statehood. The crisis effectively began with the 2003 invasion of Iraq, although well before then states such as Afghanistan, Somalia, and Yemen had already fractured. The fragility of statehood became especially evident when the invasion led to an effective collapse of the Baathist state, while the new regime put in place in Baghdad under Nuri Al Maliki proved little more than a Shi'a-dominated regime. By 2006–2007 Iraq had descended into an intensifying sectarian war, a conflict that not only has heavily destabilised Iraq but also has given rise to Islamic State or ISIL, which has proven to be a major factor in the continued instability of Iraq.

But one of the key dynamics has been the brutal response by a number of regimes to the Arab Spring that started in 2011. This was a movement for democratisation initiated by students and the educated middle class in December of that year in Tunisia. It rapidly spread to a number of other states in North Africa and the Middle East such as Egypt, Libya, Syria, and Yemen, while further civil disturbances occurred in a variety of states such as Morocco, Jordan, Oman, Mauritania, Kuwait, and Sudan. None of these uprisings led to the actual overthrow of the ruling regime apart from the 'dignity revolution' in Tunisia, which eventually led to the departure of the corrupt dictator Zine el Abidine Ben Ali in January 2011. In many cases, the civil disturbances were relatively easily contained by the ruling regimes, confounding the predictions of some optimistic Western news reporting, such as that of the BBC, that Tunisia was the 'Arab Gdansk' and the start of something resembling the 'velvet revolutions' in Eastern Europe in the late 1980s and early 1990s.[15]

The misreading in the West of the Arab Spring was partly due to the way that the imagined 'revolution' was transmitted globally in real time by social media, making it a fashionable example of modern civil action producing a new kind of popular politics. Its favourable reporting in the Western media can, with hindsight, be seen, largely as wishful thinking driven by a remarkable lack of understanding of the relatively narrow social base of the young would-be revolutionaries, whose adroit use of social media disguised the fact that they had weak political roots within many of the societies from which they came. This became starkly exemplified by the draconian response by the Baathist regime of Bashar al-Assad in Syria to Arab Spring demonstrations in Damascus in the spring of 2012; the conflict rapidly descended into sectarian civil war between a regime narrowly based around Alawites, Christians, and other minorities (along with small numbers of Sunnis) and the Sunni majority.

The rapid pace of events that devastated large parts of Syria over the next five years was impelled not only by a festering series of internal dynamics but external intervention by a series of powers including Iran, Turkey, and Russia that has transformed the war into a proxy war with the potential to run for many years. Leaving aside the complicated diplomatic process necessary to secure viable peace negotiations between a range of warring parties, the Syrian civil war has further eroded conventional forms of statehood in the Middle East. By August 2015 the Syrian government was estimated to control no more than 16% of the country's population, though since then its position has been partially strengthened by the brief intervention of Russia, the long-standing patron of the Baathist regime in Damascus.

The fracturing of Syria in the wake of the sectarian disintegration of Iraq between 2003 and 2011 has produced a situation almost unimaginable at the time of the 2003 invasion of Iraq. Perhaps, historians in years to come will conclude that this was the final phase of Western imperial thinking about the 'Middle East' (a term only invented in the early twentieth century by strategic writer Alfred Thayer Mahan) that underpinned the Versailles Peace Settlement of 1919. The Settlement constructed a number of new states out of the carcass of the Ottoman empire, whose demise has remained poorly understood until relatively recently by historians compared to the collapse of the other three great empires at the end of World War I – Germany, Russia, and Austria-Hungary. It was out of the areas of former Ottoman control that a number of newly invented states were forged, such as Iraq, Syria, Jordan, and Palestine (most of the latter forming after 1948 the state of Israel). None of these states had any real traditions behind them or a clear sense of identity. Several insurgent movements thus started out as local and tribal revolts against the power of the central state. It is only in more recent years that a number have become transformed into ideologically coherent jihadist insurgencies under the control, in many cases, of Salafist zealots, as some of the articles in this issue indicate – though it should be pointed out that other jihadist insurgencies emerged among Shi'as such as the Sadrist movement in Iraq led by Muqtada al-Sadr.

Studying such movements emphasises the importance of religious ideology in insurgent movements. The ultimate objective of many jihadist insurgencies is the full implementation of Islamic law on a regional if not global basis. Such beliefs are anchored in myths of single Islamic ummah, or community; they are not going to disappear even if some of the current jihadist insurgent movements such as ISIL or al-Nusra are defeated.

Notes

1. Duyvesteyn and Fumerton, 'Insurgency and Terrorism'; Lister, *The Syrian Jihad*, 59–60.
2. Lynch, *The New Arab Wars*, 19 and *passim*.
3. Filiu, *From Deep State to Islamic State*, 47–8.
4. See the critical review of Filiu's book by Hugh Roberts, 'The Hijackers', *London Review of Books*, 16 July 2015.
5. Marshall, 'From Civil War to Proxy War', 183.
6. Zakaria, *The Future of Freedom*, 147.
7. Martin Robertson, 'British terrorists from Birmingham bought "Islam for Dummies" book before traveling to Syria to join rebel fighters in Jihad', *Daily Mail*, 8 July 2014.
8. See for instance, Sullivan and Bunker, 'Rethinking Insurgency'.
9. Metz, 'The Future of Insurgency'.
10. The Spanish guerrillas fighting against Napoleon's armies before 1814 were largely Catholic-inspired rightists who would fight as reactionaries in later civil wars of 1820–1823 and 1830. See Lawrence, 'Poachers Turned Gamekeepers'. See also Chartrand et al., *Spanish Guerrillas*.
11. Balandier, *Political Anthropology*, 121.
12. Laqueur, *Guerrilla*; Ellis, *From the Barrel of a Gun*; Boot, *Invisible Armies*; Beckett, *Modern Insurgencies and Counter-Insurgencies*; Porch, *Wars of Empire*. Laqueur discusses the guerrilla insurgencies in Poland and Italy, though one would have thought that the centrality of the Catholic Church in both societies would have led at least to some discussion of religion (Laqueur *Guerrilla*, 132). Beckett acknowledges the role of the Catholic Church to have been of some importance in the Spanish and Polish revolts in the nineteenth century as well as the Tyrolean revolt under Andreas Hofer and the revolt of the Kingdom of Naples between 1806 and 1811, though in the latter instance Beckett considers that religion amounted to little more than banditry (Beckett, *Modern Insurgencies and Counter-Insurgencies*, 6–7). Porch emphasised the centrality of 'national liberation' in the history of guerrilla insurgencies, erecting in the process a sort of radical Whig view of history by which to judge their growth and development.
13. Miller and Aya, *National Liberation*.
14. Bell, *The Myth of the Guerrilla*.
15. BBC News, 15 January 2011.

Disclosure statement

No potential conflict of interest was reported by the author.

References

Balandier, Georges. *Political Anthropology*. Harmondsworth: Penguin Books, 1972 (1st edition, 1970).
Beckett, Ian. *Modern Insurgencies and Counter-Insurgencies*. London and New York: Routledge, 2001.
Bell, J. Bowyer *The Myth of the Guerrilla*. New York: Knopf, 1971.
Boot, Max. *Invisible Armies: An Epic History of Guerrilla Warfare from Ancient Times to the Present*. New York and London: Norton, 2013.
Duyvesteyn, Isabelle and Mario Fumerton. 'Insurgency and Terrorism: Is there a difference?' In *The Character of War in the 21st Century*, edited by Caroline Holmquist and Christopher Coker, 27–41. London: Routledge.
Ellis, John. *From the Barrel of a Gun: A History of Guerrilla, Revolutionary and Counter-Insurgency Warfare from the Romans to the Present*. London: Greenhill Books, 1995.
Filiu, Jean Pierre. *From Deep State to Islamic State: The Arab Counter-Revolution and its Jihadi Legacy*. London: Hurst, 2015.
Laqueur, Walter. *Guerrilla*. London: Weidenfeld and Nicolson, 1977.
Lawrence, Mark. "Poachers Turned Gamekeepers: A Study of the Guerrilla phenomenon in Spain, 1808–1840." *Small Wars and Insurgencies* 25, no. 4 (2014): 843–857.
Lister, Charles R. *The Syrian Jihad: AL Qaeda, The Islamic State and the Evolution of an Insurgency*. London: Hurst, 2015.
Lynch, Marc. *The New Arab Wars: Uprising and Anarchy in the Middle East*. New York: Public Affairs, 2016.
Marshall, Alex. "From Civil War to Proxy War: Past History and Current Dilemmas." *Small Wars and Insurgencies* 27, no. 2 (2016): 183–195.
Metz, Steven. 'The Future of Insurgency'. Strategic Studies Institute, Carlisle, PA, 1993. http://www.strategicstudiesinstitute.gov.mil/pfffile/00333.pdf.
Miller, Norman, and Roderick Aya. *National Liberation: Revolution in the Third World*. New York: The Free Press, 1971.
Porch, Douglas. *Wars of Empire*. London: Cassell, 2000.
Sullivan, John P, and Robert Bunker, 'Rethinking Insurgency: Criminality, Spirituality, and Societal Warfare in the Americas'. *Small Wars and Insurgencies* 22, no. 5 (2011): 742–763.
Zakaria, Fareed. *The Future of Freedom: Liberal Democracy at Home and Abroad*. New York and London: Norton, 2007.

The Islamic State and the Return of Revolutionary Warfare

Craig Whiteside

ABSTRACT
The rise of the Islamic State (ISIS/ISIL) is not well understood at this point. This paper starts by comparing the Islamic State to the Vietnamese communists in a revolutionary warfare framework and makes a causal argument that the Islamic State's defeat of the Sahwa (Awakening) movement in Iraq was the key to its successful establishment of control of most Sunni areas and the mobilization of its population for support. Islamic State operational summaries and captured documents are used to quantitatively establish the impact of the subversion campaign against the Sahwa and Iraqi government and trace the efforts of operatives in tribal outreach and recruiting. This research provides a valuable insight into the return of a powerful method of insurgency as well as a glimpse into the vast clandestine network that provides the strength of the Islamic State movement.

Introduction

The descent into disorder began years before the crisis, with whispers of the return of veterans from the previous war and the announcements from a political front representing a competing shadow government opposed to the incumbent. The murky deaths of political figures in the hinterlands are written off as banditry, local blood debts, and revenge killings unremarkable in a society long riven by internecine conflict. Seemingly random in pattern, the deaths soon become part of the rhythm of everyday life in the country, as unexplainable as they are inconsequential. The rising criminality in these areas soon block many government services in the area, a fact buried by the bureaucracy and invisible to the leaders of the state who believe that what they see in the capital is the reality of the state. Villages have no officials, taxes go uncollected, and schools have no teachers. By the time the state's police and military units lose the ability to operate in these same rural areas, the crisis has matured to an existential crisis for the state.

This generic vignette is an amalgamation of several accounts of the Vietnamese People's Revolutionary Party campaign to defeat the Diem regime during 1959–1963, but it also could easily pass for a description of what happened in the Sunni provinces of Iraq from 2008 to 2013 – long before the world discovered the Islamic State. Often incorrectly described as an ex-Baathist cabal that invaded Iraq from Syria and easily defeated an unmotivated and corrupt Shia Army of occupation, the Islamic State is better understood as a revolutionary movement that has learned, practiced, adjusted, and honed a successful politico-military doctrine in their state-building campaign. They have deep roots in the population and are determined to win the competition of governing with the Iraqi government. In short, they are very real and here to stay.

The inspiration for this research came from Bernard Fall, whose writings about the Vietnam wars often reflected an amazement of the subversive nature of revolutionary warfare and its paralyzing effect on government. Fall delighted in contrasting public pronouncements of government control by French military or American political observers who counted secure provinces instead of obscure assassinations or uncollected taxes.[1] The cumulative results of this subversion and an associated fear led others to claim that the exhaustion effect of revolutionary warfare was unbeatable, 'a dynamic that will take over the world!'[2] Surely this was overstated, and the end of the Cold War heralded an end to ideological warfare, and the return of power and interest based conflict now that the war of ideologies was over – it was the end of history.[3]

The demise of revolutionary warfare turned out to be a fantasy.[4] A little known movement known as Salafi–jihadism adopted it after the Afghan–Soviet War, due to the similarity of its struggle against powerful enemies and proxies that dominated an international system inherently incompatible with their ideology. The Salafi–jihadist movement suffered a long series of trials as it stumbled from failed revolution to crushed revolt, so much so that one of its adherents who later founded the Islamic State movement[5] called it 'the sad, recurrent story in the arenas of jihad'.[6] Abu Musab al Zarqawi too failed, but his successors continued to adapt and evolve and implemented a doctrine that, in a series of operational campaigns, finally produced a pseudo-state[7] with a reasonably effective conventional army and political apparatus. This interweaving of political actions with military ones is a clear indicator of an understanding of revolutionary warfare, a phenomenon rarely mentioned today in reference to the Islamic State.[8] A careful study of the rise of the Islamic State will demonstrate that its adaptation of Mao's revolutionary warfare concept – as executed by the Vietnamese communists and modified it to fit its Islamist ideology – best explains how the Islamic State rose to power.

To support this argument, I will first examine the revolutionary aspects of the Islamic State in accordance with revolutionary warfare theory. Next, I will trace the development of revolutionary warfare doctrine in the Salafist–jihadist movement to its current state of execution by the Islamic State. In the third part, I will conduct a structured comparison between the Vietnamese communists campaign in South Vietnam from 1959 to 1964 with the Islamic State's campaign in Iraq from 2008 to 2013. Finally, I will test a hypothesis concerning the Islamic State's defeat of the Sahwa (Awakening) movement as a necessary condition for their return to prominence in Sunni Iraq.[9]

Islamic State as a revolutionary movement

While often described as a 'terror group',[10] the Islamic State actually fits the definition of a movement conducting an insurgency, defined as an armed struggle dedicated to replacing the government.[11] Revolutionary warfare is a more specific version of an insurgency, designed to use guerrilla warfare combined with political action to further an ideology in place of the incumbent government.[12] While wars are always fought for political purposes, the French counterinsurgent Galula argued that in conventional warfare political goals run parallel to military efforts and play the decisive role in strategy formulation at the beginning and in deciding war termination alternatives in the end of conflict. In contrast, revolutionary warfare is primarily political in nature, with political efforts integrated into all operations at the tactical and operational levels of war.

The Islamic State movement has two political goals: the establishment of a caliphate in the place of the current governments that rule over majority Muslim populations and a subsequent expansion across the world. While some observers label this vision unrealistic or simply aspirational,[13] historian Ibn Khaldun believed in the natural expansionistic nature of a truly Islamic state.[14] The creation of a polity where Muslims can exercise the correct practice of their religion is a key narrative in Islamic State messaging. Therefore, the Islamic State is revolutionary in two different aspects: in its desire to replace state governance in a long list of countries, as well as in a recognition that it can never integrate socially, politically, or economically with an international order of states that will always be at war with it.

In addition to its revolutionary nature, the Islamic State has adopted the jihadist version of irregular warfare, which is described as action by small groups conducting independent operations.[15] Due to the powerful nature of the state and the system it is rebelling against, the Islamic State conducts robberies, assassinations, acts of terror, sabotage, and other attacks termed 'war out of the dark'. There are no conventional battles and no blitzkrieg in this 'long attritional struggle' to wear down the will of the enemy.[16] These activities took place in the first two of what McCuen described as the four phases of revolutionary warfare: organization, terrorism, guerrilla warfare, and mobile warfare.[17] These phases can occur at different times in different locations, and are conditions based, meaning that setbacks could force the revolutionaries back into a lower stage of operations out of weakness.

The advantages of a credible and established network in an irregular warfare setting are seen in McCuen's early stages, where smaller and nimbler organizations with a widespread set of associates linked together in small nodes can work with greater autonomy and anonymity, while a smaller central nervous system creates and disseminates broad policies and strategy for the movement.[18] The Islamic State has existed from the very beginning in 2002 as a growing network of foreign Islamists that recruited a strong core of ansar (local supporters) and later related tribesmen, former Saddam regime members, and Sunni rejectionists.

A revolutionary movement can achieve its end state in several different ways, including massive uprisings or coups d'état, but the choice of irregular warfare is often dictated by the strength of the system.[19] Cuba's revolution required minimal action by a small cohort to overthrow the government, whereas the Islamic State faced a majority Shia population in Iraq and a global hegemon supporting the local Iraqi government. This fact made the choice of irregular warfare a wise one.

One critique of viewing the Islamic State through a revolutionary warfare lens is that it is simply an outdated construct. Metz argued that modern insurgencies are in essence a complex internal conflict, with a need to generate income for operational purposes, which leads to the development of patronage networks and a widely diffusive set of alliances.[20] This reduces the requirement to mobilize the population for support and removes incentives for engagement with prospective supporters, with the result that contemporary insurgencies are more focused on violence and coercion. While this is a valid description of the Islamic State's early years as it struggled to grow and dominate the resistance movement in Iraq from 2004 to 2007, the post-surge Islamic State made some important attitudinal changes to how they engendered support within its target population.

Evolution of revolutionary Salafist–jihadism

It might seem farfetched to attempt to trace the influence of a group of progressive atheists on reactionary religious zealots, but it is a valuable exercise if one wants to understand the Islamic State movement. It should not be surprising that a group that venerates the salaf of early Islam would claim a heritage of irregular warfare including trickery, small numbers, and a reliance on superior morale to win the day. Ibn Khaldun, who described this way of warfare in the *Muqadimmah*, wrote 'Muhammad won with small numbers over the polytheists during his lifetime' because of what the historian called asabiyah, or special group feeling.[21]

The Islamic State's consistent use of historical narratives and concepts is often overlooked by observers who focus on the tactic of terror and the brutality of the group, and it also obscures the deep roots of its doctrine in previous generations of jihad.[22] While others focus on the formative experiences of many Salafist–jihadists in the Soviet–Afghan war when analyzing doctrinal evolution, it was the failed Syrian uprising against Hafiz al Assad from 1976–1982 that seems to have most influenced the development of Salafi–jihadi revolutionary warfare. Abu Musab al Suri, a Syrian fighter turned theorist, wrote an influential training book titled 'Lessons Learned from the Armed Jihad Ordeal in Syria'. The work is an insightful litany of the problems of an unorganized and poorly structured resistance movement that was routed by the security services of a totalitarian regime. Al Suri wrote:

> the struggle for the sake and path of Allah is not called 'jihad' for nothing, the term 'jihad' literally means: 'exerting a tiring effort to set up.' The enemy is strong and powerful, we are weak and poor, the war duration is going to be long and the best way to fight it is in a revolutionary jihad way for the sake of Allah. The preparations better be deliberate, comprehensive, and properly planned, taking into account past experiences and lessons.[23]

By revolutionary al Suri meant in the way of what he termed the 'gang warfare theorists', who advocated waging war on behalf of the masses who nurtured and sustained insurgents. A fan of Taber's *The War of the Flea*, Suri also referenced the metaphor of the insurgent as a fish in the sea of the people (without citation) in his work. Al Suri's omission of Mao was a clever dodge to avoid tainting the message with the messenger for virulent Salafi–jihadis who hated communism as a source of disbelief and atheism.[24]

Suri's document was captured in one of al Qaeda's camps in Afghanistan during the American invasion. Since 1996, the Taliban had hosted various Arab jihadist training camps, and Suri's document was available for study. Bin Laden had led his organization back to Afghanistan from Sudan, and a young and upcoming Jordanian named Abu Musab al Zarqawi had recently arrived to establish his own training camp.[25] Saif al Adl, an al Qaeda advisor, courted Zarqawi on behalf of al Qaeda in order to gain influence in the Levant region. Al Adl set up Zarqawi in Herat, Afghanistan, away from the prying eyes of the Pakistanis and closer to their future operating area – reachable through Iran. Zarqawi had collected many Syrians as part of his early group, brothers who had all been through the 'misery' of the failed uprising against Hafez Assad.[26] Since the camp in Herat functioned as a place to exchange ideas with other Salafist–jihadists in the current, it is highly probable that Zarqawi was influenced during this time by the Suri's lessons learned work.

Hypothesis

Zarqawi's Tawhid wal Jihad, established in Iraq in 2002,[27] became a dominant element of the subsequent resistance to the American occupation and the Iraqi government, establishing de facto control of Anbar province by 2006. Why were they so successful compared to the homegrown and more numerous competitors like Jaysh al Muhammed and the 1920s Revolution Brigade? To frame the argument for the rest of this paper, I constructed two assumptions and one hypothesis.

Assumption 1

Zarqawi's early attempts at insurgency in Jordan were an unqualified disaster.[28] Between his release from prison in 1999 and the 2001 scattering of Arab jihadist camps in Afghanistan due to the American invasion, Zarqawi secured an education on how to establish a successful group. That education came mostly from Abu Musab al Suri's work on the failed Syrian rebellion and Suri's advocacy of revolutionary warfare. Zarqawi and his early advisors especially focused on these particular lessons:

(1) Maintain a covert organization and avoid temptation of going public, even when seeing success.
(2) Push a centralized strategy in a decentralized organization that is compartmentalized to avoid compromise.
(3) Do not prioritize military activities over public opinion.
(4) Safeguard all communications as this is the 'weak link'.
(5) Quality over quantity, and ideology over military experience works best. Jihadists will learn in the college of war.
(6) Adopt a clear pattern of publicizing operations. Don't publicize the killings of Muslim informers.
(7) Stay true to the Muslim banner and avoid the draw of secularism.
(8) To avoid factionalism, emphasize the indoctrination of members.[29]

These lessons learned set Tawhid wal Jihad apart from all other insurgent groups and helped them achieve an early dominance. Scholars of the Iraq insurgency from 2003 to 2006[30] support this assumption with one exception: the controversial killings of Muslims. The Islamic State relied heavily on Zarqawi's interpretation of the takfir concept, and their response to criticism was to simply deny or fail to claim attacks with significant civilian deaths. For example, Zarqawi's group denied bombing the Samarra mosque in February 2006, despite strong evidence to the contrary.[31]

Assumption 2

Despite substantial success in 2006 and in the middle of a sectarian war between the Shia and Sunni of Iraq, the Islamic State movement was devastated by a split in the Sunni community, which turned on them in the form of the Awakening movement. Like Ho and Giap, Zarqawi's successor Abu Omar al Baghdadi and his deputy Abu Hamza al Muhajir found themselves facing catastrophic defeat before adapting their organization to leverage the advantages of a revolutionary movement. The blueprint that the Islamic State used, consciously or not, was proven successful by the Viet Cong in their assassination campaign against village chiefs in South Vietnam from 1959 to 1963, which allowed them unfettered access to a majority of the rural population for mobilization purposes. This leads to my hypothesis:

Hypothesis 1

If the Islamic State succeeded in winning support from the Sunni community after 2010, then it was because it adapted the tactics of subversion and revolutionary warfare to remove its Sunni rivals and their government supporters from its core areas and regain a base of political support in the Sunni community.

This hypothesis runs counter to the narrative that Iraqi Prime Minister Maliki alienated and neglected the Awakening movement, or allowed militias and security forces to kill them off as part of a sectarian campaign.[32] Instead, I argue that the Islamic State ran a skillful campaign to eliminate Sunni partisans of the Iraqi government in large numbers, while coopting and wooing other Sunnis back into the fold. Islamic State ability to control territory after 2010 facilitated this collaboration.[33] Once pro-government Sunnis were eliminated from key areas, Iraqi Security Forces stood little chance of defeating an underground subversive movement, and their COIN practices suffered in direct correlation with rising casualties from an unseen enemy.

To validate these two assumptions, I will compare and contrast the initial communist campaign in Vietnam to disconnect the Diem government from the population with the Islamic State campaign to defeat the Sahwa following the Surge. This will establish to what degree the Islamic State adopted principles of revolutionary warfare from the advocacy of the Suri school of Salafist–jihadism. Next, I will test the hypothesis that the Islamic State was the primary agent for the collapse of the Sahwa movement as an effective security force for Sunni areas by conducting a quantitative analysis of the Islamic State's assassination campaign targeting the Sahwa from 2007 to 2013.

Comparing the Vietnamese communists (1960–1964) to Islamic State (2008–2013)

Assassination as a political weapon is not a new tactic, but its role in revolutionary warfare is underdeveloped compared to the importance of mobilizing and harnessing the power of the people and the asymmetric battle between weak insurgent and powerful incumbent government. In reality, the three are often tied together using a common tactic that embraces all three elements of revolutionary warfare: terror. The most recent issue of al Qaeda's *Inspire* has an instructional section on assassination operations, a subconscious and belated homage to the rampant success of the campaign of their rival and former affiliate, the Islamic State.[34] The removal of the links tying the government to the people is a key aspect of the foundation for a successful insurgency, a tactic proven by the Vietnamese communists.

The early years

The assassination campaign in South Vietnam began with an acknowledgment of weakness, an alternate means for the Vietnamese communists to carry on the fight against the Diem government when hopes of a general insurrection were dim. Prior to the Treaty of Paris in 1955, 60% of villages in the South were under communist control.[35] By 1958, an effective campaign by the Diem government had severely damaged local communist cadres in the rural areas. In one village, all 20 members of the People's Revolutionary Party had been arrested and imprisoned.[36] Denying a request to start open warfare in the South by its former Vietminh cadres – now called the People's Revolutionary Party – the Ho Chi Minh regime in the North approved a subversion campaign in 1958 against village chiefs called the 'extermination of traitors'.[37] The purpose of the campaign was to eliminate government interference of party activities in villages, to create fear in their enemies, and to build the faith of its supporters. The inspiration for this campaign came from previous purges of Trotskyites in 1945–1946 as well as the liquidation of 'reactionaries' in the North following the 1955 peace treaty.[38]

The Islamic State movement enjoyed a similar strength in the majority Sunni areas of Iraq in 2006 according to one highly publicized American intelligence assessment[39], and it had experimented with controlling territory in Fallujah, Ramadi, Mosul, and al Qaim. Ironically, its success in achieving this domination inspired a backlash among its own Sunni base, mostly from rival insurgent groups that were feuding with Islamic State fighters[40] and tribes that refused to submit to Islamic State governance and its takeover of the local black markets.[41] Zarqawi's strict policy of killing collaborators with the government encouraged local Sunni tribes, while still fearful of the consequences of collaboration with the government,[42] to work with American units in Ramadi and Fallujah to establish local security militias and local police that would secure tribal areas against Islamic State fighters.[43] This grassroots movement, a mix of tribes and select resistance groups known as the Awakening, spread to other Sunni areas in Diyala and North Babil province and made it impossible for the Islamic State to retain control over core areas. The result was a dramatic and sudden defeat for the Islamic State movement, which like the Vietnamese communists had lost the ability to operate freely in rural areas and to recruit proselytize, tax, and hide.

Campaign against the Traitors

The primary targets of the Vietnamese communist assassination campaign in South Vietnam beginning in 1959 were village chiefs and school teachers. The 'destruction of oppression' campaign highlighted what the People's Revolutionary Party called 'selective' terror, which included disemboweling village chiefs, their wives, and decapitating children in front of entire villages.[44] These killings were carefully vetted by party officials, and were deemed a political act first and foremost. Once authority was removed, local grievances such as land reform could be acted on. Again, the purpose of this was political – not economic in this case. The land was not permanently awarded to peasants because this would remove or solve the grievance, which had to be maintained for continued support for the movement.[45]

Once the government's local representatives were eliminated from the village, the communists moved to expand control through the establishment of liberation committees that consisted of military affairs, recruitment, security, finance, propaganda, and civil affairs.[46] Taxes were collected, less for financial needs and more as an implicit recognition of party legitimacy in the area.[47] Fall used this same logic to investigate who truly dominated the villages of the Red River Delta in 1953 and found that 'the bulk of the Delta was no longer paying taxes'. Fall also found an inverse correlation between the presence of teachers and Viet Minh control.[48]

Vietnamese Communist Party legitimacy was expanded by the use of mass political organizations that were separate from the party so as not to dilute its purity. Instead, the party maintained a carefully concealed control of these front organizations – representing women or farmers united for land reform – while using them to expand the exposure of the population to indoctrination of party principles and stressing popular local grievances.[49]

In contrast to this popular outreach, the assassination campaign of government associated 'counter-revolutionaries' was not about terrorizing a population into submission, which has limited effect and undermines the legitimacy of the future regime. This distaste for extreme violence was expressed by the Chinese communists who were openly critical of the Vietnamese for their reliance on terror.[50] However, this did not dissuade the Vietnamese communists; the intent of the campaign was to create an unfair advantage in the competition for governance, which cannot be won in an absentee fashion and therefore the insurgents win by default.

Compared to the politically advanced People's Revolutionary Party, the Islamic State movement was a military organization with a highly functioning public relations office and little governance outside of small local areas. These attempts at governance had focused on the strict imposition of the Islamic State's religious ideology and had not been considered successful. Furthermore, the foreign roots of the organization had allowed rivals to paint the group as unrepresentative of the true wishes of Iraqi Sunnis.[51]

The natural advancement of Iraqi ansar (supporters) of the Islamic State drove the organization to create a political union that allowed Salafist groups to join with the Islamic State movement in a front called the Mujahideen Shura Council

(MSC) in January 2006. Several months after Zarqawi was killed in the summer of 2006, Abu Omar al Qureshi al Baghdadi[52] became the leader of the newly proclaimed Islamic State of Iraq in October. Abu Hamza al Muhajir, an Egyptian al Qaeda veteran, became Omar's deputy and the military leader of the movement. The Islamic State claimed in a subsequent press release that the group known as al Qaeda in Iraq no longer existed.[53]

The significance of this transition was the establishment of a political body with Iraqi leadership and one with a historical tie to the Salafist community that had grown in Iraq since the 1980s. This move, which took place too late to prevent the defeat of the movement in 2007 at the hands of the Sahwa and Coalition forces, played a large role in the later resurgence of the Islamic State. The creation of various committees signified a more serious approach to matching the type of political organization required for the success of a revolutionary movement – as seen in the success of the Vietnamese communists.

Abu Omar and Abu Hamza publicly discussed the reasons for their failure to capture public support and admitted to certain failures. A captured letter from 2007 – a 38-page strategy document by someone close to the leadership – decried the rigidity of the movement's doctrine and recommended improvements in organization and a more flexible strategy of revolution[54] – a very Leninist approach.[55] In addition to pushing the concept of an Islamic State when they controlled no territory, the new leaders of the movement prioritized a subversion campaign directed at their Sunni rivals who had pushed them out of their core areas. Abu Omar announced a campaign called al Karamah (Dignity) in 2008 followed by the Hasad al Khayr (Harvest of the Good) in 2009, focusing on eliminating Sunni Sahwa, Shia militias, and Iraqi government officials and political candidates. It was frequently referred to as the 'Campaign against the Traitors'. To test my hypothesis that these campaigns were a major factor in the return of the Islamic State, the following case study is presented.

Turning the tables: Testing the hypothesis

The abrupt fracturing of the Sunni resistance in 2007 saw a significant amount of fighting between rival groups, an end to robust sanctuaries for the Islamic State movement, and the death and desertion of large numbers of fighters. Pressure from below (Sahwa) and above (US Special Operations Forces) meant the organization had to operate in small cells with little guidance other than the establishment of open worded campaign plans. To measure the impact of these campaigns, I used the Iraqi Body Count database[56] to ascertain a baseline of Awakening deaths from 2006 to 2013. I compared this estimation with an analysis of all of the Islamic State operational summaries from the same period in four key locations with varying population sizes and makeup: Jurf ah Sakhr, Garma, Baqubah, and Mosul. These summaries had been posted by the official media outlets of the movement, systematically since 2004, on jihadist websites for dissemination to supporters. The four locations in Iraq cover Babil, Anbar, Diyala, and Nineveh provinces and represent the southern, western, eastern, and northern regions of Sunni Iraq. What the locations shared in common was a pattern of Islamic State activity that highlighted their importance as core areas of support by the population.

Four samples

Jurf ah Sakhr (pop. 80,000)[57] is a small agricultural area along the Euphrates river that had been the home to the Republican Guard Medina Division, with a corresponding ammunition supply point looted after the invasion that provided enough explosive material to supply the insurgency for decades. Almost exclusively Sunni, it sat on the border of the Sunni–Shia fault line that ran south of Baghdad and was close to the highway that Shia pilgrims used to walk to Karbala. Sectarian control of this area was a major concern for both sides of the divide.

Garma (pop. 116,000) is a medium-sized village outside of Fallujah described as the 'hardest nut to crack' by the Marines assigned to pacify Anbar province in 2006.[58] Garma (sometimes spelled Karma) is also almost exclusively Sunni, but its location in Sunni Anbar province left sectarian tensions somewhat lower, with the exception of the Shia Army unit from Basra that had failed to pacify it prior to the Awakening, when security was put into local Sunni hands in early 2007.

Baqubah (pop. 220,000) is the capital of Diyala, a mixed sect province northeast of Baghdad with a high residual level of violence. Shia militia activity was heavy in the region, and it took some time and effort for the Awakening to be established in the city. The measurements for Baqubah included the nearby towns of Buhriz and Khalis, and all three had functioning Sunni Awakening units in a diverse population of Sunni and Shia. Like Garma and Jurf, it was a historic stronghold for the Islamic State; it took most of 2008 to clear out the large number of militants that had fled from other areas due to the Sahwa/Surge.

Mosul (pop. 2,000,000)[59] is also a provincial capital and a large ethnically diverse city in Nineveh, the north of Iraq. The ancient city astride the Tigris River was the second largest city in Iraq before 2014 and had a large Sunni population which had often been at odds with the local Kurds. Efforts to establish an Awakening in Mosul had been frustrated by an Islamic State movement that maintained an extensive extortion network that had taxed oil and other normal economic activity since 2005.

The benchmark: Iraqi Body Count

The Iraqi Body Count database uses multiple media reports of deaths along with morgue data to report casualties and helpfully reports the special status of victims such as Awakening members or Shia pilgrims. This victim count is

Table 1. Awakening deaths in Iraq, 2007–2013 (data from IraqiBodyCount.org).

Year	Deaths
2007	149
2008	677
2009	254
2010	262
2011	204
2012	221
2013	546
Total	2313

certainly understated due to the nature of civil wars and the fact that some bodies are not reported or found. To establish a benchmark, I screened for all reported Awakening/Sahwa references across the country from 2007 to 2013 (see Table 1). Awakening deaths at the national level peaked early in 2008 at 677 as the Islamic State movement adjusted to its loss of control of core areas, then leveled out evenly from 2009 to 2012 before rising dramatically again in 2013 as the Islamic State began to control more and more territory throughout Iraq, including Fallujah in December 2013. It is striking, however, that Awakening deaths are relatively constant between high points, at a time when the Islamic State movement is often declared non-existent or in Syrian sanctuaries. The total deaths of Sahwa members is 2313, a significant number considering that the Sahwa consisted of 90,000 members.[60] The benchmark doesn't measure the number of Sahwa that were wounded, incapacitated, fled the country, or defected to the Islamic State.

The pattern of nationwide Sahwa deaths shows that after the first full year of the Awakening's existence (2008) was also the record high; after this, deaths leveled out at between 200 and 250 per year until 2013, when deaths again spiked in the year before the Islamic State made its move to permanently control and administer territory. In accordance with my hypothesis, 2008 marked a turning point and a diminished capability for the Islamic State movement to take action against the Sahwa, which then manifested itself in a patient campaign to undermine the organization for the next four yours. By 2013, the organization was strong enough to push out of its newly established core areas and expand influence in all Sunni areas of Iraq, and this results in twice as many Sahwa deaths than in any year since 2008. By very early 2014, the Islamic State had achieved success in Anbar and many other areas. The four sample locations: Jurf, Garma, Baqubah, and Mosul allow a glimpse into the actual strategy the Islamic State took in establishing control.

Islamic State operational reports

To test my hypothesis that the Islamic State was responsible for this carnage, and not the Maliki administration or Shia militias, I extracted claims from the

Islamic State's wilayat (provincial) monthly operational summaries and compared them to the Iraqi Body Count data for the four cities described above. The veracity of the claims does vary by province, but for the most part the movement seemed to follow Abu Musab al Suri's guidance to be honest in order to maintain credibility.[61] The press releases noted when the operators were unsure of the target's status or had missed the target, chalking it up as God's will. They often gave descriptions of exact locations and names, making verification with press reports achievable.

Often, I found that the Islamic State had claimed an assassination that remained an unsolved mystery in the press. For example, according to an NPR report, Sunni Islamic Party member and elected official Samir Safwat al Hadithi[62] was gunned down outside his home in southern Baghdad on 18 February 2009.[63] The news report insinuated that either Shia militias had assassinated him or his own Sunni political rivals had. He was the third Islamic Party member assassinated that month. There was no mention in the newscast of the possibility that the Islamic State had killed a Sunni rival for participating in a democratically elected government, an act of apostasy according to Islamic State doctrine. The Islamic State claimed his death in May of 2009 – unnoticed by the same media that reported on it in February.[64]

Jurf

The benchmark Iraqi Body Count (IBC) Sahwa deaths suggests a bell-shaped distribution with a slow start to the campaign, peak deaths in 2009–2011, and a reduction afterwards. A parallel analysis of Islamic State claims shows a similar pattern with peak attacks and most deaths claimed in 2011 (13), which mirrored the benchmark. Attacks and deaths drop off after 2011. The correlation between Islamic State claims and the benchmark was close to 80% (see Table 2 and Figure 1).

Garma

According to the benchmark, Sahwa deaths in this key Anbar town were unremarkable until 2013, when an increase in Islamic State activity in Anbar corresponded with the high. With some minor exceptions, Islamic State claims

Table 2. Comparison of IS claimed attacks to Benchmark (IBC) in Jurf ah Sakhr.

Jurf	Sahwa killed (IBC)	ISI claimed (Sahwa kill)	ISI claimed (Sahwa wounded)	ISI claimed attacks
2007	1	NR	NR	NR
2008	5	4	4	6
2009	17	8	6	14
2010	14	11	4	10
2011	13	13	6	20
2012	4	1	0	2
2013	1	9	0	6
Total	55	46	20	58

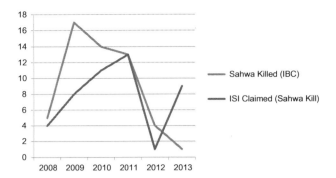

Figure 1. Comparison of IS claimed attacks to Benchmark (IBC) in Jurf ah Sakhr.

Table 3. Comparison of IS claimed attacks to Benchmark (IBC) in Garma.

Garma	Sahwa killed (IBC)	ISI claimed (Sahwa Kill)	ISI claimed (Sahwa wounded)	ISI claimed attacks
2007	0	NR	NR	NR
2008	4	25	0	1
2009	7	8	9	10
2010	2	0	1	1
2011	0	2	1	3
2012	0	0	0	1
2013	31	11	7	9
Total	44	46	18	25

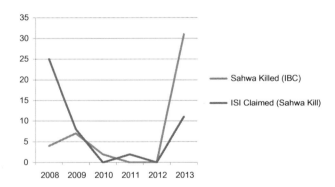

Figure 2. Comparison of IS claimed attacks to Benchmark (IBC) in Garma.

matched the output of the benchmark as well as the pattern (see Table 3 and Figure 2). Anbar was the home of the Sahwa movement, and it seemed to maintain its strength there longer than it did in the other sample cities. While other Sahwa associated tribes, particularly in the Ramadi region, held fast against the return of the Islamic State, Garma returned to the Islamic State fold in early 2014.[65]

Table 4. Comparison of IS claimed attacks to Benchmark (IBC) in Baqubah.

Baqubah	Sahwa killed (IBC)	ISI claimed (Sahwa Kill)	ISI claimed (Sahwa wounded)	ISI claimed attacks
2007	23	40	1	17
2008	95	19	14	7
2009	23	4	7	6
2010	23	6	5	10
2011	54	35	25	48
2012	41	33	22	44
2013	53	16	13	20
Total	312	153	87	152

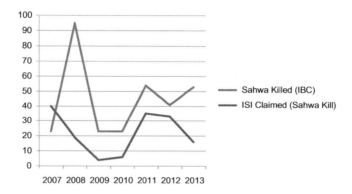

Figure 3. Comparison of IS claimed attacks to Benchmark (IBC) in Baqubah.

Baqubah

The pattern of Sahwa deaths differs from both the national level benchmark and the other cases in that it remained constant throughout, with a spike in violence in 2008 as the Islamic State movement, which had consolidated in Diyala during the Surge operations, was defeated. While the pattern for ISI claims is similar to the benchmark (see Table 4 and Figure 3), it suffers from incomplete data from missing operational summaries in 2008 (missing 10 months out of 12), 2009 (missing 9), 2010 (missing 8), and 2013 (missing 5). The other provinces reliably reported their activities, but the Islamic State Diyala media organization for whatever reason either failed to post its data or I was unable to collect it. Nonetheless, despite missing 32 months of data during this period, the Islamic State still claimed almost half the number of Sahwa deaths compared to the benchmark. It is possible that Shia militias operating in Diyala also targeted the Sahwa for sectarian reasons and are responsible for the deaths reported in the benchmark. This possibility aside, there are several press reports that indicate that many of the Sahwa deaths that occurred during the period of missing operational reports were inflicted by the Islamic State.

In late 2009, Ramzy Mardini of the Jamestown Foundation noted that 'AQI' had reformed the Islamic State of Iraq in Diyala province that September and 'recently opened a campaign of assassination' against senior Sahwa leaders there. There is plenty of evidence to believe that the Islamic State movement was active before 2009 due to its own claims of a substantial number of Sahwa kills (59) prior to this (see Table 4), but Mardini's claim could explain the absence of the periodic operational summaries that were so consistently produced in the other provinces. According to Mardini,

> On November 17, AQI-associated operatives assassinated Hameed Khaleel al-Obeidi, the leader of the Sahwa council of the Bab al-Darb district of Baaquba, the capital city of Diyala province. The next day, AQI affiliates fired upon Shaykh Houssam Ulwan al-Majmaai, the commander of Sahwa forces for all of Diyala, after intercepting his vehicle on the major road leading to the Kanaan district (*Awsat al-Iraq*, November 18). Though the operation failed to kill al-Majmaai, it was the second assassination attempt on his life within a month. In late October, a bomb wounded the Sahwa leader in the Bahraz district, south of Baaquba (*Awsat al-Iraq*, October 22). Only days earlier a suicide bomber killed the Bahraz Sahwa leader Leith Mashaan and other members of the Awakening movement. Mashaan was reported to have contributed to the arrests of numerous AQI leaders, including the individual the Iraqi government claims to be Abu Omar al-Baghdadi – the alleged commander of the ISI (*Awsat al-Iraq*, October 13).[66]

The suicide bomber and the revenge motives all point toward Islamic State involvement in these deaths. In the claims I do have, the Islamic State claimed three other attacks on Sheik Houssam's aides in the Majmaai clan in Buhriz town, just south of Baqubah, with Jasim Suhayl being killed on 4 March 2011,[67] a failed attempt on 29 September 2011,[68] and Ahmad Nada killed on 24 May 2012.[69]

The *New York Times* documented the disintegration of the Baqubah Sahwa movement in October 2010, which happened earlier than Jurf (2011) and Garma (2013), noting that the Sahwa was caught between an aggressive Islamic State that could infiltrate the movement and an untrusting government that often disrespected them and occasionally arrested them in cases of mistaken identity or suspicion of involvement in insurgent activities. One Islamic State member was quoted saying 'many of those who called themselves the Awakening felt remorse... They believed they were making a mistake by helping the occupiers and have returned to Al Qaeda. I can say this number is increasing every day.'

The article also quoted the same Sheik Houssam Majmaai as receiving a phone call from his cousin, a jailed Islamic State member, who advised him to rejoin the insurgency. Sheik Majmaai declined, but acknowledged that the effort was an example of an 'ongoing seduction' by men who 'had no doubts' about their future success.[70] Pairing these news reports with an extrapolation of Islamic State activities for the missing months, and the results come close to the patterns of the other three cases.

Mosul

The final case was the provincial capital of Nineveh. The benchmark for Sahwa deaths reveal very few in number (4) over a seven-year period, and the Islamic

Table 5. Comparison of IS claimed attacks to Benchmark (IBC) in Mosul.

Mosul	Sahwa killed (IBC)	ISI claimed (Sahwa kill)	ISI claimed (Sahwa wounded)	ISI claimed attacks
2007	1	NR	NR	NR
2008	0	2	2	7
2009	1	1	0	1
2010	0	0	0	0
2011	0	0	0	0
2012	0	1	1	4
2013	2	3	0	3
Total	4	7	3	15

State claims are similar (see Table 5). Considering that Mosul is the second largest city in Iraq, this scarcity of Sahwa deaths is puzzling. There are several reasons that the Islamic State did not conduct an anti-Sahwa campaign in Mosul, the most obvious being that there was never an Awakening movement there.[71] The weight of the evidence leads me to believe that this failure was due to the deep entrenchment of the Islamic State in Mosul and a lack of desire of Sunnis there to rally to the government, unlike in Anbar and elsewhere.

The presence of the Islamic State in Mosul grew in late 2004 after the battles of Fallujah forced some Zarqawi elements to relocate to Mosul.[72] From 2005 to 2008 the Islamic State movement established a strong extortion network[73] that soon replaced Anbar province as its strongest revenue generator.[74] In one short period in early 2010, the counterinsurgents killed or captured an Islamic State economic security emir, three 'extortion personalities', an oil minister and his deputy, and an oil extortion leader all in the Mosul area.[75] This economic infrastructure, a level of development that belies the criticism of the Islamic State's 'fake state', allowed the group to be completely self-funded by 2006[76] – with a resultant independence from external interference that al Suri stressed in his lessons learned.[77]

The Islamic State's strong presence in Mosul was manifested in two important ways, one politically and the other militarily. Captured Islamic State of Iraq documents[78] from Mosul in 2007 demonstrate early attempts by Wilayat Ninewa to govern the population as a shadow government, including regulation of billiards and music halls,[79] crime,[80] and sexual harassment.[81] These decrees provide evidence of the Islamic State's early nation-building desires not only in Mosul but also Diyala, Anbar, and Saladin provinces, and foreshadow the nation-building efforts that took place once the Islamic State secured territory in these same provinces in 2014.[82]

While attacks on Awakening in Mosul were negligible, attacks on the Iraqi Security Forces in Nineveh province were the highest in the nation during this time period. A sample of Islamic State claimed operations in three provinces demonstrate that without an Awakening presence to collaborate with the state for security maintenance and intelligence gathering, insurgent activity as early

Table 6. Islamic State attacks during the month of Dhu-al Hijjah (28 October – 24 November) 2011. (Documented Military Operations in Mosul (17 January 2012), Anbar (3 January 2012), and Diyala (18 December 2011)).

	Attacks
Mosul	73
Anbar	52
Diyala	20

as 2011 was significantly higher in Mosul than elsewhere (see Table 6). This factor will be investigated in more detail by returning to the Jurf ah Sakhr case study and comparing the Islamic State campaign against the Sahwa with its parallel effort against the Iraqi Security Forces operating in the area.

Jurf Part II

Security for Jurf ah Sakhr district in 2008 consisted of a small Awakening detachment of 200 local Sunnis from a diverse group of clans in the area, mostly from the Janabi federation. Iraq Security Forces consisted of local police, an Army battalion, and an Emergency Response Force regiment (SWAT). This was a significant increase in forces since the Awakening movement took root in Jurf in mid-2007, at which time there were no police, one Iraqi Army platoon, and one US Army platoon. The Awakening movement which reduced violence in the area had been mostly made up of Sunni professionals, tribal elements, and former resistance members from the Islamic Army and other insurgent groups. Sabah al Azab al Janabi was appointed by the local Janabi tribe to lead the Awakening movement, and he eventually became the mayor of Jurf ah Sakhr district, which included half a dozen small villages (Fadiliyah, Farisiyah, Owesat, Sunydij, Hamiya, and Abd Ways). American forces remained in support of local Iraqi Army units in Hamiya through the very end of the American presence in the country (2011).[83]

In four years there were only two attacks against American forces and both happened early in 2008. Given the amount of Islamic State activity during this time period, there can be little doubt that the Islamic State movement was deliberately avoiding targeting American forces because their focus was on defeating the Sahwa. The earliest attack on a key Sahwa leader occurred in October 2008 when Abd al Hadi was assassinated by the Islamic State. Hadi had been active in the resistance against the government and the United States, and was wanted for the killing of an American paratrooper.[84] He had also led the fight against the Islamic State in 2007 but was denied participation in the Sahwa at the time due to his past. By 2008 he had joined the Sahwa in some leadership capacity, partnering with Sabah al Azab before his death. The Islamic State claimed the assassination of Hadi as part of Abu Omar's Al Karamah (Dignity) campaign.[85]

Attacks increased steadily in Jurf, with most targeting the Sahwa in 2008 (6 of 9) and 2009 (14 of 21). Attacks were more evenly spread in 2010 (10 of 23)

Table 7. Breakdown of Sahwa attacks, January 2008 – February 2013, claimed by Islamic State of Iraq (ISI).

	Jurf	Garma	Baqubah	Mosul
Awakening date	June 2007	Spring 2007	Late 2007	None
Sectarian makeup	Sunni	Sunni	Mixed	Mixed
Sahwa attacks	58	25	152	15
Close kill	29	11	44	5
IED/sticky	14	6	72	5
Named target	26	9	76	7
Sahwa leaders targeted	23	9	73	7
Houses destroyed	3	1	17	1
Killed	46	46	153	4
Wounded	20	18	87	3

and 2011 (20 of 45) despite the fact that Jurf had a heavy Iraqi Security Force presence during many times of the year in order to protect the various pilgrimages to Karbala on the highway that skirted the town to the south. In addition to a heavy Sahwa focus, the Islamic State's strategy hinged on eliminating key Sahwa leaders in a discriminate manner while pressuring tribal leaders to withdraw their participation in the local militia. Of the 58 attacks on Sahwa during the period, exactly half were close-kill assassinations in the middle of the night and another quarter of them were IEDs of the normal type, or more frequently, sticky bombs that were magnetically attached to the engine of a Sahwa vehicle and detonated while driving. In 26 of the 58 attacks the victim was named, and 23 targets were leaders or key tribal sheiks supporting the movement. Targeting the leadership, instead of lower ranking Sahwa sitting on check points, was designed to allow future recruitment of Sahwa members to the Islamic State at a future date (see Table 7).

Of the many Jurf Sahwa leaders targeted by Islamic State, Sabah al Azab survived one assassination attempt in July 2009 due to mistaken identity[86] and was seriously wounded in June 2010 in an IED attack.[87] By the end of 2011 Sabah had fled the country, due to both Islamic State pressure and the state's security forces which no longer seemed to trust Sabah to keep Jurf secure.[88] The campaign against the Awakening began to taper after his absence, but not before claiming a distinguished tribal leader from Jurf ah Sakhr named Ahmad Muzahim al Janabi, who was assassinated while returning from a meeting in Baghdad of the National Reconciliation Committee in October 2012.[89] By this time, the Islamic State had shifted its focus in the Jurf area from the Sahwa to the Iraqi Security Forces.

Without a functioning Awakening unit providing information and context on the local Sunni dynamics in Jurf, attacks on security forces increased after 2010 and were characterized by attacks using mortars and IEDs, both activities that require some military skill and a population that is either supportive or unwilling

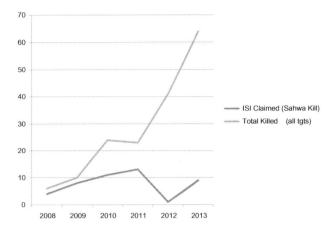

Figure 4. Comparison of Awakening deaths to other targets (ISF, US, Civ) in Jurf.

to inform. After 2011, casualties among security forces operating in Jurf skyrocketed (see Table 8 and Figure 4). The early Sahwa intensive campaign gave way to a focus on security that struggled to operate in a suddenly unfriendly area. Large Army sweeps to find Islamic State insurgents in Jurf were not only failures, but the local Army unit lost its division commander and several other key leaders in an IED attack in Abd Ways in December 2013 that killed a total of 10.[90]

Discussion

The Islamic State demonstrated a mastery of irregular warfare in their subversion of a tightly controlled Jurf run by an effective, tribally supported local Sahwa militia. While the irregular warfare campaign described above documents the damage done to the Sahwa and supporting governmental forces, it does not measure how the Islamic State was able to mobilize the population in preparation for taking control of core areas. To establish control, the Islamic State would have to master the techniques of political outreach to the local population coupled with an effective messaging campaign to popularize Islamic State solutions to local grievances in order to establish legitimacy for the movement. After a short period of adjustment and debate, Abu Omar al Baghdadi and Abu Hamza al Muhajir did just that.

Gartenstein-Ross recently described the Islamic State's revolutionary warfare approach as less Maoist and instead closer to the Focoist approach, where the 'political foundation necessary for revolution can be crafted through violence'.[91] Certainly the leaders of the Islamic State movement had and continue to have a cultural and cognitive preference for using violence to shape the environment and achieve the Caliphate. However, a focus on the excessive violence and terror

Table 8. Comparison of Sahwa attacks and total attacks in Jurf with casualty figures.

Jurf	Sahwa Killed (IBC)	ISI Claimed (Sahwa Kill)	ISI Claimed (Sahwa Wounded)	ISI Claimed Attacks	Total Killed (all tgts)	Total Wounded (all tgts)	Total Attacks (all tgts)
2007	1	NR	NR	NR	NR	NR	NR
2008	5	4	4	6	6	4	9
2009	17	8	6	14	10	10	21
2010	14	11	4	10	24	19	23
2011	13	13	6	20	23	15	45
2012	4	1	0	2	41	22	21
2013	1	9	0	6	64	45	69
Total	55	46	20	58	168	115	188

produced by the Islamic State – while understandable – diverts our attention from its less visible but crucial mobilization of the support of the Sunni nation.

Social movement theory provides a framework to explain how the Islamic State accomplished the mobilization of supporters in its core areas of Iraq to successfully gain control of territory by 2014. McAdam's political process model, consisting of antecedent conditions, mechanisms, and effects, explains how resistance movements develop. Lee's social movement approach to resistance dynamics adapted the model for irregular warfare, with conditions that included political disunity, ungoverned economics, socio-ethnic divides, and identity grievances.[92] The Islamic State emphasized a narrative of Maliki's oppression of Sunnis and its view of the historical and cultural inferiority of the Shia, exploited the divided Sunni polity, and its domination of the economy in Sunni areas attracted recruits and followers.

The mechanisms the Islamic State used to rebuild their Sunni base included co-option and conversion of political elites, resource generation and usurpation of state resources, recruitment and network expansion, and framing using media platforms.[93] The elimination of pro-government Sunni tribal and Sahwa leaders allowed increased recruiting within the tribes and in rural areas. Islamic State media shifted its strategy to produce more products at the local level while focusing on what Ingram calls pragmatic and perceptual factors. Pragmatic factors focus on security and livelihood, while perceptual factors play on identity conflicts between the Sunni Iraqis that Islamic State was pursuing and the predominant sectarian makeup of the government, which is Shia.[94]

The effects of the process are increased political legitimacy, economic self-sufficiency, organizational and operational resiliency, and increased popular support.[95] The Anbar Sunni protest movement created the appearance of a crisis that the Islamic State leveraged for additional legitimacy in their argument against the incumbent government, and their growing military strength in core areas allowed them to demonstrate the potential for governance. By the end of 2013, the Islamic State was seizing and holding territory for the first time since 2007. To demonstrate how the Islamic State mobilized its target population,

I used Lee's social movement approach to trace the Islamic State's rise in the areas in an around Jurf ah Sakhr using documents from the Conflict Records Research Center (CRRC).[96]

Balancing coercion, co-option, and carrots

In August 2011, Islamic State of Iraq spokesman Abu Mohammed al Adnani highlighted how the anti-Sahwa campaign was used as a psychological weapon designed to instill fear:

> How long are you going to live in fear? No one among you dares to leave his house, travel, or even sleep peacefully in his own home. When will you enjoy peace again? How long are you going to stay alert day and night? Do you think we will go away? Do you think we will cease to exist or get bored? No! Repent quickly before it is too late, for the results of the battle have been already decided, and it is only a matter of days![97]

The Sahwa had much to fear from the Islamic State, but there was often another message broadcast to the Sunni community – particularly the lower ranking members of the Sahwa – and this one is from Abu Bakr al Baghdadi, Omar's successor:

> As for those who were misled by chieftains and members of our tribes and thus sided with the ranks of the Crusader United States and became servants and stooges of the Safavid government, I tell them that I swear to God you will not be harmed if you follow the truth and support the religion of God, just as you fought against it. Thus, repent and reform your mind because God will forgive you and replace your sins with good.[98]

These two messages illustrate the dual-tone strategy that Abu Omar al Baghdadi crafted in 2008–2009 with his war minister and partner, Abu Hamza al Muhajir. As Lee's social movement model suggests, the dynamics were much more than just addressing a grievance or developing a slick media program. Such a change would require new institutions and the communication of the vision throughout the ranks.

The idea of repentance for the Sahwa was controversial among the upper ranks of the Islamic State. Captured correspondence from Abu Hamza to Al Qaeda Central in 2008 exposed a dispute between Abu Sulayman, the head of the Islamic State's legal branch, and Abu Hamza. Sulayman left the Islamic State to return to Pakistan where he complained to al Qaeda Central's leadership that Abu Hamza and Abu Omar had offered amnesty to the 'criminals of the tribes who went back and formed the Awakenings'.[99] The letters paint a picture different than the caricature of the Islamic State of as rigid, instead providing key evidence that the Islamic State's leadership was flexible and willing to change course, even in the face of the defection of key religious leaders. Furthermore, it exposes the breakdown in communications between the two groups.

Once the difficult leadership decision was made to offer repentance to the tribes and convince them to return to resistance, Abu Omar al Baghdadi created a tribal outreach office.[100] A RAND Corporation examination of captured Islamic State documents prior to 2008 does not show such a tribal outreach department in Anbar province's organization chart.[101] By 2009, captured letters retrieved from the strike that killed Abu Omar and Abu Hamza revealed the efforts of an emir named Abu Khaldun from the 'Southern Belt'[102] who was reporting back to a centralized tribal engagement office.

The institution of a tribal outreach office was a belated recognition that ignoring the importance of tribal leaders in the traditional Sunni society had been a primary factor in the rise of the Sahwa – particularly considering that the Islamic State movement was an economic competitor to Sunni tribes.[103] Islamic State had ignored the tribes originally because they were a rival to their future implementation of Sharia and the rule of the Islamic State appointed emir in local areas. This changed in 2008. Abu Khaldun's post-engagement reports, addressed to someone who reported directly to both Abu Omar and Abu Hamza, described his outreach to Sunni tribal leaders in Jurf ah Sakhr, Yousifiyah, Amiriyah al Fallujah, and other former ISI sanctuaries. The emir brought the tribal leaders gifts of fine robes and headdresses, and played on their Sunni ties and suspicions of the government. He reported who was amenable to the ISI, who was willing to sabotage Sahwa participation in the tribe, and who was stalling and maintaining ties to the government. In one case, he asked his superior in the letter for permission to move against one prominent sheik who had spurned his engagements and elected to run for government under the Maliki ticket.[104]

In Jurf ah Sakhr in the fall of 2009, Abu Khaldun met with a very prominent Jurf Sheik (name withheld) and reported that his contact:

> was a high ranking officer in former Army but refused to be part of al Alqami's state. Abu Asim visited him previously. As for me, I sat with him for five minutes after Ramadan prayers and introduced myself and told him about my mandate, and he welcomed me and I conveyed your best regards for him and gave him the gift I was taking to him. He told me to convey his allegiance to the sheikhs for best or worst and conveyed to me the leadership should avoid the type of mistakes committed in the past (target quality not quantity), and he repeated this last phrase three times and implored Allah to preserve you and grant you victory. We then parted.[105]

The sheiks referred to were Abu Omar and Abu Hamza, and the reference to 'al Alqami's state' was a historic reference to the Caliph's Shia vizier al Alqami who allegedly conspired to assist the Mongols in the catastrophic sack of Baghdad that ended the Abbasid empire. The entire engagement emphasized similar identity (Sunni Arab) loyalties and religious ties. The tribal sheik was advising the emir to respect the tribes and work through them in their efforts to contest the Maliki government, and to be discriminate in the elimination of their enemies.

The network expanded throughout the Southern Belt in the Sunni farmland among a population vulnerable to their identity and tribal ties to the Islamic

State. The Iraqi state was simply incapable of competing with Abu Khaldun's social networking. From another of his reports:

(1) After arrangements and communications, a meeting was held with Sheikh X[name withheld], the chief of al-'Imran sub-tribe of al-Gharir [or al-'Azir] tribe who lives in Shishbar region near by A1-Ghuwaythat, who is a popular man in his tribe, well known, and has good reputation. He is also supportive of the Islamic State and is ready to accommodate the State members. Several issues have been discussed, some of which are:

(a) Dismantling the al-Sahwah [Awakening Councils] groups, which is an Awakening of both apostasy and hypocrisy, and he told us that would be achieved by eliminating the al-Sahwah Sheikh, [name withheld] and the Al-Ghuwaythat al-Sahwah Sheikh, [name withheld]. He also showed readiness to cooperate with the brothers to work and accommodate them for any project.

(b) He told us he has three fighters who wish to pledge their allegiance and work with the Islamic State.

(c) The brothers in Al Latifiyah have been informed about Sheik X's stance and the cooperation with him.

The meeting was conducted by our brother Abu-Hazim

(1) A meeting was held with one of Zawba' tribal chiefs, Sheikh [name withheld] al-Zawba'i, who is kind, courageous, and supportive to the State, who literally told me: 'I wish for the Islamic State men to return so they can chase away those traitors, the men of the al-Sahwah groups of apostasy and hypocrisy who gave up their faith and honor for the infidel Occupier.

(2) The discussion topic was about dismantling of the al-Sahwah groups, which is an al-Sahwah of apostasy and hypocrisy, as soon as possible. Also, he told me that he is going to do his best working with Sheikhs and good and prominent individuals to enlighten and advise the people to return to their right sense.

The meeting was conducted by our brother Abu-Hisham.

(3) A trip to our brother [name withheld] has been conducted, whereas the conditions of the homes and the tribes around the Expressway between alMu'in and Albu-Hamdan have been discussed with him. He also has been tasked to move on with the matter of coordinating with other sheikhs in the region.

(4) A communication took place with Hajji [name withheld] al-Qarghuli who is the uncle of Al-Qarghul sub-tribe leader Sheikh [name withheld], who is completely opposite to his brother's son and he is

supportive to the Islamic State. A meeting has been arranged soon with him.[106]

The tribal outreach and network extension by leaders in the Islamic State movement was a slow process that took five years to develop, and only accelerated at the end when the Islamic State tapped into a parallel but independent Sunni protest movement in Anbar that reinforced their messaging about Shia oppression of Sunnis. Despite the empirical evidence suggesting that the Islamic State emphasized the elimination of its Sunni rivals, the leadership understood that co-option and engagement of the remainder of those networks was crucial in fashioning the foundations for the creation of a real Islamic State, one that remains and expands.

Conclusion

While many factors influenced the environment that enabled the Islamic State to rise to control large areas in both Syria and Iraq, the Islamic State's defeat of the Sahwa in Iraq is a primary factor that allowed it to upend government control of their core areas and mobilize its target population. The hypothesis testing confirms a strong correlation between the elimination of the Sahwa elements in the Jurf test case and the ability of the Islamic State to move from the Maoist organizational phase to mobile warfare against state security forces. While this is an important finding in explaining the rise of the Islamic State, this research presents several questions for future research.

If the Vietnamese communists and the Salafist–jihadists were able to adapt different ideologies to irregular warfare tactics, then how important is ideology as a factor in both successes? While it is possible that there are similarities between communism and Salafist–jihadism that could account for the compatibility between ideology and irregular warfare tactics, it seems intuitive that these would still be special cases. Are these ideologies similar enough to work in combination with the tactics to produce success? What role does insurgent leadership play in adapting to changing dynamics for success in this combination of violent social movement formation?

Another area that could be developed further is the idea of the two networks – the Sahwa and the Islamic State – at war with each other. An argument could be made that the Islamic State's multiple networks: Salafist–jihadists, outcasts from the Sahwa movement and Sunni resistance rejectionists, Camp Bucca alumni, former Ba'ath regime members, and foreign fighters combined to create a deep, overlapping network that was impenetrable to the Sahwa once they realized they were under attack. In contrast, the Sahwa were at odds with Sunni political leadership of the provinces and were localized networks that had odd strands across the country that could not be described as a national network. The previous war had damaged the structure of the tribes and the tribes were hopelessly divided in most cases between supporting the Iraqi government or the resistance. The Islamic State did have this national character and could easily surge assets as they attacked different parts of the Sahwa network in detail. Islamic State assassination squads created patterns of attacks in this town, followed by a series of attacks in a nearby town, and so on. With perfect local intelligence by clandestine stay-behind networks, the Islamic State could achieve the discrimination demanded of them by their prospective Sunni tribal leaders sitting on the proverbial fence. In the battle of networks, the deeper and more connected network might have won.

Finally, the battle of narratives in this decade-long struggle by the Islamic State is fascinating. Analysts and reporters often describe the Islamic State as too brutal for even al Qaeda, and that this violence was supposedly crucial in instigating the Sahwa backlash in 2006. Yet in 2009 and 2010, Sunni tribal leaders are once again sending their men to join the Islamic State. I would suggest that Mao's concept of contradictions can explain this confusing juxtaposition of narratives and truth. Mao recommended that all grievances be attended to but not solved, while according to one observer: 'the secret behind revolutionary successes in winning the people is to tell them what they want to hear, irrespective of whether or not this happens to vary from the long term rebel objectives.'[107] I would add that the other secret is to take a kernel of truth, such as Iranian influence among some Shia politicians, and conflate it, manipulate it, and exaggerate it until it becomes what Ingram calls the crisis – a crisis that is manufactured, and that only the revolutionary can solve. After that, the revolutionary simply has to manage the savagery before establishing new governance ... and a new truth.[108]

Notes

1. Fall, 'Theory and Practice', 50–6.
2. Taber, *The War of the Flea*, cover.
3. Fukuyama, *The End of History*, xiii.
4. Marks, *Maoist Insurgency Since Vietnam*, 1. Marks studied four insurgencies (Thailand, Philippines, Sri Lanka, and Peru) that were inspired by Mao's revolutionary doctrine. All were long-standing insurgencies whose lack of success after the Vietnam period might have confirmed the opinion that revolutionary warfare had lost its magic.
5. I use the term 'the Islamic State movement' to describe the group that Abu Musab al Zarqawi formed in Iraq in 2002 from remnants of his original camp in Afghanistan (founded in 1999) that he named Tawhid wal Jihad (Monotheism and Struggle). Zarqawi renamed the group Tanzim Qaidat al Jihad fi Bilad al Rafidayn (Organization of Jihad's Base in Mesopotamia, a.k.a. al Qaeda in Iraq – AQI) in 2004 after pledging allegiance to Osama bin Laden. The group joined the Mujahideen Shura Council (MSC) in January 2006, which was a political– military front of several jihadist groups but so dominated by AQI to the point that it is possible MSC was a sham organization used to convince Iraqis of its indigenous nature. Nevertheless, MSC lasted eight months before transforming

from a group into a shadow government with a variety of cabinet positions (at least in name if not function). The Islamic State of Iraq lasted from 2006 to 2013, when Abu Bakr al Baghdadi reclaimed the al Nusra franchise as an Islamic State element and changed the name of the organization to the Islamic State of Iraq and al Sham (Levant). The group left that name behind when it established the caliphate known as the Islamic State in 2014. Zarqawi's often stated intent in Iraq and the Levant as early as 2004 was to establish an Islamic state in the region once the coalition was expelled.
6. Abu Musab al Zarqawi, 'Zarqawi's Cry', 3.
7. The Islamic State controls territory in areas that are also claimed by Syria and Iraq, while administering services to the remaining population and claiming a monopoly on the legitimate application of violence in the same area. The legitimacy of such a state remains to be evaluated, although it is still in power after two years. No other state has recognized the Islamic State, nor has any international organization.
8. Exceptions are Kalyvas, *Logic of Violence*; Goldstone, 'What is ISIS?'; and Gartenstein-Ross et al., *The War between the Islamic State and al-Qaeda*.
9. The Sahwa (Awakening) movement was/is a grassroots movement of Sunni tribes in Anbar that fought Al Qaeda in Iraq/Islamic State of Iraq in 2006–2007 for control of Sunni areas. They were joined by elements of insurgent groups and other Sunnis and the movement spread outside Anbar to other Sunni areas of Iraq and elements still exist today, particularly around Ramadi. Cottam and Huseby's book *Confronting al Qaeda; The Sunni Awakening and US Strategy in Al Anbar* contains interviews and a scholarly analysis of changing identities and images for both the Americans and the Sunni of Iraq from 2003 to 2010.
10. Two popular books about the Islamic State are Stern and Berger, *ISIS: The State of Terror* and Weiss and Hassan, *ISIS: Inside the Army of Terror*. Both sets of authors present the group as a state and an army respectively that centers on terror, as opposed to a movement that uses terror instrumentally to achieve its end state – the creation of a 'new' type of state in the international system.
11. Galula, *Counterinsurgency Warfare*, 4.
12. Fall, 'Theory and Practice', 46.
13. Fromson and Simon, 'ISIS: The Dubious Paradise of Apocalypse Now', 44.
14. Ibn Khaldun, *The Muqaddimah*, Vol. I, 473. This is important because IS describes themselves in this image and this end state drives their strategy.
15. Arquilla, *Insurgents, Raiders, and Bandits*, 8.
16. Ibid., 9.
17. McCuen, *The Art of Counter-Revolutionary Warfare*, 40. These phases are an adaptation to Mao's original stages as modified by the Vietnamese communists.
18. Arquilla, *Insurgents, Raiders, and Bandits*, 274.
19. Marks, *Maoist Insurgency Since Vietnam*, 7.
20. Metz, *Rethinking Insurgency*, 13.
21. Ibn Khaldun, *The Muqaddimah*, Vol. II, 86.
22. Hafez, 'Lessons from the Arab Afghans Phenomenon'.
23. Abu Musab al Suri, 'Lessons learned from the armed Jihad in Syria', 16.
24. Lia, 'Abu Musab al Suri's critique of hard line Salafists in Jihadist current'.
25. Hamid and Farrall, *The Arabs at War in Afghanistan*, 257.
26. al Adl, My experience with Abu Musab al Zarqawi, 10.
27. Weiss and Hassan, *ISIS: Inside the Army of Terror*, 13.
28. Brisard and Martinez, *Zarqawi*, 226–7.

29. These concepts can be found throughout Abu Musab al Suri's 'Lessons learned' document.
30. Hafez, *Suicide Bombers in Iraq*, 69; Hashim, *Insurgency and Counterinsurgency in Iraq*, 47.
31. Whiteside, *The Smiling, Scented Men*, 141–4.
32. Even an informed observer with a decade of Iraq experience and the former Special Inspector General for Iraq Reconstruction claimed that the Maliki administration was responsible for 'killing all those Sunnis in the Awakening movement . . . they were met with murder'. This is a patently untrue statement but a common belief. This research proves the claim is baseless, while not disputing that Awakening members were at times arrested by the government under suspicion of collaboration with Islamic State – a charge that is hard to evaluate. Sometimes it was true. Bowen and Hamid, 'Discussion about Islamism', minute 44.
33. Kalyvas, *Logic of Violence*, 112–13.
34. Al-Qaidah Organization in the Arabian Peninsula, 'Assassination Operations', 64–87.
35. Lomparis, *From People's War to People's Rule*, 95.
36. Andrews, *The Village at War*, 44.
37. Moyer, *Triumph Forsaken*, 79.
38. Ibid., 18.
39. Russell, *Innovation, Transformation, and War*, 54.
40. Islamic State of Iraq, 'Analysis of the State of ISI', 3–4.
41. Russell, *Innovation, Transformation, and War*, 57.
42. Ibid., 105.
43. Green and Mullen, *Fallujah Redux*, 118.
44. Andrews, *The Village at War*, 57.
45. Ibid., 68.
46. Ibid., 73–103.
47. Ibid., 96.
48. Fall, 'Theory and Practice', 46–57.
49. Andrews, *The Village at War*, 72–95.
50. Lomparis, *From People's War to People's Rule*, 69.
51. Abu Omar, 'The Religious and Political Crime of the Election and Our Duty Toward It', 5.
52. The Qureshi indicated a lineage tie to the House of Muhammad, a legitimizing factor for a would-be caliph.
53. Abu Hamza, 'The command is for none but Allah'.
54. Islamic State of Iraq, 'Analysis of the State of ISI'. ID: NMEC-2007–612449
55. Lomparis, *From People's War to People's Rule*, 68.
56. Database available at iraqibodycount.org.
57. These population estimates are very rough due to the lack of reliable surveys since 2000. Baqubah's number includes Buhriz and Khalis numbers to reflect the mixed nature of Diyala province.
58. Green and Mullen, *Fallujah Redux*, 118.
59. The United Nations believes that over half a million Maslawis left the city in 2014 as refugees. UNAMI/OHCHR, *Report*, 4.
60. Williams and Adnan, 'Sunnis in Iraq Allied with U.S. Rejoin Rebels', A1.
61. Abu Musab al Suri, 'Lessons learned from the armed Jihad in Syria', 33.
62. Iraqi Body Count incident: k12246-ef1611.
63. Flintoff, 'Violence in Iraq Takes a Political Turn'.

64. Islamic State of Iraq, 'Harvest of operations in Al Rusafa and the Southern Sections (Baghdad), 1 Feb to 16 Mar 2009', item 1.
65. Ghazi and Arango, 'Qaeda-Linked Militants in Iraq Secure Nearly Full Control of Falluja', A8.
66. Mardini, 'Al-Qaeda in Iraq Operations Suggest Rising Confidence Ahead of U.S. Military Withdrawal', 6.
67. Islamic State of Iraq, Documented Military Operations in Diyala Province, 17 Feb-26 Mar 2011.
68. Islamic State of Iraq, Documented Military Operations in Diyala Province, 26 Sep-17 Oct 2011.
69. Islamic State of Iraq, Documented Military Operations in Diyala Province, 22 Apr -19 Jun 2012.
70. Williams and Adnan, 'Sunnis in Iraq Allied with U.S. Rejoin Rebels', A1.
71. Al Umar, 'Al-Hamadani'.
72. Weiss and Hassan, *ISIS: Inside the Army of Terror*, 38–9.
73. Al Tamimi, 'Violence in Iraq', note 47.
74. Allam, 'Records show how Iraqi extremists withstood U.S. anti-terror efforts'.
75. Roggio, 'Iraqi forces strike blow to al Qaeda in Iraq's northern leadership cadre'.
76. Bahney et al., *Economic Analysis*, 75.
77. Abu Musab al Suri, 'Lessons learned from the armed Jihad in Syria', 19.
78. This research relied on many captured documents authored by the Islamic State of Iraq. I found these to be a very reliable source, and this claim is supported by the excellent work done by Jung et al. in 'Managing a Transnational Insurgency' as part of the Harmony Program for the Combatting Terrorism Center at West Point, NY. For a convincing theory on why an insurgent group would expose themselves to risk by producing such a voluminous administration, see Shapiro's *The Terrorist's Dilemma*, a chapter of which focuses on the 'Al Qaeda in Iraq'.
79. ISI, State of Ninewa, Mosul Sector, 'Warning to the owners of billiard halls, laser CD stores'.
80. ISI, Governor of Mosul, (No Title).
81. ISI, Warning No 106.
82. Al Tamimi, 'Archive of Islamic State Administrative Documents'.
83. Interview with TW (20 March 2015), who served as a U.S. Army platoon leader in the Hamiya/Jurf area in 2010–2011.
84. Sergeant First Class Christopher Brevard of Apache 1-501 Parachute Infantry Regiment was killed in March 2007, allegedly at the direction of Abd al Hadi and his Islamic Army of Iraq cell in Jurf ah Sakhr.
85. ISI, 'Harvest of military operations in the Southern belt sector of the Baghdad Province', 19 October 2008 entry.
86. ISI, 'Documented Military Operations in the South Province', 3 July 2009 entry.
87. ISI, 'Documented Military Operations in the Southern Governorate', 9 June 2010 entry.
88. Interview with FJ (14 July 2015), an Awakening coordinator in Jurf from 2007–2012.
89. ISI, 'Documented military operations in the South Governorate', 15 Oct 2012 entry.
90. ISI, 'Statement detailing some documented cases in the blessed head harvesting raid in the southern province', item #2.
91. Gartenstein-Ross et al., *The War between the Islamic State and al-Qaeda*, 5.
92. McAdam, *Political Process*, 40–55. Brought to my attention by Professor Doowan Lee of the Naval Postgraduate School. Lee adapted the model for use in

analyzing the social movement aspect of unconventional warfare and shared his unpublished paper 'Resistance Dynamics' with me.
93. These are subsets of the mechanism element in Lee's model.
94. Ingram, 'Strategic Logic', 2.
95. These are the subsets of the effects element in Lee's model.
96. The Conflict Records Research Center at National Defense University was closed in late June 2015 due to a lack of funding. There are plans to reopen the center soon in a different venue.
97. Adnani, 'The Islamic State of Iraq will Remain', minute 35–46.
98. Abu Bakr, 'But Allah will not allow but that his light should be perfected', words addressing 'O Sunni Tribes ...'.
99. Anonymous Al Qaeda Central official writing to Abu Hamza, portion of the correspondence dated 25 January 2008.
100. Abu Omar al Baghdadi had the personal credibility to establish a tribal outreach among Iraqi Sunnis, not Abu Hamza who was Egyptian. The relationship between the two partners and Abu Omar's considerable influence is a yet untold story that hopefully will be further developed by additional research.
101. Anbar province had a legal, media, medical, prisoners, support battalion, security, treasury, and mail section overseen by an administrative emir council. A spoils group reported to the administrative emir. The general emir reported to the Mujahidin Shura Council (prior to the Islamic State formation) according to Bahney et al., *Economic Analysis*, 35. These documents came from the Harmony Batch ala Daham Hanush and Harmony Batch MA 7029-5.
102. The Southern Belt was a term developed during the Zarqawi era to describe an area which stretches from south of Fallujah to just beyond the Tigris River south and east of Baghdad. This included Jurf ah Sakhr, one of the towns in the case study.
103. Bahney et al., *Economic Analysis*, xvi.
104. Abu Khaldun, 'Synopsis of the Relations Committee in Baghdad's Southern Belt'.
105. Ibid.
106. The names of the Sahwa sheiks were in the original document but withheld in this paper to protect them from possible harm. Abu Khaldun, 'OPSUM from Abu Mustafa of Southern Belt trying to overturn Sahwa'.
107. McCuen, *The Art of Counter-Revolutionary Warfare*, 55–6.
108. Haji Bakr Naji, *The Management of Savagery*, 31–3.

Disclosure statement

This research was inspired by a series of articles published by the author on the website "War on the Rocks." This work reflects the views of the author, and in no way represents the opinions of the United States Naval War College or the United States government.

Funding

This work was supported by Naval War College Foundation.

References

Abu Bakr al Baghdadi. 'But Allah will not allow but that his light should be perfected'. Al Furqan Media, audiotape (21 July 2012).

Abu Hamza al Muhajir. 'The command is for none but Allah'. Jihadist websites (10 November 2006).

Abu Khaldun, 'Synopsis of the Relations Committee in Baghdad's Southern Belt'. CRRC Document AQ PMPR-D-001–717 (2009).

Abu Khaldun. 'OPSUM from Abu Mustafa of Southern Belt trying to overturn Sahwa'. CRRC Document AQ-POAK-D-001–695 (9 September 2009).

Abu Mohammad al Adnani. 'The Islamic State will Remain' (video). Al Furqan Media (7 August 2011).

Abu Musab al Suri. 'Lessons learned from the armed Jihad in Syria'. CTC West Point collection, document #AFGP-2002-600080, 2002. https://www.ctc.usma.edu/v2/wp-content/uploads/2013/10/Lessons-Learned-from-the-Jihad-Ordeal-in-Syria-Translation.pdf (accessed 1 September 2015).

Abu Musab al Zarqawi. 'Zarqawi's Cry'. Captured document released by the CPA Iraq, Haverford College Global Terrorism Research Project (14 February 2004). https://ds-drupal.haverford.edu/aqsi/aqsi-statement/596 (accessed 1 September 2015).

Abu Musab al Zarqawi. 'Al-Zarqawi Declares "Total War" on Shi'ites, States that the Sunni Women of Tel'afar Had "Their Wombs Filled with the Sperm of the Crusaders"'. Retrieved from the Haverford College Collection (16 September 2005).

Abu Omar al Baghdadi. 'The Religious and Political Crime of the Election and Our Duty Toward It'. Haverford College Global Terrorism Research Project (13 February 2010).

al Adl, Saif. 'My experience with Abu Musab al Zarqawi'. Trans. L. Othman, ed. H. Ingram. Accessed from a jihadist website, 2005.

Al-Qaidah Organization in the Arabian Peninsula. 'Assassination Operations'. Inspire no. 14 (Summer 2015): 64–87.

Al Tamimi, Aymenn. 'Violence in Iraq'. Middle East Review of International Affairs (Fall 2012). http://www.aymennjawad.org/12557/iraq-violence.

Al Tamimi, Aymenn. 'Archive of Islamic State Administrative Documents' (2015). http://www.aymennjawad.org/2015/01/archive-of-islamic-state-administrative-documents.

Al Umar, Umayah. 'Al-Hamadani: Mosul does not need awakening councils'. Niqash (3 June 2008). http://www.niqash.org/en/articles/politics/2211/Mosul-does-not-need-awakening-councils.htm.

Allam, Hannah. 'Records show how Iraqi extremists withstood U.S. anti-terror efforts'. McClatchy DC (23 June 2014). http://www.mcclatchydc.com/news/nation-world/world/middle-east/article24769573.html.

Andrews, William. The Village at War: Vietnamese Communists Revolutionary Activity in Dinh Tuong Province 1960–1964. Columbia, MO: University of Missouri Press, 1973.

Anonymous official, Al Qaeda Central. 'Intercepted Letters from al-Qaeda Leaders Shed Light on State of Network in Iraq'. Trans. and ed. Tony Badran, with analysis by Bill Roggio. Foundation for Defense of Democracies (12 September 2008). http://www.defenddemocracy.org/media-hit/intercepted-letters-from-al-qaeda-leaders-shed-light-on-state-of-network-in/.

Arquilla, John. *Insurgents, Raiders, and Bandits: How Masters of Irregular Warfare have Shaped Our World*. Chicago, IL: Ivan R. Dee, 2011.

Bahney, Benjamin, Howard Shatz, Carroll Ganier, Renny McPherson, and Barbara Sude. *An Economic Analysis of the Financial Records of al-Qa'ida in Iraq*. Santa Monica, CA: RAND Corporation (2010).

Bowen, Stuart Jr. and Shadi Hamid. 'Stuart Bowen Jr. and Dr. Shadi Hamid in discussion about Islamism. Perilous Situation in Iraq'. Video. Chautauqua Institution, 19 August 2015. https://www.youtube.com/watch?v=jwGPtCUelz0.

Brisard, Jean-Charles, and Damien Martinez. *Zarqawi: The New Face of Al Qaeda*. New York, NY: Other Press, 2005.

Cottam, Martha and Joe Huseby. *Confronting al Qaeda; The Sunni Awakening and US Strategy in al Anbar*. Lanham, MD: Rowman & Littlefield, 2016.

Fall, Bernard. *Street Without Joy*. Mechanicsburg, PA: Stackpole Books, 1994.

Fall, Bernard. 'The Theory and Practice of Insurgency and Counterinsurgency'. Naval War College Review (Winter 1998): 46–57. http://www.au.af.mil/au/awc/awcgate/navy/art5-w98.htm.

Flintoff, Corey. 'Violence in Iraq Takes a Political Turn'. NPR.org (24 February 2009). http://www.npr.org/templates/story/story.php?storyId=101050719.

Fromson, James and Steven Simon, 'ISIS: The Dubious Paradise of Apocalypse Now'. Survival: Global Politics and Strategy 57, no. 3 (2015): 7–56.

Fukuyama, Francis. *The End of History and the Last Man*. New York, NY: Perennial, 1992.

Galula, David. *Counterinsurgency Warfare: Theory and Practice*. New York: Frederick A. Praeger Publishers, 1964.

Gartenstein-Ross, Daveed, Jason Fritz, Bridget Moreng, and Nathaniel Barr. *The War between the Islamic State and al-Qaeda: Strategic Dimensions of a Patricidal Conflict*. Washington DC: Valens Global, September 2015.

Ghazi, Yasir and Tim Arango. 'Qaeda-Linked Militants in Iraq Secure Nearly Full Control of Falluja'. The New York Times (5 January 2014). http://www.nytimes.com/2014/01/05/world/middleeast/shelling-in-iraqi-city-held-by-qaeda-linked-militants-kills-at-least-8.html?_r=1 (accessed 1 September 2015).

Goldstone, Jack. 'What is ISIS?' Political Violence @ a Glance website. http://politicalviolenceataglance.org/2014/09/10/what-is-isis/ (accessed 1 September 2015).

Green, Daniel, and William Mullen. *Fallujah Redux: The Anbar Awakening and the Struggle with Al Qaeda*. Annapolis, MD: Naval Institute Press, 2014.

Hafez, Mohammed. 'Lessons from the Arab Afghans Phenomenon'. CTC Sentinel 1, Issue 4 (2008). https://www.ctc.usma.edu/posts/jihad-after-iraq-lessons-from-the-arab-afghans-phenomenon (accessed 1 September 2015).

Hafez, Mohammed. *Suicide Bombers in Iraq: The Strategy and Ideology of Martyrdom*. Washington DC: USIP, 2007.

Haji Bakr Naji. *The Management of Savagery: The Most Critical State Through Which the Ummah Will Pass*. Trans. Will McCants. Harvard University John M. Olin Institute of Strategic Studies, 23 May 2006.

Hamid, Mustafa, and Leah Farrall. *The Arabs at War in Afghanistan*. London: Hurst Publishers, 2015.

Hashim, Ahmed. *Insurgency and Counterinsurgency in Iraq*. Ithaca, NY: Cornell University Press, 2006.

Khaldun, Ibn. *The Muqaddimah; an Introduction to History (three volumes)*. Trans. Franz Rosenthal. New York: Pantheon Books, 1958.

Ingram, Haroro. 'The Strategic Logic of Islamic State Information Operations'. Australian Journal of International Affairs (25 Aug 2015). http://www.tandfonline.com/doi/abs/10.1080/10357718.2015.1059799#.VgTKcUZM6iw.

Islamic State of Iraq. 'Analysis of the State of ISI'. Harmony Collection, CTC West Point: Captured Document ID: NMEC-2007-612449 (est 2007).

Islamic State of Iraq. 'Harvest of operations in Al Rusafa and the Southern Sections (Baghdad), 1 Feb to 16 Mar 2009'. al Fajr Media (11 May 2009).

Islamic State of Iraq. 'Documented Military Operations in Diyala Province, 17 Feb–26 Mar 2011'. Al Fajr Media (7 April 2011).
Islamic State of Iraq, 'Documented Military Operations in Diyala Province, 26 Sep–17 Oct 2011'. Al Fajr Media (2 November 2011).
Islamic State of Iraq, 'Documented Military Operations in Diyala Province, 20 Oct – 23 Nov'. Al Fajr Media (18 Dec 2011).
Islamic State of Iraq, 'Documented Military Operations in Diyala Province, 22 Apr –19 Jun 2012'. al Fajr Media (18 Jul 2012).
Islamic State of Iraq, Governor of Mosul. (No Title). ISI Ministry of Information, CRRC Document AQ-MCOP-D-001–666 (3 Nov 2007).
Islamic State of Iraq, State of Ninewa, Mosul Sector. 'Warning 104: Warning to the owners of billiard halls, laser CD stores'. CRRC Document AQ-MCOP-D-001–672 (2007).
Islamic State of Iraq, Mosul. 'Warning No 106: This is a warning to the young men who gather on the road leading to the girls' Middle school, Fatimah al-Zahra', at al-Ta'mim Neighborhood'. CRRC Document AQ-MCOP-D-001–665 (2007).
Islamic State of Iraq. 'Harvest of military operations in the Southern belt sector of the Baghdad Province'. al Fajr Media (10 December 2008).
Islamic State of Iraq. 'Documented Military Operations in the South Province, 21 June–13 July'. al Fajr Media (30 Jul 2009).
Islamic State of Iraq. 'Documented Military Operations in the Southern Governorate, 15 May–12 June 2010'. al Fajr Media (20 Jul 2010).
Islamic State of Iraq, 'Documented military operations in the South Governorate 19 Aug–16 Oct'. al Fajr Media (25 Nov 2012).
Islamic State of Iraq and Levant. 'Statement detailing some documented cases in the blessed head harvesting raid in the southern province'. Hanin Network (2 Jan 2014).
Jung, Danielle, Pat Ryan, Jacob Shapiro, and Jon Wallace. *Managing a Transnational Insurgency: The Islamic State of Iraq's 'Paper Trail', 2005–2010*. West Point, NY: Combatting Terrorism Center 15 (December 2014).
Kalyvas, Stathis. *The Logic of Violence in Civil War*. Cambridge: Cambridge University Press, 2006.
Kalyvas, Stathis. "Is ISIS a Revolutionary Group and if Yes, What are the Implications?" *Perspectives on Terrorism* 9, no. 4 (2015): 42–47.
Lee, Doowan. 'Resistance Dynamics and Social Movement Theory: Conditions, Mechanisms, and Effects'. Unpublished paper, Naval Postgraduate School.
Lia, Brynjar. 'Abu Musab al Suri's Critique of Hard Line Salafists in the Jihadist Current'. CTC Sentinel 1, no. 1 (2007). https://www.ctc.usma.edu/posts/abu-musab-al-suri%E2%80%99s-critique-of-hard-line-salafists-in-the-jihadist-current (accessed 1 September 2015).
Lomparis, Timothy. *From People's War to People's Rule: Insurgency, Intervention, and the Lessons of Vietnam*. Chapel Hill, NC: University of North Carolina Press, 1996.
Mardini, Ramzy. 'Al-Qaeda in Iraq Operations Suggest Rising Confidence Ahead of U.S. Military Withdrawal'. *Terrorism Monitor* by The Jamestown Foundation (25 November 2009): 4–6.
Marks, Thomas. *Maoist Insurgency Since Vietnam*. London: Frank Cass, 1996.
McAdam, Doug. *Political Process and the Development of Black Insurgency, 1930–1970*. Chicago, IL: University of Chicago Press, 1982.
McCuen, John. *The Art of Counter-Revolutionary War*. St. Petersburg, FL: Hailer Publishing, 1966.
Metz, Steven. *Rethinking Insurgency*. Carlisle, PA: Strategic Studies Institute, 2007.
Moyer, Mark. *Triumph Forsaken: The Vietnam War, 1954–1965*. Cambridge: Cambridge University Press, 2006.

Roggio, Bill. 'Iraqi forces strike blow to al Qaeda in Iraq's northern leadership cadre'. The Long War Journal (2 April 2010). http://www.longwarjournal.org/archives/2010/04/iraqi_forces_strike.php.

Russell, James. *Innovation, Transformation, and War: Counterinsurgency Operations in Anbar and Ninewa, Iraq, 2005–7*. Stanford, CA: Stanford Security Studies, 2011.

Shapiro, Jacob. *The Terrorist's Dilemma: Managing Violent Covert Organizations*. Princeton: Princeton University Press, 2013.

Taber, Robert. *The War of the Flea: A Study of Guerrilla Warfare Theory and Practice*. New York, NY: L. Stuart, 1965.

UNAMI/OHCHR. *Report on the Protection of Civilians in the Armed Conflict in Iraq: 6 July – 10 September 2014*. Baghdad, 18 Aug 2014.

Whiteside, Craig. *The Smiling, Scented Men; The Political Worldview of the Islamic State of Iraq, 2003–2013*. Dissertation, Washington State University, 2014.

Williams, Timothy and Duraid Adnan. 'Sunnis in Iraq Allied with U.S. Rejoin Rebels'. The New York Times (16 October 2010).

How revolutionary are Jihadist insurgencies? The case of ISIL

Paul B. Rich

ABSTRACT
This paper examines the rise of ISIL in the context of wider debates in the first half twentieth century on the nature and political direction of the early Bolshevik state model of Lenin, Trotsky, and Stalin. It argues that there are some parallels between the Trotskyite internationalist tendency in Soviet Russia and of ISIL given the latter's calls for revolutionary jihad against both 'apostate' states in the Islamic world and, in the longer term, against the Western world as a whole. ISIL though is distinguished by its attempt to carve out a new state formation of its own in parts and Iraq and Syria, a project that may well end in failure. However, even if its so-called caliphate fails, it cannot be expected to vanish from the scene since it can either re-emerge elsewhere in a region of weak or failing states or merge with its current rival Al Qaeda.

Radical jihadist movements have gripped international attention over the last two decades or more. They are examples of what Hegghammer has termed 'militant sunni activism' in contrast to wider patterns of Islamic activism incorporating radical Shi'ite revolutionary ideology similar to the Iranian revolutionaries who overthrew the Shah in 1979.[1] Many of the more recent examples of these radical jihadist movements such as self-proclaimed Islamic State (ISIL), the Al-Nusra Front in Syria, Al Qaeda in the Maghreb (AQIM), and Boko Haram in West Africa have involved violent insurgent guerrilla warfare with a range of battlefield strategies and tactics, though for the last couple of years or more it has been ISIL, under its mysterious self-proclaimed caliph Abu Bakr al-Baghdadi, which has gripped international media attention.

The amazingly swift rise of Islamic State in parts of Syria and northern and western Iraq has been accompanied by a series of gruesome videos of public beheadings and crucifixions, the mass kidnapping and rape of women, and the wanton destruction of priceless archaeological sites such as Palmyra. Such spectacles have certainly succeeded in shocking international humanitarian opinion, though ISIL has not been especially concerned to keep all its atrocities secret, seeing considerable propaganda payoffs by publicising its activities as part of a wider strategy aimed at mobilising international support and recruitment of jihadi fighters among angry young men and women in marginalised Islamic communities in the West, as well as in the broader Islamic world. Many of these young supporters have come to admire the ISIL brand it for its fanatical commitment to armed struggle and strict implementation of sharia law. There are features here of a revolutionary process that still remains to be worked out but which could have profound implications in the future stability and functioning of the international system, even if the actual quasi state structure established by ISIL is eventually defeated and destroyed.

In this paper I shall focus mainly on ISIL in Iraq and Syria in a fluid situation of interlocking civil wars and sectarian conflict. At the time of writing, the movement is on the defensive and the regime of Basher al-Assad, with some Russian military support, has recaptured extensive territory including Palmyra. However, ISIL continues to display several intriguing features: it appears to confound evidence that few guerrilla movements, such as North Korea and later Cuba, manage to attain control of the state without some wider cross class national coalition.[2] Indeed, the pattern of conflict in Iraq and Syria suggests that it is possible for a modern insurgent movement such as ISIL to create the basic structures of a state more or less *de novo*, using claims to statehood as major propaganda asset in a far more wide-ranging agenda for a global jihadist revolutionary movement. To this extent, ISIL seeks the overthrow of order of states established in the Middle East after World War I: it has demonstrated this all too clearly by destroying the formal border between Iraq and Syria.

Broadly speaking, therefore, it is possible to see ISIL as having embarked on a challenge to the Westphalian order of sovereign states by creating its own distinct *khilafah* or Islamic political system. Under this, all Muslims become members of one community or *ummah* and pledge allegiance to a caliphate governed by sharia law, restored after its abolition in 1924 following the collapse of the Ottoman Empire.[3] This might of course be viewed simply as a guerrilla insurgency infused with millenarian 'end of days' features, though the analysis of the movement's emergence and leadership suggests that much of its strategy is formulated by leaders displaying considerable political and military acumen.[4]

The rapid emergence of ISIL means that many long-standing assumptions about the jihadism as well as the politics of the Middle East will need substantial revision. Long treated as an exotic revolutionary ideology, jihadism has come into renewed focus given the extraordinary success of Islamic State in capturing large swathes of territory in Iraq and Syria since the middle of 2014. What was formerly treated as just another example of a regional jihadist terrorist movement competing with other rival movements in the region for support among Sunni Muslims has emerged into a far more serious player given that it has displayed many of the basic features of statehood, certainly those centred on what Rana Khalaf has termed the 'governance model' of effectiveness, security, and legitimacy, though this can also be undermined by terrorist attacks in the Middle East and Europe which to some degree threaten the movement's longer-term goals.[5]

This is exemplified all too starkly on the question of ISIL's status in international law where it started out initially as simply a non-state actor. There were thus some problems for the US-led coalition in terms of justifying military action against it, even though this did not prevent some 5500 air strikes against ISIL targets in Iraq and Syria between August 2014 and August 2015 (leading to an estimated 15,000 ISIL deaths). The coalition justified the strikes on grounds similar to those used against Afghanistan prior to the invasion at the end of 2001, namely that the host state (Syria) was unwilling or unable to suppress ISIL's activities. Such arguments failed to secure the support of some other Security Council members such as Russia and China, and it was events on the ground that eventually led to change in international opinion, especially ISIL's shooting down of a Russian airliner on 3 October followed by a terrorist attack in Paris on a rock concert on 13 November. These terror attacks led to the UN Security Council passing unanimously Resolution 2249 on 3 December 2015 describing ISIL as a 'global and unprecedented threat to international peace and security' and calling for 'all necessary measures' to be taken to remove its safe haven in Syria.[6] Here was a stark example of terrorist attacks not really being particularly well calibrated with the movement's ongoing guerrilla insurgency on the ground in Iraq and Syria since they led to ISIL being even more internationally isolated than it might otherwise have been.

This example suggests that the zealous pursuit of ideological aims can win out over a more cautious military strategy. It suggests that ISIL is, in the end, a recent manifestation of a much longer tradition of jihadism that has waxed and waned in the Middle East since at least the early twentieth century. The movement is complex in the way it presents itself to the world; as Fromson and Simon have suggested, it has four primary ways of revealing itself: as a 'guerrilla army', a 'revanchist political movement', a 'millenarian Islamist cult', and an 'administrator of territory'. Despite this multifaceted nature, ISIL embodies many of the features of mainstream or 'classical' jihadist thought including a narrative of righteous war against apostates to regain Muslim honour by securing a territorial caliphate destroyed by Kemal Ataturk's regime in Turkey in 1924.[7] To this extent it can be seen as departing from the alternative 'globalist' jihadist ideology that was long espoused by Al Qaeda and anchors itself more in the idea of waging guerrilla and irregular warfare in certain defined territorial zones.[8]

This territorial imperative is what really distinguishes ISIL from its Al Qaeda rival and, even if it is eventually defeated in Iraq and Syria and its caliphate destroyed, there are good grounds for thinking that it will resurface in another form in some other region or failing state such as Libya or parts of Afghanistan that have recently been won by ISIL from the Taliban. We see here features of a 'postmodern' state form that can be relocated across the globe in a manner unimaginable within traditional conceptions of the state and the Westphalian model of international order. This adaptability of the ISIL implies an innovative form of statehood that belies the image of a completely backward-looking and reactionary movement aiming to restore a lost medieval world along with brutal codes of punishment. If there are medieval features in its ideology, it is a manufactured medievalism reminiscent in some ways of the counter-revolutionary groups that surfaced in opposition to the French Revolution at the end of the eighteenth century. As Arno Mayer has pointed out, these counter-revolutionaries invented a largely chimerical past of apparent medieval order in order to cope with a world of disorder brought on by war and military intervention.[9]

There is a highly contrived dimension to ISIL's apparent restoration of the caliphate in Mosul in June 2014. This was a good example of media spectacle aimed at a global audience linked through social media. The exercise was modern myth-making in the sense that ISIL was essentially grafting on to the Western state model a myth of pristine Islamic state righteousness anchored in Islamic prophecy. Prophecies of one kind or another litter Islamic history, providing a kind of prophetic residue which can always be turned to when current politics fail.[10] For ISIL the prophetic myth stretched back to an imaginary period of *salaf-al-salih* encompassing the four decades after 622 when the Prophet and his ancestors were believed to have exercised power, despite considerable evidence that this was a period of considerable turbulence, with three of the first four caliphs being killed and a fundamental theological split in Islam emerging between Sunnis and Shi'as.[11] Nevertheless this myth of a puritanical past is one that has continually attracted conservative Islamic scholars. It is, after all, a means of maintaining links to a noble and pure history that includes the Ummayad Caliphate of 661–750 and the Abbasid Caliphate that succeeded it. The Abbasids are widely seen as ushering in a 'golden age' of Islamic history and culture, while caliphates of some kind or another continued more or continuously until the final abolition of 1924, a result of a tragic period of violent intrusion by Western imperialism into the Middle East.[12] Espousing this view of history thus strengthens the political legitimacy of ISIL, which uses such a sacred past to affirm the one true pattern of Islamic history compared to which all others are heretical and morally contaminating: it is from this standpoint that classical and pre-Islamic ruins such as those at Palmyra can be destroyed in a cleansing iconoclasm that confirms, at the same time, the true moral worth of ISIL and its own historical lineage.

The revolutionary model of ISIL also recalls previous revolutionary movements in Europe from the eighteenth century onwards, most notably Leninist vanguard parties in the twentieth century, though the Bolsheviks never resorted to quite the same iconoclasm towards artistic artefacts and historical monuments.[13] As a number of analysts, including Craig Whiteside in this issue, have pointed out, there are some obvious comparisons between various groups of Marxist revolutionary internationalists and revolutionary jihadist elites seeking to develop a global movement to overthrow not so much Western capitalism but Western 'imperial' Christian states and their 'apostate' Middle Eastern allies. These divisions between jihadist movements replicate aspects of earlier ideological conflict among the Marxist revolutionaries, especially those in Russia in the aftermath of the Bolshevik revolution of October 1917. The regime of Lenin and Trotsky in Moscow professed little interest in its early years in any serious accommodation with the surrounding powers, and the Soviet Commissar of Foreign Affairs Trotsky went as far as declaring in 1917 'there exists for us only one unwritten but sacred treaty, the treaty of the international solidarity of the proletariat.'[14] This did not prevent the Bolshevik state signing a peace accord with Germany at the Treaty of Brest Litovsk in March 1918 ceding vast tracts of territory to save the revolutionary state; however, the Soviet Commissariat of Foreign Affairs continued to act as a revolutionary state seeking the ultimate overthrow of the norms of the existing states system. The state, however, avoided being defeated militarily and progressively accommodated to the norms of the international system. By 1930, the Commissariat had evolved into an institution that was patterned on similar grounds to its Tsarist predecessor, while the project for overthrowing the global state system was put on hold as the practitioners of Soviet diplomacy found little to guide them in the workings of Marx and Engels. In effect, the Soviet state established what Armstrong terms a 'dual identity' in the form of diplomatic respectability, on the one hand, while keeping, on the other hand, the state's Marxist Leninist revolutionary goals in reserve, for use whenever possible. Despite the abolition of the Comintern in 1943, this situation continued until the Gorbachev area of the mid to late 1980s when the Soviet state's revolutionary goals became finally abandoned.[15]

The failure of the Bolshevik revolutionary regime to prosecute its global goals has often served as a model through which to judge other transnational or global revolutionary movements: in a study of the evolution of modern war published in 2001, for instance, Paul Hirst argued that the 'have not' powers would continue to be hindered by the absence of any unifying ideology to challenge the dominant powers of the international system.[16] It is, of course, still early days by which to evaluate the achievements of the current wave of revolutionary jihadists and ISIL. Unlike the future-orientated utopian ideology of Marxism–Leninism, which looked towards the eventual creation of a global workers' state, many of the strands of jihadist ideological thought, for all their dependency upon cyberspace for disseminating propaganda and recruiting new followers, are, as we have seen, backward looking in the sense of seeking a past golden age of an Islamic state governed by a caliph. Moreover, unlike the earlier Soviet revolutionary model, contemporary jihadist movements have so far failed to evolve into a full-fledged military state with advanced weaponry, though it has moved, as we shall see later in this paper, to some degree beyond simple insurgent warfare.

Interestingly, splits reminiscent of the international communist movement in the late 1920s and 1930s between Trotskyite revolutionary internationalists and Stalinist exponents of 'socialism in one country' have already emerged within global jihadism. A bitter struggle has ensued between an Al Qaeda orientated strategy of global terrorism and a territorially focused strategy of ISIL, especially following the creation on 1 July 2014 of a caliphate with its leader Abu Bakr al-Baghdadi as first caliph. Since then what might be termed the 'quasi state' of IS has issued its own currency and flag and created a police force in the areas under its control, which amounted at one point to a land area of some 200,000 sq. km – only 40,0000 sq. km smaller than the United Kingdom. Within its boundaries were some 6 million people in a state which might, in some ways, be likened to the original Soviet workers state struggling to survive in the civil war of the early 1920s.[17]

This paper will address these issues in the next three sections: the first section looks at the failure of doctrines of national liberation in the Middle East and the resulting spread of tribal and clan-based sectarianism; the second section examines the crisis surrounding the state in Iraq after the invasion of 2003 and the circumstances surrounding the emergence of IS/DAESH; finally, the last section will discuss how far a strategy of containment can be devised to contain the new strategic threat posed by Islamic State.

The failure of national liberation and the spread of sectarianism

The concept of 'national liberation' has never had the same resonance in the Middle East and North Africa like other regions of the developing world, beyond the obvious example of Algeria and its long insurgent war against the French between 1954 and 1962. While individual Arab leaders such as Gamel Abdel Nasser in Egypt in the 1950s and early 1960s and later Muammar Qaddafi in Libya played considerable rhetorical lip service to the concept, this never amounted to much beyond aid and support to individual insurgent and terrorist movements, including, in Qaddafi's case, the Provisional IRA in Northern Ireland. Nasser certainly sent troops to aid the regime in North Yemen, though for the most part Arab leaders were loath to get bogged down in proxy wars. There was no serious Pan-Arab movement for revolutionary insurgency given the sharp political and ideological rivalries between individual states: Morocco and Algeria, for instance, nearly came to full-scale war over the latter's support for Polisario in the Sahara in the 1970s.

The other side of the coin to a failing 'national liberation' narrative has been the growth of various forms of 'sectarianism' in the Middle East and North Africa, in some cases driven by various forms of religiously inspired ideology. The concept of sectarianism is one that has increasingly shaped much political and social analysis, though it is markedly different to earlier categories of analysis favoured by social scientists based on class, nationalism, and ethnicity. While by no means completely displacing these earlier categories, the concept marks a stronger awareness of the importance of religious language and symbols in group identities and political mobilisation: it also accords with the more subjective approach inspired by postmodernist trends in political sociology since the 1990s.

As a term, 'sectarian' stretches back to the politics of mid seventeenth-century England and the breakdown of central government in the civil war between Royalists and Parliamentarians. Revolutionary religious sects appeared in the course of the 1650s at a time of the collapse of religious hierarchies when, in some cases, millenarian expectations were raised for the destruction of any sort of state church and the fall of the papal authority of 'Antichrist'. A battle ensued for the control of the state, exemplified in a question posed by Vavasor Powell: would the Lord 'have Oliver Cromwell or Jesus Christ to rule over us'. In the event it was Cromwell and the conservatives who ended up ruling, while the Puritan radicals eventually came to accept some common ground with their rivals, leading to the restoration of Charles II in 1660. Following the restoration the radicals effectively abandoned the search, in this world at least, for the Antichrist enemy, who lived on only in sporadic puritan rhetoric, such as that of some religious zealots in the Orange Order in Northern Ireland.[18]

Despite a fairly rich historical background, the re-emergence of the concept of sectarianism in recent political sociology has been of a rather top-down nature, with a main focus being on the way political elites have mobilised sectarian religious symbols in the building of power-bases. Used in this way, 'sectarianism', as a term, is open-ended and begs a series of further questions: Just when, for instance, does a 'sectarian' political movement become so and when does it cease to manifest clearly 'sectarian' features? What criteria are involved in measuring this? Did both Sinn Fein and the Democratic Unionist Party in Northern Ireland, for example, cease to be 'sectarian' organisations following the 1998 Good Friday Agreement or the later agreement on power sharing in Belfast in 2007? Or did they remain 'sectarian' movements of a less overt and aggressive kind but with the constant potential to re-emerge?

Seen in these terms, 'sectarianism' is a rather difficult concept to pin down, given the way it is anchored in subjective and often 'irrational' attachments to group identity. In this regard, Fanar Haddad has provided a useful guide to understanding sectarianism in the Iraqi context by categorising it into three basic forms of 'active', 'passive', and 'banal' sectarianism. 'Active' sectarianism is precisely the sectarianism emphasised by many political science analysts where it is open to manipulation by key political leaders for the purpose of group mobilisation to secure a power base, often in periods of rising political and military conflict; 'passive' sectarianism, on the other hand, is less overt and defines groups where political and religious symbolism is expressed less forthrightly and often in coded language. Taken to extremes, it might even become an 'apologetic' sectarianism where someone fits in with the wider group attachment to religious or political symbols – frequently under pressure from the central state – but without any genuine commitment. Finally, 'banal' sectarianism follows the example of 'banal' nationalism where it is often there as only a vague group marker like a national flag on top of a town hall or police station, but not necessarily symbolising anything very political (unless it becomes mobilised in, say, a riot by rival football fans with strongly religious or ethnic overtones).[19]

These three categories certainly provide some insight into the way sectarian attachments can be seen to work in many Middle Eastern societies such as Iraq. They suggest that religious communities were organised at the very least around 'passive' if not 'active' sectarianism. This meant that, even under a consociational power-sharing agreement encouraging political elites to seek support outside their own narrow 'sectarian' power-bases, Western liberal democracy would always be a difficult project to get established once the Baathist regime of Saddam Hussein was removed. For this to have been properly understood before the invasion of 2003 would have required far greater attention to the attitudes and values of communities in the Iraqi society at the grass roots – broadly 'low' culture rather than the 'high' culture of the political elite. This was a problematical task given that the whole issue of sectarianism was politically taboo in Iraq for most of the twentieth century.[20] It is thus the emergence of sectarian politics in the wake of the failure of the national liberation project under the Baathist regime in Iraq that will be the focus of the next section.

Iraq and the emergence of ISIL/DAESH

The Baathist regimes in both Syria and Iraq were largely built up in the 1960s to 1980s under the guiding hand of the Soviet Union at a time of superpower rivalry in the Middle East. Both regimes borrowed from the Soviet model of a highly state-controlled economy and an authoritarian centralised dictatorship ruled through a single party and with leadership cults of personality. Both regimes, though, drew more on the symbols and language of Arab nationalism than they ever did on Soviet communism, and communist parties in both states remained outlawed and repressed. Both Iraq and Syria thus veered towards strongman regimes that managed to hold together rival tribal and religious communities in authoritarian political systems that largely destroyed the institutions of civil society. At the same time, though, both pursued programmes of secularisation ensuring social alienation from religious and clerical elites.

The Iraqi regime of Saddam Hussein proved especially resolute, until its terminal phase, in its prosecution of secular policies. The Baathist era in Iraq was one of belated state-building in a desperate effort to overcome the basic weaknesses of a state built on the cheap by the British under the League of Nations Mandate from 1919 to 1934, when rural tribal authorities were given considerable powers and privileges over communities in the cities.[21] Saddam's regime ran up against strong opposition from Shi'ites in the southern part of the country, where many communities had only converted to Shi'ism in the nineteenth century as they underwent a transition from itinerant nomadism into settled pastoral farming. Shi'ite holy places such as those at Najaf and Karbala acted as vital points of identification among these new communities of pastoralists. Social order was provided in turn by a powerful and influential clerical hierarchy. Opposition to the Baathist regime in Baghdad was expressed in a polyglot political ideology by the main Shi'ite party Dawa, containing a mixture of Marxism and religious Messianism. Its two most prominent clerical leaders, Baqir and Sadiq al-Sadr were eventually assassinated by Saddam's police in 1980 – though Sadiq's son, Moktada, would go on to lead the Shi'ite revolt against the US-led occupation after 2003, and Dawa would also become the party backing Nuri al Maliki. [22]

As the Shi'ites of the South of Iraq veered towards a form of revolutionary jihadism partly modelled on revolutionary Iran, another jihadist model emerged among the Sunni population in the wake of the collapse of the Baathist regime in 2003. Deprived of their top-dog status, which they had enjoyed more or less continually from the time of the creation of the state by Britain in the early 1920s, the Sunnis became open to the appeals of what Dodge has termed 'ethnic and sectarian entrepreneurs' in a situation of rapidly escalating sectarian conflict.[23] Sunni jihadism had not been seen as necessary under the Baathists as most Sunni communities enjoyed fairly close channels of access to central political power. This became dramatically removed with the disastrous de-Baathification policy pursued under Paul Bremer after May 2003 whereby all former Baathist civil servants lost their jobs and some 400,000 former members of the Iraq army were laid off.

Over the following years the idea of anti-governmental jihadism and a holy war against unbelievers began to surface in Iraqi society, strongly shaped by a range of jihadist thinkers such as Sayyid Qutb in Egypt before his execution by Nasser in 1966 and Abu al-Ala al-Mawdudi in 1920s' British India. Both these figures saw violent jihad and martyrdom as necessary in a holy war against unbelievers and for the creation of an Islamic state founded on sharia law. Both thinkers had helped indirectly inspired the radical Shi'ism that would emerge before the revolution in 1979 that overthrew the regime of the Shah, though this became obfuscated by the emergence in the 1980s of the theocratic doctrine espoused by Ayatollah Khomeini of the *velayat-i-faqih* (or supreme law giver).[24]

The 1980s, in fact, remained a largely unsuccessful decade for Sunni jihadis compared to their Shi'ite counterparts in Iran. The Shi'ites had mounted a successful revolution against the Shah on the basis of an alliance between university students, the clergy, and the bazaaris. By contrast, the Sunni jihadis remained at odds with the *ulema* for most of the 1980s, and it was not surprising that the decade was largely a story of failure: starting with the suppression of the

Hegira uprising in the Great Mosque in Mecca in 1979 by Saudi security forces; the suppression of the Al Jihad movement in Egypt in the aftermath of the assassination of Anwar Sadat in October 1981; and the violent suppression of the Moslem Brotherhood revolt in Hama in Syria in 1982.[25] It would not be until the emergence of the Taliban in Afghanistan in the mid-1990s that Sunni jihadism really started in earnest.

Sunni jihadism led to a revival of the idea of restoring the caliphate decades after its abolition in 1924. This had long been a dormant idea in Arab politics: in the period before World War II it had failed to lead to any serious political movement given that the Sharif Husayn in Mecca remained an important ally of British interests in the Middle East. The rise of Arab nationalism after World War II also ensured that demands for a caliphate generally remained peripheral to political debate as many Arab nationalist intellectuals became attracted to the more secular ideas of Pan-Arabism, especially following the creation by Nasser of a United Arab Republic in Egypt. Although this failed to lead to any wider Pan-Arab unification, beyond a short-lived unification with Syria, it did become later in the Muslim World League (WML), formed in Mecca in 1962, as well as the Organization of Islamic Cooperation (OIC), formed in 1969 with a permanent secretariat in Jedda.[26]

The re-emergence of the caliphate idea really started with the growing crisis of the Arab nation-state in the 1980s, as the Iraqi regime became embroiled in a long and destructive war with Iran and many jihadi fighters from the Middle East were drawn into the struggle against the Soviet armies occupying Afghanistan. It was here that Osama bin Laden defined the message globally with the formation in 1998 of the *World Islamic Front against Jews and Crusaders*. The attacks on Western interests over the next few years by Al Qaeda such as the embassy bombings in East Africa in 1998 and the attack on the USS *Cole* in Yemen in October 2000 have usually been seen as examples of global terrorism rather than insurgency, though, in Afghanistan, Al Qaeda became linked closely to the Taliban as it attempted to establish after 1995 a ramshackle state centred on the capital Kabul. The Al Qaeda leadership preferred to see the whole world as a battlefield which they could attack more or less randomly and in places and times of their own choosing. They failed to develop any sort of Maoist-type strategy of protracted guerrilla war and preferred to rely more on selective spectacular terrorist strikes against Western targets.[27] But the political–religious ideology of Al Qaeda did attack American imperialism for the violence against Muslims as well the poverty and social injustice they were felt to experience.

By contrast, the ideology of Al Qaeda in Iraq (AQI) as well as later the Islamic State evolved in a rather more conservative direction of declaring their opponents' beliefs to be *takfir* and thus heretical. This became the ideological base for a project of state-building that involved moving away from the Al Qaeda strategy of seeking a broad base of legitimacy for global jihad towards a narrower goal of conquering land as the basis for a new caliphate.[28] The ideological tendency was reinforced by wider events in the Middle East and North Africa accompanying the 'Arab Spring' from the end of 2010, starting with the mass demonstrations in Tunisia that led to the overthrow of the Zimine Ben Ali dictatorship in Tunis early the following year. The demonstrations were copied around the Arab world and provided the spark for the outbreak of the Syrian Civil War the following year in Damascus.

What started out as an 'Arab Spring' soon turned into widespread political disillusionment and an 'Arab Winter' with the apparent failure of civil society in the Arab world to overthrow repressive regimes. The demonstrations and eventual overthrow of the Qaddafi regime in Libya in 2011 led to the country eventually falling part as rival militias battled for power, while in Syria the civil war intensified as the increasingly sectarian Assad regime resisted all efforts at any form of non-violent political transformation and transfer of power to the Sunni majority. In the case of Egypt, the Muslim Brotherhood came to power in 2012 under Mohammed Morsi on a platform of building a new 'civil state' based on democratic institutions but one firmly based on Islamic values. The government was largely concerned with its own domestic issues and had no agenda to widen its influence outside its borders; however, its incompetent management of the government contributed to its overthrow the following year in a military coup.[29] By this time, an increasingly sectarian trend had already emerged in Iraqi politics as the Maliki regime after 2006 increasingly consolidated its sectarian power base in Baghdad under the auspices of the US military.

The rise of ISIL

Given the patterns outlined in the previous section, it is possible to see how Iraq after 2003 became one of the main nurseries, along with Syria, for an increasingly militant form of jihadism forged in the context of increasingly bitter sectarian civil war. Unlike the largely rural insurgency of the Taliban in Afghanistan, the jihadist movements in Iraq were largely urban in orientation and fuelled by the immense caches of weapons left behind by the regime of Saddam Hussein. One key political entrepreneur in forging an increasingly sectarian Sunni insurgency in Iraq was the Jordanian gangster Abu Musab al Zarqawi, who went initially to Afghanistan after his release from prison in Jordan in 1999. Zarqawi then joined Al Qaeda and was posted to head the movement's operation in Herat in the east, bordering Kurdistan and Iran. He was reputedly financed by Al Qaeda with the relatively small sum of $35,000, though he was able to use some Jordanian jihadists, linked to a movement known as Asbat al-Ansar (League of Partisans), as emissaries to set up new camps over the border in Iraqi Kurdistan. He also recruited a new cadre of jihadi fighters who were too young to have fought against the Soviet in Afghanistan and were more open to being moulded to his particular brand of jihadist ideology.[30] Zarqawi eventually fled into Iraq following the collapse of the Taliban regime in Kabul in late 2001.

At this stage, Zarqawi was less in charge of any coherent movement than a loose series of cells largely guided by an anti-imperialist ideology that Napoleoni has termed 'Al Qaedism'.[31] Zarqawi was fortunate in being able to take advantage of a range of underground cell contacts stretching into Iraq as well overseas into Europe; he became perhaps even more fortunate after he became exposed to global attention for the first time in the speech of Colin Powell to the UN in early 2003 justifying military intervention into Iraq. Now he was officially on the list of international top terrorists, though his activities started to move away from attacks on the secular Kurd PUK movement towards mobilising a jihadist insurrection among the communities of the Sunni Triangle once the Baathist regime of Saddam Hussein was finally toppled and the Iraq army disbanded.

Zarqawi was remarkably open about the sectarian strategy to be pursued by AQI. In a letter to Osama bin Laden in February 2004, he outlined what he saw as the main difficulties facing a Sunni insurgency. The ulema and the sheikhs represented nothing less than an obstacle to a strategy of mobilising the mass of the Sunni population behind a Maoist-style sectarian insurgency; indeed, 'their part of religion' he contemptuously dismissed as 'an anniversary in which they sing and dance to the dancing of a camel driver, with a fatty banquet at the end'. Zarqawi's main hope lay in the mujahidin, whom he saw as the 'the good sap of the country' and 'the quintessence of the sunni'. There was a strategic problem confronting any insurgency given that there was no Sunni heartland easy to defend in a country where there were no mountainous or forested regions (at least in predominantly Sunni areas). Overcoming this absence of strategic depth lay in identifying the key enemy, which Zarqawi identified as the Americans, the Kurds, the soldiers, police and agents of the Iraqi government in Baghdad, and the Shi'as. It was the Shi'as who were the main enemy, not only because they were 'depraved infidels' but because they were the key to the transformation of the Sunni population from what might be termed 'passive' into 'active' sectarianism

> If we succeed in dragging them [the Shi'as] into the arena of sectarian war, it will become possible to awaken the inattentive Sunnis as they feel imminent danger and annihilating death at the hands of these Sabaeans [a people inhabiting Yemen cited in the Koran as pagan worshippers of the son – PR].[32]

In December 2004 Zarqawi became recognised by bin Laden as the head of AQI, reflecting perhaps his emergence as a relatively successful military commander as opposed to being an organiser of terrorist cells. Doctrinal rifts with the parent organisation in Afghanistan, however, became increasingly evident as Zarqawi formed his own armed following known as *al Tawid al Yihad*. His main strategy remained largely a terrorist one of car bombings and murder of hostages in order to undermine the credibility of the coalition government in Baghdad as well as to foment sectarian hostilities between Sunnis and Shi'as and prevent a non-sectarian national resistance emerging.[33] Indeed, Zarqawi saw that the only way to stop a Shi'a-dominated government establishing itself was through civil war. The takeover of the city of Falluja, west of Baghdad during 2004 enabled this strategy to be put to the test. It also drew in the Al Qaeda leadership even further behind Zarqawi's sectarian strategy since they could provide a mantle of legitimacy that could not be so readily found among the mainstream Sunni ulemas in Iraq. But the protracted siege of the city led to a progressive widening of the Sunni–Shi'a chasm as initial Shi'a support for the resistance in April 2004 became transformed into support for the US attack on the city by November the same year.[34]

Zarqawi's sectarian strategy needs to be seen in the context of a failing state unable to deliver basic services as well as one seen by many Sunnis as falling increasingly under the control of a Shi'ite-dominated coalition established by the Americans. As the state's authority collapsed, so the geographical borders of the state appeared increasingly permeable as vital decision-making appeared to come less from Baghdad than from Tehran, Amman, and Damascus.[35] Between 2003 and 2006, when he was killed by a US bomb, Zarqawi was a key entrepreneur in creating a strategy for Iraqi Sunnis geared towards establishing a separate state ruled by a caliph, though in practice AQI did not amount to more than 10% of the total numbers of people involved in the Iraq insurgency.[36] The movement's sectarian strategy did not sit easily with the more globally inclined strategy of the Al Qaeda leadership. Ayman al Zawahiri had already launched a forthright attack on the idea that a 'Muslim state' could be 'launched as a regional struggle' given the likely opposition of the 'Crusader Alliance' of the United States and Israel to any such venture. '... to adjust ourselves to this new reality,' he wrote 'we must prepare ourselves for a battle that is not confined to a single region, one that includes the apostate domestic enemy and the Jewish-Crusade external enemy.'[37]

AQI had superior funding as well as good media and propaganda skills compared to its Sunni rivals, though its escalating attacks on Shi'ites in Iraq, including some of their most revered holy sites, made him an increasing obstacle to the Al Qaeda leadership in Afghanistan. From the vantage point of the Al Qaeda leadership around bin Laden, Iraq was only one of a number of battlefronts including Saudi Arabia, and there was some anger at the way that Zarqawi's strategy was leading to rising tensions with Iran, who even handed over some captured Al Qaeda operatives to Saudi Arabia and Egypt.[38] Zarqawi had the upper hand with the Al Qaeda leadership in Pakistan, though this hardly strengthened the movement's wider reputation given its failure to prosecute any sort of protracted insurgent war in Afghanistan. Along with the strategy of global terrorism, Al Qaeda had trained at least 1000 or more guerrilla fighters, many of Saudi origin, whom it thought would be a good match for any American-led invasion by replicating some of the mujahidin warfare against the Russians in the 1980s. This proved not to be the case in late 2001, as Northern Alliance forces supported by just 110 CIA officers and 350 Special Forces succeeded in dislodging the Taliban from Kabul and chasing Al Qaeda out of Afghanistan completely after Operation Anaconda in March 2002.[39]

It remained broadly the case that both Al Qaeda in Afghanistan and AQI under Zarqawi looked towards the establishment of a caliphate as the one true state. But they had significantly different approaches towards achieving this, and the Al Qaeda leadership was more than relieved when Zarqawi was finally killed in 2006.[40] His removal did not really solve anything in Iraq, though on a wider plane the rifts between Al Qaeda and Iran were partially resolved when the Iranians released several Al Qaeda detainees, including bin Laden's daughter, Iman bin Laden, in 2010.[41] Al Qaeda continued to view Iraq as a relative diversion from the apparently more central conflict in Afghanistan between the Taliban and the Kabul regime of Hamid Karsai, and it would require an increasingly radical jihadist Sunni insurgency in Iraq to challenge this dominant view.

This came as the escalating sectarian conflict in Iraq reached civil war proportions by the latter part of 2006, prompting a change of course by the United States in the direction of a troop surge and the resort to a strategy of counterinsurgency under General Petraeus in early 2007. Though in many ways a return to a more old-fashioned form of imperial expeditionary warfare, the surge had the effect of calming the situation down between 2007 and 2010, especially as it enabled the winning back of support from some of the Sunni tribes in the form of the 'Anbar Awakening'. The problem was that the strategy remained incongruent with wider developments at the level of the Iraqi state; no matter how much the United States sought to enforce a legal framework through the Baghdad Security Plan (known in Arabic as the *Fard al-Qanoon* or 'enforcing the law') its credibility continued to be undermined by the resistance from the Iraqi state to the release of funding to support the development of the infrastructure in Sunni communities. Dodge reports that in some instances US colonels took Sunni representatives into the Green Zone in Baghdad to lobby for funding, only to be rebuffed.[42]

The problem was one that the United States was only too familiar with from the earlier experience in South Vietnam with the Diem regime. Here, once more, was a narrowly based regime in Baghdad that was fatally flawed from the very moment of its inception, given the way that it had been conjured into existence by what Dodge has termed an 'exclusive elite bargain', largely under the auspices of exiled Iraqi political leaders who had few if any connections to politics at the local level. The Iraqi Governing Council (IGC) that was formed in 2003 after the initial invasion became the vehicle for these groups to seize control of the Iraqi state and drive through the elections in January 2005 displaying widely differing levels of turnout – from 61–71% in southern Shi'a districts to only 2% in Anbar province where 95% of the population was Sunni.[43] Following this, a new constitution was drafted by a drafting committee that was not even representative of the new assembly, though this in turn provided the basis for the ascendancy of Nuri al Maliki as prime minister in 2006.

Maliki was actually only the deputy leader of the Shi'a Islamist Dawa party, though he also had the advantage of links with the Shi'a militias. Once in power, he was able to use the office of the prime minister to establish an effective shadow state based on a strong grip on the army, the security services, and special forces. Controlling these bodies gave at least the appearance that the state under Dawa was less under the influence of the Shi'a militias than those of his rivals such as the Sadrist followers of Muktada al Sada and the Islamic Supreme Council of Iraq (ISCI).[44] This also enabled him to rule in an increasingly extra-constitutional manner, especially through the office of the commander in chief where he proceeded to do long-term damage to the chain of command in the new Iraqi Security Forces by imposing his own political appointees as senior army chiefs.

These trends within the Iraqi state escaped widespread notice in the period 2006–2008 as the US military waxed lyrical about a series of victories against AQI in the 'Anbar Awakening'. With this success some analysts have suggested that there was one last window of opportunity for Maliki with the departure of US troops from Iraq in 2011. He could then have begun a process of integration of the Awakening members into the Iraq national military and secured a course towards a more secular type of state with Maliki, perhaps, as a new Saddam type of strongman.[45] However, given what we have seen, this was highly unlikely, and the reverse soon happened when Maliki arrested the bodyguards of the Sunni finance minister Rafi al-Issawi in December 2012 in a move aimed at marginalising potential political rivals. The arrests led to widespread protests across the Sunni heartland including Anbar, Ninawa, and Kirkup and the Sunni neighbourhoods in Baghdad. This was then followed by the Iraqi Security Forces (ISF) attacking a Sunni protest camp at Hawija killing 20 protesters. More violent protests followed and the country descended again into sectarian conflict.

The Sunni resistance at this stage contained a number of different organisations including the 1920 Brigades, the Islamic Army of Iraq, Jaysh al-Mujahadin, Ansar al Islam, as well as the Baathist General Military Council of the Iraqi Revolutionaries. However, AQI soon rebranded itself in April 2013 as the *Islamic State of Iraq and al Sham* both to gain control of the revived Sunni militarism as well as to link it to its cross-border activities in Syria. By the end of the year it was able to demonstrate its apparent military competence by killing 23 senior ISF officers in the Horan Valley. But far more important than this in symbolic terms was Maliki's decision to pull his forces out of Falluja on 1 January 2014, allowing the ISIS to secure the city that had been at of the heart original sectarian conflict stretching back to 2004.[46] The stage was now effectively set for *Islamic State*, as it was increasingly becoming known, to seize the initiative in the Sunni resistance and direct it into the completely new agenda of a radical anti-imperialist caliphate.

Can the jihadist revolution be contained?

So far ISIL has confirmed the general assumption held by many analysts of guerrilla war, especially when waged in cities rather than rural terrains, that the chief objective is not so much outright victory over its enemies as the ability not to lose.[47] The movement has managed over the last year to establish itself as a considerable player in Iraq and Syria as well as establishing a large array of supporting organisations worldwide: indeed, it is estimated that it has at least 32 partner organisations and has recruited between 20,000 and 30,000 foreign fighters, though many of these have minimal military skills or training.[48] It appears that, unless it is at least contained both militarily and politically, the movement will continue to threaten instability in the whole Middle East region with the prospect of escalating military conflict that could eventually draw in Israel.

There are certainly some contradictions in IS/DAESH strategy that might increasingly undermine the organisation with the passage of time. The objective of conquering and controlling territory forces what had hitherto been a guerrilla insurgency into positional warfare, with ISIL in some instances building defensive trench fortifications reminiscent of World War I. On the other hand, ISIL has attempted, where possible, to overcome this strategic limitation by maintaining an element of surprise and rapid manoeuvre warfare on a number of separate fronts. It has clearly been helped by its use of trained senior officers from the former Iraqi army, though this dimension to its operations should not be exaggerated. The former Baathist officers did not necessarily bring any especially new military doctrine since the hierarchical nature of Saddam's army and fear of extreme consequences for any unorthodox behaviour made this a cautious and unimaginative military machine. The role of the contingent of Chechen fighters who had fought the Russians in two wars of 1994–1996 and 1999–2000 seems equally important, given that in the first war a Chechen guerrilla of some 10,000 men had surrounded a much larger Russian force of 24,000 men in Grozny inflicting on them a humiliating defeat. Chechen guerrilla tactics involved the use of highly mobile light infantry units together with the agile use of mortars that never stayed too long in the same place but could inflict deadly fire on more static troop concentrations.[49]

Overall, ISIL has forged a rather successful hybrid of guerrilla and conventional tactics, though it has also been aided by its ability to recruit large numbers of untrained but highly motivated fighters to replenish its losses. Over time, it may become increasingly difficult for it to maintain this rapid rate of recruitment, especially as it starts to appear incapable of maintaining the territory it conquered in 2014–2015. This problem is likely to be exacerbated if the surrounding states, especially Turkey, become increasingly successful in imposing restrictions on the movement of aspiring jihadi fighters trying to enter ISIL territory. It is also hard to see how ISIL can continually replenish much of the weaponry it has captured, and many of these assets will degrade if no spare parts for them can be obtained. Some analysts have suggested that the caliphate has already lost up to 75% of its former finances, and the movement will find it increasingly hard to function as a serious state once it is unable to obtain the constant supplies of new revenue; it may be forced at this point to extort more and more resources from the population under its control, so possibly undermining its popular base among Sunnis.[50]

Nevertheless, this is not a movement simply reacting to external events; its considerable military gains in the middle of 2014 appear to have been well planned. The collapse of the ISF came in the wake of a long 'soldiers harvest' campaign involving attacks on checkpoints, assassinations of soldiers off duty, as well as the destruction of soldiers' homes. The campaign was concentrated in Mosul and Ninawa, the main targets of the advance in June 2014.[51] The movement has also been remarkably successful in maintaining its momentum by opening up new surprise attacks even when it has been thrown back on other fronts. This was seen when a small ISIL force of some 200 well-trained militants took the city of Ramadi after earlier losing Tikrit following a protracted assault by the ISF with its Shi'a militia allies. The attack on Ramadi was aided by the use of massive suicide-bomb attacks which had the effect of demoralising the poorly led ISF forces, numbering some 2000 against a highly motivated IS enemy of only 200. The capture of the town proved highly symbolic, for it was here that the local leaders were especially important in mobilising the support of the Sunni tribes behind the 'Anbar Awakening' against the AQI in 2006–2007.[52]

An apocalyptic jihadi ideology acts as a very effective force multiplier for a military formation that can flexibly adopt a range of battlefield tactics. This is a movement that has an army that has gained extensive battlefield experience across a variety of regions. Western states have preferred a policy of containment to direct military engagement, though a number of analysts continue to maintain that any final defeat of the organisation will require Western boots on the ground in one form or another. The containment policy has amounted to a range of measures that include the selective bombing of IS targets, efforts to limit the external financing of the IS regime as well as the flow of jihadi fighters, in addition the United States and other powers continue to assist in building up and training of the ISF in Iraq as well as engaging in wider efforts to delegitimise the ISIL 'brand' along with that of Al Qaeda and other extremist jihadi movements. It has also adopted surprise attacks by both drones and special forces to assassinate middle level ISIL cadres: these threaten the continuity of command in the organisation and appear to have had some impact on the overall morale of ordinary fighters, given some recent defections.[53]

The containment strategy can be judged a success to the extent that it has effectively ended any immediate threat to any of the major cities in the region, especially Baghdad and Damascus. In the latter case, though, it was the short-lived intervention by Russia which served to bolster the Assad regime rather than the rather more restrained response from the West. However, unless there is an escalation of military pressure to effectively end the ISIL control of its territorial area, the threat posed by the movement in the Middle East remains.

Any ultimate end state remains hard to work out at this moment in time. A continuing, if only gradual, limiting of the ISIL land area is likely to precipitate a number of possible outcomes. As the coalition forces in Iraq make access to key resources such as oil harder to obtain, it will become increasingly difficult for ISIL to maintain the limited state infrastructure it has built up, even with tightening pressure and extortion of the inhabitants it controls. Thus one clear possibility is some sort of political transformation in the ruling elite which will end the current antipathy between the supposed caliph Baghdadi and the Al Qaeda leadership. Bruce Hoffman has recently suggested that the two organisations might at this point merge, a scenario he finds a nightmare for Western anti-terrorism strategy.[54] This scenario is clearly possible, but it is driven by a mode of analysis that sees both Al Qaeda and ISIL as essentially terrorist-type organisations with similar ideological programmes and only divided by personal antipathies of their two respective leaders. The argument overlooks the fact that the two movements have both different military strategies as well as different rates of success in recruitment of cadres: Al Qaeda has generally failed to 'bleed out' by securing a real grip on Middle Eastern and North African communities in Europe or even to secure a large number of 'clean skin' passport holders held by second- and third-generation migrants. By contrast, ISIL has been comparatively successful in recruiting fighters in Europe as well as terrorist militants and suicide-bombers to launch attacks such as those in Paris and Brussels.[55] The contrasting strategies of the two rival organisations linked to radically divergent narratives of jihad suggest that an early merger is not very likely.

Moreover, even if ISIL is ultimately defeated, it would be foolhardy to overlook the powerful ideological impact it has exerted on the Islamic world. There will be 'lessons learned' in jihadist debate on social media. The historical fact of a radically inclined Islamic 'state' capable of surviving for some years will almost certainly exert a major influence on jihadist strategic thought. So far, this thought has not been taken especially seriously by Western strategic theorists – an example of what some critics have for years seen as the inherent ethnocentrism of strategic studies. It has often been based on a reading of texts by such figures as Sayyid Qutb and Ayman Zawahiri, suggesting a strategy more or less completely dominated by a dogmatic Salafism that more or less obliterates any possibility for pragmatic forms of statecraft or any form of peaceful accommodation with the West.[56]

A careful reading of the text *The Management of Savagery* suggests a rather more nuanced pattern of strategic thinking among some jihadists and one, moreover, that might well have some bearing on the emergence in other war-torn regions of newer jihadist formations of an ISIL type. The text is widely believed to have been written by one Abu Bakr Naji, who apparently came from North Africa. Some analysts, though, have suggested the real author was Muhammed al-Hukayma, who worked for the media wing of Al Qaeda before being killed in 2008 in Pakistan in a US drone strike.[57] Whatever the case, the text certainly reveals familiarity with the power and importance of media, which the author believes has contributed to an illusion of domination by great powers such as the United States and Russia. But most importantly, the text urges jihadists to read works on strategy by non-Islamic strategic theorists such as Sun Tzu and Clausewitz as well as key works in management studies in order to build up a new state that is capable of managing the 'chaos' that he believes to exist in the era before a new Islamic state is formed. In true Hobbesian form, the author believes that this new state, infused by modern management methods, can effectively control 'savagery' like some modern terrorist Leviathan in order to establish itself in a region as well as stand up to the West, which he believes, in an analysis shaped by a reading of Paul Kennedy, is in danger of 'imperial overstretch'.[58] 'Managing', in effect, the 'savagery' of a new state becomes a rational strategy to pursue as a means of making the state's enemies 'think one thousand times before attacking us'.[59]

The interesting question that emerges from this line of reasoning is whether this is a text in the tradition of 'peoples war', stretching back possibly to Clausewitz's idea of mobilising the *Landsturm* (the civil organisations of society) against enemy invasion, or something else. In an age of massive and deadly weaponry that can easily destroy whole swathes of a society, as has been seen only too clearly in Syria, the traditional idea of protracted war involving the long-term mobilisation of the 'people' maybe rather outmoded – especially if the 'people' can be scooped up from the sea in the manner of modern deep-sea fishing and dispersed to other regions such as Europe. Naji's focus is thus important for the way it shifts to the capacity of the state to inflict terror as a political weapon, a return to the original foundations of terror as a political concept in the French Revolution. By demonstrating a capacity to raise the threshold of terror to new levels in the Middle East, ISIL has demonstrated an effective use of terror as a serious military tactic alongside other tactics such as guerrilla warfare, suicide-bombing, and assassination. As we have seen in this paper, ISIL has not always been able to calibrate these tactics especially well, given the way that the UN Security Council resorted to Resolution 2249 on 3 December 2015. It may in time, though, either modify its stand in the interests of survival or re-emerge in some new form with a more sophisticated military strategy than we have seen hitherto.

Notes

1. Hegghammer, *Jihad in Saudi Arabia*, 3.
2. Rubinstein, *Alchemists of Revolution*, 223.
3. Phillips, 'The Islamic State's Challenge'.
4. See for example O'Neill, *Insurgency and Terrorism*, 22.
5. Khalaf, 'Beyond Arms'.
6. Michael P. Scharf, 'How the War Against ISIS Changed International Law', 9–10.
7. Napoleoni, *Insurgent Iraq*, 213.

8. Hegghammer, *Jihad in Saudi Arabia*, 7. Hegghammer's analysis of classical jihadism is heavily influenced by the thinking of Abdallah Azzam, though as I shall seek to show in this paper there were far more important influences from the actual conflict in Iraq, especially via al Zarqawi.
9. See the discussion on counter-revolutionary and counter-Enlightenment thought in Mayer, *The Furies*, 59–63.
10. McCants, *ISIS Apocalypse*, 23.
11. Ayoob, 'The Myth of the Islamic State'.
12. Atwan, *Islamic State*, 132–3.
13. Walt, 'ISIS as Revolutionary State'.
14. Cited in Armstrong, *Revolution and World Order*, 227.
15. Ibid., 303; Uldricks, *Diplomacy and Ideology*; Andrei Grachev, *Gorbachev's Gamble*; Haslam, *Russia's Cold War*.
16. Hirst, *War and Power in the 21st Century*, 99.
17. Atwan, *Islamic State*, xi–xii.
18. Hill, *Antichrist in Seventeenth Century England*, 157–8; *The World Turned Upside Down*.
19. Haddad, *Sectarianism in Iraq*, 25–9.
20. Ibid., 33.
21. Dodge, *Inventing Iraq*.
22. Kepel, *The War for Muslim Minds*, 228–9.
23. Dodge, 'Seeking to Explain the Rise', 5.
24. Cook, *Martyrdom in Islam*, 137–40.
25. Kepel, *The Revenge of God*, 29–33.
26. Nafi, 'The Abolition of the Caliphate'.
27. O'Neill, *Insurgency and Terrorism*, 66.
28. See in particular Lakitsch, 'Islamic State', 12–13.
29. Kaminski, 'Comparing Goals', 44.
30. Brisard, *Zarqawi*, 74–5.
31. Napoleoni, *Insurgent Iraq*, 127.
32. Zarqawi letter to bin Ladin, February 2004. http//2001-2009.state.gov/p/nea/rls/31694.htm. Accessed 25 May 2015.
33. Napoleoni, *Insurgent Iraq*, 158.
34. Hashim, *Insurgency and Counter-Insurgency in Iraq*, 212.
35. Dodge 'Seeking to Explain the Rise', 8
36. Dodge, *Iraq*, 61.
37. Mansfield, *His Own Words*, 220.
38. Shahzad, *Inside Al Qaeda*, 57.
39. Hegghammer, *Jihad in Saudi Arabia*, 162.
40. Lewis, *The Islamic State*, 9.
41. Shahzad, *Inside Al Qaeda*, 193–4.
42. Dodge, *Iraq*, 87.
43. Ibid., 45.
44. Ibid., 127.
45. This is suggested in Adnan and Reese, *Beyond the Islamic State*, 10.
46. Ibid. 12.
47. Joes, *Urban Guerrilla Warfare*, 158.
48. Choksy, 'Ending the Islamic State's Siren Song'.
49. Barfi, 'The Military Doctrine of the Islamic State'.
50. 'The Caliphate Cracks', *The Economist*, 21 March 2015
51. Knights, 'ISIL's Political-Military Power in Iraq', 2.

52. Hassan, 'The ISIS March Continues'.
53. Derek, 'ISIS Is Not Losing'.
54. Hoffman, 'The Coming ISIS-Al Qaeda Merger'.
55. Watts, 'Why ISIS beats Al Qaeda in Europe'.
56. See for example Gorka, 'Understanding Today's Enemy'.
57. McCants, *ISIS Apocalypse*, 210, ref. 78.
58. Naji, *The Management of Savagery*.
59. Ibid., 111–12.

Disclosure statement

No potential conflict of interest was reported by the author.

References

Adnan, Sinan, and Aaron Reese. *Beyond the Islamic State: Iraq's Sunni Insurgency*. Washington DC: Institute for the Study of War, 2014.
Armstrong, David. *Revolution and World Order*. Oxford: Clarendon Press, 1993.
Atwan, Abdel Bari. *Islamic State: The Digital Caliphate*. London: Saqi, 2015.
Ayoob, Mohammed. "The Myth of the Islamic State: The History of a Political Idea." *Foreign Affairs* 3 (April 2016), www.foreignaffairs.com.
Barfi, Barak. 'The Military Doctrine of the Islamic State and the Limits of Baathist Influence'. *CTC Sentinel*, 19 February 2016. http://www.ctc.usma.edu/posts. Accessed 24 February 2016.
Brisard, Jan-Charles. *Zarqawi: The New Face of Al Qaeda*. London: Polity, 2005.
Choksy, Jamsheed K. 'Ending the Islamic State's Siren Song', 14 May 2015. http://www.e-ir.info/2015/05/14. Accessed 20 May 2015.
Cook, David. *Martyrdom in Islam*. Cambridge: Cambridge University Press, 2007.
Dodge, Toby. *Inventing Iraq: The Failure of Nation Building and a History Denied*. New York and London: Columbia University Press, 2005.
Dodge, Toby. *Iraq: From War to a New Authoritarianism*. London: Routledge, 2013.
Dodge, Toby. 'Seeking to Explain the Rise of Sectarianism in the Middle East: The Case Study of Iraq'. In *Iraq Between Maliki and the Islamic State*, George Washington University: Project on Middle East Political Science, Briefing No 24.
Gorka, Sebastian. 'Understanding Today's Enemy: The Grand Strategists of Modern Jihad'. *Military Review*, May–June 2016.
Grachev, Andrei. *Gorbachev's Gamble: Soviet Foreign Policy and the end of the Cold War*. London: Polity, 2008.
Haddad, Fannar. *Sectarianism in Iraq*. New York, NY: Columbia University Press, 2011.
Harvey, Derek. 'ISIS Is Not Losing, So the US Is Not Winning', 19 May 2015. http://derekharvey.org/2015/05/19/isis-is-not-losing-so-the-u-s-is-not-winning/. Accessed 20 May 2015.
Hassan, Hassan. 'The ISIS March Continues: From Ramadi on to Baghdad?' 19 May 2015. www.foreignpolicy.com/2015/05/19. Accessed 20 May 2015.
Hashim, Ahmed H. *Insurgency and Counter-Insurgency in Iraq*. London: Hurst, 2006.
Haslam, Jonathan. *Russia's Cold War: From the October Revolution to the Fall of the Wall*. New Haven and London: Yale University Press, 2011.
Hegghammer, Thomas. *Jihad in Saudi Arabia: Violence and Pan-Islamism since 1979*. Cambridge: Cambridge University Press, 2010.

Hill, Christopher. *Antichrist in Seventeenth Century England*. London: Oxford University Press, 1971.
Hill, Christopher. *The World Turned Upside Down: Radical Ideas in the English Revolution*. London: Penguin Books, 1991.
Hirst, Paul. *War and Power in the 21st Century*. London: Polity, 2001.
Hoffman, Bruce. "The Coming ISIS-AL Qaeda Merger." *Foreign Affairs* 29 (March 2016), www.foreignaffairs.com. Accessed 5 April 2016.
Joes, Anthony James. *Urban Guerrilla Warfare*. Lexington: University of Kentucky Press, 2007.
Kaminski, Joseph. "Comparing Goals and Aspirations of National vs Transnational Islamist Movements." In *Caliphates and Global Politics*, edited by Timothy Poirson and Robert Oprisko. Bristol: E-International Relations, 2015.
Kepel, Gilles. *The Revenge of God*. London: Polity Press, 1994.
Kepel, Gilles. *The War for Muslim Minds: Islam and the West*. Cambridge, MA and London: Harvard University Press, 2004.
Khalaf, Rana. "Beyond Arms and Local Governance of ISIS in Syria." In *Caliphates and Global Politics*, edited by Timothy Poirson and Robert Oprisko, 7–14. Bristol: E-International Relations, 2015.
Knights, Michael. "ISIL's Political-Military Power in Iraq." *CTC Sentinel* 7 (August 2014): 8.
Lakitsch, Maximilian. "Islamic State, the Arab Spring, and the Disenchantment with Political Islam." In *Caliphates and Global Politics*, edited by Timothy Poirson and Robert Oprisko. Bristol: E-International Relations, 2015.
Lewis, Jessica D. *The Islamic State: A Counter Strategy for a Counter State*, Washington DC: Institute for the Study of War (ISW), 2014.
Mansfield, Laura (ed.). *His Own Words: A Translation of the Writings of Dr Ayman al Zawahiri*. TLG, n.p. Lulu Pub. 2006.
Mayer, Arno J., and The Furies. *Violence and Terror in the French and Russian Revolutions*. Princeton and Oxford: Princeton University Press, 2000.
McCants, William. *ISIS Apocalypse: The History, Strategy and Doomsday Vision of the Islamic State*. New York, NY: St Martins Press, 2015.
Nafi, Basheer M. 'The Abolition of the Caliphate in Historical Context'. In *Demystifying the Caliphate: Historical Memory and Contemporary Contexts*, edited by Madawi Al-Rasheed et al., 31–56. London: Hurst, 2013.
Naji, Abu Bakr. *The Management of Savagery: The Most Critical Stage Through Which the Umma Will Pass*, translated by William McCants. Harvard University: John M. Olin Institute for Strategic Studes, 23 May 2006. http://azelin.files.wordpress.com./2010/08. Accessed 10 June 2016,
Napoleoni, Loretta. *Insurgent Iraq: Al Zarqawi and the New Generation*. London: Constable, 2005.
O'Neill, Bard E. *Insurgency and Terrorism: From Revolution to Apocalypse*. Washington DC: Potomac Books, 2005.
Phillips, Andrew. "The Islamic State's Challenge to International Order." *Australian Journal of International Affairs* 68, no. 5 (2014): 495–498.
Poirson Timothy and Robert Oprisko (eds.). *Caliphates and Global Politics*. Bristol: E-International Relations, 2015.
Rubinstein, Richard E. *Alchemists of Revolution: Terrorism in the Modern World*. New York, NY: Basic Books, 1987.
Scharf, Michael P. 'How the War Against ISIS Changed International Law'. Case Research Paper Working Paper 16 in Legal Studies, School of Law, Cape Western Reserve University, March 2016.
Shahzad, Syed Saleem. *Inside Al Qaeda and the Taliban*. London: Palgrave Macmillan, 2011.

Uldricks, Teddy J. *Diplomacy and Ideology: The Origins of Soviet Foreign Relations, 1917–1930*. London and Beverly Hills, CA: Sage, 1979.

Walt, Stephen M. 'ISIS as Revolutionary State: New Twist on an Old Story'. *Foreign Affairs*, November–December 2015. www.foreignaffairs.com. Accessed 20 January 2016

Watts, Clint. 'Why ISIS beats Al Qaeda in Europe: A New Recruitment Strategy for a New World'. *Foreign Affairs*, 4 April 2016. https://www.foreignaffairs.com/articles/2016-04-04/why-isis-beats-al-qaeda-europe.

Global Jihad and Foreign Fighters

George Joffé

ABSTRACT
One question that has been unresolved since the current phase of extremism began in the early- to mid-1990s has been whether or not there is a global structure to the jihadi phenomenon. This paper argues that no such definable structure exists, although regional, national, and local networks may well share common objectives and ideological ambitions. There has, in short, been a process of global branding that has developed that, in structural terms, corresponds to a 'network of networks'. These objectives and the related praxis, moreover, have evolved over the years, going through three distinct stages of development, encapsulated in the strategic distinctions between al-Qa'ida, Ansar al-Shar'ia, and the Islamic State (Da'ish). Allied to this is a second consideration; namely that the formal ideological inspiration and justification for extremist activities is a set of integrated common insights that form a coherent ideology derived from a literalist interpretation of Islam, Salafism. A further aspect of the Salafi–jihadi phenomenon is to what degree this formal ideology is the real explanation of the appeal of these movements to their adherents, particularly to the so-called 'foreign fighters' – those who volunteer from countries not directly implicated in the specific conflicts in which they participate. This paper will argue that the phenomenon is far more complex than the superficial appeal of jihadist ideology would suggest. Finally, the paper will attempt to sketch out what the underlying causes of the intense wave of extremism sweeping the Middle East and North Africa might be and to what extent 'blow-back' from returning jihadis should be of concern to home governments.

David Rapoport has argued that violent extremism has been an accompaniment of European civilisation since at least the 1880s.[1] He suggests that there was, first, an anarchist wave of violence, followed by an anti-colonial wave, itself succeeded by what he calls a 'New Left' wave and now replaced by a wave of religious terrorism with each of these waves lasting for 40 to 45 years. Jeffrey

Kaplan, writing at the end of the first decade of the twenty-first century has suggested a fifth wave which seeks to re-create a lost golden millennium and is characterised, inter alia, by being, 'chiliastic in nature, deeply religious with eclectic or syncretic religious tropes assembled and interpreted by the leaders in support of a millenarian dream to be realized through a campaign of apocalyptic violence'.[2]

If these two comments are relevant to the contemporary phenomenon of *Salafi–jihadi* extremism and violence, then they suggest that it is not *sui generis*, a unique event that could not have been anticipated and, as such, a threat to the structure, beliefs, and practices of modern society. Rather, it is an inevitable concomitant of a long history of often unhappy interactions between governments and the societies over which they rule and of interstate conflict and domination. Despite current claims that contemporary terrorism reflects a conflict of civilisations of the type proposed by Samuel Huntington, it forms part of the long historical pattern of populist responses to autocratic government and state intervention.[3] What is unique about it, then, is the structural form it adopts and the ideological justifications it mobilises.

Content, form, and structure

Contemporary terrorism relies for its ideological underpinnings on the doctrines of Salafi–jihadism, which essentially originates in the mujahidin resistance to the Soviet invasion of Afghanistan in the 1980s, although other events at around the same time also contributed to its growth. Rapoport, for instance, suggests that the Islamic Revolution in Iran in 1979 – which coincided with the advent of a new Muslim century – was also a major driver of the violent extremism that has characterised radical political Islam.[4] Nonetheless, the codification of an ideology of violence emerged from the widespread recruitment and armament of Muslims to support the Afghan resistance. This process, encouraged by Saudi Arabia and funded by the United States, was paralleled by the development of an ideology of resistance rooted in the Islamic tradition of jihad, of defence of the integrity of the Islamic world against external threat, as restated by, among others, Abdullah Azzam in his two fatwas, *The Defence of the Muslim Lands* and *Join the Caravan*, the first written in 1979 and the second eight years later. The importance of jihad had been emphasised by the Egyptian activist, Muhammad Faraj, in his book, *The Neglected Duty*, published in Arabic in 1982 and in English in 1986, after he had been executed by the Egyptian authorities for his role in the assassination of President Anwar Sadat.

Ideology

The doctrine of *jihad* they revealed was one of an individual duty, incumbent on all Muslims (*fardh al-ayn*), to defend the Muslim world and its religious culture if any part of it were threatened.[5] The religious culture they endorsed was a literalist restatement of Islamic society in the Rashidun period – that of the first four rightly guided caliphs after the death of the Prophet Muhammad. It is a vision that is normally described as Salafist, although in its political activism, it is far removed from conventional Salafism – *salafiyya-ilmiyya*.[6] It was, however, a very particular vision that allowed no space for deviance from a rigidly narrow canon of belief and regarded deviance as apostasy and therefore punishable by death. It implied, furthermore, a literalist interpretation of shar'ia law, with all the repressive potential that that could imply.

In two senses, however, the doctrines of praxis that emerged from the Afghani maelstrom were innovative. One made a distinction between what it called the 'near enemy' and the 'far enemy', the former being corrupt, autocratic – and thus un-Islamic, *jahili* – governments in the Middle East and North African region, and the latter being those governments outside the region (and, by definition, non-Muslim governments) that had supported and nourished their corrupt regional counterparts.[7] Among the *mujahidin*, it was al-Qa'ida, the successor organisation to Abdullah Azzam's Maktab al-Khidma reception centre, that decided to target the latter, while the many national movements focused their attentions exclusively among the former. The second characteristic that was novel was that jihad was now interpreted as a pre-emptive obligation; in other words, the Islamic world did not need to wait to be attacked, it could (and should) pre-emptively attack its expected opponents if it believed that they would attack it. This also became an intrinsic aspect of al-Qa'ida's doctrine. This, incidentally, fitted well within the classic doctrine of offensive jihad, whereby the caliph was expected to undertake offensive strikes into the *Dar al-Harb* once or twice a year both to collect booty and to discourage attacks on the Muslim community inside the *Dar al-Islam*, as Abdullah Azzam had made clear in his own fatwas on jihad.

Allied to this was the doctrine of decentralised jihad, as put forward by Abu Mus'ab al-Suri in his major work, *The Global Islamic Resistance Call*.[8] His ideas were challenged by those of Abdul-Bakr Naji, who argued instead that the purpose of jihad was to convince Muslims in the 'grey zone' – the region of mixed Muslim and non-Muslim populations, as well as in *takfiri* (apostate) Muslim states – to reject their non-Muslim and *takfiri* compatriots and to solidify the Muslim community there by exemplary violence; the strategy espoused by Abu Musab al-Zarqawi in his organisation of al-Qa'ida in Iraq, to the consternation of al-Qaida's leaders themselves.[9] In effect, these three sets of doctrines, taken together, provided a complete agenda through which extremists could challenge the established political order within the Muslim world, as sanctioned by its external non-Muslim partners who could therefore also be subject to attack.

Indeed, over the past 20 years, these basic doctrines have become the core of *Salafi–jihadi* ideology worldwide. Associated with them has been the cult of martyrdom, which previously was much more closely associated with Shi'a

Islam and the emulation of the death of Imam Husayn.[10] Sunni jihadism is, in theory an inevitable by-product of jihad in that the loss of life it implies is an incidental, not an intended, consequence of a heroic act in defence of the Islamic ideal – although this distinction has become blurred as suicide attacks have become a preferred mode of aggression. Yet it is also a vehicle of powerful propaganda in that, within the jihadi context, it is also associated with the media glorification of the act itself through the formality of the martyr's filmed farewell and commemoration of his sacrifice.[11] It is also, in a sense, a negation of the Divinity, the very entity that it is meant to glorify, for it ignores the ethical and moral principles it transgresses, as defined by the Divinity, justifying itself on the practical objectives it achieves to reinstate the Divinity and to restore its moral and religious status.[12] In this respect, it is worth remembering that, initially, such altruistic suicide attacks in Ceylon, Lebanon, and Palestine were primarily the prerogative of secular resistance groups, not religious ones.[13] In essence, however, this compendium of ideological elements – jihadi ideology, the near and far enemy differential targeting, pre-emptive defence, decentralised jihad, savagery, and altruistic suicide – strongly suggests that the formal intellectual and religious justification for violent, extremist jihad comprises a global ideology and strategy.

Strategy: the initial challenge

This transnational ideology does not, however, imply that the strategies or targets adopted by the movement have remained universal or, indeed, invariant as well, for there were clear divergences over the ultimate objective. Indeed, over the lifetime of the movement to date, there have been at least three, if not four iterations of the strategy that it has adopted, each of which reflects one or other aspect of the ideology outlined above. These iterations also reflect a certain degree of fragmentation of the movement, which was apparent from its inception within the mujahidin movement that developed in Afghanistan in the 1980s, although organised transnational jihadi violence really only begins at the end of that decade, after the Soviet withdrawal.

The initial distinction lay between those who sought national objectives – the replacement of un-Islamic national governments and the reorientation of society through violence – and those who sought to attack states outside the region whom they held responsible for supporting national governance practices within it – the 'near' and 'far' enemy dilemma. Al-Qa'ida, of course, became the pre-eminent exponent of the attack on the 'far enemy', but it is often forgotten that it only did this in coalition with or with the support of other movements as well. Thus although the first of its two initial declarations of intent in 1996 and 1998 – a declaration of war on the foreign presence in Saudi Arabia after the Iraqi invasion of Kuwait in 1990 – was made in his own name, the second – a fatwa directed against the United States and Israel – brought together a heterogeneous collection of extremist religious movements; two from Egypt and several from the Indian subcontinent.[14] At least one of the Egyptian signatories, Ayman Zawahiri, was to become an integral part of the movement and Bin Ladin's eventual successor in 2011.

There was another alternative, too, a kind of 'nomadic jihad' that emerged in the wake of the Afghani experience. Here former mujahidin who were not repatriated – often to face a vengeful home government, well aware of the ideologies the returnees might have adopted – sought, instead, new arenas in which to pursue jihad. Thus, Bosnia-Herzegovina and Chechnya became prime objectives in which the aim was not so much to confront Western violence but rather to protect outliers of the Islamic world irrespective of the nationalities involved, on the argument that the Islamic world, as a single *umma*, a Muslim community, did not recognise the salience of nationality. This again diluted the ability of al-Qa'ida to control a single movement by itself because of the cooperation that was necessary, an initiative resisted by both Abdullah Azzam and as-Suri despite Bin Ladin's clear desire to do so quite apart from the impossibility of doing so in organisational terms, even though ideology and objectives might have been shared on a transnational basis.[15]

Many other movements present in Afghanistan, however, did not accept this approach. Instead they sought to concentrate on removing their own corrupt national governments. Indeed, until the Mubarak government in Egypt successfully suppressed the campaign of violence against it in the second half of the 1990s and its leaders fled to Afghanistan, this had been true of both *Islamic Jihad* and the *Jamiyat Islamiyya* there as well. Certainly throughout the 1990s, groups in Libya (the *Libyan Islamic Fighting Group*) and in Algeria (the *Groupes Islamiques Armés* – GIA – and, later, the *Groupe Salafiste de Prédication et du Combat* – GSPC) sustained such positions, as did other less extreme religious movements, such as *Hizbullah* and *Hamas* in the Middle East, as well as in the Gulf, particularly in Saudi Arabia with *al-Qa'ida in the Arabian Peninsula*. And, of course, the classic example, was to prove to be *al-Qa'ida in Iraq* between 2003 and 2006.[16]

This distinction in targets implied a difference in tactics as well, even if all extremist groups shared a common ideology. Al-Qa'ida became a decentralised network, with its leadership increasingly harassed and isolated, particularly after its most successful operation to date, on September 11, 2001 in Washington and New York. It also became increasingly difficult for it to mount operations, with those it did undertake often being contracted out to autonomous groups, although it continued to be able to provide funding for them.[17] This seems to have been the case quite early on, with the bombings of American embassies in Nairobi and Dar es Salaam in 1998 and with the bombing of the USS *Cole* in Aden harbour in 2000. It was certainly so after 2001 with many of the potential airline bombers and with abortive attacks on facilities in the developed world being organised increasingly by independent groups, even if they did claim affiliation with al-Qa'ida itself. Al-Qa'ida, in short, seemed to have been transformed from a global network, if indeed it ever was, into a global brand.

As such, as al-Qa'ida's utility as an independent transnational jihadi group directed against the West faded, its utility as the symbol of a global brand significantly increased. Other, independent groups, whether they were primarily concerned with the near or the far enemy sought the affiliation to give themselves increased credibility. Nor were these groups only in the Arab world; Indonesia and the Philippines also featured their al-Qa'ida affiliates, as did Pakistan and Bangladesh, and, later on, North Africa (*al-Qa'ida in the Islamic Maghrib*), Nigeria (*Boko Haram*), and Somalia (*al-Shabaab*). Yet, despite a shared ideology, organisational links were minimal and al-Qa'ida's ability to set the extremist agenda also began to fade, being replaced by national objectives instead. Control of territory became more important than diminishing the 'Great Satan' and its Western acolytes. One of the ironies was that al-Qa'ida had also sought to set out territorial objectives as well; Ayman Zawahiri had set a detailed plan for Abu Musab al-Zarqawi in Iraq in which, after expelling the US forces from the country, his movement was to set about constructing an Islamic caliphate there.[18]

A strategic alternative

Nonetheless, by 2011 it appeared as if the extremist groups had lost much of their global appeal as social movements throughout the region, enunciating demands that had little to do with Islamic values or objectives had come to the fore. Coincidentally, shortly before the Arab Spring exploded at the end of 2010, at least one al-Qa'ida affiliate seems to have decided that the objective of combating Western interference inside the Middle East and North Africa was no longer viable, not least because of the growing loss of popular support within the region for such initiatives. Both al-Qa'ida in Iraq's experiences of being marginalised as a result of the *Sahwa* movement in 2007, when its attempts to root itself within the Sunni tribes of Anbar ran up against tribal hostility to its brutal methods, and warnings from the al-Qa'ida leadership over the dangers of excessive violence (warnings that had also been given to the GIA in Algeria in the late 1990s), seem to have persuaded al-Qa'ida in the Arabian Peninsula to develop a new approach. It was tried first in Zinjibar, in South Yemen until the Yemeni army abruptly terminated the experiment in May 2011.[19]

The new approach was to offer the idea of good governance in place of the Islamic caliphate or the expulsion of Western influences, through a new organisation, *Ansar al-Shar'ia*. The same agenda and organisation was subsequently to emerge in both Libya and Tunisia, as an alternative to the purist jihadi vision and as one in which violence did not necessarily, at least not initially, have to play a part. Thus, in Libya, for example, after the collapse of the Qadhafi regime in October 2011, Ansar al-Shar'ia emerged in Benghazi both as a vehicle for local administration and as a militia that was to be responsible for the assassination of the rebel Libyan army commander, Abdulfattah al-Obaydh, in July 2011 and for the death of Ambassador Christopher Stevens in Benghazi on 12 September 2012 – old habits, evidently died hard![20]

The important point about the new model agenda was not that it prevented the groups concerned from engaging in violence in pursuit of the traditional transnational or national agendas. What it did was to make them far more difficult for government to control, since they operated in social situations of acute need or the absence of state authority and, in Libya in particular, provided security guarantees that the nascent state could not. Popular sentiment, in addition, would not consent to their suppression because of the social services they provided, even if they also engaged in violence against those of whom they disapproved, including symbols of Western influence or takfiri behaviour. Nonetheless, in Tunisia in particular, the harder-edged agenda of violent disruption of the state began to reassert itself, with two assassinations of leading secular politicians in February and July 2013, and with the growth of rural-based violent extremism along the border with Algeria, in which Tunisian and Algerian extremists collaborated in building up an increasingly effective movement.

The third way

It was at this stage that the strategic picture of violent extremism was to be complicated by events in Iraq and Syria. Up to 2014, it had appeared that the four variants through which the global Salafi–jihadi ideology could be expressed – targeting the far enemy, nomadic jihad, targeting the near enemy, and seeking Islamic good governance – had been able to coexist, and even if no unified organisation of violence had proved to be possible, al-Qa'ida had maintained its re-eminence as the global brand. This was now to be abruptly disrupted, both by the evidence of the effectiveness of social movements in the region with quite different agendas from Islamist extremism and by the objectives of the resurgent extremist movement in Iraq, now calling itself *Islamic State* or *Da'ish*, which had captured control of most of Anbar in January 2014 and Mosul in June 2014 while, at the same time, expanding into Syria.

The social movements of the Arab Spring had framed the issues confronting the populations of the Middle East and North Africa in quite different ways from the extremists. Rather than pinpointing the breakdown of Islamic observance as the cause of the region's problems and an extremely narrow, literalist explanation of the issue in terms of essentialist Islam as its means of resolution, the vast bulk of the Arab world was now primarily concerned with removing autocratic, corrupt, and incompetent kleptocracies from power.[21] They were also aware of the adverse consequences of chronic Western interference in regional affairs and bitterly resented the way in which Iraq had been victimised and Iran isolated (despite Gulf antipathies towards the Sunni–Shi'a divide), but they did not see Islam, at least in the form expressed by al-Qa'ida and its affiliates, as the solution.

Indeed, in some countries, such as Algeria and, surprisingly, Libya, there was a strong antipathy towards such approaches.[22]

In Iraq, however, the movement that was to become the Islamic State was to be revitalised after its near-annihilation in 2010 by the civil war in Syria, where it had been able to promote a new movement, the *Nusra Front* (*Jabhat an-Nusra li Ahli ash-Sham* – the 'Support Front for the people of Sham (Syria)'), to challenge both the Assad regime and the Free Syrian Army and its associates among the moderate Islamist movements supported by Turkey, Qatar, and Saudi Arabia. It had also introduced a new feature into its tactics, of seeking alliances with other irredentist opposition groups inside Iraq, notably the *Naqshbandi Order* in the form of the *Jaysh Rijal at-Tariqa an-Naqshbandiyya* (JRTN), which also acted as a cover for the powerful remnant of the Ba'ath Party which was determined to undermine the post-2003 Iraqi state.[23] Alongside such an alliance, the Islamic State also sought other alliances with tribal groups, which it enticed into its orbit by offering them material advantages, provided they did not threaten it, and the promise of extreme exemplary violence if they did.[24]

These new tactics were combined with a new set of objectives; namely the deliberate construction of an Islamic Caliphate to be controlled by itself, as its primary purpose. This was to be accompanied by the creation of an administration to control the new state and a military strategy that would exploit very effectively the weaknesses of its opponents. The movement also ensured that it had adequate funding and weaponry for this ambitious agenda, which anticipated nothing less than the capture of both Syria and Iraq for the nucleus of its new political creation. It has certainly been supremely successful in these objectives, having allegedly amassed up to $8 billion in funds and having conquered to date 25% of the territorial extent of Syria and a similar area in Iraq.[25] It also financed itself through oil sales from the oilfields it controlled around Deir ez-Zor in Syria, as well as from expropriations, the sale of antiquities, extortions, and taxation (canonical taxes including *jiziya*[26] that it charges over the areas it controls). It has also extended its territorial control from north-eastern Syria and western and northern Iraq to include Sinai in Egypt and central Libya. Territory, rather than straightforward geopolitical power and influence, appears to be its main driver.

Alongside these successes have been new perspectives for the global jihadi movement. Now Islamic State claims that it, rather than al-Qa'ida, isolated in its mountain fastnesses in Afghanistan or Pakistan, is the true embodiment of the extremist ideal for it is engaged in actual combat and it should be combatants who actually determine policy and strategy for all of the transnational movements, not the marginalised legacy of Usama bin Ladin, now under the control of the ageing Ayman Zawahiri. It has also sought to recall the Nusra Front to its banner, although the Front's leadership persists in regarding itself as part of al-Qa'ida.[27] Its rank-and-file, however, has tended to drift away, attracted to Islamic Front's evident military prowess and territorial acquisition. Al-Qa'ida has also protested against the Islamic State's usurpation of its pre-eminent position but to no avail.

The Islamic State has also demonstrated a surprising energy in trying to capture global leadership, despatching selected members to sow extremism elsewhere. As mentioned above, the result has been a rash of eruptions of incipient Islamic State organisations, all claiming local affiliation to the parent organisation, particularly in North Africa, with Egypt (Sinai) and Libya as primary targets but with rumours that there is an actual Islamic State presence in Algeria too. Beyond this, the Islamic State has been immeasurably helped by two other factors. The first is a veritable rush among other, often isolated, extremist groups to brand themselves with its characteristic brutality, violence, and universalist ambitions. And the second has been a spontaneous rallying to its colours from Muslim communities throughout the Middle East and North Africa, as well as from the Muslim minority communities in the wider non-Muslim world. Nothing, in short, seems to succeed like success, whatever the means used or the objectives sought!

In late 2015, however, the Islamic State appeared to have shifted its strategic approach significantly as it expanded its activities in Europe itself. Its declared objective was to eliminate the 'grey zone', that sociocultural environment where Muslim and non-Muslim shared the same physical environment and political institutions in a common social context, as Naji had defined it.[28] It typically chose to do so in the most violent and brutal way available to it, by launching suicidal violence against civilian populations in public settings, as it demonstrated in Paris on 13 November 2015. It mobilised disaffected youth from ethnic minority communities in European countries for this purpose, particularly from among the North African second generation communities in France and Belgium. In fact, similar tactics of mobilisation had also been used by some of the Islamic State's predecessors, such as the GIA in the 1990s, but those occasions had tended to involve isolated individuals or small, self-motivated locally based networks like the Buttes-Chaumont or the Chasse-sur-Rhone groups.[29] The Islamic State's attacks, however, were coordinated within a general strategy directed from its headquarters in Syria and mobilising European nationals. In reality, this was not really a change in strategy but an extension of its existing approach for it was designed to exclude non-Muslims from its territorial domain and to encourage the Muslim community to see the Islamic State as its sole and proper protector.

The foreign fighter syndrome

Indeed, one of the most striking consequences of the success of the Islamic State has been its ability to attract supporters from abroad. They are currently estimated to be at least 25,000 strong and may even be as many as 30,000 in total. The majority are probably from the Middle Eastern and North African region, despite the curbs placed upon them by their home states, but there is, however, a significant number from European states and further afield – as far away as Australia and the United States – as well. During 2015, detailed estimates of the numbers involved began to emerge.

Thus, at the start of the year the International Centre for the Study of Radicalisation and Political Violence at Kings College in London University estimated that there were 20,730 'foreign fighters' worldwide, more than there had been in Afghanistan during the Soviet occupation there. Some 11,000 came from the Middle East and North Africa and 3000 from the former Soviet Union.[30] A subsequent estimate by the United Nations Security Council in April 2015 suggested that there were 22,000 in Syria and Iraq, 6500 in Afghanistan, and 'hundreds' in Pakistan, Yemen, Somalia, and Libya. The numbers had risen by 71% between mid-2014 and March 2015.[31] A report for the United States Congress calculated that there were 6540 foreign fighters from Europe and Russia alone in Syria and Iraq in April 2015. The major source countries were France (1200) and Russia (1500).[32] A House Homeland Security Committee report in September 2015 claimed that six Middle Eastern and North African countries had supplied 12,775 foreign fighters, four European countries had provided a further 4350, Russia 1700, and the United States just 250. In the Middle East, Tunisia headed the list with 5000 foreign fighters, followed by Saudi Arabia with 2275, Jordan with 2000, Turkey with 1400, and Morocco with 1200. In Europe, France provided 1550 fighters, followed by Germany (700) and Britain (700).[33]

Despite the disparities between these figures, they do, nevertheless, show some clear trends. The Middle East and North Africa are the major source of foreign fighters, with Europe as the second most important source, and the majority, as might have been expected, are in Syria and Iraq. Their numbers are rapidly growing; as the United Nations reported the accretion rate is accelerating, a trend that is confirmed by the Homeland Security Committee report as well. It suggests that, from a base of more than 1000 in 2011, the numbers increased to 3500 a year later. By 2013 there were 8500 foreign fighters from 74 countries, a total which rose to 18,000 from 90 different countries by the end of 2014 and which, by September 2015 had reached 25,000 individuals from over 100 countries.[34] Up to 7000 persons are believed to have rallied to Syria and Iraq in the first six months of 2015 alone.[35] There are also very clear local reasons that determine levels of recruitment; otherwise how can one explain the fact that such a high number of people have joined the foreign fighter exodus from Tunisia and Morocco, while Algeria – a country of comparable size to Morocco – generated only 18% as many extremists in 2014, a figure which halved in 2015?[36] It also seems clear that the reasons that impel individuals in the Middle East and North Africa to join the jihadi struggle are different from those that generally drives those who come from the West. Governance in the region, as revealed by the Arab Spring, leaves much to be desired and is far from any Islamic ideal. In Europe, on the other hand, governance is ostensibly democratic, with great attention paid to individual rights.

The question then is why would those foreign fighters who come from Europe rally to an organisation whose values and objectives appear to be so far removed from the objectives of states and societies that reflect the essentially normative and moral values of the Enlightenment. One obvious reason lies in the way in which that question has been posed. Enlightenment values may seem very different, depending on where the observer is situated, for what may appear to Westerners to be humane reflections of universal principles may appear to be the coercive consequences of repeated interventions in Middle Eastern and North African affairs stretching back over 200 years, back indeed to Napoleon's invasion of the region in 1798. This has been particularly true of two instances of Western interference: the abject failure of Western powers to resolve the Palestinian issue since at least 1993, if not far longer, and the American invasion of Iraq, which basically destroyed the Iraqi state and failed to institute a viable alternative. Allied to that is the question of Sunni attitudes towards Iran and the way in which Iran has been the major beneficiary from Western attempts to regulate regional problems over the past two decades.

The anger felt over what is seen in the region as double standards and casual and brutal interference in regional affairs is today vast, and, therefore, any organisation that highlights and targets Western intervention is likely to attract considerable support. The problem, though, is far wider than that; the outcome of the Arab Spring has been, in large part, a huge disappointment for regional populations; economic circumstances have worsened, and the parallel crises in Europe and the United States have meant that little attention beyond rhetorical support has been voiced by Western powers for the consequences inside the region itself. There is thus a profound distrust of Western imperatives and concerns and a corresponding willingness to embrace radical alternatives, even if the concomitant violence is a significant disincentive.

Then there is the enormous resentment felt by youth over the way in which it has collectively been the primary victim of the economic collapse throughout the region. Since it is increasingly denied access to an alternative in Europe, for example, its resentments turn inwards and become directed towards regional government for its evident failure to offer employment and fulfilment. Islamic State at least offers employment and other benefits, too, some of which, like marriage and family life, however debased in practice, are increasingly important to a youthful population deprived of opportunities for independent life outside the confines of the family. Allied to this is the natural exuberance of youth seeking to remake the world in a better image, even if – to outside observers – the model to be achieved is palpably worse than its precursors! After all, it worked very effectively to dynamise international support for the Spanish Republic during the Spanish civil war and achieved a similar outcome within North Africa during the Algerian war for independence.[37]

Quite apart from these factors, however, there are some factors that are unique to the situation of Muslim minority communities, particularly in Europe, the United States, and the Dominions. First of all, there is a profound sense of anomie and alienation which is a consequence of the relative failure of initiatives designed to integrate minority communities within the host communities inside which they live, whether through the French model of *laïcité* or the British vision of multiculturalism. This is, in part, a European failure to realise Jacques Derrida's vision of 'hospitality'.[38] It is, in part, too, an attempt to share in a lost identity, that of parents frozen in an interstitial location between an identity of origin and an identity of displacement. The result is a search for authenticity in which the rejection of Western paradigms plays a major role, a sentiment which is fully satisfied by the Salafi–jihadi vision.

Yet ideological or religious knowledge or commitment do not seem to play a major role in recruitment, even if they become the rhetoric through which commitment is expressed; instead active grooming, social media, and, as Sageman has shown, peer pressure seem to have been key.[39] It can be reinforced, strangely enough, by generational tensions, themselves the reflection of contradictions between the paradigms of the host society and the country of origin.[40] Then, finally, there is the sense of the purity of commitment to an ideal which transcends the commonplace, the day-to-day, and offers a vision of personal sacrifice – however perverted the ideal may be – that ordinary life can never offer. It is an ideal that Mohamed Tozy has captured in his description of Abdullah Azzam's account of his meeting with Mahmoud Shah Abbas with its evocation of homoerotic idealism in the purity of such commitment.[41]

Even if these factors provide an explanation of what has emerged as an apparently predominant threat to the integrity of state and nation, both in Europe and in the Middle East and North Africa, they do not explain why often well-educated young men and women choose to endorse an obscurantist, literalist, and brutal ideology to express their alienation. It has been notable, for instance that a disproportionate number of individuals who have been educated in the STEM subjects (science–technology–engineering–mathematics) tend to adopt Salafi–jihadi views, as compared with those who have been educated in the humanities. It has been suggested that the reason for this is that those educated in the natural and applied sciences have been accustomed to the simplicities of the certainties inherent in scientific truth and thus seek parallel certainties and simplicities within the politics of identity, whereas the humanities inculcate scepticism, complexity, and uncertainty, sentiments which in themselves insulate the individual from the literalist determinism of the Salafi vision.[42] It is certainly the case that many who adopt the literalist vision express their admiration and commitment to the ideological certainties they espouse, whether they do so through education or through the actions of facilitators, and it is equally clear that the nature of education they have received can facilitate this process, not least because many converts have not been religiously active previously, nor do they necessarily have the basic knowledge to question the ideas they inculcate.

Conclusion

The phenomenon of transnational jihad today thus seems to be a complex phenomenon. Despite sharing a common ideology, it has lacked a shared organisational structure. More than that, it has undergone a series of tactical transmutations which have alienated its original objectives from those that today inform its basic intentions. Its structural patterns have also changed profoundly over the years, with the result that, today, it seeks to resemble much more a social movement that the network it originally sought to be. The common feature that allies it with its origins in the 1980s and 1990s is the resentment that it expresses, resentment at the long-term Western interference and abuse of the worlds of Islam, the Middle East, and North Africa. In this respect, therefore, it is an extension of the colonial experience and of the violence that Franz Fanon argued was the essential means by which a subjugated world recovers its sense of agency.[43]

Yet, how viable is the project of the Islamic State, of creating a permanent reality mirroring its ideological dream rather than simply trying to adjust geopolitical realities as al-Qa'ida sought to do? The problem that the movement faces is multifaceted. On the one hand, it is driven by a vision that admits of no compromise but which it seems to believe is achievable by virtue of its religious status alone. Dabiq may be the village where the final conflict is to be fought and won in its version of Muslim chiliasm, but the certainties of eschatological visions are rarely achievable in reality. The Islamic State seems likely, therefore, to create a geopolitical environment dedicated to its destruction, rather than creating one that would adjust to its continued existence. Its vulnerability to hostile action is, interestingly enough, intensified by the bureaucracy that it must create to administer its new-found caliphate for that provides information upon which its enemies can plan action against it.[44] Indeed, the problems that it will face are compounded by the economy that underpins its political and military activities for it has created what is essentially an aggressive comprador rentier state, dependent on acquisition of assets as 'gifts-of-nature' rather than through their production. Its caliphate must continually acquire the assets it needs to survive through conquest or extortion as it has not created the economic means by which it can reproduce itself and the financial mechanisms that it regards as licit are inadequate to support it.[45]

On the other hand, its opportunism in mobilising Sunni sentiment against Shi'a or Alawi domination and in buttressing its support base through alliances with local tribes, reinforced by the threat of extreme violence should the tribes wish to end alliances, will ultimately prove to be a self-defeating approach. As it alienates its supporters – through aggression or deprivation – so its support base will shrink despite increasingly violent attempts to preserve it. Its disappearance, however, does not mean that the phenomenon of Salafi–jihadi inspired violence will be eliminated from the Middle East and North Africa, it will merely transform, phoenix-like, into a new movement will a slightly different agenda but driven by the same absolutist, intolerant dream.

Notes

1. Rapoport, 'Four Waves'.
2. Kaplan, 'Terrorism's Fifth Wave'.
3. Huntington, 'The Clash of Civilisations?'.
4. David Rapoport points out that a long-standing tradition in Sunni Islam anticipates the intervention of a 'mahdi', a religiously inspired charismatic and chiliastic personality, who will lead the Muslim community to an era of social justice and prosperity, is often associated with the dawn of a new century. He cites the violent occupation of the Great Mosque in Mecca in 1979 in this connection, alongside the Islamic Revolution in Iran which, although Shi'i in nature, nonetheless persuaded Sunni Muslims that religiously inspired populist political change was possible. A few years later, this was to be followed by Hizbullah's attacks on French forces and US marines in Lebanon, which also introduced the weapon of suicide bombing. Rapoport, 'Four Waves'.
5. The classic view was that jihad was a collective duty (*fardh al-kifaya*) upon the Muslim community – not an obligation incumbent upon all – unless that community were directly threatened; only then did it become *fardh al-ayn*. The reinterpretation proposed by Abdullah Azzam, therefore, was innovative and a challenge to the community at large.
6. The term 'Salafism', as conventionally used, is ambiguous. It initially referred to the Salafiyya Movement, founded in the 1870s and 1880s by Jamal al-Afghani and codified at the start of the twentieth century by Muhammad 'Abduh in Egypt. They argued that Islam and modernity were not only compatible but that the dynamism of European civilisation could be more than mirrored by the Islamic world by returning to the essential Islamic message of activism and unicity, contained in the Qur'an, the Sunna and the Hadith, as articulated in the Rashidun caliphates. Cleveland and Bunton, *A History of the Modern Middle East*, 125–8. The neo-Salafiyya or Salafi Movement espouses a modernised variant of Wahhabism, Salafism, which emerged in Saudi Arabia in the 1960s and provides a literalist interpretation of Islam as practised in the Rashidun era as a paradigm for contemporary practice. It is this latter vision that forms the core of *salafiyya-ilmiyya* and which, in more extreme variants developed largely in the non-Arabic Islamic world, have emerged as the essence of *salafiyya-jihadiyya*. See Devji, *Landscapes of the Jihad*.
7. Gerges, *The Far Enemy*, 119–50.
8. Lia, *Architect of Global Jihad*, 102, 313–16, 347–484.
9. Naji's major vision, as expressed in *The Administration of Savagery*, is discussed in Brachman, *Global Jihadism*, 94–5 and in Ryan, *Decoding Al Qaeda's Strategy*, 148, 168–78. It should be noted that the original book is also sometimes entitled *The Management of Savagery*.
10. Devji, *Landscapes of the Jihad*, 21.
11. Ibid., 87–111.
12. Ibid, 118–24.
13. Pape, 2005, 210.
14. Lewis B, 'License to Kill'.
15. Lia, *Architect of Global Jihad*, 103–5.

16. Joffé, 'The Fateful Phoenix'.
17. Sageman. 'Confronting al-Qaeda'.
18. Zelin, 'Jihad 2020'.
19. Council on Foreign Relations, 'Al-Qaeda in the Arabian Peninsula'.
20. Zelin, *Rise and Decline*.
21. Joffé, 'The Arab Spring'.
22. Interestingly enough, moderate Islamist movements also took no formal part in the events of the Arab Spring, although some, such as the Muslim Brotherhood in Egypt, did provide covert support to the social movements that actually organised the demonstration in 2011. They did, however, benefit from the radical changes that occurred afterwards, in terms of electoral success, except in Libya and Algeria.
23. Knights, 'The JRTN Movement'.
24. Joffé, 'Barcelona'.
25. Joffé 2016, 'The fateful phoenix', 1–21.
26. A canonical head tax charged on non-Muslims but now used a punitive measure to coerce conversions to Islam. The normal canonical taxes are *jiziya* as head tax on non-Muslims, *zakat* (on personal wealth), *kharaj* (on land), and *'ushur* (on agricultural produce).
27. CISAC, *Jabhat al-Nusra*.
28. See note 4.
29. Joffé 2007, 'Europe and Islam', 100.
30. ICSR, 'Foreign fighter total'.
31. BBC, 'United Nations says 25,000 foreign fighters joined Islamic militants'.
32. Archick et al., *European Fighters in Syria and Iraq*, 10.
33. Homeland Security Committee, *Final Report*.
34. Ibid., 11.
35. According to the Institute for Economics and Peace's Global Terrorism Index, 30,000 persons have gone to Syria and Iraq alone since 2011, 7000 of them in the first six months of 2015. Norton-Taylor, 'Up to 30,000 foreign fighters'.
36. According to a report in the *Al-Khabar* newspaper on 20 November 2015, the number of jihadists in Algeria halved from 220 to 100 over the year up to the end of 2015.
37. Indeed, the Algerian struggle had a much wider mobilising effect, offering a model for national liberation movements throughout the French colonial empire and inspiring Franz Fanon's vision of the purifying effects of violence. See Fanon, *The Wretched of the Earth*.
38. Derrida, *Politics of Friendship*.
39. Sageman, *Understanding Terror Networks*, 107–34.
40. Schmidt et al., 'The Psychology of Political Extremism'.
41. Tozy, 'Desir de guerre'; Chafiq, 'Pourquoi l'offre'.
42. Rose, *Immunising the Mind*, 13–16.
43. Fanon, *The Wretched of the Earth*, 72–4.
44. Shapiro, *The Terrorist's Dilemma*, 3–7.
45. An examination of Islamic State accounting for revenues and expenditure in the Wilayat Deir ez-Zor for the Islamic month Rabi al-Awal 1436AH (23 December 2014–22 January 2015) reveal that 44.7% of the revenue base relied on confiscations and 27.7% came from oil and gas sales. Taxation provided only 23.7% of the revenue base. Expenditures were dominated by fighters' salaries (43.6%), expenditure on military infrastructure (19.8%), and the police (10.4%). Services caused 17.7% of total expenditure. Al-Tamimi, 'The Archivist'.

Disclosure statement

No potential conflict of interest was reported by the author.

References

Archick, K., P. Belkin, C. M. Blanchard, C. E. Humud, and D. E. Mix. "*European fighters in Syria and Iraq: Assessments, Responses and Issues for the United States.*" Washington, DC: Congressional Research Services 27 (April 2015).

Azzam, A. *Defence of the Muslim Lands*. Birmingham, AL: Maktabah al-Ansaar Publications, 1979 and 2002.

Azzam, A. *Join the Caravan, (Amman), trans*. J. Jansen. New York: Macmillan, 1986.

BBC. 'United Nations says 25,000 foreign fighters joined Islamic militants', 2 April 2015. http://www.bbc.co.uk/news/world-middle-east-32156541. Accessed 22 November 2015.

Brachman, J. *Global Jihadism: Theory and Practice*. London: Routledge, 2008.

Center for International Security and Cooperation (CISAC). *Mapping Militant Organizations Project: Jabhat Al-Nusra*. Stanford, CA: Stanford University, 2015. https://web.stanford.edu/group/mappingmilitants/cgi-bin/groups/view/493. Accessed 19 November 2015.

Council on Foreign Relations (CFR). 'Al-Qaeda in the Arabian Peninsula (AQAP)', CFR Backgrounder (June 19, 2015), Council on Foreign Relations, New York, NY. http://www.cfr.org/yemen/al-qeda-arabian-peninsula-aqap/p9369. Accessed 17 November 2015.

Chafiq, C. "Pourquoi l'offre islamiste séduit une jeunesse en mal d'héroisme." *Le Monde* 6 (February 2015).

Cleveland, W. L., and M. Bunton. *A History of the Modern Middle East*. 4th ed. Boulder, CO: Westview Press, 2009.

Derrida, J. *The Politics of Friendship*. London: Verso, 2006.

Devji, F. *Landscapes of the Jihad: Militancy, Morality, Modernity*. London: Hurst, 2006.

Fanon, F. "*The Wretched of the Earth*, trans." C. Farringdon. Harmondsworth: Penguin 1967 (1963).

Faraj, M. *The Neglected Duty*. http://www.jungensmeyer.com/files/Faraj_The_Neglected_Duty.pdf, Accessed 26 May 2015.

Gerges, F. A. *The Far Enemy: Why Jihad Went Global*. Cambridge: Cambridge University Press, 2005.

Homeland Security Committee. *Final Report of the Task Force on Combatting Terrorist and Foreign Fighter Travel*. Washington, DC: US House of Representatives, September 2015. https://homeland.house.gov/wp-contents/uploads/2015/09/TaskForceFinalReport.pdf. Accessed 18 November 2015.

Huntington, S. P. 'The Clash of Civilisations?' *Foreign Affairs* (Summer 1993). 22–49.

International Centre for the Study of Radicalisation and Political Violence (ICSR). 'Foreign Fighter Total in Syria/Iraq Now Exceeds 20,000; Surpasses Afghanistan Conflict in the 1980s'. Department of War Studies, Kings College, London University, 26 January 2015. http://icsr.info/2015/01/foreign-fighters-total-syriairaq-now-exceeds-20000-surpasses-afghanistan-conflict-1980s. Accessed 18 November 2015.

Joffé, George. "The Arab Spring: Origins and Prospects." *Journal of North African Studies* 16, no. 4 (December 2011): 517–532.

Joffé, George. "Barcelona, Twenty Years On." In *North African Politics: Change and Continuity*, edited by YH Zoubir and G White. London: Routledge, 2015. 309–328.

Joffé, George. 'Europe and Islam: Partnership or Peripheral Dependence?' In *Geopolitics of European Union Enlargement: The Fortress Europe*, edited by W. Armstrong and J.Anderson, 90–107. London: Routledge, 2007.

Joffé, George. "The Fateful Phoenix." *Small Wars & insurgencies* 27, no. 1 (February 2016): 1–21.

Kaplan, J. 'Terrorism's Fifth Wave'. *Perspectives on Terrorism* 2, no. 2 (2008). http://www.terrorismanalysis.com. Accessed 25 May 2015.

Knights, Michael. 'The JRTN Movement and Iraq's Next Insurgency'. *CTC Sentinel* 4, no. 2 (July 2011): 1–6.

Lewis, B. 'License to Kill: Usama bin Ladin's Fatwa on Jihad'. *Foreign Affairs* (November 1998).

Lia, B. *Architect of Global Jihad: The Life of al-Qaida Strategist Abu Mus'ab al-Suri*. New York, NY: Colombia University Press.

Naji, A.-B. *The Management of Savagery: The Most Critical Stage through Which the Umma Will Pass*, trans. W.McCants. Cambridge, MA: John M. Olin Institute for Strategic Studies, Harvard University Press, 2004. https://azelin.files.wordpress.com/2010/08/abu-bakr-naji-the-management-of-savagery-the-most-critical-stage-through-which-the-umma-will-pass.pdf. Accessed 16 November 2015.

Norton-Taylor, R. "Up to 30,000 foreign fighters have gone to Syria and Iraq since 2011 – report." *Guardian* 17 (November 2015).

Pape, R. *Dying to Win: The Strategic Logic of Suicide Terrorism*. North Carlton, Australia: Scribe Publications, 2005.

Rapoport, D. 'The Four Waves of Rebel Terror and September 11'. *Anthropoetics – the Journal of Generative Anthropology* 8, no. 1 (spring/summer 2002): 1–19.

Rose, M. *Immunising the Mind: How Can Education Reform Contribute to Neutralising Violent Extremism?*. London: British Council, November 2015.

Ryan, M. W. S. *Decoding Al Qaeda's Strategy: The Deep Battle Against America*. New York, NY: Columbia University Press, 2013.

Sageman, M. 'Confronting al-Qaeda: Understanding the Threat in Afghanistan'. *Perspectives on Terrorism* 3, no. 4 (December 2009).

Sageman, M. *Understanding Terror Networks*. Philadelphia, PA: University of Pennsylvania Press, 2004.

Shapiro, J. N. *The Terrorist's Dilemma: Managing Violent Covert Organisations*. Princeton, NJ: Princeton University Press, 2013.

Schmidt C., E.Davar, and E.G.H.Joffé. 'The Psychology of Political Extremism'. *Cambridge Review of International Affairs* 18, no. 1 (April 2005).

Al-Tamimi, A. J. 'The Archivist: Unseen Islamic State Financial Accounts for Deir az-Zor Province', GLORIA Center, Rubin Center, IDC Herzliya (Israel), 5 October 2015. http://www.rubincenter.org/2015/10/the-archivist-unseen-islamic-state-financial-accounts-for-deir-ez-zor-province. Accessed 18 November 2015.

Tozy, M. "Desir de guerre et quête de justice." *Actes Sud: la pensée du midi no*. 4 (2008): 22–30.

Zelin, Aaron Y. 'Jihad 2020: Assessing al-Qa'ida's 20-Year Plan'. *World Politics Review*, 11 September 2013. Washington, DC: Washington Institute for Near East Policy. http://www.worldpoliticsreview.com/articles/13208. Accessed 31 October 2014.

Zelin, Aaron Y. *The Rise and Decline of Ansar al-Sharia in Libya*. Washington, DC: Hudson Institute, 2015. http://www.hudson.org/research/11197-the-rise-and-decline-of-ansar-al-sharia-in-libya. Accessed 17 November 2015.

A Fratricidal Libya: Making Sense of a Conflict Complex*

Mikael Eriksson

ABSTRACT
This study explores the development of Libya's security situation following the so-called Arab Spring in 2011 up to March 2016. It provides an overview of Libya's main warring parties and the struggles they are engaged in. The analysis covers both domestic groups and the main external stakeholders. The study finds that the security dynamics are changing quickly and that Libya has many political hurdles and security challenges to overcome before a more durable situation of stability can be achieved.

Introduction

Colonel Muammar Qaddafi ruled Libya for nearly 42 years before being toppled and killed in an armed revolt which erupted with the so-called Arab Spring in 2011. However, five years into Libya's transition, the country finds itself in a second civil war with two rival governments and parliaments vying for power: the Tripoli/ General National Congress [GNC]/Dawn side vs the Tobruk/House of Representatives [HoR]/Dignity side. More precisely, the existing conflict in Libya could be understood seen as a multi-layered conflict involving: (1) the presence of two competing governments and parliaments; (2) the manifestation of numerous rival armed groups partly born out of the so-called Arab Spring as well as the subsequent NATO intervention (on 19 March 2011); (3) rivalry between nationalists and federalists; (4) societal tensions that exist between local villages and tribes; and (5) a proxy war between different Arab states supporting

---
*This article is based on previous research presented in Eriksson, A Fratricidal Libya; Eriksson, 'Towards Selective Regionalization?'

either of the two sides. More recently, the expansion of the Islamic State of Iraq and the Levant (ISIS) in 2015 has added another layer of complexity to the conflict in Libya. The expansion of ISIS has even changed the security dynamic among adversaries, bringing combatants together to confront this new threat. The geopolitical bird's nest that Libya has become over recent years warrants a closer examination. Thus the purpose here is to disentangle some of the main parties, their goals, and the overall dynamic. With this ambition in mind though, it goes without saying that the dynamic in the region has been well covered in recent publications.

It is pertinent to say that recent research on the Middle East and North Africa (MENA) is undergoing a rebirth. Old notions are being reassessed as a result of the geopolitical turmoil currently taking place across the region.[1] Particularly noteworthy books here include Gerges's *The New Middle East* (2014), a book that takes a comparative and thematic approach to explaining recent developments in MENA, and the regional overview by Kadhim et al., *Governance in the Middle East and North Africa* (2013). In addition, recent studies have tried to capture the phenomenon of the Arab Spring from different thematic perspectives,[2] including those seeking to analyse democratic evolutions, political governance practices, and how these as changes have the region's security environment.[3] As for more specific studies on Libya's political and security developments, several books and articles have been published in the period 2011–2015. Four categories stand out: the modern history of Libya;[4] the Arab Spring in Libya and the violent revolt;[5] the NATO intervention in Libya, including the notion of 'responsibility to protect';[6] and the post-Qaddafi political and security chaos that has come about.[7]

To build on these observations, the aim of this study is to provide an analysis of the main events leading to the existing security developments in Libya. To limit the scope, the focus here is on the main actors fighting in Libya's second civil war and what security implications the ongoing turmoil has for the region. Overall then, the focus is to better understand how Libya has become a geopolitical top priority.

The point of departure in this article is NATO's intervention in 2011. Then follows an analysis of how Libya's road to partition unravelled. In the second part an analysis and overview of Libya's main domestic and external parties are made. The article ends with a number of concluding observations and lessons learned.

Libya and the NATO intervention 2011

In 2015 the people and states of North Africa entered their fifth year after the Arab Spring following its outbreak in 2011. The geopolitical impact continues to reverberate both inside and outside the region. What key developments following the NATO intervention followed and how has the narrative surrounding this intervention been shaped ever since?

With the 17 March 2011 UNSC Resolution 1973, the UN Security Council called upon its member states to take all necessary measures to protect Libyan civilians, including the establishment of a no-fly zone and an arms embargo. The guiding political principle for the Security Council mandate was what was known as Protection of Civilians, i.e. providing support for those targeted by one-sided violence by the Qaddafi regime.[8] As commentators at the time suggested, the resolve of the UNSC was further stiffened by battlefield losses of the opposition in the battle for Benghazi and equally hardened by harsh government reprisals.[9]

Consequently, the military campaign against Libya was launched in mid-March 2011. Key intervening states at the times were France, the UK, and the United States. While France and the UK took the political and military initiative, US involvement soon followed (Operation Odyssey Dawn).[10] The operation was later transferred to NATO's Operation Unified Protector.[11] The official goal of the military operation was to protect civilians and curb violence, though the campaign increasingly turned into a de facto process of removing Qaddafi. Once Qaddafi had been ousted, the NATO Operation Unified Protector was officially declared terminated (23 March–31 October 2011).

Five years later, the legacy of the NATO intervention in Libya continues to haunt not only Libyans but also the international community at large. The debate about what implications the Libya intervention had for the ensuing violence is receiving considerable academic and policy attention.[12] In essence five strands of critique have been raised against the intervention.

The first category of critique deals with the issue of how the military intervention was actually carried out, i.e. how different parties intervened in Libya without a unified command. This structure led different states to operate on their own mandate, with complicating consequences for external actors' military responsibilities.

A second strand of criticism suggests that the role played by the League of Arab States (LAS), i.e. as provider of a regional mandate to the UN and thereby a green light to military engagement, was mostly an agenda that was driven by the West. In this line of thinking key Western powers had well-defined interests, but these had to be legitimised by LAS acceptance.

Perhaps a more extensive third critique deals with the actual military rationale for intervention Libya. This critique also suggests that the existing narrative of a 'Benghazi moment', i.e. when Qaddafi was about to crush the opposition on the battlefield, never actually existed and that the international community was simply misled by the anti-Qaddafi opposition.[13] As for instance argued by Kuperman and others, the United States and other Western states would have been better off not intervening in Libya.[14] First of all, 'Libyan civilians were not actually being targeted'. Claims could be made that Qaddafi's forces were refraining from using indiscriminate violence. Thus as the argument goes, Libya would have been better off had Qaddafi's son Saif al-Islam been allowed to govern. Part of the critique put forward by Kuperman and others is that the White House had greatly overestimated the level of violence (death toll of citizens), which was one main argument for the mission rationale.[15] A counter-argument to this critique is that it is a view shaped in retrospect and that at the time of intervention other dynamics were at stake. World opinion called for intervention to side with what was perceived as a democratic opposition being crushed by an authoritarian ruler. Data on the use of indiscriminate violence inside Libya at the time may not even have been available to Western decision-makers. Western powers and others thus acted on the best information available at the time.

A fourth critique has to do with how the principle of protection of civilians was overstepped in practice by a regime-change agenda.[16] According to the well-renowned international law specialist Professor Richard Falk, the idea of establishing a 'no-fly zone' over Libya was never really serious.[17] The protection of civilians in this perspective was simply a political pretext for national strategic interests to get rid of Qaddafi.

Finally, there has been a strand of critique that questions the absence of any plans for the post-intervention phase. While the military engagement in Libya came quickly, no real and credible post-intervention plan for the stabilisation of Libya was ever prepared. This is an abysmal failure, as most interventions nowadays testify to the need for post-intervention stabilisation mechanisms to protect a military armistice and political transitions.

In all then, the NATO intervention has increasingly come to be questioned. A main reason for this is that the intervention left Libya with a severe security vacuum. The legacy of the intervention and the lack of a follow-up post-conflict recovery plan are currently building a negative narrative of NATO's Libya engagement. Recently though a number of US officials have begun to push back on the criticism. For instance, the previous US National Security Council official Ben Fishman (2009–2013) suggests that the critical narrative being constructed 'is misinformed and rife with simplicities' and that the Obama administration, for example, 'was neither naïve nor ill prepared when it became involved in Libya'.[18]

In sum, in a situation of a complete breakdown of security arrangements, power vacuums across the country allowed various militias to claim interests in what was to become the 'new' Libya. While the international community backed the new NTC, there was yet no overall plan for how to support the newborn state (especially in the area of demobilisation of armed actors). As Syaigh and others have noted, a post-uprising reconstruction plan would have decisively altered security.[19] However, the lack of political will, the paucity of the resources invested for stabilisation, and false expectations of what Libya could do on its own severely limited the potential for positive change. [20]

Libya partitioned 2014–2015

On 7 July 2012 national elections were held in Libya for the first time, leading to the transfer of power from the NTC to the democratically elected GNC (lasting between 8 August 2012 and 4 August 2014), thereby formally dissolving the NTC. The election held in July 2012 brought numerous political actors on to the political scene, all jockeying for power. In seeking to influence and profile each political cause, support and liaisons were sought and secured in the security sector.[21] In this context, a question to further address is what main conflicts divided the parties?

Despite political processes taking Libya towards greater political inclusion and political stability, the situation increasingly deteriorated in the period 2011–2013. One of the chief conflicts was over how the future state of Libya would determine the role of former members of the Qaddafi regime, as well as what role anti-Qaddafi rebels would have in Libya's newborn security sector.

In principle, the more conservative Islamist parties in the existing GNC in Tripoli aligned themselves with Libya's thuwar, revolutionaries. These pushed for the political isolation law, effectively calling for the exclusion of former Qaddafi regime loyalists from government posts.[22] They further worked to set in motion the Integrity and Reform Commission (June 2013) that would seek to identify and exclude members of the military loyal to Qaddafi's regime. This of course was clearly unacceptable both to former members of Libya's elite and to those who did not accept Islamist political rule, i.e. nationalist members later with the HoR in Tobruk.

Another way to deal with the security threats posed by thuwar and other militia members was a government-sponsored payment programme to several militia members having been part of the revolt (despite conflicting interests). The programme, still existing in early 2016, has been criticised for prolonging existing conflict layers in the country.

The political and security turmoil continued to intensify during the autumn of 2013 and early 2014 with an increasing number of armed attacks across the country. One of the more significant events was the 14 February 2014 challenge to the incumbent Libyan leadership by General Haftar.[23] The challenge, described by some media accounts as an alleged coup d'état, sharpened the rift between Islamists in the west and nationalist groups in the east of Libya. This push for power was later followed in March by the ousting of then acting Prime Minister Ali Zeidan by the GNC.[24] A key development took place on 16 May 2014, when forces loyal to General Haftar launched a large-scale air and ground offensive codenamed Operation Dignity (also known as Operation Karama) against the Islamist coalition in Tripoli. The goal of Operation Dignity was to dismantle the Libyan branch of the Muslim Brotherhood and other conservative Islamist movements.

On 18 May 2014 Haftar's forces and loyal militias such as al-Qaaqaa, Sawaaq, and Zintan entered Tripoli and challenged the GNC. In a statement Haftar gave the GNC an ultimatum to dissolve itself. While Zintani groups staged armed attacks, their allies under Haftar challenged the GNC politically with a policy of seeking to establish a House of Representatives (HoR). In the following weeks, demonstrations were held demanding that the GNC take part in new elections as its mandate had expired in February.

In response to the critique, elections were held on 26 August 2014 to the 200 seats allocated to individual candidates. In theory, the election was democratic. However, there are questions both about how representatives were chosen and about what legitimacy the turnout gave the election. Voters generally selected candidates on the basis of tribal affiliations. In the elections, the 'federalists' did well while Islamist candidates suffered a major defeat. Turnout was only 18%, mainly because people were outright disillusioned with the political process.[25]

Following the 25 June 2014 elections, Islamists (e.g. the Justice and Construction Party (JCP) and those associated with al-Wafa who had dominated the Congress after the liberals pulled out) have been seeking to discredit the outcome. A main reason for this was that the JCP did not want to reverse the Isolation Law, and parties and movements in this bloc were also afraid of tougher anti-terror laws, and afraid that the new government would cut militia funding and force a demobilisation process upon them. Another factor was that they were afraid that the HoR would provide increased support for Operation Dignity.[26]

Subsequent to the election, on 10 July 2014, the Dawn coalition (mainly backed by the Misratan militias) loyal to the new GNC in Tripoli appeared for the first time. In a sense the movement was born as a reaction to the loss of political influence in the elections, as well as being a result of the challenge posed to Islamist parties by Haftar, his men, and the Zintani militias in Tripoli.

Following a six-week armed confrontation, the Dawn coalition emerged victorious and de facto reinstated what was left of the GNC and on that basis formed a 'government of national salvation'.[27] In this process, the Dawn coalition pushed a demand that the HoR be dissolved because it constituted a political challenge to the GNC.

On 6 November 2014, the Supreme Court ruled that the HoR was illegal and unconstitutional.[28] As international media noted at the time, the Supreme Court decision effectively left Libya without an officially recognised government.[29] The GNC for its part claimed that it was the only legal and democratically elected legislature in the Country. Critics of the GNC claim that its mandate had expired in February 2014 and that the Supreme Court had been intimidated into passing its ruling on the HoR.

However, given the level of violence in Tripoli, only about 46 elected parliamentarians (mainly Islamists in the JCP and al-Wafa bloc) out of the 120 needed for passing laws were able to meet in session.[30] This in turn was the result of the spiralling conflict in Tripoli, the fact that several political representatives had earlier resigned due to the dominance of Islamists, and because some had turned to backing the HoR.

Libya was consequently divided between two rival parliaments. While the government, supported by the majority of the newly elected HoR, relocated to

Tobruk, those members and political parties that recognised the GNC stayed in Tripoli. The Tobruk government was recognised by most members of the international community even though the Tripoli government had de facto been given legal backing by the Supreme Court.

As a result of the split of power and the division of Libya into two competing parliaments and government representatives, outside actors began to side with one or the other government more forcefully. In October 2014 the HoR in Tobruk officially allied itself with Haftar and his men.[31] Up to this point it had merely been a supportive ally. This official support escalated the conflict and contradicted previous political statements by the HoR about helping to restore order, rebuild the Libyan state, and demobilise armed actors in a more non-confrontational way.[32]

During the remainder of 2014 and the early months of 2015 the conflict continued to spiral with various attacks occurring against each bloc and their supporters. An important turn of events came with the armed involvement in Libya's conflict by regional stakeholders. Having followed the negative events in Libya since 2011, on 18 August 2014, the United Arab Emirates (UAE) and Egypt launched an attack on opposition forces in Tripoli. Egypt was allegedly also raiding Derna using its special forces.[33] The attack, however, did not change the position of the GNC in Tripoli. The intervention in Libya has to be read from a larger geopolitical dynamic in which sets of alliances in region have responded to security developments taking place depending on how respective administrations favoured different outcomes in conjunction with national interests.

Moreover, in October 2014, Haftar conducted Operation Snake's Sting against Islamic radicals in Benghazi. Public reports suggest that Egypt gave the operation considerable military and intelligence support.[34] Around the same time, the Libyan Army also decided to recognise Operation Dignity. This in turn gave further legitimacy to Haftar and his men.

Aside from the armed conflict between the various groups, the UN is making a vigorous diplomatic push to unite Libya's political fractions, i.e. the GNC and the HoR. Overall the diplomatic push towards some sort of an agreement has been extremely complicated. Nonetheless, during 2015 a number of important meetings were held between the HoR in Tobruk and the GNC in Tripoli. Subsequently, the UN Support Mission in Libya (UNSMIL) unveiled a six-point plan, including the need to establish a transitional government of national unity that would seek to design and adopt a new constitution.[35] The plan for a government of national unity has since been a key vision for UN and diplomatic backers. With the growing threat of ISIS, part of the negotiation strategy has been to press parties on possibility of an increasing instability in the absence of a unity government. Further to this, no real foreign support can be provided to Libya unless parties agree on a new government.

Warring parties

Having analysed some of the key dynamics that subsequently led to the breakdown of Libya's security order, this part of the article will disentangle the role of domestic security actors as well the interest of external actors.

The domestic scene

During 2014–2015 the security situation in Libya turned from bad to worse. By autumn 2015 there were in all five major warring sides: (1) the HoR and Operation Dignity in Tobruk; (2) the new GNC and Operation Dawn in Tripoli; (3) the Islamist Shura Council of Benghazi; (4) al-Qaeda forces; (5) ISIS; and (6) ethnic and tribal forces. However, since the beginning of 2016, the two rival parliaments have come closer as a result of UN negotiation efforts and the threat posed by an expanding ISIS.

The House of Representatives (Council of Deputies/Dignity) in Tobruk

As noted previously, the HoR (also known as the Council of Deputies, CoD) is a political bloc consisting of different individual candidates with its base in the city of Tobruk. The HoR has officially formed a government that currently enjoys considerable international recognition. Since the parliament in Tripoli split away, the HoR has had backing from General Khalifa Haftar (on 2 March 2015 Haftar was officially confirmed as the commander of the HoR forces, i.e. the Libyan Army). The HoR and its secular and nationalist camp have set up their support base in Tobruk.

Operation Dignity

Following the overthrow of the Qaddafi regime in October 2011, former General Haftar sought to claim a post in the national transitional government, though with little success. On 16 May 2014, forces loyal to General Haftar launched a large-scale air and ground offensive codenamed Operation Dignity.

An important ally in Operation Dignity is the Zintani Brigade. It consists of several dozen local militias formed in the midst of the uprising against Qaddafi in 2011 and mainly operating out of eastern Libya (including the Zintani Revolutionaries Military Council, the Tripoli Revolutionary Council, the Qa'qa' Brigade, al-Madani Brigade, the Sawa'iqa brigade, etc.). Its members are largely linked to the city of Zintan and are first and foremost opposed to more radical Islamist governance. During the uprising it formed part of the international coalition to overthrow Qaddafi. It enjoys the support of the Libyan National Army and forms an integral part of Operation Dignity. Also allied to the Zintani Brigades is the Tribal Army (mainly members of the Wershefana tribe). Since the split of the GNC in late June 2014 the Zintan Brigade, siding with the HoR in Tobruk, has been in open armed conflict with the Misratans and the Dawn coalition in Tripoli.

Tripoli and the (reinstated) General National Congress (GNC)

The reinstated GNC is formed from the remnants of those representing the original GNC following the 25 June 2014 elections. It is dominated by the JCP (i.e. the Libyan Muslim Brotherhood's party) and the Loyalty to Martyrs Bloc (i.e. political parties with Islamist leanings). The political parties are indirectly supported by Operation Dawn.

Operation Dawn

The GNC relies on the support provided by a coalition of armed actors working under the Operation Dawn alliance. Broadly, the coalition consists of a number of Misratan brigades, including the Libya Shield Middle, a host of Islamist brigades and militias in Tripoli (including the Libya Revolutionaries Operations Room), other Libya Shield forces including Libya Shield West, and various other Islamist brigades and militias.

Albeit the Operation Dawn alliance is made up largely of supporters of an Islamist agenda, they are far from united. One explanation has to do with the ideology of the group and/or ethnic/tribal affiliations. On 6 July 2015, the Tripoli-based Prime Minister Khalifa al-Ghawi (elected on 31 March 2015) declared a reorganisation of its armed forces into '11 brigades including militiamen who fought in the country's 2011 revolution'. The goal was to establish a 5000-strong army.

The Libya Shield Force

The Libya Shield Force was formed six months after the fall of Qaddafi and the establishment of the NTC. It was formed by the Libyan Ministry of Defence on the basis of existing cadres of anti-Qaddafi militias. The goal was to set up a national force with the aim of protecting the Libyan Arab Spring and to insulate the new government from being penetrated by those forces that had supported or fought alongside Qaddafi. In principle, the Libya Shield Force has an agenda of promoting political Islam. The Shield Force forms the backbone against Haftar's anti-GNC agenda.

The Libya Shield Force comprises three largely independent main subdivisions: (1) the original Libya Shield 1 (currently based in Benghazi) but whose members are now part of (2) the Western Shield (at the disposal of the new GNC) and (3) the Central Shield, which is largely built on the Misrata brigades. All forces are operating around Tripoli and in pockets around key cities like Benghazi. The main headquarters is said to be Misrata.

The Misrata militias are considered to be key protectors of the anti-Qaddafi revolution. A principal reason for this is their long-standing mistrust of Qaddafi and his main followers in Zintan (Zintan has been considered a stronghold of the Qaddafi regime, while Misratans have generally mistrusted Qaddafi deeply). Indeed, historically there has been mistrust between different regions and cities in Libya.[36] The long-standing conflict between Misratans and Zintanis re-surfaced following the Arab Spring.

The Islamist Shura Council of Benghazi

The Islamist Shura Council of Benghazi Revolutionaries is a military coalition that came together under this umbrella to fight Haftar. The council is led by Ansar al-Sharia (Libya) with the support of the reinstated GNC. The coalition consists mainly of Ansar al-Sharia and Libya Shield 1 and has a total strength of approximately 400–500 members.

Ansar al-Sharia

Ansar al-Sharia Libya is one of Libya's largest armed groups. It made its first appearance after the outbreak of the Arab Spring in 2012. Some members are former Libya Islamic Fighting Groups (LIFG) members that existed in Libya before the so-called Arab Spring. Its main bases have been in Benghazi, Derna, and Sirte since 2012 (though it withdrew from Benghazi for a period). Following Haftar's Operation Dignity in May 2014, Ansar al-Sharia has fought under a loose coalition named the Shura Council of Benghazi Revolutionaries. Its principal targets have (at times) been Operation Dignity forces, nationalists and secular-oriented movements, and ISIS (as some members of the Shura Council had refused to pay allegiance to ISIS leader Abu Bakr al-Baghdadi).[37]

The group is a coalition of Islamist and Salafist groups active mainly in eastern Libya. Its members fight under different alliance formations mainly against the forces of Haftar, though increasingly also against rival Islamic groups. Ansar al-Sharia has different factions with different moderate-jihadist tendencies. For instance, Ansar al-Sharia – Derna (a more hard-line faction) in July 2012 considered the GNC un-Islamic; Ansar al-Sharia – Benghazi was claimed by the United States to be involved in the 11 September 2012 attack on the US Mission to Libya. Leading up to this development there were several reports of fighting against ISIS. Later in 2015 media reports suggested that segments of Ansar al-Sharia (and possibly the entire group) had pledged allegiance to ISIS.[38]

The Islamic State of Iraq and the Levant (ISIS)

ISIS has been present in Libya since early autumn 2014.[39] The exact timing of its establishment is open to debate. There have been a number of radical forerunners to ISIS in Libya. Rosenthal suggests that al-Qaeda forces were an integral part of the anti-Qaddafi rebellion (that was indirectly supported by Western states intervening under a UN mandate).[40] Nonetheless, by mid-2015, ISIS had been able to locate itself in at least four cities across Libya. Having initially established itself in Benghazi and Derna in 2014 (see below), in 2015 it later moved into Sirte and to Tripoli (2015). During the spring of 2015, ISIS was no longer only operating through different cells but had declared the presence of a local ISIS caliphate in local provinces in Libya: Wilayat al-Barqah in the east, Wilayat al-Tarabulus in the west, and Wilayat al-Fizan in the south.[41] Since its emergence, open media reports suggest that ISIS has actively been recruiting supporters in different parts of Africa to shore up its support in Africa.[42]

The chain of ISIS expansion is not yet fully clear. According to Wehrey and others, a group of Libyans travelled to fight in Syria in 2011.[43] Records testify that the group established an armed group calling itself the Battar Brigade (deployed at first in Deir Ezzor in Syria and then at Mosul in Iraq).[44] The group expressed thanks on social media to the citizens of Derna for their support for the struggle in Syria. At some point in the period 2011–2014, it expressed its loyalty to the Nusra Front.

During the first part of 2014, about 300 members of the Battar Brigade returned to Libya and Derna. Some of their members teamed up with a local group named the Islamic Youth Shura Council (IYSC). The IYSC had previously declared loyalty to al-Baghdadi of ISIS and eventually, during the autumn, also claimed eastern Libya as part of the ISIS 'Wilayat al-Barqah' caliphate. Scholars and experts have examined why radicals have been able to root themselves and gained local support in Derna.

One explanation provided in a recent study by Eljarh is that for many decades Derna was politically and economically neglected by the Qaddafi regime.[45] This led to high levels of unemployment, a lack of economic opportunities, and a lack of prospects for those living there. Neglect of the region has marginalised local communities and made them susceptible to radicalisation. This is not to say that there is much support for extremist versions of Islam (such as ISIS ideology), but there is a case of resentment at the lack of social order. Citizens have minimal representation and local elections have been systematically prevented. Another factor that may have spurred radicalisation is the existence of several militias operating in Derna, partly rivalling each other.

One interesting side-effect of ISIS's expansion though is that it seems to be having a unifying effect on the warring parties in Libya. The threat of ISIS in many ways pre-empts other threats as it has a completely different and radical political and religious agenda for Libya.

Al-Qaeda in the Islamic Maghreb (AQIM)

One of the most significant groups operating inside and outside Libya is al-Qaeda in the Islamic Maghreb (AQIM). AQIM has been around in North Africa since 1998 (at that time called the Salafist Group for Preaching and Combat; it was renamed in 2007). In recent years AQIM and al-Qaeda on the Arabian Peninsula (AQAP) have sought a role in North Africa.

In 2015 news reports suggested that AQIM (as well as other radical Islamic groups such as Ansar al-Sharia) has a presence in north-eastern Libya. Reports also suggest that one of its strongholds is around Benghazi and Derna. These territorial locations can partly be explained by long-term historical reasons related to the type of governance and levels of economic development, but also by more contemporary policies of Qaddafi. For instance, the region around Benghazi was widely neglected by Qaddafi, which led to widespread poverty, a lack of developed infrastructure, less political representation, etc. This in turn, according to some experts, led to a marginalisation of the region and thereby laid the ground for resentment and support for alternative support structures offered by Islamic groups.

Since its establishment ISIS has increasingly rivalled AQIM. The rivalry between the two groups has led to a number of skirmishes (a rivalry that needs to be read from their competition over power in the wider Middle East). As further noted below, ISIS is seeking to dominate AQIM and the al-Qaeda movement, Ansar al-Sharia Libya, and their followers (by fighting them and by buying over their followers). The rivalry between ISIS and al-Qaeda should not be overplayed. Rather, ISIS is increasingly winning over supporters from the Ansar al-Sharia group.

The overview of domestic armed actors above is of course not complete, but it testifies to the fragmentation of Libya's social order. While some of these groups are struggling for political and economic compensation for having taken part in the uprising that removed Qaddafi from power, others make reference to root causes such as lack of equitable political representation and prospects of a stable social and economic life. Adding to this complexity is the growing crime–terror–war nexus, in which groups burgeon, as well as the increasing presence of ideologically motivated groups that are competing for power in Libya.

To understand Libya's security scene, it is crucial to cover the regional dynamics. Below follows an overview of the posture of key stakeholders vis-à-vis Libya.

External actors

The security turmoil in Libya has had several repercussions for the stability of the region over the past years, in two notable ways.

First, instability in Libya has had negative security spillover effects including societal stress among all of Libya's neighbours. Notably, the violence in Libya has been a source of armed groups, arms flows, illicit trade, migration and trafficking, etc. This in turn has contributed to the undermining of political stability in a region already suffering from volatility.

Second, the conflict in Libya has been propelled by external powers meddling in Libya's domestic affairs. Although it is accurate to talk about the domestic turmoil in Libya as a second civil war, it is a civil war with external interference, i.e. to a large extent a proxy war. Indeed, external actor engagement has fuelled domestic conflict and augmented the rivalry between Libya Dawn and Libya Dignity and other groups.

Egypt and the United Arab Emirates (UAE)

The civil war in Libya has been a top security concern for Egypt since 2011. The possibility of the civil war bringing the Libyan Muslim Brotherhood into power would be one of Egypt's worst fears. Thus, following Islamist rule in Tripoli, President Sisi engaged in a more active foreign policy and sided with the anti-MB bloc.

As the political process in Libya developed unfavourably for Egypt, Egypt increasingly engaged in Libya's internal conflict by siding with Haftar's forces. During the first half of 2015, Egypt scaled up its support for the anti-government side, first and foremost providing backing to General Haftar and his Operation Dignity. However, Egypt was not alone. Fearing the same unfavourable outcome, the UAE also took an active role in the Libyan conflict. Egypt and the UAE have allegedly provided Operation Dignity with training, ammunition, and intelligence support.[46]

Qatar, Turkey, and Sudan
Meanwhile, whereas Egypt and the UAE favour the Tobruk government, Turkey and Qatar are siding with the government in Tripoli. Qatar has provided support to the Tripoli government as part of seeking to influence the regional balance in a way that reflects its political engagement across the Middle East. Early on there were reports in the media of arms shipments to Misrata militias.[47] In other media reports Qatar and Sudan have provided support to the Tripoli government.[48]

Tunisia, Algeria, and Morocco
The policies of Tunisia, Algeria, and the Sahel states towards Libya have mainly been policies of containment. The historical presence of armed groups in the region, notably AQIM, but also more recently MUJAO and Ansar al-Dine, has challenged governments and kept them on the alert for potential attacks.

Tunisia for its part is absorbing many fleeing Libyans. Over the course of the conflict it has maintained a policy of openness towards Libyans wanting to leave Libya. A more immediate consequence of the Libyan turmoil is that Libya has turned into a breeding ground for armed jihadist groups. Following the Tunisia Bardo museum attack, several European states began to provide support to Tunisia to safeguard against the spread of ISIS. Algeria and Morocco meanwhile have taken on the role of powerbrokers in Libya. Although the two countries may prefer different political outcomes for Libya, a unity government and stability are preferable. A stable Libya would reduce several security challenges, including putting pressure on armed groups such as Ansar al-Dine, AQIM, and MUJAO, which can hide arms and fighters in Libya.

Aside from Libya's most immediate neighbours there are other key external actors with interests in Libya. Below follows a brief overview of their main concerns and activities.

The EU and its southern member states
Security developments in Europe's southern neighbourhood are of great concern for the European Union and its member states. Following the Arab Spring, security developments have become increasingly acute. A raging civil war in Libya, the increase of terrorism and radicalisation, a worsening humanitarian situation, a sharp increase of migration, and authoritarianism among North

African leaders (e.g. Egypt) have required a constant political attention to security developments.[49]

Following the growing migrant crisis and by mid-2015 the EU sensed an increasing pressure to tackle Libya's conflict. Another pressure followed the growing threat of armed jihadist groups such as ISIS and AQIM; and for the growing frustration among regional actors (notably Egypt and some Gulf states which would otherwise risk intervening more actively in Libya).

In responding to the humanitarian situation, on 18 May 2015 the EU launched an EU Maritime Force – EUNAVFOR Med (Operation Sophia in the Mediterranean Sea) – to act 'against human smugglers and traffickers in the Mediterranean'. However, neither of the rival parliaments accepts the EU force penetrating its territorial waters, which effectively limits the force to patrolling only EU states' and international waters. This may hinder the force going after those vessels that enter Libyan territorial waters. As a consequence, the EU has not been able to do much because Libya does not have a unity government in place. The EU's top priority has therefore been to support the UN-led talks. On the other hand, the threat posed by armed jihadist groups could potentially become so great that the EU cannot wait indefinitely until the national government is set up.

Worth noting though are indications that key Western governments, notably the United States, the UK, and France have begun different forms of military intervention using both air and ground forces.[50]

The United States and NATO

As a result of the breakdown of Libya's security order in 2014–2015 (as well as the generally deteriorating situation across MENA), the United States is becoming increasingly concerned about the growing presence of armed jihadist groups in Libya and the potential challenge these may pose. This in turn has led to an increase in counterterrorism cooperation with most states in North Africa.

Over recent years NATO have closely monitored the political rivalry of the two parliaments (including the multilateral talks) as well as the the dynamics of the local violence, including the activities and expansion of ISIS. Pending the development of these two areas, NATO may need to revisit its strategy for dealing with Libya. Depending on the progress of UN held talks, the position of NATO is that it will have to await further UN Security Council developments before any other action can be undertaken if the conflict situation becomes more pressing.

The African Union (AU)

The African Union has been playing a rather limited role in Libya. It has mainly contributed to settling the various conflicts in Libya by offering diplomatic initiatives to resolve the Libyan crisis. For example, the AU has initiated the international contact group on Libya and has been hosting a number of regular meetings in the role of facilitator.[51]

Conclusion

Following the end of the Qaddafi era, the security turmoil in Libya moved from a political transitional process with pockets of violence to a situation of full-blown second civil war. A complex web of domestic actors has been jockeying for power and influence. From being a first civil war with fairly united parties, the security situation in Libya has changed into a fragmented second civil war involving many different types of armed actors. The descent into chaos should be understood in terms of both the absence of functioning state institutions that were able to deliver minimum state services and the absence of a legitimate and national police and army that would safeguard public order and a sense of public security.

Beyond a functioning state and trust in the state on the domestic level, Libya has been driven into further chaos by regional interests. Regional powers are currently propelling the conflict by siding with actors they want to boost as the calculation rests on the assumption that states would favour their own national interests.

A lesson for the future from the Libyan conflict is that practitioners and decision-makers need to look more closely at the dynamics that follow military intervention. While general experiences from war-torn societies (ended by outside intervention) call for a rethinking of the need for post-intervention plans, more specific lessons from Libya suggest the need for a strategy on how to help rebuild political institutions and economic infrastructure (including providing support to war-distressed regions, promoting trade and welfare, reviving domestic industry, and support for energy diversification). To help further thinking about what measures the international community can offer in terms of post-intervention stability programmes of this sort, the conflict dynamics as well as the existing grievances and root causes have to be better understood.

To further understand why Libya's security situation looks the way it does, this study has taken particular note of the following conflict enablers: the complete breakdown of central power, the absence of a functioning security sector, the availability of arms, and the lack of territorial and border control.

Putting the situation on a different analytical level, Libyans do not yet have an existing social contract. There is simply no legitimate political authority in which the whole of the people is represented, including different political and religious interests. In the absence of a well-functioning state, there is a security dilemma and a spiralling cycle of violence. Because of the erosion of the state under Qaddafi, Libyans are today forced to harvest the fruit of decades of divide-and-rule tactics which paved the way for deep social mistrust – a mistrust that has been used by different political parties and armed movements inside and outside Libya. In the event of an external military intervention in Libya, the long-term mission goal needs to be that of enabling Libyans to establish a new social contract.

Notes

1. Ayoob, *Will the Middle East Implode?*; Pollack et al., *The Arab Awakening*; Dabashi, *The Arab Spring*; Fosshagen, *Arab Spring*; Haas and Lesh, *The Arab Spring*; Danahar, *The New Middle East*; Marcovitz, *The Arab Spring Uprisings*; Inbar, *The Arab Spring, Democracy and Security*.
2. Mhenni, *Tunisian Girl*; Joffé, *North Africa's Arab Spring*.
3. Lynch, *The Arab Uprisings Explained*.
4. St John, 'Libya'.
5. For a comprehensive coverage of Libya's armed conflict 2011–2013 (mainly from an international law perspective), see Bassiouni, *Libya, from Repression to Revolution*; Dalton and Lobban, *Libya: History and Revolution*; and Chorin, *Exit Qaddafi*.
6. Hehir and Murray, *Libya*.
7. Pack, *The 2011 Libyan Uprisings*.
8. Gartenstein-Ross and Barr, 'Dignity and Dawn'.
9. See for instance the so-called 'cockroach' speech by Qaddafi on 22 February 2011.
10. Several commentators have convincingly argued that the US government took a 'leading from behind' position in the intervention.
11. Lindvall and Forsman, *Internationella insatser i Libyen 2011*.
12. See the 'positive' analysis of the Libya intervention by Ivo Daalder (former US Permanent Representative to NATO) and James Stavridis (at the time Supreme Allied Commander of Europe), Daalder and Stavridis, 'NATO's Victory in Libya'. See also Hehir and Murray, *Libya*; and for a very critical and comprehensive view of how the international community has handled Libya (including, NATO, the AU, the EU, the LAS and the United States), see Campbell, 'Failure in Libya'.
13. See Roberts, 'Who Said Qaddafi Had to Go?'.
14. Kuperman, 'Obama's Libya Debacle', 67–72.
15. Ibid.
16. Hehir and Murray, *Libya*; Eriksson, 'Towards Selective Regionalization?'.
17. Falk, 'Chaos and Counterrevolution'.
18. Fishman, 'How We Can Still Fix Libya'.
19. Sayigh, 'Crumbling States'.
20. The fact that Libya was left to its own destiny is further exemplified by the 2015 UK Parliamentary report, a public document revealing that the UK spent 13 times as much money (£320 million) bombing Libya as it provided for rebuilding after the NATO intervention (a cost of £25 million, of which most went to humanitarian support). Although each country has its own reasons for investing money and resources in post-conflict intervention programmes, the asymmetric proportions mentioned in this UK example are likely to mirror the same lack of post-intervention reconstruction interest by other states, see MiddleEastEye, 'UK spent 13 times more money bombing Libya'.
21. As noted by Sayigh, 'Crumbling States', groups included '. . . secular opposition activists, some of whom had recently returned from exile; the Muslim Brotherhood and its parliamentary vehicle, the JCP; Salafist Islamists; and the 'liberal' National Forces Alliance'. Cf. note 19.
22. Gartenstein-Ross and Barr, 'Dignity and Dawn', 17.
23. Haftar was previously a serving general under Qaddafi who defected after coming into personal conflict with him. Haftar left the region for the United States. During

the Arab Spring he came back to side with the anti-Islamist coalition in Libya under the sponsorship of countries like the UAE and Egypt; *The Independent*, 'Libyan Government Should Be Suspended'.
24. The aim was to target groups such as the Shura Council of Benghazi Revolutionaries in Benghazi (of which Ansar al-Sharia and other armed Islamists were part), which largely rejected the formal political process at the time (the Islamists were at the time influential and in control of parts of Tripoli). Internal Displacement Monitoring Centre, 'Libya', 3.
25. Cf. note 17; Internal Displacement Monitoring Centre, 'Libya', 3.
26. Gartenstein-Ross and Barr, 'Dignity and Dawn', 23.
27. Kuperman, 'Obama's Libya Debacle', 68.
28. Members of the HoR, having recognised the Supreme Court up to this point, rejected the court ruling on two bases, arguing (1) that Tripoli, where the Supreme Court operates, was under the control of Islamist and Misratan militias, and (2) that the electoral law to which the Supreme Court referred in its ruling was put in place by the GNC (having been dominated by Islamist and pro-militia blocs and therefore biased). See Eljarh, 'The Supreme Court Decision'.
29. Ibid.
30. Ibid.
31. Reuters, 'Libya Parliament Allies with Renegade General'.
32. Ibid.
33. The New York Times, 'Arab Nations Strike in Libya'.
34. Gartenstein-Ross and Barr, 'Dignity and Dawn', 23.
35. Institute of Security Studies, 'World Attention on Libya as Migrants Die'.
36. Vandewalle, *History of Modern Libya*.
37. United Press International, 'Egypt seeks U.S. Gear'.
38. Newsweek, 'Spiritual Leader of Libya's Biggest Jihadi Group'.
39. Wehrey, 'Rising out of chaos'.
40. Rosenthal, *The Jihadist Plot*, ch. 3.
41. The Washington Post, 'The Islamic State's Model'.
42. The New York Times, 'Arab Nations Strike in Libya'.
43. Cf. note 39.
44. CNN World News, 'ISIS Comes to Libya'.
45. Eljarh, 'A Snapshot'.
46. Gartenstein-Ross and Barr, 'Dignity and Dawn', 40.
47. Guardian, 'Libyan Rebels'.
48. International Business Times, 'Libyan Prime Minister Accuses'.
49. However, Libya is also important for Europe for many other traditional geopolitical reasons, notably when it comes to migration from Africa, as an important supplier of energy, and for the challenges posed by radicalisation. Serwer, 'Libya's Escalating Civil War'.
50. See for instance France Soir, 'Le gouvernement de Tripoli'; The Telegraph, 'British "Advisers" Deployed to Libya'.
51. Institute of Security Studies. 'World Attention on Libya'.

Disclosure statement

No potential conflict of interest was reported by the author.

Funding

The original work was supported by the Swedish Defence Research Agency.

References

Ayoob, Mohammed. *Will the Middle East Implode?*. London: Polity Press, 2014.
Bassiouni, M. Cherif, ed. *Libya, from Repression to Revolution: A Record of Armed Conflict and International Law Violations, 2011–2013*. Leiden: Martinus Nijhoff Publishers, 2013.
Campbell, Horace. *NATO's Failure in Libya: Lessons for Africa*. Africa Institute of South Africa: Pretoria, 2012.
Chorin, Ethan. *Exit Qaddafi: The Hidden History of the Libyan Revolution*. London: SAQI, 2012.
CNN World News. 'ISIS Comes to Libya', 18 November 2014. Accessed 5 August 2015. http://edition.cnn.com/2014/11/18/world/isis-libya/.
Daalder, Ivo H., and James G. Stavridis. *Nato's Victory in Libya: The Right Way to Run an Intervention*. March/April: Foreign Affairs Magazine, 2012.
Dabashi, Hamid. *The Arab Spring: The End of Postcolonialism*. London: Zed Books, 2012.
Dalton, Christopher H., and Richard A. Lobban. *Libya: History and Revolution*. London: Praeger, 2014.
Danahar, Paul. *The New Middle East: The World after the Arab Spring*. London: Bloomsbury, 2013.
Eljarh, Mohamed. "A Snapshot of the Islamic State's Libyan Stronghold." *Foreign Policy* 1 (April 2015).
Eljarh, Mohamed. 'The Supreme Court Decision That's Ripping Libya Apart'. *Foreign Policy*, 6 November 2014. Accessed 3 March 2015. http://foreignpolicy.com/2014/11/06/the-supreme-court-decision-thats-ripping-libya-apart/.
Eriksson, Mikael. "Towards Selective Regionalization? The Intervention in Libya and the Emerging Global Order." In *Regional Organisations and International Peacemaking: New Actors and New Roles for the UN*, edited by Peter Wallensteen and Anders Bjurner, 217–236. London: Routledge, 2014.
Eriksson, Mikael. *A Fratricidal Libya and its Second Civil War: Harvesting Decades of Qaddafi's 'Divide and Rule'*. FOI-R–4177—SE, December 2015.
Falk, Richard. *Chaos and Counterrevolution*. Charlottesville, VA: Just World Books, 2015.
Fishman, Ben. 'How We Can Still Fix Libya'. *Politico Magazine*. Accessed 3 March 2011. http://www.politico.com/magazine/story/2016/02/libya-intervention-hillary-clinton-barack-obama-213686#ixzz41q3zXv8I.
Fosshagen, Kjetil (ed.). *Arab Spring: Uprisings, Powers, Interventions*. New York, NY: Berghahn, 2014.
France Soir. 'Le gouvernement de Tripoli confirme la présence de commandos français en Libye'. 25 February 2016. Accessed 3 March 2016. http://www.francesoir.fr/politique-monde/le-gouvernement-de-tripoli-confirme-la-presence-de-commandos-francais-en-libye
Gartenstein-Ross, Daveed and Nathaniel Barr. 'Dignity and Dawn: Libya's Escalating Civil War'. International Centre for Counter-Terrorism, the Hague, ICCT Research Paper, February 2015.
Gerges, Fawaz A. (ed.). *The New Middle East: Protest and Revolution in the Arab World*. New York, NY: Cambridge University Press, 2014.
Haas, Mark L., and David W. Lesh. *The Arab Spring: Change and Resistance in the Middle East*. Boulder, CO: Westview Press, 2012.

Hehir, Aidan, and Robert Murray (eds.). *Libya, the Responsibility to Protect and the Future of Humanitarian Intervention*. New York, NY: Palgrave Macmillan, 2013.

Inbar, Efraim (ed.). *The Arab Spring, Democracy and Security: Domestic and International Ramifications*. Abingdon: Routledge, 2013.

The Independent. 'Libyan Government Should Be Suspended, Says Military Commander', 14 February 2014. Accessed 3 June 2015. http://www.independent.co.uk/news/world/middle-east/libyan-government-should-be-suspended-says-military-commander-9127861.html.

Institute of Security Studies. 'World Attention on Libya as Migrants Die Leaving Its Shores'. *Security Council Report*, 4 May 2015. Accessed 15 July 2015 .https://www.issafrica.org/pscreport/situation-analysis/world-attention-on-libya-as-migrants-die-leaving-its-shores.

Internal Displacement Monitoring Centre. 'Libya: Uprising and Post-Qadhafi Tribal Clashes, Displacement in a Fragmenting Libya', 30 March 2015. Accessed 5 May 2015. http://www.internal-displacement.org/search?q=libya.

International Business Times. 'Libyan Prime Minister Accuses Qatar, Sudan of Supporting Rebel Forces with Arms and Ammunition'. Accessed 15 September 2014. http://www.ibtimes.com/libyan-prime-minister-accuses-qatar-sudan-supporting-rebel-forces-arms-ammunition-1688620.

Joffé, George (ed.). *North Africa's Arab Spring*. London: Routledge, 2013.

St John, Ronald Bruce. *Libya: continuity and change*. London: Routledge, 2011.

Kadhim, Abbas K., (editor of compilation.) *Governance in the Middle East and North Africa: a handbook*, 1st ed. London: Routledge, 2013.

Kuperman, Alan.'Obama's Libya Debacle'. *Foreign Affairs Magazine*, . March/April 2015.

Lindvall, Fredrik and David Forsman. *Internationella insatser i Libyen 2011 – En analys av den militära kampanjen mot Qaddafis regim*. FOI-R—3447—SE. Stockholm: Swedish Defence Research Agency, 2012.

Lynch, Marc (ed.). *The Arab Uprisings Explained: New Contentious Politics in the Middle East*. New York, NY: Columbia University Press, 2014.

Marcovitz, Hal. *The Arab Spring Uprisings*. San Diego, CA: Reference Point Press Inc., 2014.

Mhenni, Lina Ben. *Tunisian Girl: En bloggares berättelse om den arabiska våren*. Stockholm: Sekwa förlag AB, 2012.

MiddleEastEye. 'Uk Spent 13 Times More Money Bombing Libya Than Rebuilding It, Documents Reveal', 27 July 2015. Accessed 1 August 2015. http://www.middleeasteye.net/news/documents-reveal-uk-spent-13-times-more-bombing-libya-rebuilding-it-1532581617.

Newsweek. 'Spiritual Leader of Libya's Biggest Jihadi Group Pledges Allegiance to ISIS', 8 April 2015. Accessed 11 August 2015. http://europe.newsweek.com/top-judge-libyas-biggest-jihadi-group-pledges-allegiance-isis-320408.

Pack, Jason (ed.). *The 2011 Libyan Uprisings and the Struggle for the Post-Qadhafi Future*. New York, NY: Palgrave Macmillan, 2013.

Pollack, Kenneth M. et al. *The Arab Awakening: America and the Transformation of the Middle East*. Washington, DC: Brookings Institution, 2011.

Reuters. 'Libya Parliament Allies with Renegade General, Struggles to Assert Authority', 20 October 2014. Accessed 10 August 2015. http://www.reuters.com/article/2014/10/20/us-libya-security-idUSKCN0I91B620141020.

Roberts, Hugh. 'Who Said Qaddafi Had to Go?' *London Review of Books* 33, no. 22 (November 2011): 8–18. Accessed 15 April 2015. http://www.lrb.co.uk/v33/n22/hugh-roberts/who-said-Qaddafi-had-to-go.

Rosenthal, John. *The Jihadist Plot: The Untold Story of Al-Qaida and the Libyan Rebellion*. New York, NY: Encounter Books, 2013.

Sayigh, Yezid. 'Crumbling States: Security Sector Reform in Libya and Yemen'. Carnegie Middle East Center Paper, 18 June 2015. Washington, DC: Carnegie Endowment for International Peace, 2015.

Serwer, Daniel. 'Libya's Escalating Civil War'. Council on Foreign Relations, Center for Preventive Action, Contingency Planning Memo Update. 18 June 2015. Accessed 3 June 2015.http://www.mei.edu/content/at/libya%E2%80%99s-escalating-civil-war?print.

The Guardian. 'Libyan Rebels Supplied with Anti-Tank Weapons by Qatar'. 20 April 2011. Accessed 8 August 2011. http://www.theguardian.com/world/2011/apr/14/libyan-rebels-supplied-weapons-qatar.

The New York Times. 'Arab Nations Strike in Libya, Surprising U.S.', 25 August 2014. Accessed 2 March 2015. http://www.nytimes.com/2014/08/26/world/africa/egypt-and-united-arab-emirates-said-to-have-secretly-carried-out-libya-airstrikes.html

The New York Times. 'U.S. Scrambles to Contain Growing ISIS Threat in Libya', 21 February 2016. Accessed 2 March 2016. http://www.nytimes.com/2016/02/22/world/africa/us-scrambles-to-contain-growing-isis-threat-in-libya.html?_r=0.

The Telegraph. 'British "Advisers" Deployed to Libya to Build Anti-Isil Cells', 27 February 2016. Accessed 3 March 2016. http://www.telegraph.co.uk/news/worldnews/africaandindianocean/libya/12176114/British-advisers-deployed-to-Libya-to-build-anti-Isil-cells.html.

The Washington Post. 'The Islamic State's Model', 28 January 2015. Accessed 1 August 2015. http://www.washingtonpost.com/blogs/monkey-cage/wp/2015/01/28/the-islamic-states-model/.

United Press International. 'Egypt Seeks U.S. Gear to Help Secure Border with Libya'. 5 June 2015. Accessed 11 August 2015. http://www.upi.com/Business_News/Security-Industry/2015/06/04/Egypt-seeks-US-gear-to-help-secure-border-with-Libya/9621433446286/?st_rec=7871434121739.

Vandewalle, Dirk. *A History of Modern Libya*. Cambridge: Cambridge University Press, 2006.

Wehrey, Frederic. 'Rising Out of Chaos: The Islamic State in Libya'. In *Syria in Crisis*. Carnegie Endowment for International Peace, 5 March 2015. Accessed 11 August

Belgian and Dutch Jihadist Foreign Fighters (2012–2015): Characteristics, Motivations, and Roles in the War in Syria and Iraq

Edwin Bakker and Roel de Bont

ABSTRACT

In recent years, Belgium and the Netherlands have been confronted with relatively many citizens or residents who have traveled to Syria and Iraq to join and fight with jihadist groups — 388 Belgian and 220 Dutch as estimated by the respective authorities. This article provides an overview of the phenomenon of jihadist foreign fighters in the Low Countries, analyzing their characteristics, motivations, and roles in the war in Syria and Iraq. It compares the Belgian and Dutch cases, focusing on key aspects, such as age, sex, and geographical and socioeconomic background.

Introduction

In recent years, many European countries have been confronted with citizens or residents that have traveled to Syria and Iraq to join jihadist groups such as Jabhat al-Nusra (JaN) and Islamic State (IS). The larger European countries, most notably France, the United Kingdom, and Germany, have 'produced' the highest number of these jihadist foreign fighters. But smaller countries have also seen high numbers of young Muslims leaving for the battlefields in the Middle East. Two of them, Belgium and the Netherlands, have been confronted with relatively many of them compared to the size of their populations. Belgium is in fact the European country with most of these fighters per capita with 388 confirmed cases.[1] The Netherlands' authorities estimate the number of Dutch jihadists in Syria and Iraq at 220, including 70 women.[2]

Why have these two countries produced relatively many jihadists? This question is difficult to answer as there are many possible factors that play a role, ranging from national and local political contexts, and the existence of networks and leadership, to demographics and individual push and pull factors. This article aims to offer a first attempt to shed light on this question by providing an overview of the phenomenon of jihadist foreign fighters in the two Low Countries, by analyzing their characteristics, motivations, and roles in the war in Syria and Iraq, and by comparing the cases of Belgium and the Netherlands. Thus, the article contributes to the discussion on the topic of foreign fighters which is hampered by a lack of empirical data on the phenomenon in general and detailed information on individual cases in particular. Linked to this, there are many assumptions regarding European foreign jihadist fighters – e.g. they are very young, they are single, mainly of migrant background, and part of the lower strata of society — that need to be confronted with empirical data.

This study of Dutch and Belgian jihadist foreign fighters is based on media reports, governmental documents, court proceedings, media reports, as well interviews with key actors in relation to jihadist foreign fighters including governmental officials, Syrian refugees, friends and family members of those that have left for Syria or Iraq, and a number of active supporters of the violent jihad. In this article, the term 'jihadist foreign fighter' is used to describe persons who have joined a fighting group in a foreign conflict with a jihadist agenda. The term refers to both Dutch and Belgian citizens and residents of the Netherlands and Belgium. The part on the characteristics of these fighters uses the methodological framework developed by Mark Sageman[3] and is based on a dataset consisting of 370 cases (of which 211 are from Belgium and 159 from the Netherlands).[4]

The outline of the article is as follows: First we provide a number of historical examples of foreign fighters from the Low Countries before focusing on cases of jihadist foreign fighters until the outbreak of the civil war in Syria in 2011. Secondly, it looks into key characteristics of these jihadists, such as age, sex, and geographical and socioeconomic background. This is followed by an attempt to explain why more than 600 men and women from the Netherlands and Belgium have joined the jihad in Syria and Iraq. What were their motivations? In order to answer this question, we focus on push and pull factors that have been mentioned in scholarly and governmental reports. Next the article deals with their roles in the conflict in Syria and Iraq. Based on open sources,[5] it describes the process of vetting and training after their arrival, the role of the men in the violent conflict, and the specific role of women in territories occupied by the organizations IS and JaN. In the final section, we reflect on the limitations of this research and arrive at a number of general observations.

The phenomenon of (jihadist) foreign fighters

The phenomenon of foreign fighters is not new to the Low Countries. The first type of foreign fighters the recently independent state of Belgium and the country it separated from, the Netherlands, were confronted with were the so-called Papal Zouaves. These were Catholic youngsters who gave heed to the call of Pope Pius IX to assist him in his struggle against the Italian Unificationists in the 1860s. Some 1910 Dutch and 686 Belgians left for Rome to fight.[6] More than half a century later, in the 1930s, some 1700[7] Belgians and 650[8] Dutch joined the International Brigades that fought in Spain to help the Republican cause against the Nationalists headed by general Franco. During World War II, thousands joined the ranks of the Waffen-SS: between 22,000 and 25,000 Dutch[9], and 10,000 Flemish speaking Belgians and 6700 Francophone Belgians.[10] Such high numbers seem to be a thing of the past. In the decades after World War II until recently, the phenomenon of foreign fighters had shrunk to just a few individuals who joined groups abroad, ranging from Palestinian organizations in the Middle East to left-wing groups in Latin America. In the Netherlands, the most famous non-jihadist foreign fighter is Tanja Nijmeijer, who got engaged in the Fuerzas Armadas Revolucionarias de Colombia (FARC), and who is currently part of the FARC delegation in the peace talks with the Columbian government in the city of Havana, Cuba.[11]

The phenomenon of jihadi foreign fighters is relatively new. It started at the turn of the century when individuals or small groups of friends tried to join the violent jihad in places such as Kashmir, Afghanistan, Iraq, Chechnya, and Somalia. Some died just after their arrival. Such was the case of two Dutch youngsters of Moroccan background who went to India in December 2001 and who were killed in the streets of Srinagar in Kashmir, apparently before they could make contact with local jihadist groups.[12] Many failed to even reach the war zones where they wanted to fight. In 2003 two other Dutch youngsters were arrested in Ukraine while trying to cross the border with Russia, allegedly on their way to Chechnya.[13] Some did manage to reach the battlefields and join jihadist groups. Among them was at least one woman: Muriel Degauque, a Belgian convert to Islam who committed a suicide car bomb attack on US soldiers in Iraq in December 2005.[14] The total number of these 'early' jihadist foreign fighters was relatively small – perhaps only a dozen who managed to join a jihadist group. Hence, until 2012, the authorities in the Low Countries were not very worried about the phenomenon of jihadist foreign fighters. It was seen as an isolated phenomenon of individuals and small local networks mostly characterized by their inactivity and limited size.[15] In the fall of 2012, the situation changed drastically. Partly as a result of extensive media and Internet attention to the conflict in Syria, rather suddenly, dozens of jihadists started to travel from the Low Countries to Syria.[16]

It took until early 2013 before the authorities publicly sounded the alarm bell. In February 2013, the head of the Dutch secret service, the General Intelligence and Security Service (AIVD), went on television warning about a rapid growth in the number of Dutch youngsters going to Syria to join the armed struggle against the regime of Bashar al-Assad, among others on the side of JaN, an organization linked to Al Qaeda. This warning was followed by the quarterly Terrorism Threat Assessment (DTN) of March 2013,[17] which raised the threat level from 'limited' to 'substantial', the second-highest threat level on a scale of four. Around the same time, the European Union's judicial cooperation unit Eurojust officially confirmed that Belgians were also fighting in Syria. In Belgium in 2013, the jihadist foreign fighter phenomenon became front page news, and reports and articles on these fighters appeared weekly. Many of these fighters were affiliated with a Belgian organization called Sharia4Belgium.[18] This organization has been described as an 'atypical but extremist Salafist organization'.[19] Sharia4Belgium was founded by Muslim youngsters in Antwerp on 3 March 2010 and was declared a terrorist organization by the Antwerp Correctional Tribunal in February 2015. Despite its short existence, it contributed significantly to the growth of the Belgian jihadist scene[20] and may be regarded as an important factor in explaining why Belgium has 'produced' relatively many jihadist foreign fighters.

The growth of the number of these fighters in Belgium was spectacular: from about 70 according to the first official estimate in March 2013,[21] to 388 according to data provided by the Belgian minister of the interior in February 2016.[22] In the Netherlands it grew from a few dozen in early 2013,[23] to an estimated 220 by early 2016.[24]

Who are they?

Who are these jihadist fighters from the Low Countries, and what are their characteristics? Using Sageman's methodological framework, we have looked at a number of characteristics that make up the 'biographies' of the men and women from Belgium and the Netherlands who have joined a jihadist organization in Syria or Iraq. The database, consisting of 370 cases, serves as the empirical basis for the overview below. In addition, occasionally, we refer to other relevant sources that add insight into the question of who these jihadists are.

Geographical origin

The Belgian and Dutch jihadist foreign fighters generally have the nationality of, were born in, or resided in Belgium or the Netherlands. Most persons have parents who were born in Morocco or were born there themselves (46%), followed – at a distance – by persons of Belgian, Dutch, Turkish, Syrian, Russian (Chechen), Somali, and Algerian extraction (Table 1). Other sources speak of an

Table 1. Family of origin.

	Dutch jihadists (N = 66)	Belgian jihadists (N = 54)	Total sample (N = 120)
Parents born in Morocco or born there themselves	41%	50%	46%
Parents born in Turkey or born there themselves	13%	5%	8%

Table 2. Average age (measured at the time of departure).

	Dutch jihadists (N = 82)	Belgian jihadists (N = 85)	Total sample (N = 167)
Average age	23.2	23.8	23.5

even higher percentage of people of Moroccan descent – up to 80% according to the Soufan Group in the case of Belgium.[25]

Their place of recruitment proved difficult to determine. For those cases for which we could find reliable information, it often coincided with the last known place of residence. This place of residence could be determined for 122 Dutch jihadists. More than 70% of those resided in one of the four main urban agglomerations in the Netherlands: Amsterdam, Rotterdam, The Hague, and Utrecht. The majority of them lived in the greater The Hague area, which also includes the cities of Delft and Zoetermeer. With regard to the Belgian cases, of which we could determine the place of residence for 203 persons, more than 65% were from Antwerp or Brussels. Another significant number of Belgian jihadists came from the city of Vilvoorde located in Flanders, just north of Brussels. Other cities and towns with a sizable group of jihadist foreign fighters include Maaseik, Kortrijk, Ghent, and Genk (all located in Flanders), and Liège (the biggest city of Wallonia).

Age

The average age of the jihadist foreign fighters is 23.5 years old (Table 2). Their statistical distribution is very spread out: the youngest person was only 13 years old when he left, while the oldest was already 67. Most of them are not (late) adolescents, but young adults, being in their early or mid-twenties. The female jihadists in the sample are on average younger than their male counterparts.[26] Among them are several underage jihadi-brides who joined their (future) spouse in Syria or Iraq.

Regarding age, Belgian and Dutch jihadists differ from other groups of jihadists from the past, as studied by Sageman and Bakker. Their studies show that most persons who joined the jihad in the period between the 1990s and 2009 did so while being well past adolescence. The average age in the study of global Salafi jihadists by Sageman is 25.7.[27] That of homegrown jihadists in Europe,

Table 3. Sex.

	Dutch jihadists (N = 159)	Belgian jihadists (N = 211)	Total sample (N = 370)
Male–female ratio	76–24	84–16	81–19

studied by Bakker, was 27.3.[28] Furthermore, their findings show that the average age of joining the jihad increased during these two decades.[29]

Sex

Of the 370 cases of Belgian and Dutch jihadists in the dataset, 81% are male. Although in both countries the majority is male, the share of females is a lot higher in the Netherlands (Table 3). This difference is also noted in other sources. For instance, Van Ostaeyen claims females represent less than 10% of the group of Belgian jihadists, while AIVD figures state that one in three Dutch jihadists is female.[30]

A high proportion of males among jihadists is also found by both Sageman and Bakker.[31] However, the number of females among the jihadist foreign fighters is considerably higher than in the aforementioned studies of jihadists in the past. It should also be noted that nearly all of those that have been reported to have died in Syria and Iraq are male.[32]

Faith

Approximately half of the jihadists were raised as Muslims. Some were raised in orthodox families. Of the cases for which we could find reliable information on their faith as youth, many were not strict observers of all traditions and obligations. The dataset of Belgian and Dutch jihadists also shows that 6% of the persons converted to Islam before traveling to Syria or Iraq. This number reflects official figures as provided by the OCAD, which also speak of 6% being converts.[33] According to van San, most of these Dutch and Belgian converts are women.[34]

Of the jihadists for which information could be collected on religious devotion prior to traveling to Syria or Iraq, most of them showed signs of intensification of religious beliefs. This manifested itself in for instance wearing traditional clothes, increased visits to mosques or praying, and/or increased interest in the study of religious texts. Similar manifestations of more intense religious devotion were found by Weggemans, Bakker, and Grol who, for instance, observed stricter compliance with Islamic dietary laws.[35]

Table 4. Background.

	Dutch jihadists (N = 30)	Belgian jihadists (N = 15)	Total sample (N = 45)
Lower class origin	67%	47%	60%
Middle class origin	33%	47%	38%
Upper class origin	0%	6%	2%

Table 5. Occupational status.

	Dutch jihadists (N = 32)	Belgian jihadists (N = 34)	Total sample (N = 66)
Employed	21%	27%	25%
Unemployed	41%	32%	36%
Student	38%	41%	39%

Socioeconomic background and education

The data on the socioeconomic status of the families of the Belgian and Dutch jihadists indicate that they almost exclusively stem from the lower and middle strata of society (Table 4). The distributions among the three classes in society somewhat differs between the two groups. In the case of the Netherlands, the majority are of lower class origin (67%) and a minority from middle class background (33%). In the case of Belgium, the jihadists are evenly spread over these two classes (47%) and a small minority is of upper class origin (6%).

Regarding education, some of the jihadists had only finished primary education. For others, a high school diploma was the highest achieved degree. Relatively many had at least vocational training, and a few had followed education at a higher level (together they represent 47%). Of this group, however, most did not finish their education. Some dropped out just before traveling to Syria or Iraq – either as the result of bad grades, bad behavior, or by their own decision. Others were still enrolled at the time of their departure. Others were too young to have either vocational or higher educational experience. This explains the relatively low level of those that finished education beyond the level of high school. According to Coolsaet, in Belgium, only a small minority held a college degree.[36]

Regarding occupational status, of those for which we could find reliable information, many were unemployed (Table 5). Of those that were employed, their occupational status was mainly within the category unskilled worker.[37] There were also a few within the category of professionals.[38] A few jihadists, both among the Belgian ones and the Dutch, were known to have served in the military before joining the jihad. Many were students at the time they left for Syria and Iraq.

Finally, data on relative deprivation proved difficult to collect. Signs of economic, social, and/or political deprivation have nonetheless been identified in 6% of the cases in the database – comparable with Bakker's findings.[39]

Table 6. Marital status.

	Dutch jihadists (N = 50)	Belgian jihadists (N = 37)	Total sample (N = 87)
Married	64%	78%	70%

Psychological make-up

In his study of the psychological make-up of 140 Dutch jihadists, Weenink showed that 60% of them had psychological problems.[40] Using a very wide definition of such problems, he found problems as diverse as a 'problematic social setting', petty and serious criminal offenses, and diagnosed mental health issues. The latter is found in almost 9% of the sample. This is a lot higher than the data in our sample – using a narrower definition — that suggest that 2% of the Dutch and Belgian jihadists had some sort of psychological disorder before traveling to Syria. These disorders include feeble-mindedness, attention deficit hyperactivity disorder, schizophrenia, and claustrophobia. This 2% is in line with earlier findings by both Sageman and Bakker.[41] However, according to Coolsaet, the foreign fighters 'yearning to place themselves at the centre of events [...] reflects a degree of narcissism that was largely absent among their older predecessors'.[42]

Regarding criminality, based on our data, roughly 20% of the Belgian and Dutch jihadists has been suspected of criminal activity prior to departure. In the case of Belgium, a distinction should be made between the first group of jihadists that left for Syria and later groups. The first group was composed mainly of members from pre-existing networks, mainly Sharia4Belgium which was regarded as a terrorist organization by a Correctional Tribunal in Antwerp in 2015.[43] According to Coolsaet, whereas most individuals of the first group were known to the police (partly because of their link to Sharia4Belgium or because of ordinary crimes), this was less so for those that followed the first wave. Those that left at a later stage 'showed no signs of deviant behavior and nothing seemed to distinguish them from their peers'.[44]

Social affiliation

Most of the jihadists for which information on marital status could be collected were married,[45] despite being relatively young – on average 23.5, including quite a few teenagers. Among Belgian jihadists, 78% were married, compared to 64% among the Dutch (Table 6). This might be explained by the fact that, on average, the Dutch were a bit younger than their Belgian counterparts. Among the married were also women who went together with their husbands or joined them later on.

In many instances, the jihadist foreign fighters were closely connected to one another by way of family bonds and/or friendships. The latter category includes both larger groups – sometimes networks of radicals — and smaller groups of two or a few friends. Such pre-existing social affiliations often seem to have played an important role in (collective) recruitment – as will be discussed in the next section.

Why did they go?

What has caused more than 600 men and women from Belgium and the Netherlands to join the jihad in Syria and Iraq? There seem to be many factors that play a role, which can be divided into push and pull factors. In addition, propaganda and recruitment that stress both types of factors also seem to have contributed to the growth of this phenomenon. Moreover, the first jihadists with combat experience that returned to the Low Countries also seem to form a source of inspiration for potential fighters.

Push factors

As mentioned in the previous section, many of the Belgian and Dutch jihadists are part of the lower strata of society and have relatively low levels of education (which is partly related to their young age). However, jihadists do not solely stem from the lower socioeconomic strata of society, nor are they all poorly educated. Therefore, socioeconomic characteristics alone do not explain the phenomenon of jihadist foreign fighters. There are however factors that are partly linked to these characteristics that seem to hold more explanatory value. Research on Dutch jihadist foreign fighters showed that many of the jihadists grew up in deprived neighborhoods, that they had difficulties at school or at work, confrontations with the authorities, traumatic experiences, and (the perception of) being confronted with all kinds of injustice.[46] Against this backdrop, some of the Dutch jihadists showed strong frustrations about their own societal position in the Netherlands or that of their ethnic group.[47] Some of them also showed feelings of apathy and a lack of meaningfulness in their lives prior to traveling to Syria. As a consequence, some persons no longer felt they had a future in the Netherlands.[48] This also seems to be the case for the Belgian jihadists. According to Coolsaet,

> one cannot fail to notice how frequently [the Belgian jihadists] refer to the absence of a future, to personal difficulties that have to be coped with in everyday life. Often these stories point to a desire to leave all this behind, to be 'someone', to be accepted.[49]

Coolsaet also stresses the importance of feelings of injustice and discrimination as the decision to join the jihad in Syria seems to a large extent found in how one feels.[50] Such feelings also played a role in the Netherlands, and not only for those on the fringes of society. Based on her research on Dutch and Belgian jihadist foreign fighters, Van San states that those that are well integrated raise their societal expectations, and consequently are more susceptible to social exclusion and (perceived) discrimination.[51] Such feelings seem to be strongly felt among those from Moroccan families.[52] For others, leaving the Netherlands or Belgium presented an opportunity to break with their criminal, corrupted, Western lifestyle. In some cases, this meant escaping prison sentences or debts. In other instances, it meant leaving a place where nothing really happened, in pursuit of excitement.[53]

Pull factors

Jihadist foreign fighters are not only persons who leave their place of residence, but are, perhaps first and foremost, persons who go to a certain place abroad to fight. In the case of Syria, especially during the early stages of the conflict, (images of) the brutality committed by the al-Assad regime in combination with the 'international paralysis'[54] served as an important justification to pick up arms against the Syrian regime.[55] Extensive media coverage of the Syrian conflict also played a role.[56] According to the Dutch National Coordinator for Security and Counterterrorism (NCTV), Sunni Muslims increasingly came to see the regime of Bashar al-Assad as representing an infidel sect that brutally repressed the majority Sunni population.[57] In Belgium, this narrative was propagated by Sharia4Belgium and like-minded groups.[58] In the Netherlands it was propagated by groups like Behind Bars/Street Dawa, Sharia4Holland, and the 'Context group'.[59] As the war progressed, the religious and sectarian aspect became the dominant narrative. The rise of jihadist groups and the conflicts between these and other groups further contributed to the chaos and bloodshed in the country. To some, this infighting meant that they could no longer identify with the battle fought in Syria and hence they decided not to travel abroad.[60] For many others, the rapid ascent of ISIS, the establishment of the caliphate, and the impression of unstoppable expansion boosted the appeal to join the jihad.[61] According to Bakker and Grol, among the Dutch jihadists there is a strong – often persistent – conviction that traveling to Syria is the right thing to do, now or in the future. This conviction can be based on ideals or on specific personal needs and desires, and it is often a mixture of both.[62] Among the personal factors that contribute to the appeal of joining the violent jihad are the need for a sense of belonging, fraternity and comradeship, respect, recognition, acceptance by a group, identity, adventure, heroism. Factors of a more religious and ideological nature include the appeal of living under strict Islamic law, contributing to an ideal state, and that of martyrdom.[63] In particular, living under Islamic law in the self-proclaimed caliphate of ISIS seemed an important motivation for a number of Dutch jihadists that were studied by Weggemans, Bakker, and Grol.[64] Some regard migrating to the caliphate as a religious obligation – referred to as *hijrah*. It is however important to stress that the role of religion and the extent to which persons see the idea of joining the jihad as a religious duty is difficult to assess. According to a French judge specializing in terrorism cases, 90% of the jihadists traveled to Syria because of various personal motives, and only 10% did so out of religious beliefs.[65] Still, as noted earlier, many Belgian and Dutch jihadists showed an increased interest in religion in the period before they left for Syria or Iraq. These people proved to be susceptible to the idea of the violent jihad and that of organizations such as JaN and ISIS. Another religious pull factor is the apocalyptic vision that the Syrian conflict heralds the end of the world as foretold in seventh-century prophecies.[66]

These 'attractions' of the jihad in Syria and Iraq are propagated by various jihadist groups, both in the two countries and outside the region. According to Hegghammer, Syria is probably the most 'socially mediated' conflict in modern history.[67] In particular, ISIS seems to have been successful in propagating the 'caliphate narrative'.[68] It also managed to present a 'romantic' idea of the caliphate as well as of the jihadist battlefield.[69] For instance, al-Baghdadi's call to those with certain specific occupations (e.g. doctors and technicians) to join ISIS suggests employment opportunities of a supportive nature. Furthermore, jihadist parties are in control of large areas in Syria, which suggests that it is possible to take part in the jihad while to some extent avoiding both combat and deadly enemy raids.[70] This has made joining the violent jihad in Syria and Iraq attractive for an unusually diverse group of people when compared to the situation in the past.[71] These dynamics might help explain the diversity within the group of Belgian and Dutch jihadists, which consists of both very young and very old persons, of male and female jihadists, and even families with children.

Social dynamics

Many of the Dutch and Belgian jihadists that have traveled to Syria had contact with ideologically like-minded people in person, via the Internet, and/or via social media. As noted in the previous section, many of them were connected through friendship, kinship, or both. During the early stages of the Syrian conflict, a number of jihadist networks also played an important role, enhancing the push and pull factors and bringing them together, in particular in Belgium.[72] Their role seems quite clear as the main places of residence of the Belgian and Dutch jihadists to a large extent coincide with the presence of these networks in these towns and urban regions. In many cases, these organizations did not shy away from the public spotlight. They openly promoted their jihadist and anti-democratic views. Among these groups were inspiring or charismatic figures or 'facilitators' who managed to underline the push factors and strengthen the 'attractiveness' of the jihad in Syria.[73] Furthermore, through social dynamics such as group think and peer pressure, those that participated in these networks were conditioned to go on jihad.[74] These organizations seem to have played a decisive role in the case of Belgium. According to the head of the Belgian State Security Service (VSSE), Sharia4Belgium can be considered as the main incubator of departures.[75] This organization also had an impact in the Netherlands.

According to the AIVD, the first wave of jihadist departures from the Netherlands to Syria 'was probably attributable to the close contacts between Behind Bars/Street Dawah and Sharia4Belgium. Individuals associated with the two movements were at the heart of that sudden exodus.'[76]

Another important social dynamic is 'chain migration' or peer recruitment. This dynamic has been observed by both Belgian and Dutch authorities.[77] Most of those who decided to travel to the Syria or Iraq already know someone inside territory controlled by ISIS: family, friends from their old neighborhood, friends with whom they played soccer together, former classmates, etc.[78] Often, the would-be jihadists are persuaded to come by those that are already there.[79] Concrete examples of this form of peer recruitment are the departures of relatively large groups of friends from the Dutch cities of Delft and The Hague and the Belgian city of Vilvoorde who left for Syria and Iraq in different waves.

What do they do out there?

Belgian and Dutch jihadists travel to Syria and Iraq mainly through Turkey, usually via the Turkish province of Hatay.[80] After crossing the Turkish–Syrian border, the foreigners are picked up by a contact and taken to a safe house. The jihadist groups operate safe houses for specific groups of foreigners, based on a common language. The Belgian (Flemish) and Dutch jihadists are often accommodated at the same location.[81] There, the men and women will be separated, and possessions will be confiscated and searched for chips and GPS equipment.[82] For a period of approximately two or three weeks, the new recruits will be interrogated and closely monitored to identify possible spies.[83]

After this interrogation phase, the men will undergo several training courses at a training camp. This separation between time spent at a safe house and time spent at a training facility may vary. At times, interrogation and training seem to happen rather simultaneously. The entire 'preparatory phase' (i.e. inquiries as well as training) seems to take two or three months on average.[84] Training includes lessons in the Arabic language, religion, and military training.[85] The latter covers training to improve one's physique, to cope with hunger and cold, to learn how to use various weapons (mainly the Kalashnikov, rocket propelled grenades, and hand grenades), and to become familiar with combat techniques and strategies.[86] Usually before taking part in this military training, new recruits need to swear an oath of allegiance (*bay'ah*). This pledge of allegiance occurs before entering the ranks of either ISIS[87] or JaN,[88] and entails that one will comply with the assigned duties, regardless whether one agrees or disagrees with the given tasks. While in training, the recruits are generally not send to the frontlines, yet they can be assigned with guard duties (*ribat*). This serves as a first practical experience in being part of an army and taking part in an armed struggle.

After the training phase, recruits will, in principle, be deployed on the basis of their competences and wishes, and will be prepared accordingly.[89] Most recruits can choose between becoming a fighter, committing a suicide attack, or fulfilling certain supporting activities.[90] The options for the latter seem diverse, and include jobs as an engineer, a hacker, a doctor, an administrative worker, a cook, a driver, or a job at the religious police or a Sharia court.[91]

The Dutch jihadists generally appear to choose the life of a fighter.[92] Similarly, most Belgian jihadists can be found at all the ISIS fronts.[93] After completing the training courses, the foreign fighters will be assigned to a battalion under the command of an *emir*. These battalions seem, like the safe houses, to be organized on the basis of a shared language. Hence, Belgian (Flemish) and Dutch jihadist fighters are often within the same 'battalion'. These battalions are not continuously engaged in combat. A considerable amount of time at the front lines is spent on other armed tasks, such as guarding checkpoints and patrolling.[94] Moreover, as in all armies, periods at the front lines are alternated with duties in the hinterland, including performing tasks in pursuit of the jihadist cause, such as guard duty or *dawah* (i.e. inviting others to Islam through dialog).[95]

The salary of the jihadists from Western countries varies between $300 and $800 per month.[96] Other 'benefits' of being a soldier can include war loot and female slaves.[97] According to the AIVD, when ISIS conquers a village or area, it is not unusual that its members – whether ordered to do so or not – resort to torture and rape.[98] The extent to which Dutch and Belgian jihadists are involved in these or other war crimes is difficult to tell. There is a video of Dutch-speaking jihadists who take part in a beheading.[99] Others have committed suicide attacks against civilian targets. Those that do not have a role as a soldier are primarily tasked with supporting activities. For instance, a Dutch boy told his parents that he was a cook,[100] and a Belgian jihadist is assumed to be in charge of the religious police (*al-Hisbah*) in Raqqa.[101] Such supporting activities are nonetheless often difficult to see separately from the violent jihad. Violence seems to be inherent to certain supporting jobs. For instance, this is the case with *al-Hisbah* agents, who are engaged in addressing, arresting, and punishing those who have violated the rules of ISIS. The boundaries between a violent and non-violent role are also blurred by the fact that almost all men receive a rifle (usually a Kalashnikov) and are expected to be armed.[102] Finally, as new recruits need to swear an oath of allegiance to the jihadist organization that they have joined, they can – regardless of their assigned role – be called upon to engage in combat or in other violent activities. Everyone who has sworn this oath and is not primarily a fighter is thus in fact a reservist. Young boys, viewed as the fighters of the future, are prepared for this role from an early age. The doctrine of ISIS is taught at schools, and the necessary weapon and combat skills are practiced at training camps for boys.[103]

Among the Dutch and Belgian jihadists are persons that hold relatively important positions.[104] There are indications that some have risen to the rank of *emir*, i.e. commander of a unit. Others are believed to hold high supportive positions, such as the earlier mentioned *al-Hisbah* example, or play a focal role in spreading propaganda for ISIS or other jihadist groups.

The life of women is rather different than that of men. Their primary role is to quickly marry, raise children, and to obey their husband. They serve society from behind the scenes, in principle being only able to leave the vicinity of their house while being veiled and in the company of a male relative.[105] The Belgian and Dutch wives in Raqqa often visit each other when their husbands are away during the day.[106] They have only a few options to regain some of the liberties they lost after joining ISIS. As education and health care is separated according to gender, some female jihadists are teachers and nurses.[107] Women can also join the ranks of the all-female religious police unit: the *al-Khansaa* brigade. This brigade controls the adherence of women to moral conduct according to ISIS standards. Like the *al-Hisbah*, it has the mandate to enforce ISIS's rules and to punish those that disobey the rules, among other sanctions using whipping.[108] *Al-Khansaa* agents are armed, yet women in general – in contrast to male jihadists – do not receive a weapon. They do however have the opportunity to arm themselves, and many allegedly carry a firearm in their purses.[109] Many ISIS women also play an important role in ISIS propaganda and are active in recruiting other women.[110] It should be noted that Dutch jihadists seem more often than their Belgian peers to have been involved in disseminating propaganda to a targeted audience or a wide public.[111]

General observations

Above, we have provided an overview of the characteristics, motivations, and roles of Belgian and Dutch jihadists that have left for Syria and Iraq. It is based on data that we gathered for just over half of the total amount of cases as estimated by the Dutch and Belgian authorities. Hence, it does not provide a complete overview. Moreover, the N is relatively small, which also limits the possibility of making generalizations regarding this phenomenon. Against this backdrop, and stressing the need for more research, we would like to conclude this article with a number of preliminary general observations.

First of all, the phenomenon of foreign fighters is not new to Belgium and the Netherlands. That of jihadist foreign fighters, however, is relatively novel, although both countries saw examples before 2012. Both Belgium and the Netherlands experienced a rapid growth of jihadists starting late 2012 and early 2013.

Second, many of the general assumptions regarding European foreign jihadist fighters are more or less supported by the data collected on Dutch and Belgian fighters. They are indeed relatively young (23.5), though not (late) adolescents, but rather young adults. They are mainly of migrant background (46% have parents born in Morocco) and are part of the lower strata of society

(60%). Despite their relatively young age, a surprisingly high number are not single, but married (70%), or even married with children. According to figures of the AIVD, there are about 70 Dutch children in ISIS-controlled territories.

Comparing Dutch and Belgian jihadists, we see that the two samples are very similar when looking at the following characteristics: geographical origin, age, education, and occupational status. When looking at the motivations to join the jihad, we note that both groups are believed to have done so for a wide variety of reasons ranging from a lack of meaningfulness to social exclusion and (perceived) discrimination. Their activities and roles in the conflict in Syria and Iraq are also very similar for Dutch and Belgian jihadists.

Dutch and Belgian jihadists differ when looking at the size of the phenomenon (Belgium 'producing' almost twice the number of jihadist foreign fighters compared to the Netherlands) as well as the percentage of women, which is a lot higher among the Dutch. They also differ somewhat when looking at marital status (78% of the Belgians are married compared to 64% of the Dutch) and socioeconomic background (that of the Belgian fighters being higher than that of the Dutch). Regarding motivations to leave for Syria and Iraq, the role of networks in propagating the jihad has been more important in Belgium than in the Netherlands.

These empirical data and the comparison between the jihadists from Belgium and the Netherlands provide more insight in the who, why, and what questions surrounding the phenomenon of jihadism in Europe. Comparison with other countries is needed to be able to explain why some countries have 'produced' more jihadists than others and what factors may be more important than others in explaining the characteristics and development of the phenomenon in general. To that end, we should not only focus on other European countries, but also non-European countries, such as Tunisia, Morocco, and Saudi Arabia from which thousands have left for the battlefields in Syria and Iraq and whose citizens fight alongside their jihadist comrades from Europe.

Notes

1. Those that are fighting in the region and those that have returned, see '117 Syriëstrijders in België'.
2. AIVD, 'Leven bij ISIS', 6. The report also speaks of about 70 children – of whom one-third were born in Syria or Iraq and two-thirds were brought there by one or both parents.
3. Sageman, *Understanding Terror Networks*, 69–120.
4. This figure represents more than half of the number of 608 jihadists as estimated by Dutch and Belgian authorities by early 2016. We would like to point out Reinier Bergema's role in collecting the data on Dutch jihadists.
5. Based on interviews and a variety of open sources including newspapers, governmental reports, academic literature, weblogs, and social media (e.g. Twitter, Facebook, Telegram), we have gathered information on the life of (mainly Dutch-speaking) jihadists in Syria and Iraq.

6. *New York Herald*, 10 June 1868, quoted in Marraro, 'Zouaves in Papal Army', 83.
7. Lefebvre, quoted in Beevor, *The Spanish Civil War*, 468.
8. Ibid.
9. In 't Veld, *De SS en Nederland*, 406.
10. De Wever, 'Militaire collaboratie in België', 36–7.
11. Stock, 'A Dutch Guerillera'.
12. Karskens, 'De laatste dagen van'.
13. Bakker, 'Islamism, Radicalisation and Jihadism', 174.
14. For more information on this case, see De Stoop, *Vrede Zij met U*.
15. E.g. see De Koning et al., 'Een zee van ongeloof', 73–4; NCTV, 'Dreigingsbeeld Nederland September 2012', 2.
16. AIVD, 'Jaarverslag 2012', 10; Zelin, 'ICSR Insight'.
17. NCTV, 'Terrorism threat level raised'.
18. Ibid.
19. Moniquet, 'Sharia4Belgium Atypical but Extremist'.
20. Raes, 'Lessons Learned from Verviers'; Van Vlierden, *How Belgium Became Top Exporter*.
21. Coolsaet, 'What Drives Europeans to Syria, and to IS?', 3.
22. See note 1.
23. NCTV, 'Dreigingsbeeld Terrorisme Nederland 32'.
24. NCTV, 'Dreigingsbeeld Terrorisme Nederland 40', 1.
25. Barrett, 'Foreign Fighters in Syria', 17.
26. The average age of women whose age could be determined (N = 41) is 21.5 years old: two years younger on average than their male counterparts.
27. Sageman, *Understanding Terror Networks*, 112.
28. Bakker, 'Jihadi Terrorists in Europe', 41.
29. Sageman, *Understanding Terror Networks*, 92; Bakker, 'Jihadi Terrorists in Europe', 41; Bakker, 'Characteristics of Jihadi Terrorists', 141.
30. Van Ostaeyen, 'February 2016 Statistical Update'; AIVD, 'Leven bij ISIS', 6.
31. Sageman, *Understanding Terror Networks*; Bakker, 'Jihadi Terrorists in Europe', 36; Bakker, 'Characteristics of Jihadi Terrorists', 141.
32. NCTV, 'Dreigingsbeeld Terrorisme Nederland 40', 1; Van Ostaeyen, 'February 2016 Statistical Update'. Of the Dutch jihadists, between 2012 and 2016, 42 have been reported dead by the authorities – all male. Of the Belgian cases, according to Van Ostaeyen, 81 have been killed. This count includes two females. The death of at least one Belgian women has been confirmed by the Belgian authorities.
33. De Bont, 'Belgian and Dutch Fighters', 39.
34. Van San, 'Lost Souls Searching for Answers'.
35. Weggemans, Bakker, and Grol, 'Who Are They', 108.
36. Coolsaet, 'Facing the Fourth Wave', 9.
37. Unskilled workers include cleaners and factory workers, etc.
38. Professionals (highly skilled workers) include medical doctors, army officers, scientists, etc.
39. Bakker, 'Jihadi Terrorists in Europe', 42; Bakker, 'Characteristics of Jihadi Terrorists', 142.
40. Weenink, 'Behavioral Problems and Disorders'.
41. Sageman, *Understanding Terror Networks*, 80–1; Bakker, 'Jihadi Terrorists in Europe', 40; Bakker, 'Characteristics of Jihadi Terrorists', 141.
42. Coolsaet, 'What Drives Europeans to Syria, and to IS?', 8.
43. AIVD, 'Jaarverslag 2012', 24, 29–30; Coolsaet, 'Facing the Fourth Wave', 3; De Koning et al., 'Een zee van ongeloof', 78, 265.

44. Coolsaet, 'Facing the Fourth Wave', 3.
45. Under Dutch or Belgian law or under Islamic law.
46. E.g. see: Coolsaet, 'What Drives Europeans to Syria, and to IS?'; Weggemans, Bakker, and Grol, 'Who Are They'; De Graaf, 'Nederlandse strijders in buitenland'.
47. Weggemans, Bakker, and Grol, 'Who Are They', 107.
48. Bakker and Grol, 'Motives and Considerations', 13; De Koning, *Waar hebben we het over*.
49. Coolsaet, 'What Drives Europeans to Syria, and to IS?', 17.
50. Coolsaet, 'Facing the Fourth Wave', 3.
51. Van San, *Hoe beter geïntegreerd*.
52. Coolsaet, 'Facing the Fourth Wave', 34.
53. Weggemans, Bakker and Grol, 'Who Are They'; Bakker and Grol, 'Motives and Considerations', 13; De Koning, 'Waar hebben we het over'.
54. OHCHR, '"paralysis" on Syria'. UN High Commissioner for Human Rights referring to the international indifference.
55. Hegghammer, 'Syria's Foreign Fighters'; Coolsaet, 'What Drives Europeans to Syria, and to IS?', 17.
56. Boeke and Weggemans, 'Destination Jihad'.
57. NCTV, *Analysis of the Phenomenon*.
58. Coolsaet, 'What Drives Europeans to Syria, and to IS?', 17.
59. In December 2015, the high-security court in Amsterdam declared that the Context group's 'inner circle' formed a 'criminal organization with terrorist intent' – a terrorist organization. Suspects were sentenced up to six years in prison.
60. Bakker and Grol, 'Motives and Considerations', 13.
61. Coolsaet, 'What Drives Europeans to Syria, and to IS?', 19.
62. Bakker and Grol, 'Motives and Considerations', 13.
63. Coolsaet, 'What Drives Europeans to Syria, and to IS?', 19; De Koning, 'Waar hebben we het over'.
64. Weggemans, Bakker and Grol, 'Who Are They', 14.
65. 'Le judge Trévidic'.
66. E.g. see Wood, *What ISIS Really Wants*. It is, according to the Prophet, in the Syrian city of Dabiq where the armies of Rome will set up their camp and where the armies of Islam will meet them for a decisive battle. The Muslim victory will mark the beginning of the end of the world.
67. Hegghammer, 'Syria's Foreign Fighters'.
68. AIVD, 'Leven bij ISIS', 3.
69. Bakker and Grol, 'Motives and Considerations', 13.
70. Hegghammer, 'Syria's Foreign Fighters'.
71. Ibid.
72. Coolsaet, 'What Drives Europeans to Syria, and to IS?', 21.
73. Bakker and Bergema, 'Impact of Jihadist Insurgencies'.
74. Coolsaet, 'What Drives Europeans to Syria, and to IS?', 21.
75. Raes, 'Lessons Learned from Verviers'.
76. AIVD, 'The Transformation of Jihadism', 13.
77. AIVD, 'Leven bij ISIS'; Raes, 'Lessons Learned from Verviers'.
78. AIVD, 'Leven bij ISIS', 5; Raes, 'Lessons Learned from Verviers'.
79. Raes, 'Lessons Learned from Verviers'.
80. AlDe'emeh and Stockmans, *De jihadkaravaan*, 114–15; Weggemans et al., 'Bestemming Syrië', 48.
81. Weggemans et al., 'Bestemming Syrië', 48.
82. Groen, 'Wat zich werkelijk afspeelt'.

83. Weggemans et al., 'Bestemming Syrië', 48–9.
84. Ibid., 51.
85. Ibid., 49–50.
86. Ibid.; AIVD, 'Leven bij ISIS', 7; Hassan, 'Secret World'; Al-Tamimi, 'Principles in the Administration'.
87. AIVD, 'Leven bij ISIS', 7; Speckhard and Yayla, 'Eyewitness Accounts from Defectors', 97.
88. Benotman and Blake, 'Jabhat al-Nusra', 7.
89. AIVD, 'Leven bij ISIS', 7; Weggemans et al., 'Bestemming Syrië', 50.
90. AIVD, 'Leven bij ISIS', 7.
91. Weggemans et al., 'Bestemming Syrië', 51.
92. AIVD, 'Leven bij ISIS', 7.
93. Raes, 'Lessons Learned from Verviers'.
94. AIVD, 'Leven bij ISIS', 17; Weggemans et al., 'Bestemming Syrië', 53.
95. Weggemans et al., 'Bestemming Syrië', 53.
96. Ibid., 67–8.
97. Ibid., 67–8, 71.
98. AIVD, 'Leven bij ISIS', 8.
99. 'Video: Belgian Fighters Behead Man'.
100. Weggemans et al., 'Bestemming Syrië', 51.
101. E.g. see: 'Rechterhand Belkacem'.
102. Weggemans et al., 'Bestemming Syrië', 53.
103. AIVD, 'Leven bij ISIS', 9; Weggemans et al., 'Bestemming Syrië', 57; Al-Tamimi, 'Principles in the Administration'.
104. Weggemans et al., 'Bestemming Syrië', 53.
105. Winter, 'Women of Islamic State', 7; Weggemans et al., 'Bestemming Syrië', 56.
106. Weggemans et al., 'Bestemming Syrië', 58.
107. Neurink, *Vrouwen van het kalifaat*, 66–7.
108. Weggemans et al., 'Bestemming Syrië', 54.
109. Ibid, 70.
110. Ibid, 54.
111. Bunnik and De Zoete, 'The Gloves Come Off'.

Disclosure statement

No potential conflict of interest was reported by the authors.

References

'117 Syriëstrijders terug in België'. *Het Laatste Nieuws*, 22 February 2016. http://www.hln.be/hln/nl/33982/Islamitische-Staat/article/detail/2624782/2016/02/22/117-Syriestrijders-terug-in-Belgie.dhtml.
AIVD. 'Jaarverslag 2012'. 2013. https://www.aivdkennisbank.nl/FbContent.ashx/Downloads/Jaarverslag_2012_AIVD.pdf.

AIVD. 'The Transformation of Jihadism in the Netherlands'. 2014. https://www.aivd.nl/publicaties/publicaties/2014/06/30/the-transformation-of-jihadism-in-the-netherlands.

AIVD. 'Leven bij ISIS: De mythe ontrafeld'. 2016. https://www.aivd.nl/over-aivd/documenten/publicaties/2016/01/12/aivd-publicatie-leven-bij-isis-de-mythe-ontrafeld.

Al-Baghdadi, Abu Bakr. 'A Message to the Mujahedin and the Muslim Ummah in the Month of Ramadan'. *Al Hayat Media Center.* https://ia902501.us.archive.org/2/items/hym3_22aw/english.pdf.

AlDe'emeh, Montasser and Pieter Stockmans. *De Jihadkaravaan – Reis naar de Wortels van de Haat*. Tielt: Lannoo, 2015.

Bakker, Edwin. "Characteristics of Jihadi Terrorists in Europe (2001–2009)." In *Jihadi Terrorism and the Radicalisation Challenge: European and American Experiences*, edited by Rik Coolsaet, 131–144. Farnham: Ashgate, 2011.

Bakker, Edwin. 'Islamism, Radicalisation and Jihadism in the Netherlands: Main Developments and Counter Measures'. In *Understanding Violent Radicalisation: Terrorist and Jihadist Movements in Europe*, edited by Magnus Ranstrop, 168–190. Abingdon: Routledge, 2010.

Bakker, Edwin. *Jihadi Terrorists in Europe – Their Characteristics and the Circumstances in Which They Joined the Jihad: An Exploratory Study*. The Hague: Netherlands Institute of International Relations Clingendael, 2006.

Bakker, Edwin and Reinier Bergema. 'The Impact of Jihadist Insurgencies in Syria and Iraq on Jihadist Mobilization: The Case of the Netherlands'. Forthcoming.

Bakker, Edwin and Peter Grol. 'Motives and Considerations of Potential Foreign Fighters from the Netherlands'. ICCT Policy Brief, 2015. http://icct.nl/wp-content/uploads/2015/07/ICCT-Bakker-Grol-Motives-and-Considerations-of-Potential-Foreign-Fighters-from-the-Netherlands-July2015.pdf.

Barrett, Richard. 'Foreign Fighters in Syria'. *The Soufan Group*, 2014. http://soufangroup.com/wp-content/uploads/2014/06/TSG-Foreign-Fighters-in-Syria.pdf.

Beevor, Antony. *The Battle for Spain: The Spanish Civil War 1936–1939*. London: Weidenfeld & Nicolson, 2006.

Benotman, Naeraldin and Roisin Blake. 'Jabhat al-Nusra: Jabhat al-Nusra li-ahl al-Sham min Mujahedi al-Sham fi Sahat al-Jihad'. *Quilliam Foundation Strategic Briefing*. https://www.quilliamfoundation.org/wp/wp-content/uploads/publications/free/jabhat-al-nusra-a-strategic-briefing.pdf.

Boeke, Serge and Daan Weggemans. 'Destination Jihad: Why Syria and not Mali?' *ICCT*, 10 April 2013. http://icct.nl/publication/destination-jihad-why-syria-and-not-mali/.

De Bont, Roel. 'Belgian and Dutch Foreign Fighters in the Syrian War: Their Characteristics and Conditions in Which They Joined the Jihad in Comparison to the Jihadi Generations Before Them'. MA diss., Leiden University, 2015.

Bunnik, Arno and Thomas de Zoete. 'The Gloves Come Off: The Dutch Response to Jihadists in Syria and Iraq'. *Terrorism Monitor* 13, no. 16 (2015). http://www.jamestown.org/programs/tm/single/?tx_ttnews%5Btt_news%5D=44383&cHash=4eccded7ab98f2df1086c87a6e33a050#.VtgUCU0UW70.

Coolsaet, Rik. 'Facing the Fourth Foreign Fighters Wave. What Drives Europeans to Syria, and to Islamic State?: Insights from the Belgian Case'. *Egmont Paper* 81, 2016. http://www.egmontinstitute.be/wp-content/uploads/2016/02/egmont.papers.81_online-versie.pdf.

Coolsaet, Rik. 'What Drives Europeans to Syria, and to IS?: Insights from the Belgian Case'. *Egmont Paper* 75, 2015. http://www.egmontinstitute.be/wp-content/uploads/2015/03/75.pdf.

De Graaf, Beatrice. 'De Vlam van het Verzet. Nederlandse Strijders in het Buitenland, Vroeger en Nu'. Hand-out lecture Anton de Komlezing, 2014. http://www.verzetsmuseum.org/uploads/media_items/de-vlam-van-het-verzet-nederlandse-strijders-in-het-buitenland-vroeger-en-nu.original.docx.

Groen, Janny. 'Wij Laten Zien wat Zich Werkelijk Afspeelt in het Kalifaat'. *De Volkskrant*, 5 November 2015. http://www.volkskrant.nl/buitenland/-wij-laten-zien-wat-zich-werkelijk-afspeelt-in-het-kalifaat~a4178503/.

Hassan, Hassan. 'The Secret World of Isis Training Camps: Ruled by Sacred Texts and the Sword'. *The Guardian*, 25 January 2015. http://www.theguardian.com/world/2015/jan/25/inside-isis-training-camps.

Hegghammer, Thomas. 'Syria's Foreign Fighters'. *Foreign Policy*, 9 December 2013. http://foreignpolicy.com/2013/12/09/syrias-foreign-fighters/.

'Le judge Trévidic. "La religion n'est pas le moteur du jihad"'. *Le Télégramme*, 28 June 2015. http://www.letelegramme.fr/bretagne/le-juge-trevidic-la-religion-n-est-pas-le-moteur-du-jihad-27-06-2015-10682946.php.

Karskens, Arnold. 'De Laatste Dagen van Ahmed en Khalid (1)'. *Reporters Online*, 2 April 2013. http://reportersonline.nl/de-laatste-dagen-van-ahmed-en-khalid-1/.

De Koning, Martijn. 'Radicalisering – Waar hebben we het eigenlijk over?' 7 February 2015. http://religionresearch.org/closer/2015/02/07/radicalisering-waar-hebben-we-het-eigenlijk-over/.

De Koning, Martijn, Carmen Becker, Ineke Roex, and Pim Aarns. 'Eilanden in een Zee van Ongeloof: Het Verzet van Activistische Da'wa-netwerken in België, Nederland en Duitsland'. *IMES Report Series*, 16 December 2014.

Marraro, Howard R. 'Canadian and American Zouaves in the Papal Army, 1868–1870'. *CCHA Report* 12 (1944–1945): 83–102. http://www.umanitoba.ca/colleges/st_pauls/ccha/Back%20Issues/CCHA1944-45/Marraro.pdf.

Moniquet, Claude. '"Sharia4Belgium": An Atypical but Extremist Salafist Organisation Steps on the Belgian Stage'. *European Strategic Intelligence and Security Center Briefing 21/05*, 2010. http://www.esisc.org/upload/publications/analyses/sharia4belgium-an-atypical-but-extremist-salafist-organisation-steps-on-the-belgian-stage/5.%20Sharia4Belgium.pdf.

NCTV. 'Global Jihadism: Analysis of the Phenomenon and Reflections on Radicalisation'. 2014. https://english.nctv.nl/Images/globaljihadism-uk-webversie_tcm92-575175.pdf.

NCTV. 'Samenvatting Dreigingsbeeld Terrorisme Nederland, September 2012 (DTN30)'. 2012.

NCTV. 'Samenvatting Dreigingsbeeld Terrorisme Nederland 32'. 2013.

NCTV. 'Samenvatting Dreigingsbeeld Terrorisme Nederland 40'. 2015.

NCTV. 'Terrorist Threat Level Raised'. 13 March 2013. http://english.nctv.nl/currenttopics/news/2013/terrorist-threat-level-raised.aspx?cp=92&cs=66050.

Neurink, Judith. *De Vrouwen van het Kalifaat*. Amsterdam: Jurgen Maas, 2015.

OHCHR. 'Pillay castigates "paralysis" on Syria, as new UN study indicates over 191,000 people killed'. 22 August 2014. http://www.ohchr.org/EN/NewsEvents/Pages/DisplayNews.aspx?NewsID=14959&LangID=E.

Van Ostaeyen, Pieter. 'February 2016: A new statistical update on Belgian fighters in Syria and Iraq'. 2 February 2016. https://pietervanostaeyen.wordpress.com/2016/02/02/february-2016-a-new-statistical-update-on-belgian-fighters-in-syria-and-iraq/.

Van San, Marion. 'Hoe beter geïntegreerd, hoe meer kans op radicalisering'. *De Standaard*, 2 February 2015. http://www.standaard.be/cnt/dmf20150201_01504894.

Van San, Marion. 'Lost Souls Searching for Answers? Belgian and Dutch Converts Joining the Islamic State'. *Perspectives on Terrorism* 9, no. 5 (2015). http://www.terrorismanalysts.com/pt/index.php/pot/article/view/460/html.

Raes, Jaak. 'Lessons learned from Verviers and European co-operation in the field of Counter-Terrorism'. Speech at a symposium of the German domestic intelligence service, 4 May 2015. https://www.verfassungsschutz.de/de/oeffentlichkeitsarbeit/symposium/symposium-2015.

'Rechterhand Belkacem is nieuw hoofd religieuze politie IS'. *Het Laatste Nieuws*, 8 April 2015. http://www.hln.be/hln/nl/960/Buitenland/article/detail/2197921/2015/01/28/Rechterhand-Belkacem-is-nieuw-hoofd-religieuze-politie-IS.dhtml.

Sageman, Marc. *Understanding Terror Networks*. Philadelphia, PA: University of Pennsylvania Press, 2004.

Speckhard, Anne and Ahmed S. Yayla. 'Eyewitness Accounts from Recent Defectors from Islamic State: Why They Joined, What They Saw, Why They Quit'. *Perspectives on Terrorism* 9, no. 6 (2015). http://www.terrorismanalysts.com/pt/index.php/pot/article/view/475.

Stock, Jonathan. 'A Dutch Guerillera: The Foreign Face of FARC's Civil War'. *Spiegel Online*, 2 May 2014. http://www.spiegel.de/international/world/a-meeting-with-dutch-farc-member-tanja-nijmeijer-a-966813.html.

De Stoop, Chris. *Vrede Zij met U, Zuster: De Jihad van Muriel*. Amsterdam & Antwerpen: De Bezige Bij, 2010.

Al-Tamimi, Aymenn Jawad. 'Principles in the Administration of the Islamic State': Full Text and Translation. 7 December 2015. http://www.aymennjawad.org/18215/principles-in-the-administration-of-the-islamic.

In 't Veld, Nanno. 'De SS en Nederland: Documenten uit SS-archieven 1935–1945'. PhD diss. The Hague: Martinus Nijhoff, 1976.

'Video: Belgian Fighters Behead Man in Syria'. *Al-Akhbar*, 8 June 2013. http://english.al-akhbar.com/node/16049.

Van Vlierden, Guy. 'How Belgium Became a Top Exporter of Jihad'. *Terrorism Monitor* 13, no. 11 (2015). http://www.jamestown.org/single/?tx_ttnews%5Btt_news%5D=43966&no_cache=1#.VurzYU0UW71.

Weenink, Anton. 'Behavioral Problems and Disorders among Radicals in Police Files'. *Perspectives on Terrorism* 9, no. 2 (2015). http://www.terrorismanalysts.com/pt/index.php/pot/article/view/416/html.

Weggemans, Daan, Edwin Bakker, and Peter Grol. 'Who Are They and Why Do They Go? The Radicalization and Preparatory Processes of Dutch Jihadist Foreign Fighters'. *Perspectives on Terrorism* 8, no. 4 (2014): 100–110. http://www.terrorismanalysts.com/pt/index.php/pot/article/view/365/718.

Weggemans, Daan, Edwin Bakker, Ruud Peters, and Roel de Bont. 'Bestemming Syrië: Een exploratieve studie naar de leefsituatie van Nederlandse 'uitreizigers' in Syrië'. 2016.

De Wever, Bruno. 'Militaire collaboratie in België tijdens de Tweede Wereldoorlog'. *BMCN* 118 (2003): 22–40.

Winter, Charlie. 'Women of the Islamic State: A Manifesto on Women by the Al-Khanssaa Brigade'. *Quilliam Foundation*, 2015. https://www.quilliamfoundation.org/wp/wp-content/uploads/publications/free/women-of-the-islamic-state3.pdf.

Winter, Charlie. 'Documenting the Virtual "Caliphate"', *Quilliam Foundation*, 2015. http://www.quilliamfoundation.org/wp/wp-content/uploads/2015/10/FINAL-documenting-the-virtual-caliphate.pdf.

Wood, Graeme. 'What ISIS Really Wants'. *The Atlantic*, March 2015. http://www.theatlantic.com/magazine/archive/2015/03/what-isis-really-wants/384980/.

Zelin, Aaron. 'ICSR insight: European foreign fighters in Syria'. ICSR, 2013. http://icsr.info/2013/04/icsr-insight-european-foreign-fighters-in-syria-2/.

Who Goes, Why, and With What Effects: The Problem of Foreign Fighters from Europe

Lasse Lindekilde, Preben Bertelsen and Michael Stohl

ABSTRACT
This article explores the phenomenon of Islamist foreign fighters, more specifically the movement of European Muslims to participate in the insurgencies in Syria and Iraq connected to the Islamic State/Daesh as well as the anti-Assad forces in Syria and the implications for European state stability. Drawing on personal psychology, social psychology, and social movement theory the article offers an integrated theoretical framework to analyze the radicalization of Islamist foreign fighters. Building on Danish data of Islamist foreign fighters, the article provides a first test of the analytical usefulness of this framework. The article further considers what distinguishes the Islamists that go from those that under similar circumstances stay behind, and whether this is a differences of kind or a difference of degree. Finally, we discuss the question of how much of a threat foreign fighter returnees pose to European states.

This article explores the phenomenon of Islamist foreign fighters, more specifically the movement of European Muslims to participate in the insurgencies in Syria and Iraq connected to the Islamic State/Daesh as well as the anti-Assad forces in Syria and the implications for European state stability.

Despite its horrific methods, brutal oppression of the local population, beheading of hostages, and planned terror attacks in the West, Islamic State continues to recruit thousands of voluntary fighters from the Muslim population in Western Europe and from Muslim populations across Southwest Asia and North Africa. Denmark is second, after Belgium, on the list of countries within Europe that sends most foreign fighters to Syria as a percentage of their total population. Since the civil war broke out, more than 110 Danish Muslims have gone to Syria to fight – many under Islamic State's banner. At least 17 Danes have perished, several of them as suicide bombers for Islamic State in Iraq, and around 50 foreign fighters have returned from Syria.[1]

After discussing the methods and data on Danish foreign fighters utilized in the article, the first section examines how these foreign fighters are radicalized and mobilized and what motivates young Danish Muslims to go to war for an ultra-violent, revolutionary movement like Islamic State. Drawing on elements of personal psychology, we scrutinize individual motivation to and risk factors associated with traveling and violent engagement, in particular the significance of personal challenges in everyday life and perceived self-uncertainty. Engaging insights on mobilization and recruitment within social movement theory, we next look at how contact to radicalizing milieus is established, highlighting particularly three relational, causal mechanisms: self-selection, social selection, and organizational outreach/recruitment. Building on social-psychological studies of group polarization, we focus on the interaction in radicalizing milieus and examine how this interaction contributes to radicalization, specifically radicalization of actions, i.e. developing preparedness for violence. We then examine how group dynamics as well as direct and indirect encouragement to action affect the decision to go.

The article's second section asks the much less researched question of who stays behind and why. We know from studies of terrorism and radicalization that the distribution of people with seemingly like demographic and motivational profiles who turn to violence is long. In 'long-tailed' distributions a high-frequency or high-amplitude population is followed by a low-frequency or low-amplitude population which gradually 'tails off' asymptotically. The events at the far end of the tail – in our case people developing a propensity for political violence – have a very low probability of occurrence. Put differently, we take a look at not only why and how those we know became radicalized and violent, but also why most under similar circumstances do not and what factors may remove the obstacles and inhibitors that help explain why in fact there is such a long tail.

Before the concluding remarks, the third section of the article turns to foreign fighter returnees and the question of how much of a threat they pose to European states. Drawing on unique qualitative data from counseling sessions offered to a number of Danish returnees and their families (conducted by one of the authors, Preben Bertelsen), we draw psychological profiles of returnees and discuss the risk to European societies by returned foreign fighters compared to 'failed joiners' among those that stay behind.

In the following section the article's methodology and data is outlined. However, before turning to this, let us briefly define the core concepts in the article. 'Radicalization' here means to develop a propensity for political violence, to develop a mindset in which political violence is established as an option likely to be taken.[2] We define a 'foreign fighter' as a person who travels from a Western to a non-Western country to participate in a conflict via combat action, combat training, or logistic support to combat actions.[3] We focus specifically on foreign fighters whose destination is the Syrian civil war zone and neighboring areas. Note that our definition includes persons whose departure was imminent or failed (they did not enter the conflict zone). Finally, we define a 'radicalizing milieu' as a more or less bounded locality or set (mosque, study circle, club, apartment, web forum, etc.) where a relatively closed group of persons with a shared identity meet regularly and where political violence is discussed as an option.

Methods and data

We have chosen to focus exclusively on Danish foreign fighters. First, Denmark is a major supplier of foreign fighters, relative to its population, and its program for preventing travel to Syria and aftercare for returned fighters is a model for other countries. The city of Aarhus has developed a mentor-based initiative for potential foreign fighters as well as an exit strategy including, among other things, psychological aid for returned fighters.[4] The Danish government's new action plan for prevention of radicalization proposes nationwide implementation of these initiatives.[5] Denmark thus qualifies as a critical case in terms of European foreign fighters. Second, we have chosen Denmark as a case because we have privileged access to data about these foreign fighters. One of the authors, Preben Bertelsen, has trained the Danish anti- and deradicalization mentors who work with potential foreign fighters, and, in connection with the exit strategy for returned foreign fighters in Aarhus, he has personally conducted counseling sessions with returned fighters and their families. Via these initiatives, we have access to unique data for about 15 foreign fighters.

More specifically, the data consist of anonymized and confidential case summaries prepared by the mentors and Preben Bertelsen. We have selected three cases, Mahmoud, Amir, and Martin (all pseudonyms), for our analysis. Mahmoud was on his way to Syria when he was assigned a mentor. We chose Mahmoud's case because his development before the mentor initiative in many ways is typical of the other cases – also for those who eventually went to Syria. Amir went to Syria and returned, and the convert Martin went to Syria and perished. The two latter cases have been in the media and the data is thus open-source material (media coverage, essays, reproduced interviews with the fighters, their friends, or families). These three cases make up the core of the data for the analysis and were chosen based on the representativeness of the radicalization process, diversity in terms of non-travel, travel, and return, and level of detail in the material. In addition, we draw on restricted data on cases from Aarhus and publicly available material for seven additional cases. Publicly available case material has been gathered via systematic online searches in the newspaper database Infomedia and supplemented with information from non-classified intelligence reports. In total, the article draws on data on 22 Danish foreign fighters. The analysis of the Danish data is supported by and compared to foreign data and analyses of foreign fighters.[6]

Despite privileged access to data, the data upon which our analysis is based has obvious limitations. We have data of varying quality for only 22 Danish foreign fighters out of at least 110 (significantly more if we count those who for different reasons did not depart). Our data may therefore contain biases of which we are unaware. As a consequence, our conclusions are preliminary and their scope limited.

Who goes and why?

The search for life embeddedness as leitmotif

Theoretically our point of departure is life psychology. Life psychology is based on two fundamental assumptions, namely that all people aspire to create a solidly embedded life and that perceived life embeddedness – having a firm grasp on life – is achieved by possessing the life competences required to handle everyday life tasks.[7] Life embeddedness requires that the individual possesses the competences to and is capable of (a) participating in intimate communities and society in general; (b) balancing values and practical matters with reality and one's surroundings; and (c) putting their own and others' self-perception and philosophy of life into perspective. Good life embeddedness can be defined as a good match between life tasks (including everyday routines and major life choices) and life competencies. Threatened life embeddedness can thus be defined as a mismatch: either because the tasks are too overwhelming and/or because the life competencies are underdeveloped or not fully formed. Threats to basic life embeddedness are experienced when persons for different reasons (exclusion, disregard of knowhow, non-recognition, loss of dear ones, economic crisis, migration, etc.) lose their grip on life and these fundamental life tasks. Threatened life embeddedness is often associated with self-uncertainty, i.e. you are not sure who you are, where you belong, and what direction to follow in life.[8] According to life psychology, people who experience threats to their life embeddedness will strive to (re)establish embeddedness, i.e. a state of flow where life tasks, life competencies, and resources are in harmony.[9] Likewise, people who experience self-uncertainty will search for new certainty.[10] Most people who experience threats to their life embeddedness and perhaps related self-uncertainty manage quite peacefully to reestablish embeddedness, for example by establishing new or reestablishing old belongings (friends, family, work, school), developing self-knowledge and identity (subcultural, political, religious), or acquiring new life competencies/resources (via education, therapy, coaching, etc.).

In rare cases, the search to (re)establish life embeddedness and reduce uncertainty can lead to political or religious radicalization. Several studies have shown that identification with a group can effectively reduce self-uncertainty.[11] This is particularly true for identification with high entitativity groups, i.e. groups that are relatively closed, bounded, unambiguous in terms of action, instructions, and moral directions, and whose members resemble each other and have a shared destiny.[12] These traits are common to many radical groups. The argument is that under certain conditions, identification with radical groups or projects may offer a refuge from perceived threatened life embeddedness and self-uncertainty. Identifying with a radical group or project, like Islamic State and its fight for an Islamic caliphate, offers 'easy' answers to complex questions, direction, and belonging.

It is remarkable how much narratives about exclusion from intimate communities (friends, school, work, housing) and society in general (in terms of values, politically) stand out in the individual stories in our data; so do accounts about being at odds with social morals and laws (crime, street violence, gang activity) and feeling uncertain about oneself, the future, and one's role in life. Many informants describe feelings of emptiness, frustration, anger, and apathy. We interpret this empirical pattern as an expression that the vast majority of the foreign fighters in our sample have experienced some form of threatened life embeddedness with an imbalanced existence – non-flow between life tasks and opportunities for and life competencies to solve these tasks.[13] The result is an urge to reconstruct life embeddedness and reduce uncertainty.

In Mahmoud's case (enters mentor project, does not go to Syria), a key factor of change appears to be when he moves with his family from a predominantly ethnic Danish, middle-class neighborhood to an area with a majority of Danes with immigrant background. Religion suddenly becomes an accessible and constant element in the form of religious symbols and in people's conversations. Mahmoud explains that after being separated from his familiar circle of friends and everyday life, he finds renewed peace, direction, and reference points in Islam. In his own words, he falls in love with his religion, which engulfs him and his interest more and more. His life becomes exclusively focused on religion – it becomes a monomaniac project.[14] Shortly after, Mahmoud encounters a group that works actively to recruit young people to go to Syria. Mahmoud quickly bonds with the group and expresses great joy with the fellowship (experiences renewed life embeddedness).

In Amir's case (goes to Syria, returns to Denmark), there are no sudden threats to his life embeddedness; his life was never really embedded (for personal reasons and due to the 'little' everyday exclusions he perceived). Amir had a relatively normal childhood in subsidized housing in Copenhagen with a Pakistani father and a Danish mother. From the age of 12–13 he hangs out with a group involved in petty crime.[15] When he is 17, his parents divorce and he has a falling out with his brother. Amir feels empty and looks for comfort elsewhere. He starts attending a moderate mosque and soon makes contact with a small, radical group, which guides Amir through religious preaching. Amir's identity complexity shrinks to the role of Muslim as he distances himself from non-believers (family, friends, etc.). Like Mahmoud, Amir explains how the group gives him a sense of fellowship, pride, and the feeling that he can unfold his life competences in a meaningful way (experiences life embeddedness and uncertainty reduction). He also describes his time in Syria as happy and as a time when everything fell into place and made sense.[16]

The young convert Martin's story is in many ways parallel (goes to Syria, perishes). Martin's life embeddedness has been challenged since his childhood by Asperger's and ADHD diagnoses.[17] Martin has a hard time in school and growing up he feels restless and rootless, he runs away from home several times, hangs out in the streets, and becomes involved in petty crime at a young age. In Islam, Martin finds peace for the first time in his life. Religion puts order in his everyday life, and he gives up petty crime. However, religion quickly becomes an all-engulfing project, and Martin loses the ability to put his own and others' philosophy of life into perspective. He avoids contact with non-Muslims and tries to convince his mother to convert.[18] Just as in Amir's case, his identity complexity shrinks to the role of Muslim (no room for the role of son, etc.), and he develops ambiguity intolerance.[19]

The three cases have several things in common. The pivotal point in all three stories is a craving for life embeddedness. All three experience immediate uncertainty reduction when they join a religious community, and they quickly encounter radicalizing milieus where they are introduced to new religious interpretations and demands, where travel to Syria is established as a duty, and Syria is established as the place where dreams about meaning, solidarity, marriage, heroic deeds, etc. come true. Going to Syria as a foreign fighter becomes a way to (re)construct life embeddedness – a way to cement a relatively newfound religious identity and live the dream about a new life, a fresh start, and an everyday life that is easy to understand (life/death, friend/enemy, right/wrong, etc.).

This pattern reappears – partly or completely – in almost all the cases for which we have data. The search for life embeddedness, rather than religion and political convictions as such, is a leitmotif for many foreign fighters beyond Denmark as Rik Coolsaet's analysis of Belgian foreign fighters in Syria demonstrates.[20]

Self-selection, social selection, and recruitment to radicalizing Islamist milieus

It is far from certain that a person who experiences threatened life embeddedness and is exposed to several other risk factors will become radicalized. And even if that person does become radicalized, a propensity to see political violence as an option is not necessarily acted upon. This often requires a form of contact with a radicalizing milieu with which the person identifies and that pushes actual action preparedness.[21] Foreign fighters thus rarely travel to Syria without discussing it with others first.

Building primarily on social movement theory about mobilization and recruitment, we next highlight three mechanisms that may facilitate encounters with radicalizing milieus: social selection, organizational outreach/recruitment, and self-selection.

One of the most solid conclusions in the study of social movements is that everybody who knows somebody who already participates in political protest and activism is far more likely to become active than people without such relations.[22] The costs of participation are reduced via existing social relations, and the benefits increase because you get to spend time with people about whom you care. Social relations with friends or family who are involved in radicalizing milieus may predispose an individual to follow this path to (re)establish life embeddedness. Persons with this type of 'privileged' access to radicalizing milieus are thus more vulnerable. Several studies have shown that social selection is the primary form of mobilization to high-risk activism, including violent groups.[23]

Martin's case underlines these insights. Martin converts to Islam via friends and begins to attend the mosque where he is later introduced to a radical group. When Martin decides to run away from the institution where he lives, he moves in with three men from the radical group. In Amir's case, his friendship with Fadi plays an important role. Amir and Fadi frequent the same radicalizing milieu, and Fadi leads the way by going to Syria before Amir. Our material also offers examples of how family relations bring persons into contact with radicalizing milieus. In two cases, one brother and then the other brother leave for Syria via Islamist milieus.

Radicalizing milieus also sometimes use direct recruiting outreach, i.e. radicalizing entrepreneurs make contact with young, often searching individuals via different recruitment strategies. Studies of radical Islamist milieus in Europe demonstrate use of front organizations like language courses or standard Quran lessons.[24] Others point to the role of charismatic leaders, often imams or self-appointed sheiks in recruitment.[25] Social movement theory theorizes this outreach between activist groups and potential supporters under the heading 'framing'. Framing theory claims that for mobilization to turn into activism, activism must be framed as both necessary and possible. A frame typically consists of a diagnosis (what's the problem), a prognosis (what has to be done), and a motivation (a register of motivation for action). 'Framing' is thus about creating resonance (recognition and sympathy) among potential supporters and motivating them to participate.[26]

The relevance of this perspective is shown in both Mahmoud's and Amir's cases. Mahmoud is contacted in the street by a group that is actively recruiting for Syria. Amir is spotted in a moderate mosque and invited to a home where he receives religious material that shows the 'real' interpretation of the messages he hears at the mosque. In both cases, recruiters exploit their existential and religious search to make contact and offer some of what they are looking for: fellowship, clear answers, and direction.

Finally, there is the mechanism of self-selection, i.e. individuals reaching out to radicalizing milieus. Self-selection is often triggered by framing activities, general references, or specific activities (social events, speeches, study circles, etc.). Media coverage of certain milieus plays an important role in this context as it informs searching individuals about radicalizing milieus and their framing. The general mobilization level and political climate also affect self-selection. Studies of social movements thus demonstrate that when mobilization has reached a certain level – critical mass – other participants often join on their own initiative.[27] The point is that self-selection to activism is more likely in a highly politicized situation (high on the political agenda) in which many have already shown the way to action. We argue below that this describes the situation with potential foreign fighters in Europe today.

Our detailed cases do not offer direct examples of self-selection to radicalizing milieus. All three actively sought out religious milieus, but were 'guided' from there by others toward radical Islam. However, there are examples of direct self-selection to radicalizing milieus in our broader material, among them a high school student who on his own initiative begins to attend the Grimhøjvej mosque in Aarhus, although he is from a city 50 miles away. Our data does not explain why he chooses to join this milieu, but it is hard to imagine, given media coverage, that he was unaware of Grimhøjvej mosque's controversial status within Denmark.

Enclave deliberation: Establishing and channeling action preparedness

It is a very clear pattern in our data that Danish foreign fighters before departure participate in intense interaction in radicalizing groups. Online interaction often plays a supplementary role, but face-to-face interaction with likeminded in small groups is dominant.[28] In all three detailed cases, interaction in the group becomes an all-important activity and project that makes it difficult to maintain old relations (friends, family, work, school, etc.). Still, they are happy. As the interaction intensifies, our case individuals express increasingly unambiguous opinions and their relations to others become more one-sided.

It is our assertion that this empirical pattern matches expectations based on social-psychological theory on group identification and group polarization. Research has shown that deliberation among persons who fundamentally identify with each other, share a series of key convictions, and are generally alike, tends to lead to group polarization, i.e. the opinions of the group become more extreme than the pre-deliberative starting point.[29]

Fellowship in and identification with a group gives the young people a sense of belonging, reduced uncertainty,[30] and thus renewed life embeddedness.[31] In the group they acquire a worldview that is simple and clear in terms of conduct, a manageable lifestyle framed as the only way to live, as God's will. Their search is given direction and meaning via fellowship with likeminded. That explains the perceived joy. Over time, the group members become increasingly sure about the truth of their convictions, and they share arguments, literature, videos, etc., which only confirm this (attitude confirmation and increasing attitude certainty). Deliberation in the group becomes closed, the pool of arguments shrinks to arguments that find corroboration in the Quran, and meaningful communication and relations with people outside the group become difficult. In all three cases, the young men's relations with family and friends deteriorate as interaction in the group intensifies. Martin's mother attempts discussions with her son, but is forced to recognize that his opinions are locked and his mind closed to counterarguments. Polarization and groupthink appears to be absolute.

However, radicalization of attitudes does not necessarily imply radicalization of actions. Establishing political violence as an option does not necessarily mean that an individual will participate in political violence. Departure to Syria as an option is established via different mechanisms in the group interaction, and religiously motivated action encouragement from scholars in the milieu plays a special role. Going to Syria is portrayed as a religious duty, a message that is repeated and shared in the group so often that it is established as a definitive truth that cannot be questioned. As Amir says: 'If I just stay home, God will punish me.' In contrast, Mahmoud says that his relation with his anti-radicalization mentor created an alternative space, a free space where, for instance, this truth could be discussed again. Congruent with other studies,[32] our material indicates that departure to conflict zones in general is legitimated in terms of religion in these milieus, whereas legitimation of terrorism against civilians in the West is contested.

Group interaction reinforces the relation between opinions (the caliphate is good, and I have a duty to help) and relevant high-risk action (travel to Syria) via development and cementing of strong feelings: political indignation, compassion, and hatred. Such strong feelings help liberate action possibilities that are otherwise morally sanctioned.[33] However, it is typical for our cases that the foreign fighters before departure carry out some preparatory, attitude-relevant actions[34]: Martin collects money for fighters in Syria; Mahmoud participates in dawa activities, a type of missionary outreach; and Amir reads and distributes violent manifestos and watches online videos of suicide actions on a daily basis. They all feel joy in doing something, in seeing themselves as doers. During these preparatory actions, they encounter additional action encouragements via direct contact with veterans. For example, Amir Skypes several times with his friend Fadi in Syria. Witnessing such exemplary behavior and hearing about life in the caliphate increases the likelihood that potential recruits will go. Both Mahmoud and Amir say that contact with veterans gives them respect for men of action and makes them feel shameful about their own petty actions, which pale in comparison and provoke even more radical action preparedness.[35] Once the decision to go to Syria is made, the necessary knowhow and resources are available in the young men's immediate environment. The distance from decision to departure is therefore often quite short in our material.

Who stays behind and why?

Of course, the explanation proposed above cannot account for all cases of voluntary departure to Syria or Iraq – there is not just one radicalization process, but many different pathways.[36] Our point is rather that the highlighted elements of radicalization in different ways and in multiple combinations are present in an overwhelming number of cases. They are robust across contexts.

As compelling as this type of explanation for going might be, it is quiet about the individuals from the same radicalizing milieus, with similar personal life stories, who end up staying behind. In most cases this group form the majority. In the following, we discuss what, if anything, sets these two groups a part. We do so pointing to two different explanations. On the one hand, the decision to stay behind can be explained as *a difference of degree*; those that stay behind are less radicalized and exhibit fewer risk factors and more protective factors (less disembedded; better life competences; more social ties outside the radicalizing milieu; fewer preparatory actions; more resilient to group dynamics, etc.). On the other hand, it might also be the case that those who stay behind are qualitatively different – *a difference of kind* – in terms of e.g. family background, perception of historical grievances, self-perception, their paths into radicalizing milieus, etc.

A difference in degree?

Two interesting findings from the social movement literature might provide insight into the drop off in size from radical to extremist movements and transitions to the use of violence and perhaps offer insight into radicals who stay in organizations vs. radicals who join terrorists. One source of the difference between members is suggested by McAdam,[37] who noted that participation in Freedom Summer in 1964 'was not correlated with individual attitudes but rather with three factors: the number of organizations individuals were members of, especially the political ones, the amount of previous experiences of collective action; and the links to other people who were involved with the campaign'.[38] Thus, it would seem that people who are most active in political and social movements, people who in Putnam's words who are less likely to Bowl Alone,[39] are potentially least likely to be marginalized or to feel marginalized by their activity. Their overlapping networks continually provide avenues for collective action.

Looking at the context of that activity and the society in which it occurs can provide further insight. Della Porta and Diani point out that 'Available evidence suggests that the more costly and dangerous the collective action, the stronger and more numerous the ties required for individuals to participate.'[40] That can lead us to two paths. First let us consider the relatively obvious. It is less dangerous in open democratic systems to organize and participate in radical social and political movements than in closed societies whether they have efficient and predictable or sporadic repressive machinery. It is also less dangerous to organize and participate in radical social and political movements if your demographic group is not a proscribed group. White South Africans more easily participated in anti-apartheid activities than black South Africans, white Americans in the civil rights movement in the South, etc. The second is that because of the danger, those who move directly from no group or organizational participation to activity with extremists are likely to be higher if participation in any group is dangerous. If we consider the difference in participation rates across nations, some explanations for the differences might emerge through the combination of integration into embedded societies, participation in civic social movement organizations, and marginalization and eventual movement to extremist organizations.

A difference in kind?

Our data does not indicate that there are significant differences in family backgrounds or historical grievances between those that stay or go. Both those that go and those that stay seem to come from all kinds of backgrounds – work migrants, refugees, converts. No pattern in terms of nationality – it is not just those with direct grievances related to the conflict in Syria that go and those without that stay behind. Perhaps the risk of ending up going abroad is greater for the 'lone seeker' who either seek out radicalizing milieus on his own or who is recruited individually as compared to those that join through social ties? Our data does not seem to support that this distinction matters. There is some indication in our data that there is a different self-perception among some of those that stay behind: they see themselves less as 'doers' and more as 'ideologues' or 'recruiters'. But this only accounts for the choice of some leading members. Age is clearly a factor in the recruitment of foreign fighters. But, interestingly, while the young are most inclined to action they still are not automatically ready to carry out violent acts for whatever cause. And here we find another possible explanation for the long tail. While Shakespeare's Henry V extolled the few, the band of brothers that were willing to sheds their blood with and for him and England, researchers since the publication of *The American Soldier* in 1949 have found that in most circumstances, most of the time, most persons won't easily shed that of others (or their own) except under particular circumstances and most importantly not until after some rigorous training. The necessary training is as much about the removal of inhibitions to do harm and why as it is about the techniques of the violence itself. Stouffer et al. found that only 15–25% of American Soldiers in World War II were able to discharge their weapons in battle.[41] Stouffer's studies indicated that soldiers had to be trained to fire their weapons and that broader calls to defend 'mom and apple pie' were not as useful as stressing the individual's relationship with, and dependence on, the band of brothers in the platoon. Men were willing to engage and shoot to defend each other to increase their chances of survival. Stouffer's analyses became the basis of US military basic training soon thereafter. That this is true beyond government military organizations is asserted more recently by Scott Atran in his analysis of religiously motivated terrorists: 'Maybe people don't kill and die simply for a cause, they do it for friends ... action pals who share a cause.'[42] And yet we know that while most persons won't commit acts of violence voluntarily, those who commit to doing so are, of course, the subject of our inquiry.

Kelman[43] provides some insight into the mechanisms which are probably at work in helping to ease the movement of recruits needed to move beyond the normal inhibitions and down the path to go and fight. These insights perhaps also offer some insight as to differences in both the numbers of 'violent perpetrators' in different types of groups. Kelman's 1973 argument in 'Violence Without Moral Restraint', is that three factors – dehumanization, routinization, and authorization – which he employs to understand what he later referred to as crimes of obedience underlie the transition of individuals who would not 'normally' act as agents of violence into organizational weapons. Jones[44] cites Bandura who building upon Kelman, argues further that some of the mechanisms by which a human being's tendencies toward empathy and compassion are disengaged are the 'redefinition of harmful conduct as morally justified', 'sanitizing language', 'diffusion of responsibility within a group', minimizing the harm done', and 'dehumanizing the victims and blaming them for the harm done to them'. Bandura[45] adds that strangers can be more easily depersonalized than acquaintances because of a lack of moral obligation to try and comprehend a stranger. Examination of the relevance of these factors awaits comparisons of the training and information received by potential recruits and the differences which exist between those that stay and those that go.

How much of a threat is posed by those that return?

At the beginning of 2015, the picture of foreign fighters and homecomings from selected European countries looked as depicted in Table 1.

Of the young men (and women) who have been traveling to the combat zones of the Middle East the last years roughly only between 20% and 30% have

Table 1. Estimated number of foreign fighters to Syria and returnees from selected European countries by the beginning of 2015.

	Foreign Fighters	Returnees
United Kingdom	700	200
Germany	650	200
Belgium	438	122
The Netherlands	190	35
Denmark	130	***

(*Source:* European Parliament, 'Foreign Fighters'.)

come home again. Most of these are not imprisoned and not participating in any exit programs. Maybe the term 'foreign fighters' should be taken with a grain of salt. In fact, most returnees have not been engaged in combat at all. There are no clear-cut typologies regarding either motives for becoming foreign fighters or the personal state, conviction, attitude, and behavior of the homecoming foreign fighter.

The profiles (not clear-cut but rather interwoven) of the homecomings can roughly be divided into (a) *Disillusioned:* They may have left as foreign fighters with romantic and/or fundamentalist ideas of and hope for a better world and being part of heroic battles, comradeship and with clear ideas of good and bad, but what they found was evilness, cruelty, corruption, perverted misuse of Islam, moral disengagement, and unreliable change of loyalties on *their* side of the front. Some of the homecomings also report boredom, not being part of the activities and excitements hoped for, but rather being stationed at unimportant (lonely) outposts, doing trivial routine jobs, and receiving endless tedious and dull religious lessons. (b) *Mental health issues*: Some have mental health problems when coming home. These can partly be due to worsening of problems that existed prior to leaving for the combat zones, e.g. due to dysfunctional families, disordered relations, or and attachment, but also identity problems, personality disorders, or disorders such as ADHD. Partly the mental health issues can be the result of traumas (not necessarily due to experienced battle, but also due to intern cruelties in one's battle group or toward civilians) resulting in PTDS. We should be especially aware of cases of moral injury,[46] i.e. a personality disorder caused by having witnessed or having been forced to engage in cruelties and inhumane actions one would not have thought possible, resulting in loss of faith in one's own and one's fellow humans' ability to act as moral beings. Without faith in fundamental human values and without a moral compass (i.e. total moral disengagement), these homecoming young men (and women) can be extremely dangerous ticking bombs. (c) *Further radicalized:* Last but not least, some of the homecomings may have been even further radicalized. That, however, seems to be the (of course dangerous) exception rather than the rule.[47]

However, we lack international cross-country studies of the different personal states of the homecomings and their ability and need of help to be re-included in society. This is even more important because we need to develop effective exit programs. There is no (politically sane) way that Europe can prosecute or jail every homecoming foreign fighter. Think of it this way: When ISIS has been defeated there will still be thousands of Western foreign fighters in the area and where should they go? If we cannot, or for political reasons don't want to, find ways to genuinely re-include them into societies, we will end up with an alarmingly large army of radicalized young nomads drifting around searching for the next and possible even worse terror organization to crystalize.

While much awareness and much political debate has been directed at homecoming foreign fighters, it has proven extremely important to be aware of those radicalized who have not yet become foreign fighters. Again there are no clear-cut profiles, but two important groups seem to stand out. (a) *Young people being radicalized in jail*: They can be politically radicalized and religiously radicalized e.g. into extremist Islamism. Obviously not all in-jail trajectories into Islam are directed at violent Jihad; on the contrary, some forms of studying Islam can in fact have deradicalizing effects because the individual is coming to a deeper and more peaceful understanding of human conditions, ethics, and politics. Another type of in-jail radicalization is pseudo-Islamism, which has little to do with genuine fate or political Islam. These people use selected Islamist catchphrases as a sort of narrative legitimation of a counter-identity which is not rooted in political or religious agendas, but rather in (social and psychological disordered) general distancing to everything else: other groups in jail, society, culture, etc. (b) *Young people 'dying to belong'* (paraphrasing the 1997 hit movie): The Copenhagen terrorist attack in February 2015, carried out by Omar Abdel Hamid El-Hussain, may very well be a tragic example of a syndrome of socio-psychological breakdown, youth crime, and what may be termed 'dying to belong': a young man just released from jail, but tragically (and unwisely) left on his own. Furthermore, Omar was multi-excluded, i.e. excluded not only from his social networks and from society but even excluded from radicalized groups and criminal gangs, but nevertheless with the human need of embeddedness (see above). Omar turned into a copycat looking for what may give him some street credit, hoping thereby to be accepted somewhere. He looked to Paris and found his desperate inspiration in the Charlie Hebdo terrorist attack. The phrase 'dying to belong' does not indicate any form of suicidal project, but rather that he, and others like him, are willing to 'go all the way' without clear ideas of what that would mean.

The conclusion here is that we are very much in need of more solid scientific knowledge combined with political willingness to invest in proper exit strategies coping both with the radicalization processes in jail as well as among desperate multi-excluded youngsters. Without this, those that stay behind may very well pose a greater threat than those who actually become foreign fighters and return.

Concluding remarks

In this article we have argued that in contrast to the common impression in media portrayals, most foreign fighters who go to Syria are not driven primarily by ideology or hatred of the West. Of course, a sense of exclusion may have nourished an us vs. them feeling. However, the underlying and the central driving force in our cases is a feeling of threatened life embeddedness, which triggers self-uncertainty and a subsequent search for embeddedness and uncertainty reduction. The young people feel excluded, alienated, and lack existential meaning – for different reasons. They do not have competences and resources to manage their lives and life tasks, and many of them harbor reinforcing risk factors like ambiguity intolerance, aggression, and absence of critical reflection. Their search for belonging and meaning brings them into contact with radicalizing milieus. They seek them out or are channeled in that direction via friends and acquaintances, and in some cases they are actively recruited by radical milieus. Via one-sided, closed deliberation, the young people's opinions become polarized, they develop a monomaniac interest in the radical project and isolate themselves from previous relations. Us/them experiences and critical opinions about life in the West have earlier been parts of a shared experience in line with other possible self-narratives. However, it is with polarization, monomania, and low identity complexity that hatred of the West is articulated purely and as the main legitimation of foreign fighting.

At the same time, the young people experience a new sense of fellowship and pride in 'doing something'. For many Danish foreign fighters, the interaction in radicalizing milieus normalizes violence and establishes departure to Syria as an option. Direct and indirect encouragements to go to Syria (for example when friends go or religious scholars portray the war as a religious duty) make attitudes and action preparedness fuse.

This account of why Danish Muslims end up participating in the insurgencies in Syria and Iraq connected to the Islamic State as well as the anti-Assad forces in Syria, we argue, is transferable to other European contexts. Our answer to the question 'who goes and why' will not account for all cases of European foreign fighters, but we contend that the explanatory ingredients highlighted by the article will be present in different combinations in the majority of cases.

Regarding the question of 'who stays behind and why' much more research is necessary. In this article we have limited ourselves to some first reflections on potential differentiations between those who go and those who under similar circumstances and with similar characteristics stay behind. One question for future research to address more thoroughly is whether to consider this a difference of degree or a difference of kind. Building on our limited data and research in neighboring areas, we are inclined to point toward a difference of degree. There is little to suggest that those who stay behind are qualitatively different in terms of ethno-national background, experienced historical grievances, or family situation than those who go. Instead it seems like those who go experience more severe lack of embeddedness, have fewer protective social ties, grow more dependent on radicalizing milieus, and, thus, are exposed to more enclave deliberation than those who stay. One potential interesting hypothesis to investigate further highlights the importance of the mechanism by which individuals enter into radicalizing milieus. Building on our data and extant knowledge, it could be hypothesized that the risk of taking the full step and going abroad as a foreign fighter is greater for those who seek out or are recruited to radicalizing milieus alone as compared to those who enter into the milieu via pre-established social ties to friends or relatives. Those who experience an overlap between friends and the radicalizing milieu might more easily find a sense of belonging, meaning, and embeddedness in the milieu at home and experience less of a need to make the radicalizing milieu a stepping-stone to communities of fighters abroad perceived to be even more rewarding. Paradoxically, good friends in the radicalizing milieu could in this case be considered a protective factor – not from radicalization as such, but from engaging in attitude corresponding risky action (going abroad). In contrast, if long-term friends chose to go (like Fadi in the case of Amir) this would increase the propensity to go.

Addressing the question of 'how much a threat is posed by those that return' we found that at least among the returnees in our study further radicalization was a relatively rare outcome. More often than not the returnees expressed disappointment and disillusionment with what they had experienced abroad or they were marked by these experiences psychologically, boosting new or old mental health issues in a way that sidetracked and made less important any political motivations or radical projects. Obviously, if left alone and not attended to, such mental health issues may become a risk factor in combination with prior radicalization and acquired knowhow. This would especially be the case if returnees were left to reintegrate into radicalized milieus where they are often received as stars.

However, as proposed in the article, maybe there is a need, in terms of building long-term security, to focus not just on returned foreign fighters, but also more on some of the groups of vulnerable youngsters who stay behind. Looking at the involvement by returned Islamist fighters in the last wave of terrorist attacks in Europe would suggest such a refocusing of attention. Special attention should be paid to radicalization in jails and the group of youngsters who are 'dying to belong', but who for different reasons do not get involved with radicalizing milieus and instead proceed toward violence as lone actors – often inspired by other successful attacks. The offender of the Copenhagen attack in February 2015 is an example in question. Omar Abdel Hamid El-Hussain was radicalized in jail (serving a two-year sentence for stabbing) to a degree that prison guards made no fewer than three reports to the Danish Prison and Probation Service about his behavior and attitudes, including a report on Omar expressing a desire to go to Syria and fight when he was released. This last report was passed on to the Danish Security and Intelligence Service. Nevertheless, when Omar was released no further steps were taken. Omar did not go to Syria or get involved with any radicalizing milieus. Instead, two weeks after his release, he carried out the Copenhagen attack alone, inspired, it seems, by the Paris attacks a month earlier.

Omar's story reminds us of the potential risk posed by those who share the experience of lack of embeddedness with many foreign fighters as well as individuals in radicalizing milieus who do not go abroad (Omar's life story is in many ways similar to that of Amir), but who for different reasons radicalize primarily alone and stay at the very fringes of radicalizing milieus – if in contact with them at all. Attacks by lone actor extremists is, as acknowledged by authorities and experts, extremely difficult to prevent and interdict. However, Omar's story also shows that it is not impossible (several 'red alerts' sounded before the attack), but that it takes effective communication between different authorities as well as political willingness to invest, not just in exit programs for returned foreign fighters, but also for certain types of released prisoners.

Notes

1. CTA, *Udviklingen i terrortruslen*.
2. Bouhanna and Wikström, 'Theorizing Terrorism', 10.
3. Coolsaet, 'What Drives Europeans to Syria', 3.
4. Bertelsen, 'Danish Preventive Measures'; Braw, 'Inside Denmark's Radical Jihadist Rehabilitation Programme'.
5. Regeringen, *Forebyggelse*.
6. Coolsaet, 'What Drives Europeans to Syria'; Barrett, 'Foreign Fighters in Syria'; Weggemans et al., 'Who Are They'.
7. Bertelsen, *Tilværelsespsykologi*; *Threatened Fundamental Life Embeddedness*.
8. Hogg, 'Self-Uncertainty'; 'From Uncertainty to Extremism'.
9. Bertelsen, *Threatened Fundamental Life Embeddedness*, 3.
10. Hogg, 'From Uncertainty to Extremism'.
11. Hogg et al., 'The Solace of Radicalism'; Hogg and Adelman, 'Uncertainty-Identity Theory'.
12. Hogg, 'Self-Uncertainty'; 'From Uncertainty to Extremism'; McCauley and Moskalenko, 'Mechanisms of Political Radicalization'.
13. Bertelsen, *Threatened Fundamental Life Embeddedness*.
14. Ibid., 9.
15. Sheikh, 'Fra barndommens gade'.
16. See also Weggemans et al., 'Who Are They'.
17. Sheikh, 'Fra barndommens gade'.
18. Compare with life story 1 in Weggemans et al., 'Who Are They'.
19. Bertelsen, *Threatened Fundamental Life Embeddedness*, 10.
20. Coolsaet, 'What Drives Europeans to Syria', 13.
21. Lindekilde, 'Abu Shaibul's Study Group'.
22. Schussman and Soule, 'Process and Protest'.
23. Wiktorovitz, *Radical Islam Rising*; della Porta, *Social Movements*; Sageman, *Leaderless Jihad*.
24. Lindekilde and Kühle, *Radicalization*.
25. Wiktorowicz, *Radical Islam Rising*.
26. Snow et al., 'Frame Alignment Processes'; Noakes and Johnston, 'Frames of Protest'.
27. Tarrow, *Power in Movement*.
28. See also Weggemans et al., 'Who Are They', 7.
29. Myers, 'Discussion-induced Attitude Polarization'; Isenberg, 'Group Polarization'.
30. Hogg, 'Self-Uncertainty'; 'From Uncertainty to Extremism'.
31. Bertelsen, *Threatened Fundamental Life Embeddedness*.
32. Lindekilde and Kühle, *Radicalization*; Hegghammer, 'Should I Stay or Should I Go', 8.
33. Abelson, 'Are Attitudes Necessary?'
34. Cf. Weggemans et al., 'Who Are They'.

35. Cf. social comparison effect, Myers et al., 'Does Learning Others' Opinions'.
36. Schmid, 'Radicalisation'; McCauley and Moskalenko, *Friction*.
37. McAdam, 'Recruitment to High-Risk Activism'.
38. See Della Porta and Diani, *Social Movements*, 117.
39. Putnam, *Bowling Alone*.
40. Della Porta and Diani, *Social Movements*, 118.
41. Stouffer et al., *The American Soldier*.
42. Atran, 'The Making of a Terrorist', 13.
43. Kelman, 'Violence Without Moral Restraint'.
44. Jones, *Blood That Cries Out*, 15; Bandura, 'Moral Disengagement'.
45. Bandura, 'Selective Moral Disengagement'.
46. Litz et al., 'Moral Injury'.
47. See also Hemmingsen, 'Bliver Syrien en skole'.

Disclosure statement

No potential conflict of interest was reported by the authors.

Funding

This work was supported by the Carlsbergfondet [grant number 2013-01-0120]; The Danish Council for Independent Research(Det Frie Forskningsråd) [grant number DFF 1329-00155].

References

Abelson, Robert. "Are Attitudes Necessary?" In *Attitudes, Conflict, and Social Change*, edited by Bert King and Elliott McGinnies. New York, NY: Academic Press, 1972: 19–32.

Atran, Scott. "The Making of a Terrorist: A Need for Understanding from the Field." *Testimony before the House Appropriations Subcommittee on Homeland Security, Washington, DC* 12 (2008).

Bakker, Edwin. "Characteristics of Jihadi Terrorists in Europe (2001–2009)." In *Jihadi Terrorism and the Radicalization Challenge*, edited by Rik Coolsaet. Farnham: Ashgate, 2011: 131–145.

Bandura, Albert. "Moral Disengagement in the Perpetration of Inhumanities." *Personality and Social Psychology Review* 3, no. 3 (1999): 193–209.

Bandura, Albert. "Selective Moral Disengagement in the Exercise of Moral Agency." *Journal of Moral Education* 31, no. 2 (2002): 101–119.

Baron, Robert et al. 'Social Corroboration and Opinion Extremity'. *Journal of Experiential Social Psychology* 32 (1996): 537–560.

Barrett, Richard. 'Foreign Fighters in Syria'. The Soufan Group, http://soufangroup.com/wp-content/uploads/2014/06/TSG-Foreign-Fighters-in-Syria.pdf, 2014.

Bertelsen, Preben. Violent Radicalization and Extremism. A review of Risk Factors and a theoretical Model of Radicalization. Translated from a Danish publication: Bertelsen, Preben. Voldelig radikalisering. i Tilværelsespsykologiens optik. I: Hansen Lund, J. (ed.).: Tværprofessionelt samarbejde om udsathed blandt børn og unge. Aarhus, Turbine, 2016. Can be found on http://psy.au.dk/pb.

Bertelsen, Preben. 'Radikaliserende mobilisering og tilværelsespsykologisk orienteret mentorforløb'. Case summary based on mentors' notes and case description, and PB's interview with mentor, 2015.

Bertelsen, Preben. *Threatened Fundamental Life Embeddedness and Violent Radicalization*. Under review at Political Psychology, 2015.

Bertelsen, Preben. *Tilværelsespsykologi. Et godt nok greb om tilværelsen*. Copenhagen: Frydenlund, 2013.

Bouhana, N. and P-O.Wikström (2010). 'Theorizing Terrorism: Terrorism as Moral Action'. *Contemporary Readings in Law and Social Justice* 2, no. 2 (2010): 9–79.

Braw, Elisabeth. 'Inside Denmark's Radical Jihadist Rehabilitation Programme'. *Newsweek*, October 17, 2014.

Coolsaet, Rik. 'What Drives Europeans to Syria, and to IS? Insights from the Belgian Case'. *Egmont paper 75*. Egmont – Royal Institute for International Relations, 2015.

CTA. *Udviklingen i terrortruslen fra personer udrejst fra Danmark til Syrien*. Center for Terroranalyse, Politiets Efterretningstjeneste, 2014.

della Porta, Donatella. *Social Movements, Political Violence and the State. A Comparative Analysis of Italy and Germany*. Cambridge: Cambridge University Press, 1995.

della, Porta D.and Mario Diani. *Social Movements: An Introduction*. Malden, MA: Blackwell, 2006.

European Parliament. 'Foreign Fighters: Member state's responses and EU actions in an international context'. Briefing, February 2015. http://www.europarl.europa.eu/EPRS/EPRS-Briefing-548980-Foreign-fighters-FINAL.pdf.

Hegghammer, Thomas. 'Should I Stay or Should I Go? Explaining Variation in Western Jihadists' Choice between Domestic and Foreign Fighting'. *American Political Science Review* 107, no. 1 (2013), doi: http://dx.doi.org/10.1017/S0003055412000615.

Hemmingsen, Ann-Sophie. "Bliver Syrien en skole for terrorister?" In *Mellemøstens nye verden*, edited by Clement Behrendt Kjærsgaard and Lars Erslev Andersen, 28–42. Ræson og DIIS: København, 2013.

Hogg, Michael (2014). 'From Uncertainty to Extremism: Social Categorization and Identity Processes'. *Current Directions in Psychological Science* 23, no. 5 (2014): 338–342.

Hogg, Michael (2012). 'Self-Uncertainty, Social Identity and the Solace of Extremism'. In *Extremism and the Psychology of Uncertainty*, edited by Michael Hogg and Danielle Blaylock, West Sussex: Blackwell Publishing, 2012: 19–35.

Hogg, Michael, and Janice Adelman. "Uncertainty-Identity Theory: Extreme Groups, Radical Behavior, and the Authoritarian Leadership." *Journal of Social Issues* 69, no. 3 (2013): 436–454.

Hogg, Michael, Christie Meehan, and Jayne Farquharson. "The Solace of Radicalism: Self-Uncertainty and Group Identification in the Face of Threat." *Journal of Experimental Social Psychology* 46 (2010): 1061–1066.

Isenberg, D. J. "Group Polarization: A Critical Review and Meta-analysis." *Journal of Personality and Social Psychology* 50 (1986): 1141–1151.

Jones, James. *Blood That Cries Out From the Earth: The Psychology of Religious Terrorism*. Oxford: Oxford University Press, 2008.

Kelman, Herbert G. "Violence Without Moral Restraint: Reflections on the Dehumanization of Victims and Victimizers." *Journal of Social Issues* 29, no. 4 (1973): 25–61.

Lindekilde, Lasse. 'Abu Shaibul's Study Group: Small Group Dynamics and Radicalization'. Paper, Multi-Disciplinary Workshop on Group Attitude Formation, Group Centrism and Extremism, University of California Santa Barbara, November 14, 2014.

Lindekilde, Lasse and Lene Kühle. *Radicalization among Young Muslims in Aarhus*. Research report, Centre for the Study of Islamism and Radicalization Processes, Aarhus University, 2009. http://cir.au.dk/fileadmin/site_files/filer_statskundskab/subsites/cir/radicalization_aarhus_FINAL.pdf

Litz, B. T., Stein, N., Delaney, E., Lebowitz, L., Nash, W.P., Silva, C., and Maguen, S. (2009). 'Moral Injury and Moral Repair in War Veterans: A Preliminary Model and Intervention Strategy'. *Clinical Psychology Review* 29, no. 8 (2009): 695–706.

McAdam, Doug. "Recruitment to High-Risk Activism: The Case of Freedom Summer." *American Journal of Sociology* 92, no. 1 (1986): 64–90.

McCauley, C. and S. Moskalenko (2008). 'Mechanisms of Political Radicalization: Pathways towards Terrorism'. *Terrorism and Political Violence* 20, no. 3 (2008): 415–433.

McCauley, C., and S. Moskalenko. *Friction: How Radicalisation Happens to Them and Us*. Oxford: Oxford University Press, 2011.

Myers, David G. 'Discussion-induced Attitude Polarization'. *Human Relations* 28 (1975): 699–714.

Myers, David G. et al. 'Does Learning Others' Opinions Change One's Opinion?' *Personality and Social Psychology Bulletin* 83 (1980): 603–627.

Noakes, John A. and Hank Johnston 'Frames of Protest: A Road Map to a Perspective'. In *Frames of Protest: Social Movements and the Framing Perspective*, edited by Hank Johnston and John A. Noakes, Lanham, Mayland: Rowman & Littlefield, 2005.

Putnam, Robert D. *Bowling Alone: The Collapse and Revival of American Community*. New York: Simon and Schuster, 2001: 1–29.

Regeringen. *Forebyggelse af ekstremisme og radikalisering. Regeringens handlingsplan.* 2014. http://sm.dk/filer/nyheder/handlingsplan-om-forebyggelse-af-radikalisering-og-ekstremisme-tilgaengelig.pdf.

Sageman, Marc. *Leaderless Jihad: Terror Networks in the Twenty-First Century*. Philadelphia, PA: University of Pennsylvania Press, 2008.

Schmid, Alex P. 'Radicalisation, De-Radicalisation, Counter-Radicalisation: A Conceptual Discussion and Literature Review'. *ICCT Research Paper*, March 2013. http://www.icct.nl/download/file/ICCT-Schmid-Radicalisation-De-Radicalisation-Counter-Radicalisation-March-2013.pdf.

Schussman, Alan, and Sarah S. Soule. "Process and Protest: Accounting for Individual Protest Participation." *Social Forces* 84 (2005): 1081–1106.

Sheikh, Jakob. 'Fra barndommens gade til kalifatets frontlinje', *Politiken*, September 21, 2014.

Snow, David A. "E. Burke Rochford, Jr., Steven K. Worden, and Robert D. Benford. 'Frame Alignment Processes, Micromobilization, and Movement Participation.'" *American Sociological Review* 51, no. 4 (1986): 464–481.

Stouffer, Samuel A. et al. *The American Soldier: Combat and Its Aftermath*. Studies in Social Psychology in World War II, Vol. 2. Princeton, NJ: A. H. Publishing, 1949.

Tarrow, Sidney. *Power in Movement*. Cambridge: Cambridge University Press, 1994.

Weggemans, Daan, Edwin Bakker, and Peter Grol. "Who Are They and Why Do They Go? The Radicalization and Preparatory Processes of Dutch Jihadist Foreign Fighters." *Perspectives on Terrorism* 8, no. 4 (2014): 1–9.

Wiktorowicz, Quintan. *Radical Islam Rising: Muslim Extremism in the West*. Oxford: Rowman & Littlefield, 2005.

A Sectarian Jihad in Nigeria: The Case of Boko Haram

Marc-Antoine Pérouse de Montclos

ABSTRACT
Boko Haram is an Islamic sect turned terrorist group. Despite its ethnic leaning, it is not a liberation front, and it does not advocate a people's revolution. From an ideological point of view, it is a jihadist movement because it fights for full implementation of strict sharia law which would require a change of political regime and the establishment of an Islamic state. But it does not really follow the Wahhabi model of Al Qaeda or Daesh, unlike AQIM in Northern Mali or Al Shabaab in Somalia. In the region of Greater Borno, which encompasses parts of Nigeria, Chad, Niger, and Cameroon, the sect remains embedded in local dynamics which this article explores through an analysis of the mobilization of its members.

[Boko Haram] is a resistance movement against misrule, rather than a purely Islamic group.[1]

Introduction

Better known under the nickname Boko Haram ('Western education is sacrilege'), the 'Sunni Community for the Propagation of the Prophet's Teachings and Jihad' (*Jama'atu Ahlis-Sunnah Lidda'awati Wal Jihad*) emerged in the Borno region of North-Eastern Nigeria, bordering Niger, Chad, and Cameroon. In March 2015, one of the factions of the group paid allegiance to Daesh and decided to be called the Islamic State in West Africa (*Wilayat Gharb Ifriqiyah*). Yet the internationalization of Boko Haram remains inconclusive and does not go much beyond video communication and the porous borders of the Sahel. Many observers jump to hasty conclusions because they rely on unverifiable information, believe in gossip, and do not have access to Borno. Based on fieldwork and a sociological investigation of Boko Haram combatants, this article seeks to provide a scholarly analysis that uses a wider range of sources and brings in new data for triangulation.[2] Indeed, the evolution of the ways of mobilizing insurgents bears witness to the importance of local dynamics.

The group has gone through four principal phases of recruitment, mainly in the region of Borno: firstly, a period of preaching (*da'awah*) under Mohammed Yusuf between 2003 and 2009; then, a descent into terrorism and hiding under Abubakar Shekau from 2010; a transformation into a guerrilla movement after the declaration of emergency rule in North-Eastern Nigeria in 2013; and finally a spatial expansion of attacks after the launch of an international coalition made up of Nigerian, Nigerien, Chadian, and Cameroonian armies in 2015. As for my investigative work, it started in 2005 along the Niger border with the 'Talebans of Nigeria', the seeds of a movement that would later be nicknamed Boko Haram.[3] After the extrajudicial killing of the founder of the sect in 2009, I visited Maiduguri, the group's fiefdom, several times, with the exception of the period 2013–2014, when the local airport was attacked and closed by the military. In the course of my investigation, I also met internally displaced persons as well as political and religious decision-makers in Kano, Zaria, and Abuja, and I interviewed refugees, Muslim clerics, and security officers in Diffa in the Republic of Niger, over 100 kilometers north of Maiduguri. To this corpus should be added 51 interviews with presumed members of Boko Haram in the Koutoukalé and Kollo prisons in Niger at the beginning of 2015.

I. From a local sect to a regional, albeit not international, threat

Many analyses oscillate between two pitfalls: on one hand, the theory of irrationality, which focuses on the cruelty and religious fanaticism of jihadist combatants; and on the other hand, the conspiracy theory that sees in the sect a well-organized, highly structured group that was planted in Nigeria by Al Qaeda or Daesh. The reality is in between the two. Before the military crackdown and the extrajudicial execution of its leader in 2009, Boko Haram first tried to convince people to join its ranks through an inner spiritual effort, the 'major jihad'. Mohammed Yusuf, a very charismatic and persuasive young speaker, began by preaching in mosques controlled by a Saudi-inspired Salafist movement called Izala. He then acquired his own religious center in the railway station district of Maiduguri. He especially drew the youth who were looking for 'the peace of the mind', to borrow the phrase of a combatant who joined the group in the little city of Geidam in 2006.[4] Others adhered to the sect because of family and generational conflicts. The possibility of marriage also attracted young men who were unable to pay for a dowry, a pre-Islamic African tradition challenged by Salafists.[5] Like every sect, Boko Haram was endogamous. Its members could only marry among themselves, with a 'discount', and some of them continued a kind of tradition of levirate marriage with widows if husbands died.[6]

The military crackdown in 2009 inaugurated a new period and exacerbated the sense of persecution of the sect. Chased from the cities, the movement went underground and fled into the countryside. In Maiduguri, Boko Haram houses were destroyed, sold, given to informers, or confiscated by district heads. Survivors sought revenge for the seizure of their goods and the murder of their relatives. With just a motorbike and an old gun, some started in 2010 to target and kill collaborators of the Borno State governor, Ali Modu Sherif, who was alleged to be very corrupt. After the brief interim leadership of Mallam Sanni Umaru, Abubakar Shekau also emerged and adopted terrorist methods such as suicide attacks and car bombings outside Borno. The 'hawks' thus took up the lead against the 'doves', who were killed by the security forces or the most radical elements in the group (see appendix). Through its brutality, the Nigerian army itself contributed to Boko Haram's recruitment. Abuse by security forces gave rise to sympathy for the victims, albeit not a true adhesion to the ideology of the sect. In spite of his total opposition to the ideas professed by Mohammed Yusuf, for example, an Izala sheikh from Sokoto, Abubakar Gero Argungu, said publicly that the members of Boko Haram killed in 2009 could be considered Muslim martyrs; following this declaration during Ramadan celebrations in Yola in 2010, his mediation was accepted by the insurgents in 2011.

Actually, inspectors generals of police and chiefs of army staff were quite aware of the perverse effects of their heavy-handed repression,[7] a position which raises serious questions about their inability to avoid abuse against civilians. Thus various investigation reports have never been published because they directly accused the security forces of responsibility for exacerbating the conflict. Established in 2011 and chaired by a former Kanuri ambassador from Nigeria to Chad, the Galtimari Commission needs to be quoted in this respect. Indeed, it has acknowledged the mistakes and 'atrocities' perpetrated by soldiers, police officers, and federal agents of the Joint Task Force (JTF). To mention but a few of its findings, it has pointed to a 'culture of impunity', the 'use of militia gangs', 'extra-judicial killings', 'incidences of rape', 'destruction of private property', violations of the rules of military engagement, lack of trust and collaboration, 'operational lapses', 'service rivalry', 'under-funding', 'under-equipment', rampant 'corruption', etc. 'In the face of such catalogue of unprofessional behavior,' wrote members of the Commission, 'it would be difficult to cultivate, let alone sustain, public support for continued military presence in the area.'[8]

As a result, it was recommended to 'replace the present troops with new ones' who would be familiar with the terrain, speak the local languages, and 'have a human touch, care and concern by avoiding unnecessary brutality and ruthlessness'. In addition, police officers linked to the murder of Mohammed Yusuf and his followers were to be tried, a judicial commission of inquiry was to look into the atrocities committed by some JTF personnel, the victims of the crisis were to be paid compensation for damaged property, and the hospital bills of those who sustained injuries were to be refunded. Finally, the authorities were to identify third parties to open dialog with the insurgents and restore their confidence by transferring 'back to Maiduguri with adequate publicity' 61 detained members of Boko Haram who were alleged to have been killed.

By way of conclusion, the members of the Galtimari Commission expressed regret that the recommendations of their predecessors were never implemented. Their own report was also dumped. In Borno and Yobe, civilians still continued to join the ranks of insurgents to seek revenge for parents killed by security forces or simply because they feared being arrested and tortured to death. In April 2013, the government inaugurated a Presidential Committee which was supposed to negotiate an amnesty. The insurgents demanded the unconditional release of the wives, children and relations of the sect's members detained by security agents, the swift trial of combatants, an amnesty for those who renounced membership of the group, and the conviction of all policemen involved in the killing of Mohamed Yusuf. However, they obtained nothing, except for a slight condemnation of junior policemen and the liberation of a few women and children in exchange for French hostages. Chaired by Malam Kabiru Turaki, a senior advocate, a gubernatorial candidate in the 2011 elections and a minister of special duties in the administration of Goodluck Jonathan, the Presidential Committee was not really committed to negotiate an amnesty and two of its members — an Islamic cleric, Datti Ahmed, and a political activist from Kaduna, Shehu Sani — declined to serve and denounced the bad faith of the government.

In fact, three months before the declaration of an emergency rule in North-Eastern Nigeria, passing of the Terrorism Act in February 2013 exacerbated the problem by authorizing the military to renew three-month detentions indefinitely and to hold suspects in custody without sending them before the police or the judicial system, which were believed to be too corrupt.[9] From this point of view, it appears that detention has been a key issue in the sect's development. The prison, rather than the mosque, has in effect become the place of recruitment, not so much because it allowed for the indoctrination of jihadists but because individuals arbitrarily arrested were likely to join the combatants who would free them. Thus, Boko Haram has destroyed or damaged 15 out of 18 prisons in Nigeria's North-East, as well as 106 out of 122 police stations and 10 out of 17 military barracks according to an official countdown for the years 2010–2015.

When Boko Haram resurfaced in 2010, its first military action was to attack the central prison in the city of Bauchi. At the time, the goal was to free members of the sect who could go back into combat and were in their thirties according to a survey of 144 suspects being held in detention.[10] But Nigerian prisons also have a characteristic in common with many others in Africa: most of their occupants are waiting for a trial that may never come. Very few of Boko Haram's combatants, for example, were convicted of terrorism and given a life sentence. In Nigeria, there were only 7 cases in 2013, 40 in 2014, and up to 110 in the first five months of 2015, statistics that should be compared with the tens of thousands of people apprehended by security forces since the beginning of the crackdown in 2009.[11] Cameroun, which was less impacted by the crisis, has been more proactive and condemned to death 89 "terrorists" in 2015 alone.[12]

By contrast, the category of ATPs (Awaiting Trial Prisoners) constituted a massive reservoir of recruits for Boko Haram. In the September 2010 attack, for instance, 721 out of 759 inmates escaped from Bauchi prison, including 150 members of the sect. While 35 illegally freed prisoners were rearrested and 30 willingly returned to serve out their short sentences, 506 thus possibly joined the insurgents.[13] Likewise, in March 2014, the Boko Haram attack on the Giwa military barracks in Maiduguri might have released between 800 and 1600 inmates who were given the option to join the insurgents; yet over 640 were recaptured and killed by the army.[14] It is certainly difficult to get details. A secretive and defiant Nigerian army refuses to give the names of its detainees to the judicial authorities; on the pretext of protecting witnesses, magistrates themselves often prefer to hold trials in camera, as in Lagos in September 2014, when a controversial judgment was passed on three alleged members of the sect. Amnesty International estimates that, in Nigeria alone, a total of 20,000 people have been imprisoned on suspicion of supporting Boko Haram.[15] Neighboring countries are equally concerned since they joined the war on terrorism. For Cameroon, unofficial sources report that around 500 people were imprisoned in Maroua at the beginning of 2015. In the Republic of Niger, the authorities have detained 200 suspects in the high security prison of Koutoukalé, to which have been added 160 others who were rounded up following battles in Bosso and Diffa in January 2015, and perhaps up to a total of 600 in May 2015. Chad has not provided any statistics.

Today, prisoners remain a major issue for Boko Haram in its demands as well as a means of recruitment. The main difference is that the group has lost social support since emergency rule was declared in Borno, Yobe, and Adamawa states in May 2013. Indeed, the Nigerian military eventually realized that they needed to win the hearts and minds of the people. So they set up local militias, called *Kato da Gora* ('the men with clubs'), who knew the terrain better and were able to root out insurgents hidden among the population. As a result, Boko Haram was no longer content with just retaliation and adopted a new strategy of terror by massacring entire villages in order to dissuade their inhabitants from joining the ranks of the Civilian Joint Task Force (CJTF). This in turn led to an escalation of violence, which took on the proportions of a civil war. In the same vein, Boko Haram began to pay 'volunteers' and coerce young recruits while using human shield to keep control of the areas it had seized. Like other guerrilla groups that did not profess Islam, Boko Haram forced children to kill their mothers and fathers so that they would be rejected by their folk and compelled to stay in their combat units. 'Collaborators', for instance, were often executed by members of their family to force parents to cooperate with the insurgents or to flee and denounce their own children to the military. According to witnesses in Maiduguri, it is also possible that combatants deliberately attacked the army in order to provoke retaliation and to push civilians toward joining the ranks of the sect.[16]

During the 2013–2014 period, the criminalization of Boko Haram basically resulted from three main challenges: thwarting local militias; making up lost revenues with pillaging; recruiting as new members 'mercenaries' who were motivated by money more than Islam. As it was no longer able to collect donations or reap the benefits of Mohammed Yusuf's investments in the microfinance sector, the sect resorted to kidnapping, extortion, and holding up banks which were accused of violating sharia by practicing usury.[17] Such criminalization is reminiscent of the path followed by other jihadist groups when their Islamic ideals were confronted with the realpolitik of managing territories. For example, the revolt of Usman dan Fodio started as a popular protest against the enslavement and forced labor of fellow Muslims, a practice that did not follow sharia rules and allowed for money payment as a substitute for conscription (*gargadi*) into the army. Consequently, recruitment of jihadist combatants was first done on a purely voluntary basis. After the death of Usman dan Fodio in 1817, however, the Caliphate of Sokoto became so institutionalized and bureaucratized that it conscripted slaves to form a permanent army in the 1860s.[18] Thus jihadists transgressed their own values by enslaving Muslims and delaying the conversion of pagans so that they would not have to enfranchise them and take labor away from the plantations that allowed the sultanate to maintain its troops.

The criminalization of Boko Haram also brings to mind the looting of Borno by Rabeh, a warlord more interested in pillage than in Mahadist doctrine at the very end of the nineteenth century. As early as July 2009, the sect was joined by thugs of the 'Ecomog' militia mobilized by Borno governor Ali Modu Shariff to win the regional elections in April 2003 and 2007. These youths, who lived in the Gidan Yashi area of Abbaganaram, very near to the religious center (*markaz*) of Mohamed Yusuf in Maiduguri, were motivated by money more than jihad. Since then, the insurgents also got connected with the armed robbers (*zargina*) of Northern Cameroon who engage in local kidnapping, smuggling, poaching in the Waza Game Reserve, and trafficking drugs such as Tramadol. In the same vein, the group attracted opportunist 'mercenaries' who were not considered Muslims, especially the Buduma of Lake Chad islands. On the other hand, the sect failed to convert Hausa fish traders, probably because the latter thought they were already Islamized and refused to pay a religious tax to the insurgents. Known for their attacks on travelers and their border trafficking, the Buduma are a non-Kanuri minority occasionally called Yedina or Kouri (from the word for their oxen).[19] They are well-versed in boat transport, raising livestock, and, to a lesser degree, fishing. Some of them joined Boko Haram to escape army raids, to take control of the fishing trade, and to get rid of the competition of Hausa 'immigrants' who came to Lake Chad in the 1970s. From this point of view, their determination to fight reveals not so much religious fanaticism as the necessity to make a living, together with the fear of being captured alive and tortured to death in prison, without any possibility of surrender.

Meanwhile, Boko Haram continued to recruit combatants because of the brutality of the military. Abuses by security forces are crucial for understanding the development of the sect. Gone is the time when policemen were described in the memoirs of a Borno colonial governor as polite, smiling, and serving the community.[20] After independence, the first military coup in 1966 and the Biafra

War in 1967–1970 gave the security forces a free license to kill. In the North, the basic police used to be a 'man carrying a baton': *dan sanda* in Hausa. Supplied with a Kalashnikov, he became much more brutal and was no longer accountable to the community since the military dismantled the Native Authorities' local militias and tried to promote an 'esprit de corps' by posting security officers outside their regions of origin in 'foreign' places where they did not speak vernacular languages. The authorities themselves approved of violence and extrajudicial killings. A governor of Niger State and a member of Muhammadu Buhari's junta in 1984, Colonel David Mark, for instance, said publicly that armed robbers ought to be burned alive.[21] Once elected president of the senate in 2007, he then advocated the death sentence for oil thieves.[22]

Thus extrajudicial killings are not collateral damage but a norm. The Nigerian security forces are trigger-happy, not to mention the practice of torture. As a result, they are unable to maintain law and order professionally and peacefully. On the contrary, the NigeriaWatch database on violence shows that the more they intervene, the bloodier the fighting. In the majority of fatalities in which they were involved, they were responsible for causing the death. The police, for instance, killed in 1561 of 2707 fatal incidents where they intervened in 2006–2014, an annual average of 58% lethal interventions which peaked at 80% in 2013–2014. The proportion is quite similar (57%) if we take into account all government security forces for the period 2006–2014, including the army, the secret services, customs, immigration, and civil defense.[23] Such a systematic pattern has a lot to do with a general culture of violence and impunity which triggered the uprising of Boko Haram in Maiduguri in July 2009.

Except for Amnesty International, however, the media and intergovernmental organizations generally find it easier and more politically correct to focus on the atrocities perpetrated by the sect. In a late 2015 report, for example, the United Nations Commission on Human Rights said it could not verify allegations about abuse by security forces. Yet it denounced Boko Haram atrocities that it could not investigate in the field either, while a press agency close to the UN lauded the merits of Nigerian prisons, which looked like Potemkin villages.[24] In fact, the army and the police have been responsible for half of the fatalities recorded by the NigeriaWatch database in the course of the conflict, especially after the extra-judicial killing of Mohammed Yusuf in July 2009. Out of 32,292 victims reported by the Nigerian press and human rights organizations between June 2006 and March 2016, 16,133 were killed by the security forces and 16,159 by the insurgents.[25] Actually, violations of the humanitarian law have not stopped even after an international coalition was put into place in January 2015. On the contrary, the security forces of Chad and Cameroon replicated the Nigerian army's mistakes, with collateral damage, arbitrary arrests, and extrajudicial executions that instigated a climate of fear likely to push civilians into the hands of the insurgents. In the villages of Bia, Doublé, and Magdeme along the border, for instance, Cameroonian forces have killed more than 71 people who were then buried in mass graves in Mindif. In turn, governmental militias took advantage of the situation to settle old scores and eliminate rivals in the areas around Amchidé and Cheripouri. In May 2015, the authorities themselves recognized that 25 prisoners had died in detention and that 192 civilians had 'disappeared', while human rights defense organizations counted 40 dead just in Maroua prison alone.[26]

Although its regime is more democratic under a president duly elected in March 2011, the Republic of Niger has also militarized its war on terror, with a 50% increase in troops in three years. In the region of Diffa, the declaration of a state of emergency in February 2015 immediately led to arbitrary arrests and two or three extrajudicial executions within the following two weeks. Officially, the objective was to control the population's movements, to create a buffer zone along the border, and to deprive Boko Haram of its financial sources.[27] Consequently, authorities of the Republic of Niger forbade selling gasoline, using vehicles registered in Nigeria, and traveling by boat or by motorcycle, both during the day and at night.[28] As a result, local peasants were no longer able to move, get fuel for their pumps, or export their pepper and their fish to Nigeria, a country that usually purchased about 80% of their agricultural products. The lack of market opportunities forced them to abandon their crops and pushed some youth to work for the insurgents. On Lake Chad, the army even ordered the total evacuation of islands after an attack that killed some 40 Nigerien soldiers in Karamga in April 2015. Forced to leave everything behind them, nearly 25,000 civilians had to walk north through the desert, up to N'Guigmi, where nothing had been prepared to receive them and from where some preferred to go south to rebel areas in Nigeria.

II. A jihadist sect with a difference

As of today, Boko Haram could thus go in one of three directions: dispersion and extinction, as happened to the Maitatsine Islamic sect after a Nigerian military crackdown in the city of Kano in 1980; recession, along the lines of the Lord's Resistance Army, who fled Uganda to hide with the remnants of combatants in the Central African Republic; internationalization in response to the regionalization of the war on terrorism under the aegis of the African Union. The first two scenarios are quite likely. At the beginning of 2015, the election in Nigeria of a Muslim from the North, Muhammadu Buhari, boosted morale and incited civilians in Borno to support the army once more, a crucial cooperation to win a war against an invisible enemy such as Boko Haram. Between resistance and collaboration, some factions of the sect may now be pushed to adopt a strategy of negotiation (*taqiyya*), which is condoned by Islam and which consists in temporarily giving up armed struggle when circumstances impose peaceful coexistence (*muwalat*) with the infidels.[29]

Because they fear arrest and torture, others might refuse to capitulate and opt to continue looting and fighting a 'low-cost' insurgency with no foreign funding but ongoing suicide attacks. The growing involvement of women and children in combat clearly shows that the group finds it more difficult to recruit new fighters and has probably no troops to send to Libya or Iraq. The first female suicide bombing to be reported was carried out on military barracks in Gombe State in June 2014. Since then, women and children have increasingly been involved in suicide attacks in Nigeria and neighboring countries, another characteristic that differentiates Boko Haram from the Islamic State in Iraq and Syria. Even if it is more millenarian and apocalyptic, Daesh has indeed governed a territory and tried to build political alliances with Sunni constituencies. On the contrary, Abubakar Shekau's group has antagonized almost all Muslims in the region and foreclosed the possibility of collaboration to run an Islamic State.[30] Also, it has been so brutal with Muslim civilians that it has lost social support and repulsed even Al Qaeda.

Thus the internationalization scenario is far less certain. In March 2015, a faction of the group paid allegiance to Daesh and took the name of the Islamic State in West Africa (*Wilayat Gharb Ifriqiyah*). But the similarities observed in the videos of the two entities cannot be interpreted as proof of an operational connection between the insurgents of Nigeria and those of Iraq, Syria, or Libya.[31] Actually, the allegiance to Daesh is first and foremost the communication war of an endogenous movement that always used references from abroad as well as from Nigeria, with the Sokoto Caliphate and the jihad of Usman dan Fodio in 1804. The 'Talebans', which were the embryo of the group, thus took their cues from Afghanistan when, in 2003, they established a rural base called 'Kandahar' at Kanama, near the Niger border. After his falling-out with the Izala movement, Mohammed Yusuf himself named his 'center' (*markaz*) in Maiduguri in honor of Ahmad Ibn Taymiyyah, a thirteenth-century Damascene theologian who came from the south of modern-day Turkey. The founder of Boko Haram also drew on the Salafi thoughts of the Palestinian-Jordanian Abu Muhammad al-Maqdisi, who mentored the leader of Al Qaeda in Iraq, Abu Mus'ab al-Zarqawi. Since then, his successors have somewhat expanded their territorial ambitions, and the new name of Boko Haram, the Islamic State in West Africa, refers to Ifriqiyah, one of the three provinces of the Maghreb in the Middles Ages.

Historically, this division only covered Tunisia, Tripolitania, and a part of Algeria including Constantine, Bijâya, and the Aurès Mountains. Thus its territory does not correspond to West Africa as it is understood today. But historical truth does not particularly concern contemporary jihadists. For example, in Mosul in July 2014, a month before the video in which Abubakar Shekau allegedly established a caliphate in Gwoza near the border to Cameroon,[32] Abu Bakr al-Baghdadi proclaimed himself great imam and commander of the faithful (*amir al-mu'mimin*) while completely ignoring Islamic jurisprudence (*fiqh*) for naming an emir to replace (*yakhlufu*) the prophet, act as his vicar, lead prayer, protect the religion, legislate on his behalf, and govern Muslims. Formerly, a caliph had to meet five conditions. He had to know Islamic science and law; show probity; prove his political and military competence; be physically apt; and, according to some, be of Quraysh descent.[33] In practice, his nomination followed strict rules of transmission.[34] In the territories of Syria and Iraq in the hands of the Islamic State today, religious norms have in fact been violated in order to construct a revolutionary discourse with a worldwide calling.

In the same line of thought, the followers of Boko Haram challenged the Nigerian Muslim establishment to legitimize their holy transnational war along porous borders. Daesh, which dates from 2014, was not their only foreign reference in this matter. As they disagreed with Abubakar Shekau, who killed mainly Muslims, certain members of the Shura (executive council) of the sect had already decided to leave the organization and follow the doctrine of Al Qaeda. For example, in August 2009, just after the assassination of Mohammed Yusuf, one of his successors, Mallam Sanni Umaru, declared to the Nigerian press:

> [Boko Haram] is just a version of the Al Qaeda, which we align with and respect. We support Osama bin Laden, we shall carry out his command in Nigeria until the country is totally Islamised, which is according to the wish of Allah.[35]

Hence in January 2012 a dissident group formed a 'Community of Defenders of Black Muslims' (*Jama'at Ansar Al Muslimin Fi Bilad al-Sudan*), criticizing Abubakar Shekau because his actions essentially targeted Muslims. Small in number but much closer to Al Qaeda in terms of doctrine, members of this 'Ansaru' faction have kidnapped and killed expatriates in Nigeria. They are also said to have participated in Mokhtar Belmokhtar's attacks against the In Amenas natural gas facility in Algeria and the Arlit uranium mine in Niger, in January and June 2013, respectively.[36] More recently, in February 2015, they again distributed a charter that confirmed their proximity to the ideology of Al Qaeda and just modified the name of their communications wing. However, it is not known if the group Ansaru is still active since the arrest of its leader by the Nigerian Army in April 2016.

Some followers of Mohammed Yusuf have thus been able to maintain individual contacts with other African or Arab jihadist groups.[37] Yet there exists no tangible evidence of any true alliance in the sense of coordinating attacks or attracting foreign combatants from Europe, America, or Asia. Specifically, none of the trials against Mohammed Yusuf in Nigeria have succeeded in proving his supposed links with an Islamist training camp in Mauritania or with the *Tablighi Jamaat* (Society for Spreading Faith) in Pakistan. Allegations of funding from a British NGO, the Al-Muntada Trust Fund, were also never proven, including in Great Britain.[38] In the same way, accusations made against Mohammed Ashafa, a follower of Boko Haram arrested in Kano in 2006, failed to prove that he received money from the Algerian Salafist Group for Preaching and Combat, the GSPC (*Groupe salafiste pour la prédication et le combat*), to recruit and train 21 combatants at a place called Agwan in Niger State. If one believes the story of Aliyu Tishau, a former commandant of the sect in Bauchi arrested by the Nigerian secret services before escaping in 2011, Mohammed Yusuf actually refused to send mercenaries to Islamist groups involved in a plot in Mauritania in 2004.[39]

Conclusion

To understand the development of Boko Haram properly, the problem is in fact to crosscheck partial or contradictory information. A first challenge is to go inside the 'haze of dust', a metaphor referring to the artificial sandstorm created by Tuareg rebels to cover combatants and confuse victims.[40] Military propaganda does not help either. The analysis is often spoiled by the storytelling of a global jihad linked to Al Qaeda or Daesh. Such narratives are not only popular in the media, they also help authoritarian and corrupt regimes to get international financial and military support in their war on terrorism.[41] Nonetheless, Boko Haram did not need any foreign instruction to rebel against the Nigerian government. The criminalization of the sect has been deeply embedded in local dynamics that now reveal the complexity of a global jihad degenerated into a multitude of micro social conflicts.

Undoubtedly, the internationalization of the response to terrorism could contribute to internationalizing the Islamic State in West Africa. But the internal dynamics of the conflict in Greater Borno also open ways for a local settlement, especially with the last waves of Boko Haram recruits: 'mercenaries', opportunist Buduma fishermen, child soldiers, captured civilians . . . Buying social peace and granting an amnesty to combatants would certainly have a high price and would not solve other issues related, for instance, to reconciliation within families torn apart by the conflict in Borno. Moreover, the core group of fanatics would remain a problem. But a realistic approach points to the fact that fighting Boko Haram in Libya, in Iraq, or on the Internet is an illusion. The solution must be local. This entails important reforms for states around Lake Chad, starting with the collateral damage and the lack of accountability of their security forces.

Notes

1. The Anglican bishop of Kaduna, Josiah Idowu Fearon, in *The Economist*, 29 September 2012.
2. Such an approach includes a systematic recording of lethal incidents involving alleged Boko Haram members. See http://www.nigeriawatch.org.
3. The name Boko Haram was coined by local journalists during the uprising of July 2009, especially on Radio Kaduna. Before, the sect bore no name and was sometimes called Yusufiyya, after its founder. Under the leadership of Abubakar Shekau, it then claimed to be the 'Sunni Community for the Propagation of the Prophet's Teachings and Jihad' (*Jama'atu Ahlis-Sunnah Lidda'awati Wal Jihad*).
4. Interview with the author, Koutoukalé prison, Republic of Niger, 27 February 2015.
5. Many young men actually marry divorced women first, because they cannot afford to pay the bride-wealth of a virgin.
6. After the extrajudicial execution of Mohammed Yusuf, for example, Abubakar Shekau allegedly adopted his children and married one of his four wives. In the Kanuri tradition of Borno, also, the payment of bride-wealth was not required in so-called "weddings of charity" (nya sadaabe), when a pious father would "give" his daughter to a Muslim scholar. Yet this was rarely the case because ulamas,

who lived from their religious activities and preferred to remain independent, were then obliged to the wife-giver for free prayers and constant officiating in his household. See Cohen, Ronald [1967], The Kanuri of Bornu, New York, Holt, Rinehart and Winston, p. 38; Cohen, Ronald [Dec. 1961], "Mariage Instability among the Kanuri of Northern Nigeria", American Anthropologist vol. 63, no. 6, pp. 1231–1249.
7. Interviews under Chatham House rule in Abuja in 2011.
8. Galtimari, *Final Report*, 10.
9. The pieces of legislation adopted by Cameroon in December 2014 and Chad in July 2015 were somewhat similar in this regard. They defined terrorism in very vague terms, which allowed the repression of all forms of political opposition and the application of death penalty for non-violent acts, for example damage to property or disruption of public services during a demonstration. In addition, they militarized justice and lengthened pre-trial detention in police custody: from 48 hours to 90 days in Chad; for periods of two weeks renewable indefinitely in Cameroon.
10. Onuoha, *Why Do Youth Join Boko Haram?*, 4.
11. In July 2013, five men were tried for their participation in bombings in Niger State in July 2011; in November and December 2013, two commandants of the sect, Kabiru Umar 'Sokoto' and Mustapha Umar, were then given life sentences for having organized various attacks, the first against the Saint Theresa Catholic Church in Madalla in Niger State, near Abuja, during Christmas 2011, the second against the offices of a newspaper in Kaduna, *This Day*, in April 2012.
12. *Jeune Afrique* 16 March 2016.
13. Ogori, 'Return of the Boko Haram'.
14. Amnesty International, *Stars on Their Shoulders*.
15. Ibid.
16. Yet the atrocities perpetrated by Boko Haram members also incited the youth to fight back with the government's CJTF (Civilian Joint Task Force). According to a small panel of 33 respondents, 60% of the militia's volunteers decided to join to revenge the killing of a relative or a friend by the insurgents. See Yusuf, Umar Lawal [2014], « The Role of Civilian JTF in tackling Boko Haram problems in Borno », Al-Mahram International Journal (Maiduguri) vol. 6, p. 66.
17. In Borno, the First Bank was often targeted, allegedly as a vengeance for the seizure of a million dollars in Mohammed Yusuf's account.
18. Smaldone, *Warfare in the Sokoto Caliphate*, 137.
19. In 1897, the explorer Emile Gentil already mentioned them as pirates. Cf. Dion, *Vers le lac Tchad*, 157.
20. Niven, Rex, *Nigerian Kaleidoscope*, 16.
21. *Daily Times* 19 March 1984.
22. *The Guardian*, 26 June 2013, 5.
23. Pérouse de Montclos, *Violence in Nigeria*, ch. 6. See also the NigeriaWatch annual reports: http://www.nigeriawatch.org/index.php?html=7.
24. United Nations High Commission for Human Rights, *Report on Violations and Abuses Committed by Boko Haram*, 12; Anyadike, 'Road to Redemption', 9.
25. Data on file with the author. See http://www.nigeriawatch.org.
26. Amnesty International, *Cameroun*; United Nations High Commission for Human Rights, *Report on Violations and Abuses Committed by Boko Haram*, 12.
27. Interestingly enough, the medieval kings of Kanem-Borno already destroyed their enemies' livestock and cut down shrubs likely to hide combatants when they fought the So of present-day Damasek in the very same region, near a river called Yo at the time. Cf. Fisher, 'The Central Sahara and Sudan', 75.

28. As early as 2010 in Nigeria, the prohibition of motorcycle taxis in Borno had also led to the unemployment of some 34,000 young men, some of whom joined the ranks of Boko Haram. Cf. Anyadike, 'Road to Redemption', 9.
29. In case of absolute necessity, compromise (*muwalat*) with infidels is justified by the Koran's Surah (III, 28) on the Family of Imran, rather than the option of war (*jihad*) or exile (*hijra*).
30. Thurston, *'The Disease Is Unbelief'*, 24.
31. In February 2016, the Nigerian secret services announced that a recruiter for the Islamic State in Iraq and Syria, Abdussalam Enesi Yunusa, had been arrested along with seven alleged members of a dissent group, Ansaru. But his nationality was not revealed, and rumors about Boko Haram combatants in the city of Sirte with the Islamic State in Libya have never been confirmed.
32. In fact, Abubakar Shekau never proclaimed a caliphate in Gwoza, which was run by a Boko Haram emir called Ibrahim Tada Nglayika 'Gooya' who was killed by soldiers in August 2014 and replaced by his elder brother Ali Gooya. According to local and anonymous sources, the main preacher is the area was a man named Adamu Rugurugu. See also Apard, 'Boko Haram'; Pérouse de Montclos, 'Boko Haram et Daech', 31–2.
33. Ibn Khaldun, *Le livre des Exemples*, 471–7.
34. The sharif of Mecca and king of Hedjaz from 1916, Hussein ben Ali, was thus deposed by Abdelaziz Al Saud in 1924 because he tried to proclaim himself caliph following the establishment of a Republic in Turkey. Since then, Saudi kings do not use the title 'Caliph' but 'Guardian of the two holy mosques'.
35. *Vanguard*, 14 August 2009. See also the statement of another spokesman, Abu Qaqa, reported by Mark, 'Boko Haram Vows to Fight'.
36. Zenn, 'Nigerian al-Qaedaism', 111.
37. According to Bernard Barrera, the General in charge of Operation Serval in Northern Mali, the French Army captured (on 2 March 2013) only one Boko Haram member who sought refuge in the mountains of the Adrar des Ifoghas and who was in charge of kidnaping Fulani young boys in the region of Gao to provide AQIM with child soldiers. This is very far from the 300 fighters mentioned by some journalists who claimed that Boko Haram had a training camp near Timbuktu in 2012. See Barrera, Bernard [2015], Opération Serval : notes de guerre, Mali 2013, Paris, Seuil, p. 216.
38. Smith, *Boko Haram*, 87. For the report clearing Al-Muntada of the accusation and written by a corporation of lawyers linked to European and Saudi oil companies, see: http://www.almuntadatrust.org/pdf/am-international-report.pdf.
39. Sahara Reporters, 21 September 2011. http://saharareporters.com/2011/09/21/punch-interview-i-told-inspector-general-police-advance-abuja-would-be-bombed-says-boko.
40. Lecocq and Schrijver, 'The War on Terror in a Haze of Dust'.
41. Pérouse de Montclos, *Nigeria's Interminable Insurgency?*, 20–2.
42. Imam and Kyari, 'Yusufuyya and the Nigerian State'; Murtada, *Boko Haram in Nigeria*, 3.
43. Interview with the author in Zaria on 2 October 2012.
44. Ogori, 'Return of the Boko Haram'.

Disclosure statement

No potential conflict of interest was reported by the author.

References

Amnesty International. *Cameroun: les droits humain en ligne de mire. La lutte contre Boko Haram et ses conséquences*. London: Amnesty International, 2015.

Amnesty International. *Stars on Their Shoulders, Blood on Their Hands: War Crimes Committed by the Nigerian Military*. London: Amnesty International, 2015.

Anyadike, Obi. 'Road to Redemption: Unmaking Boko Haram'. *IRIN News*, 1 October 2015. http://www.irinnews.org/analysis/2015/10/01

Apard, Élodie. 'Boko Haram, le jihad en vidéo'. *Politique africaine no.* 138 (2015): 135–162.

Cohen, Ronald. *The Kanuri of Bornu*. New York: Holt, Rinehart and Winston, 1967.

Dion, Isabelle. *Vers le lac Tchad: Expéditions françaises et résistances africaines 1890–1900*. Milan: Silvana Editoriale, 2014.

Fisher, Humphrey. 'The Central Sahara and Sudan'. In *The Cambridge History of Africa, Vol. 1: From the Earliest Times to c. 500 B.C.*, edited by Richard Ray. Cambridge: Cambridge University Press, 1975: 58–64.

Galtimari, Usman Gaji, ed. *Final Report of the Presidential Committee on Security Challenges in the North-East Zone of Nigeria*, Abuja, Federal Government of Nigeria, Sept. 2011. Unpublished report on file with the author.

Khaldun, Ibn. *Abd al-Rahman ibn Muhammad. Le livre des Exemples*. Paris: Gallimard, 2002.

Imam, Muhammad Sani and Muhammad Kyari. 'Yusufuyya and the Nigerian State: Historicizing the Dynamics of Boko Haram Phenomenon'. *Kaduna Journal of Liberal Arts* 5, no. 1 (2011): 27–45.

Lecocq, Baz, and Paul Schrijver. 'The War on Terror in a Haze of Dust: Potholes and Pitfalls on the Saharan Front'. *Journal of Contemporary African Studies* 25, no. 1 (2007): 141–166.

Mark, Monica. 'Boko Haram Vows to Fight Until Nigeria Establishes Sharia Law'. *The Guardian* 27 (January 2012).

Murtada, Ahmad. *Boko Haram in Nigeria: Its Beginnings, Principles and Activities*. Kano: Bayero University, Salafi Manhaj, 2013.

Niven, Rex. *Nigerian Kaleidoscope: Memoirs of a Colonial Servant*. London: Hurst, 1982.

Ogori, Abdul Kareem. 'Return of the Boko Haram'. *Politico* (18 December 2010), pp.11–16.

Onuoha, Freedom. *Why Do Youth Join Boko Haram?* Washington DC: United States Institute of Peace, 2014.

Pérouse de Montclos, Marc-Antoine. 'Boko Haram et Daech: simple alliance médiatique?'. *Les Grands Dossiers de Diplomatie* no. 32 (2016): 31–32.

Pérouse de Montclos, Marc-Antoine. *Nigeria's Interminable Insurgency? Addressing the Boko Haram Crisis*, London: Chatham House, Research Paper, 2014.

Pérouse de Montclos, Marc-Antoine, ed. *Violence in Nigeria: A Qualitative and Quantitative Analysis*. WAPOSO Series no. 3. Ibadan: IFRA-Nigeria and Leiden: African Studies Centre, 2016.

Smaldone, Joseph. *Warfare in the Sokoto Caliphate: Historical and Sociological Perspectives*. Cambridge: Cambridge University Press, 1977.

Smith, Mike. *Boko Haram: Inside Nigeria's Unholy War*. London: I.B. Tauris, 2015.

Thurston, Alex. *'The Disease Is Unbelief': Boko Haram's Religious and Political Worldview*. Washington, DC: The Brookings Institution, 2016.

United Nations High Commission for Human Rights. *Report on Violations and Abuses Committed by Boko Haram and the Impact on Human Rights in the Affected Countries*. New York: UNHCHR, 2015.

Zenn, Jacob. 'Nigerian al-Qaedaism'. In *Current Trends in Islamist Ideology: Vol. 16*, edited by Hillel Fradkin, Husain Haqqani, Eric Brown, and Hassan Mneimneh. Washington, DC: Hudson Institute, 2013: 99–117.

Appendix 1. Boko Haram key players

The doves

Mallam Abbas

A member of Boko Haram's Shura ('Executive Council'), he was the interim emir of the group when Mohamed Yusuf was away or in jail. He led the sect when some followers were buried and shot by the police in June 2009, a clash that resulted in the uprising and the extrajudicial killing of Yusuf. He then opposed Abubakar Shekau and allegedly took refuge in the Sudan, leaving his supporters in Borno.

Bugi Foi

While Mohamed Yusuf banned his followers from voting, supporting secular democracy, or working in the civil service, Bugi Foi was *the* connecting man between Boko Haram and the Nigerian state. A pious Muslim, he chaired the local government of Kaga in 1999–2003 and became the commissioner of religious affairs when Ali Modu Sheriff was elected governor of Borno. A middleman between Izala and Boko Haram, he eventually joined Mohamed Yusuf and refused to approve the release of state funding to sponsor the pilgrimage of native Christians to Jerusalem. He also tried to change the name of his ministry to a commission for Islamic affairs. Due to the opposition of the secular Barrister Association, which insisted on the religious neutrality of the state, he was then transferred to Agriculture. Just after or before the 2007 election, he asked Ali Modu Sharif to resign. As a result, the governor changed his whole cabinet. As a result, the governor changed his whole cabinet in 2008. Bugi Foi was eventually killed with Yusuf by the police in 2009.

Abubakar Hassan

The chief imam of Mohamed Yusuf's mosque and a member of Boko Haram's Shura ('Executive Council') before 2009, he was allegedly arrested in the Republic of Niger while traveling to Northern Mali to meet the leaders of AQIM (*Al Qaeda in the Islamic Maghreb*); unverified rumors claim he was then jailed in Koutoukalé high security prison near Niamey.

Mohamed Yusuf

Originally from Yobe State and an adoptive Kanuri, he was born in the countryside in 1970, either in Gigir in the Local Government Area of Jakusko, or in Na'iyyah in the Local Government Area of Yunusari, according to various versions available.[37] Some claim that his father was also an extremist who joined the uprising of the Maitatsine sect and died during the Kano riots in 1980 after being thrown out of Yobe State, first from the town of Gashua by the emir of Bade, Mai Umar Suleiman, then from Ngelzarma in the Local Government Area of Fune. In keeping with the tradition of levirate marriage, Mohammed Yusuf was thus raised by his maternal uncle, who took him to live in Bulamari and Abba Ganaram, suburbs of Maiduguri. Once in town, he married a daughter of Baba Fugu, also known as 'Bapur', a trader who imported skins from Chad, speculated in land, and had a reputation for arms trafficking, which reportedly led to his being briefly detained by police in 2004 or 2005. Accounts of what transpired at that stage differ. According to unverified information, Mohammed Yusuf began his politico-religious career among the *Yan Schia* of Ibrahim Yaqoub El Zakzaky, who has probably never met him and denies any ties to him.[38] He is even believed to have been, in Borno State, the leader of Mujahid Abubakar's *Jama'atul Tadjidi Islam*, a Kano-based dissident branch of the Shiite movement that was born in Zaria, in northwestern Nigeria. In any case, Mohammed Yusuf quickly rallied the Izala 'eradicators', Wahhabi-inspired Salafis; he followed in particular the teachings of one of their famous sheikhs, Mahamud Adam Jafar, based in Kano. Lamenting the lack of training of preachers, the latter asked Yusuf to take charge of a group of young radicals, the 'Companions of the Prophet' *(Sahaba,* or *Shabab),* founded about 1995 by Abubakar Lawan, a former Nigerian student at the Islamic University of Madinah. Officiating in the mosques of Al Haji Muhammadu Ndimi – a wealthy merchant – and Daggash, in the old colonial district of Maiduguri, Mohammed Yusuf was tasked with commenting on a compilation of verses from the Qur'an *(Riyad as-Salihin),* while others would lead sessions of exegesis of the Holy Book *(Tafsir)* or of a collection of hadiths *(Sahih Bukhari).*[39] As soon as 1997, Mohammed Yusuf was identified by the Nigerian security services as a troublemaker, taken to Abuja for questioning, released for lack of evidence and celebrated by a growing masses of followers when he would return to Maiduguri. In early 2004, however, Mohammed Yusuf had to go into exile in Mecca in early 2004 to escape prosecution; authorities accused him of supporting the rebellion of the 'Talibans' of Kanama, at the border between Niger and Yobe State in Nigeria. Brought back to Maiduguri thanks to the mediation of the deputy governor of Borno State, Mohammed Yusuf then broke his ties with the Izala, whom he criticized for compromising with a 'secular' state. This split was symbolized by the assassination in 2007 of Sheikh Mahamud Jafar Adam, which was most probably perpetrated by Boko Haram. At a time when the sect was still nameless, the ever-charismatic Mohamed Yusuf nonetheless continued to recruit new followers, which quickly enabled him to establish his own religious center *(markaz),* first in central Unguwa Doki, and then on land allocated by his stepfather near the Maiduguri railway station. Indeed, the corruption of the authorities and the harassment by the Muslim establishment strengthened the popularity of a radical movement which, in exchange for promises of a full application of sharia law, had originally supported in 2003 the election of the governor of Borno State, Ali Modu Sheriff. Arrested and released on bail several times (e.g. from 13 November 2008 to 20 January 2009), Mohammed Yusuf ultimately reached martyr status when he was extrajudicially killed by the Nigerian police in the Maiduguri police headquarters on 30 July 2009.

The hawks

Husseini Afuwa

He is a typical commander (Amir) of Boko Haram in rural Yobe State's local governments of Gujba and Gulani. He ran a patent medicine store in Buni Yadi before joining the group. A Kanuri, he succeeded the former Boko Haram Amir, who had been ambushed and killed by the Nigerian Army somewhere between Potiskum and Damaturu in 2012. Husseini Afuwa is known for its attack on the Federal Government College of Buni Yadi, where fifty-nine boys were killed on February 25, 2014. Despite the focus of the media on the Chibok girls in Borno, a greater number of schools have actually been attacked in Yobe, where the security forces claim they cannot protect them because they are not fenced.

Khalid Al-Barnawi

Nicknamed Al-Barnawi ("the man from Borno"), he was a founder and leader of the Ansaru dissent group. Possibly born in 1976 in Maiduguri or in Biu, he was also known as Mohammed Othman or Abu Hafsa. He succeeded Abubakar Adam Kambar, a jihadist who allegedly fought in Mali and was killed by the Nigerian Army in Kano in 2012. The two might have been the same person and the first spokesman of the Ansaru group was one Abu Usamatal Ansari ("the companion"). Khalid Al-Barnawi was instrumental in the kidnapping of several foreigners in Nigeria and he is said to have collaborated with Abu Mohamed, a Hausa from Bauchi killed in Zaria and succeeded by Mallam 'Bakura', a disciple who used to read the Koran during Mohamed Yusuf's sessions of exegesis of the Holy Book before 2009 ('Bakura' just means the eldest son, as opposed to the junior one called Babagana in Kanuri, Babangida in Hausa and Bawuro in Fulani). Other local sources claim that another leader of the Ansaru group, Abu Mohamed Awal, was in fact killed by Abubakar Shekau himself during the period of Ramadan in 2013. As for Khalid Al-Barnawi, the Nigerian Army said he was arrested in April 2016 in Lokoja, the capital of Kogi State.

Mahamat Daoud

Never mentioned in Boko Haram's Shura ('Executive Council'), he was presented by Chadian President Idriss Déby as the head of a faction ready to negotiate peace with the government of Muhammadu Buhari in 2015. But according to an insider in Maiduguri, he was only a fighter who contacted AQIM in Mali to get supplies and be recognized as the new leader of the group. He was disappointed that Daesh eventually preferred to deal with Abubakar Shekau, which is allegedly the reason why he offered to broker peace on behalf of the Chadian president.

Jimoh Mustapha

Nicknamed Abu Qasim, he encouraged Ebira Muslims of Kogi State to join the jihad. In 2014, he allegedly formed a group merging Ansaru and a Boko Haram cell led by Abu Suyuti in Okene Local Government Area. Inspired by the Islamic State in Iraq and Syria, he was possibly succeeded by one Asa Dullah in 2015 or 2016.

Abubakar Shekau

Allegedly born in Yobe around 1970, Abubakar Shekau (also spelled Shiku or Shikwa) is approximately the same age as Yusuf. He was an early follower of Boko Haram. Until 2009, he had his own mosque behind the El-Kanemi Cinema in the Maidokiri district of Maiduguri. He claimed to be fluent in Hausa, Fulani, Kanuri, and Arabic. A self-proclaimed imam, he was also known as Darul Tawhid, an 'expert in the oneness of Allah'. Yet he lacked the charisma of his mentor and was perceived as Yusuf's factotum, a poorly educated 'area boy' who smoked hemp when he was younger. After the killing of his master, he went into hiding and resurfaced in 2010 to take over the group with six original commanders of the former Boko Haram's Shura ('Executive Council'). Under his leadership, the movement became much more radical and violent. When Osama bin Laden was killed in 2011, Shekau took the name of his successor, al-Zaouahiri. A master of disguise, he also uses another alias, Abu Muhammad Abu Bakr Bin Muhammad Al Shakwi Al Muslimi Bishku. He was allegedly injured by the Nigerian Army in Sambisa Forest on 30 June 2013. It is not clear whether he survived, but this does not matter so much: He (or his double) remains the most mediatized leader of Boko Haram; killing him would not put an end to the violence anyway.

Abib Yusuf

Allegedly a son of Mohamed Yusuf, he is said to be the spokesman of the group since February 2015, when Abubakar Shekau no longer appeared in public. He was to be seen in videos produced by the Islamic State in West Africa in October 2015.

The opportunists

These are traders, fishermen, cattle breeders, or cultivators who joined the group during the insurgency, after the extrajudicial killing of Mohammed Yusuf in 2009. Their objective is to get their share of the booty and to settle scores. According to anonymous sources, this is for instance true of petty traders like Abba Goroma, Babba Gana Zidane, and Mustapha Bodawe, who were arrested in 2015 by the Cameroonian authorities in the smuggling complex of Banki and Amchidé along the border with Nigeria. High competition for arable land in Gwoza Hills also attracted peasants who tried to take advantage of the exodus of Christian cultivators. Led by Mustafa Chad, a hired mercenary and possibly a former Chadian military, Boko Haram invaded Gwoza in August 2014 and proclaimed 'emir of Pulka' a Mandara man called Musa Ghide. As for the Buduma fishermen of lake Chad who evicted their Hausa rivals, they were led in 2014-2015 by one Abdel Aziz. Adjacent to lake Chad in the Republic of Niger, the region of Bosso was also attacked in 2016 by the men of Bana Blachera, who was allegedly a Cameroonian in charge of supplying the group with weapons and fuel.

Operation Barkhane and Boko Haram: French Counterterrorism and Military Cooperation in the Sahel

Christopher Griffin

ABSTRACT
This article examines the current coalition campaign against Boko Haram in Nigeria in the context of French military cooperation with the Francophone countries involved. The French government is actively supporting and facilitating the offensive against Boko Haram through both structural and operational military cooperation with Chad, Niger, and Cameroon. The current effectiveness and operational state of the armies in those three countries is largely due to long-term French strategic thinking about its influence on the continent. Finally, France is also militarily active on the continent with 3000 soldiers deployed for Operation Barkhane. Barkhane, while primarily aimed at containing the threat of Al Qaeda in the Islamic Maghreb, is also designed, in cooperation with partner countries, to prevent a link-up between Boko Haram and the other terrorist groups in the Sahel.

On 17 May 2014, a little-remarked summit took place at the Elysée Palace in Paris to discuss Boko Haram. The heads of state of France, Benin, Cameroon, Nigeria, Niger, and Chad were all present, with representatives from the United States, the United Kingdom, and the European Union. The summit was intended to reinforce regional cooperation against Boko Haram, and focused on three areas: sharing intelligence (with significant technical support from France, the United States, the UK, and the EU), targeting international sanctions toward Boko Haram, and bringing economic and social development to the region.[1] French President François Hollande clearly identified the threat posed by Boko Haram, saying the group could destabilize the entire region and that France had been able to 'identify the links' between Boko Haram and other terrorist groups in the region.[2]

Starting in late 2014, France began to show signs of limited military involvement in the conflict against Boko Haram. On 4 February 2015, *Le Figaro* reported that French planes were carrying out reconnaissance missions on the Nigerian border on behalf of Chad, Niger, and Cameroon. Hollande, however, ruled out any direct French military engagement as well as any overflights of Nigerian territory (*Le Figaro*, 4 February 2015). France has taken more and more of an indirect role in the conflict in Nigeria, deploying troops to Diffa in Niger to support Nigerien forces, as well as a second detachment to Cameroon.[3]

France's interest in the Boko Haram conflict has grown significantly since 2014, and France has made considerable effort to send military aid to its allies fighting in Nigeria. Fabius said in February that 'there is a zone of stability, including Chad, Cameroon and Niger that must not be destabilized'.[4] Since its military intervention in Mali in 2013, Operation Serval, France has widened its mission to stabilize the Sahel region, and the fight against Boko Haram is part of this overall framework. French forces are engaged in Operation Barkhane, launched on 1 August 2014 to combine the ongoing French operations in Mali and Chad. It has deployed 3000 soldiers, across five countries.[5] Rather than intervening directly, however, as in Mali, France is using its military aid and presence in the Sahel to create and support a powerful sub-regional alliance to take on Boko Haram in Nigeria.

This paper will analyze the French support for the offensive by Chad, Niger, Cameroon, and, as of July 2015, Benin, against Boko Haram. The first part will consider the progress of the intervention since the beginning of 2015. The second part will examine French military cooperation in the Sahel and the state of the armies involved in the conflict. The third part will focus on French military operations, to place the Barkhane mission and the Boko Haram threat in the greater context of French military priorities in the Sahel.

The Francophone countries go to war in Nigeria: Winter–summer 2015

In January 2015, the Chadian Army, one of the most powerful in the region, began deploying troops for an offensive against Boko Haram. The military campaign also includes forces from four other African countries: Cameroon, Niger, Benin, and Nigeria (*France 24*, 12 March 2015; *Le Monde*, 2 August 2015). The involvement of neighboring countries in Nigeria has not been completely welcomed by Abuja, where the government stated that 'all efforts undertaken by foreign forces would be at best complementary to the operations of the Nigerian Army' (*France 24*, 12 March 2015). The Nigerian Army has had significant difficulties in fighting Boko Haram, however, including a mutiny in August 2014 over a lack of equipment (*BBC News*, 17 December 2014).[6]

There were limited battles in Chad, Niger, and Cameroon against Boko Haram in August and October 2014. The tipping point seems to have been the seizure of the Multilateral Joint Task Force (MJTF) base at Baga in Nigeria in January 2015.[7] Fighting began in earnest on 4 February 2015, with a battle between Cameroonian soldiers and Boko Haram at Fotokol on the border between Cameroon and Nigeria. At the same time, the Chadian Army crossed the border into Nigeria and took the city of Gamboru after heavy fighting (*France 24*, 4 February 2015). The offensives were in response to Boko Haram attacks on targets within Cameroon (*Le Point*, 3 February 2015).

On 8 March 2015, Chad and Niger began a major offensive against Boko Haram, attacking from bases in Niger into northeastern Nigeria. A number of media sources claim that the campaign was in response to Boko Haram's declaration of allegiance to the Islamic State, but it is clear that an operation of this scale had been planned for some time (*Le Monde*, 8 March 2015). Chadian President Idriss Déby set out the objectives of the operation, which were to 'annihilate' Boko Haram, and 'eliminate' its leader, Abubakar Shekau, if he refused to surrender (*Le Monde*, 8 March 2015). In the Elysée summit in May 2014, mentioned above, Déby evoked the need to wage 'total war against Boko Haram'.[8] These are exceptionally ambitious war aims, and it reflects a confidence on the part of the Chadian president in the strength of his country's army, which is starting to gain the label of the 'regional gendarme' (*France 24*, 12 March 2015).

The offensive was undertaken with what appear to be primarily regular forces from the four countries involved, with reports of attacks by fighter aircraft (mostly Chadian), heavy artillery, and 200 armored vehicles including tanks (*CNN*, 9 March 2015). Why is Chad deploying such extensive resources to fight an insurgency in a neighboring country? First, as in Cameroon, Boko Haram attacked targets in Chad in early 2015, and the Chadian government wanted to prevent further attacks. Second, Chad is worried about the ability of Boko Haram to cut its two main commercial routes to the sea via Nigeria and Cameroon (*France 24*, 10 March 2015). Third, Boko Haram leaders publicly threatened Déby, as well as the presidents of Cameroon and Niger on 20 January (*Jeune Afrique*, 21 January 2015). Finally, Chad, Cameroon, and especially Niger are also attempting to cope with an influx of refugees from the fighting in Nigeria (*Washington Post*, 29 January 2015). The UN High Commissioner for Refugees estimated, prior to the coalition offensive, that 135,000 people had already fled Nigeria, with 850,000 more displaced internally.[9]

The campaign against Boko Haram was fairly successful up to May 2015, though it was still a long way from the stated goals of annihilating the group. On 4 April, the Chadian Army said that 'phase one' of the operations had been completed, as Boko Haram fighters had been pushed back and a number of towns and villages retaken in Nigeria. The Chadian Army's Joint Chief of Staff, General Brahim Seid Mahamat, told *Euronews* that 'Boko Haram's capacity to cause trouble has been reduced' (4 April 2015). The gains were made against a backdrop of some bitter recriminations within the coalition, however. Déby and his military officers have been very critical of Nigeria's unwillingness to cooperate. Nigeria's new president, Muhammadu Buhari, indicated early on that he wanted Nigeria to retake the lead combat role (*Reuters,* 2 April 2015). In mid-May 2015, Déby stated that 'Boko Haram has been broken, but isn't finished', and indicated that there were significant problems of cooperation in the coalition (*Agence France Presse*, 12 May 2015). Chad's parliament extended its mandate for the war on 20 May (*Agence France Presse*, 20 May 2015).

In an escalation of the conflict, Chad and Cameroon became the target of Boko Haram terrorist attacks in summer 2015. Boko Haram suicide bombers attacked targets in central N'Djamena on 15 June, killing 33 people, a first in Chad's history (*France 24*, 18 June 2015). Cameroon also suffered a series of suicide attacks in the north of the country in late July 2015, and Boko Haram raided the country in early August, killing at least 9 people and kidnapping more than 100 (*International Business Times*, 5 August 2015). While it took some time for the group to reorganize after the setbacks in the initial offensives in March and April, Boko Haram was able to retaliate in strength and cause significant damage in the countries involved in the campaign. Suicide attacks have continued into 2016, especially in Cameroon (*Le Figaro*, 10 February 2016).

Chad and Cameroon, instead of ending their involvement in the war, stepped up both their internal and external responses. Cameroon sent 2000 additional troops to the north of the country to fight Boko Haram incursions (*International Business Times*, 5 August 2015). Chad changed its laws on 30 July to restore the death penalty for terrorists, as well as greatly increasing its security measures in N'Djamena (*France 24*, 31 July 2015). The Chadian Army also launched a major operation to destroy the Boko Haram presence on the islands of Lake Chad, which has resulted in a number of terrorists being killed and the loss to Boko Haram of many boats used for operations on the lake (*France 24*, 28 July 2015). The conflict clearly intensified during summer 2015 in terms of both tactics and the number of forces involved. The consolidation of forces from the five countries involved under a new, 8700-strong Multi-National Joint Task Force, would lead to the destruction of Boko Haram 'in 18 months', according to Nigerian President Buhari, speaking during an official visit to the United States in July (*France 24*, 22 July 2015).

As of writing in February 2016, the coalition's campaign continues. Boko Haram has been dealt some serious defeats and is considered by most analysts as no longer able to threaten urban areas (*AllAfrica*, 5 January 2016). Even Buhari, however, admitted in his New Year's address that there was 'still a lot of work to be done' (*International Business Times*, 1 January 2016). In a significant strategic shift, Buhari told the European Parliament at the beginning of February that Nigeria had changed to an operational approach of 'minimum force', to protect 'fundamental human rights' in the conflict (*Premium Times*, 3 February 2016). The new strategy may have to do with the damaging Amnesty International report in summer 2015 detailing what the organization called 'war crimes' committed by the Nigerian Army.[10] In any case, at the beginning of 2016, progress has been made against Boko Haram, but the war is far from finished.

The missing piece of the story in most articles and analyses of this regional conflict against the Nigerian terrorist group is the involvement of the historical 'regional gendarme', France. It is likely that the French military presence and military cooperation has substantially contributed to the increase in the effectiveness of the armies in the Sahel. President Hollande met with Déby on 15 May to discuss the campaign and congratulated the coalition nations for making significant progress against Boko Haram (*JournalduTchad*, 15 May 2015). Hollande also went to Cameroon as part of an African tour in early July and stated that 'France is at Cameroon's side in the face of the Boko Haram threat' (*Le Figaro*, 4 July 2015). France condemned Boko Haram terrorist attacks against its allies, with the French Foreign Ministry stating on 4 August, that the 'the parties responsible [for the 4 August attacks in Cameroon] must not rest unpunished'.[11] The next part of this paper will examine the structural military cooperation with France with its allies in the Sahel to face the terrorist threat.

French military cooperation in the Sahel: 1960–2015

France has an extensive military presence in Africa which facilitates aid to its Francophone allies via what the French government calls 'operational [military] cooperation' for interventions and peacekeeping, and 'structural cooperation' for routine missions of helping countries build up and maintain their military establishments.[12] This is based on three major elements: the French prepositioned forces at African bases, the RECAMP training program, and the bilateral military cooperation programs run by the French Foreign Ministry's *Direction de la coopération de sécurité et de défense* (Directorate for Security and Defense Cooperation – DCSD).

The permanent French military presence in Africa

With the decolonization of most of France's Empire in West and Central Africa in 1960, France negotiated bilateral defense and military cooperation treaties with its former colonies to maintain a permanent military presence.[13] Most French bases were initially kept open, but the number was quickly reduced following the army cuts after the end of the Algerian War in 1962.[14] The French base network was used to support military interventions in Africa, which began with an operation in Gabon in 1964 in response to an attempted coup, and continues today, as the recent operations in Mali and the Central African Republic demonstrate.

The base structure is currently being reorganized around the principle of access to the Sahel. The key permanent bases in France are Dakar, Libreville, and Djibouti (Abu Dhabi is also counted strategically as an integral part of the base network for operations in Africa)[15]. France is in the process of reducing its forces in Gabon, however, to favor Abidjan as its new main base. France is also setting up smaller permanent bases in Néma (Mauritania), Gao (Mali), Agadez and Arlit (Niger), and Zouar (Chad).[16] Niamey is also a smaller base, from which French and US forces operate drones.[17] Troops at French bases are available for immediate deployment in operations and are backed up by the *Guépard* rapid reaction force in France.[18]

French forces in Chad come under a different system than the permanent base network. The Adji-Kosseï base, which adjoins N'Djaména airport, is not considered a permanent base, but a part of active operations. French soldiers are present in the context of Operation Epervier, launched in 1986 to halt the Libyan invasion of northern Chad. There are still operational objectives for French troops in Chad, which include guaranteeing the stability and territorial integrity of the country as well as protecting the French expatriate population.[19]

The RECAMP program

In 1997, France launched the *Renforcement des capacités africaines de maintien de la paix* (Reinforcement of African Capacities for Peacekeeping Operations – RECAMP) program, which includes continental and regional military exercises (the AMANI AFRICA cycles are the most recent), several depots with available military equipment for underequipped African armies to draw on in case of need,[20] and bilateral and multilateral training programs. The training programs encompass both access for African personnel to French military schools (though there are fewer places available currently than in the past) and the creation of the *Ecoles Nationales à Vocation Régionale* (the French Foreign Ministry translates this as 'Regionally-Oriented National Schools'[21]).[22] There are 17 schools in 10 countries, which have a number of different programs, from officer training to health services to police training. France provides instructors and expertise, on the condition that the schools are open to personnel from other African countries.[23] French language instruction is emphasized for interoperability purposes.[24]

RECAMP has been internationalized since 2002. The African Union, which was launched in 2002, created the African Peace and Security Architecture (APSA). One of the goals of APSA is to create an African Standby Force (ASF) with regional response capabilities by the end of 2015.[25] RECAMP is now oriented toward helping Africans build this force as well as strengthening African capacities to contribute to UN peacekeeping missions.[26] After 2007, RECAMP became EURORECAMP to take into account the willingness of the EU to contribute, but France has been very critical of the lack of initiatives from the EU for African missions.[27]

Bilateral French military cooperation with the Sahel countries

The traditional priorities for French military aid in Africa were Djibouti, Senegal, and Chad.[28] With the problems of terrorism in the Sahel, however, France has increased its military aid to the countries of what is now called the 'Sahel G5', created in 2014 for security cooperation between Mauritania, Mali, Niger, Burkina Faso, and Chad (*Le Monde*, 16 February 2014).[29] The following sections will examine French military cooperation with three of the armies in the front line against Boko Haram, Chad, Niger, and Cameroon, with a short detour via the Malian Army.

The Chadian Army

After the last major rebel attacks on Chad in 2008 and 2009, which were defeated with the help of the French Army, the country has seen an unprecedented period of relative stability.[30] It now appears that Chad used that period, in conjunction with the French, to build up the country's army into what the French Senate called in 2013, a 'regional power'.[31] This build-up is unsurprising, as even in a period of relative internal calm, Chad faces a wide-range of external threats, including the instability in Libya and its effects on ethnic groups in northern Chad, the conflicts in Darfur and South Sudan, the conflict in the Central African Republic, terrorist groups in northern Niger (from the North Mali intervention of 2013), and Boko Haram.[32]

Chad's army is now considered as 'probably the best in the region for desert zone operations'.[33] The army consists of two different groupings, or what some analysts have labeled 'two speed'.[34] The first is a sort of republican guard loyal to Déby, from the same ethnic groups as his family, and is called the *Direction générale des services de sécurité des institutions de l'Etat* (DGSSIE). It is thought to be about 14,000 strong, and this is the force Chad has mainly used in interventions abroad.[35] The second part of the armed forces is the regular army, which is not as well equipped as the DGSSIE.[36] The French Foreign Ministry estimates total forces (including the DGSSIE) to be around 40,000 soldiers, considerably larger than the other Francophone states.[37]

The Chadian Army is modernizing, as Déby said it was made up of 'warriors rather than soldiers', but the modernization is moving slower than expected.[38] French military cooperation is playing a significant role in the rise in power of the Chadian Armed Forces. France is interested in Chad for its central location, which allows the French Army to maneuver between its other bases on the continent and respond quickly to crises.[39] The military assistance treaty with Chad (there is no mutual defense treaty) provides for French military personnel in Chadian uniforms to train the Chadian Army. France also committed to provide military equipment (both free and paid), maintenance for that equipment, and logistical support. In exchange, the Chadian government gives France the right to use its airspace and its airfields for military and civil flights.[40] Most of the military assistance treaties with the other Francophone countries have virtually the same terms.

The French National Assembly stated in 2014 that France had helped Chad develop a viable air force prior to rebel attacks in 2008 and, among other aid, provided 50% of the fuel for that air force.[41] In 2014, there were 12 DCSD *coopérants* present in the country, mostly military officers, who were helping guide the modernization and restructuring process in the army, organizing military human resources, overseeing training programs, helping manage logistics, and collecting intelligence. This number is down from the 200 *coopérants* present in the 1990s.[42] The 1070 other French forces present in the country also contribute to training programs for the Chadian Army.[43]

French military cooperation is seen to have been the most successful in Chad out of all of its African partners.[44] Chad participated in the later stages of the French intervention in Mali, taking part in some of the hardest fighting in the Adrar des Ifoghas in February–March 2013.[45] Chad lost 30 killed to France's loss of 7 soldiers.[46] Chad then sent 2250 soldiers to take part in the UN peacekeeping force in Mali after the end of French operations.[47] Chad also fought with France in the intervention in the CAR in 2014. Chad's performance on the battlefield appears to have been of mixed quality, however, and the commander of French land forces during Operation Serval, General Bernard Barrera, criticized the Chadians for the slowness of their advance and for getting repeatedly bogged down due to mines in the Adrar.[48] On the other hand, Barrera praised Chadian forces for the fact that they were the only other country to come help France in the Adrar and that they 'paid the price in blood'.[49]

The Nigerien Army

While Chad is France's most important partner in the Sahel, the French are also working closely with Niger in the fight against Boko Haram. Niger, like Chad, has been historically unstable, with four coups d'état (1974, 1996, 1999, 2010) and seven republics since decolonization. The most recent coup d'état in 2010 eventually brought to power Mahamadou Issoufou, who was prime minister in the 1990s.[50] Niger, the poorest country on the planet, faces many of the same security problems as Chad, which include the situation in Libya, Boko Haram, and the spillover from the conflict in North Mali, with the presence of armed Touareg groups and Al Qaeda in the Islamic Maghreb (AQIM).[51]

As Niger's Army recently overthrew the government, it cannot be considered as completely reliable. It is a force with a great deal of experience in desert warfare, fighting multiple Touareg rebellions during the 1990s and 2000s. It also fought AQIM near the Mali border in 2010.[52] As in Chad, the army is divided into two different elements: the regular *Forces armées nigériennes* and the better equipped and more mobile *Forces nationales d'intervention et de sécurité*. The two parts together comprise about 12,000 soldiers.[53]

As with Chad, the Nigerien Army has proved to be surprisingly effective against Boko Haram. After the initial successes of the intervention in Nigeria in 2015, Issoufou even went so far to say that 'the Boko Haram forces were overestimated . . . in the first contacts with our forces, we quickly understood that they were amateurs' (*Journal du Dimanche*, 12 April 2015). As with Chad's Army, France has helped considerably with military assistance to Niger. France also has considerable interests in Niger as it is a major source of uranium for the French nuclear power corporation Areva.[54]

French military assistance is somewhat different than that to Chad, as the focus has been more on equipment. France is helping Niger build an air force, with a gift of three Gazelle helicopters to the country in 2012, and the development of ULM capacities (in conjunction with Mali, Burkina Faso, and Senegal).[55] France has also, alongside the United States, stationed drones in Niger and works with Nigerien officers in the drone war against terrorists in the Sahel.[56]

While Niger's Army remains 'one of the most operational' in the region, it is also unstable and fragile.[57] Issoufou doubled the defense budget, but was forced to cut funds to education, health, and other social services in order to do so. He is adamant about the need, however, to 'eradicate Boko Haram and chase them out of the Lake Chad Basin' (*Journal du Dimanche*, 12 April 2015).

The Cameroonian Army

In early 2015, France sent two military advisors from the Barkhane force to help Cameroon coordinate its operations against Boko Haram (*Cameroon Tribune*, 30 March 2015). Aside from direct operational support, military cooperation is significant, at an estimated €3.95 million in 2011.[58] Vice-Admiral Gillier, director of the DCSD, said in April 2014 that 'it [Cameroon] is one of the three countries where our cooperation is the most developed' (*Cameroon-Info.Net*, 24 April 2014). France has worked with Cameroon since 2006 to modernize its armed forces with new equipment.[59] France's cooperation in Cameroon is also closely linked to naval priorities, in particular to support France's ongoing anti-piracy operation, *Corymbe*, in the Gulf of Guinea.[60] France is not the only country aiding Cameroon, and a recent official French National Assembly document stated that there is military aid coming from the United States, Israel, and China.[61] Russia promised to provide artillery and transport systems, and Germany provided other military vehicles to Cameroon.[62]

Cameroon's armed forces consist of a regular army and *Bataillons d'Intervention Rapide* (BIR), which have separate chains of command. The BIR respond directly to President Biya, much like the DGSSIE in Chad.[63] The overall strength of Cameroonian forces is estimated at 12,500 soldiers, similar to Niger. Most of Cameroon's military force is engaged at the time of writing against Boko Haram in the north of the country.[64] There is no major French base in Cameroon, but French forces have a permanent presence with a logistics unit at Douala, as it is the main seaport for access to N'Djamena. The presence is limited to 16 soldiers, who are not permitted to wear the uniform of Cameroon's Army.[65]

The Malian Army

While Mali is not engaged in fighting Boko Haram, it is useful to take a short detour to discuss French efforts to rebuild the country's army, as it helps provide information on France's overall military strategy in the Sahel region. The coup d'état in 2012 and the insurgent attacks in the north damaged the Malian Army significantly. After the French intervention in 2013, it was necessary to start over in rebuilding Mali's armed forces. The goal is to reach a 26-regiment force of 17,000 soldiers by 2019.[66] French General Lecointre told *Jeune Afrique* in March 2013 that it was not all bad, as there is 'a generation of young officers around 40–45 years old . . . who are resolved to seize what they see as a historic opportunity to sweep away the past and construct a modern army' (*Jeune Afrique*, 18 February 2013).

France delegated the training program for Mali's Army to the EU. The European Union Training Mission (EUTM-Mali) was intended to last for 15 months, but was extended and accompanied by a civilian mission to improve internal security (EUCAP Sahel Mali).[67] By January 2015, 3400 trainers were working in Mali, and the Malian Army had risen to around 8000–8200 soldiers (*Jeune Afrique*, 23 January 2015). More recent data on progress in the Malian Army remains unavailable as of writing.

At the same time, there was initial reluctance to let the Malian Army embark on stabilization missions in the north after the French departure. Both French and Malian authorities were worried about the potential for 'acts of repression' by Mali's soldiers on the populations of the north due to ethnic disputes and resentment regarding the 2012 defeat.[68] The capacity of the Malian Army to face the resurgence of terrorist groups also became an issue. On 21 May 2014, there was a major battle between Touareg rebel forces and the Malian Army at Kidal, where the Malian Army was defeated and lost a great deal of territory in the north.[69] France had hoped to give the responsibility for security to the Malian Army to deal with what has become a 'low-level insurgency' in the north of the country, but for the time being, it seems to be unsuccessful.[70] Engagements between the Malian Army, allied with the UN stabilization force, MINUSMA, and jihadist groups, continue in 2016 (*Le Parisien*, 5 February 2016).

Thus, from an overall point of view, French military cooperation in Africa seems at least partially successful, in that it has helped Chad, Niger, and Cameroon field forces that have gained some successes against Boko Haram. It permitted France to create a coalition of Francophone states which could take the operational initiative against a terrorist threat, without direct French involvement in combat.

Operation Barkhane and French military strategy in the Sahel

Operation Serval: Mali 2013

In January 2012, a number of armed groups declared independence in North Mali and began an armed offensive against the government. The long-running Touareg rebellion was initially pushed aside by a more radicalized group, Ansar Dine, which allied with AQIM and the Movement for Oneness and Jihad in West Africa (MUJWA), a splinter group from AQIM.[71] For France, AQIM was always and remains the main threat.[72] AQIM, which had its roots in the *Groupe Islamique Armée* (GIA), which attacked targets in France in 1994 and 1995, turned increasingly to kidnapping French citizens after 2007. It also bombed the French Embassy in Mauritania in January 2011.[73] In 2009, in a meeting between France, the UK, the United States, and the EU, a strategy was chosen to support the militaries of Mali, Mauritania, and Niger to fight the terrorist threat, without direct involvement of Western countries, which was called 'leading from the side'.[74]

AQIM moved into North Mali from Algeria at some point in 2009.[75] In January 2013, the allied groups in North Mali attacked into the south of the country, at which point France intervened to stop them. Ultimately, 4500 French soldiers were deployed to the country, which included forces from the bases in Chad and Abidjan as well as *Guépard* troops from France.[76] Air support, in the form of Rafales and Mirages, was used to destroy the enemy columns with French ground forces following on.[77] France intervened to stop Mali becoming a 'terrorist state' and because of the fear of the spread of the terrorist groups to other friendly countries, Senegal in particular.[78] The French military saw Serval as a major success, which retook North Mali and expelled the jihadist groups from the area, though mentioned above, there was a resurgence of the insurgency in 2014.[79]

Unlike French counterinsurgency (COIN) operations in Afghanistan,[80] Mali was fundamentally a counterterrorism campaign. French commanders were pleased that they were given the freedom to take the fight to the adversary.[81] The commander of Operation Serval, General Barrera, said that it was a great mission, because French forces could 'liberate the country and destroy the terrorists while accepting losses' (*La Voix du Nord*, 1 October 2013). Heavy firepower and Special Forces were favored to fight the terrorist groups along with close combat using regular French army units.[82] Speed was also paramount, as Hollande reportedly ordered at the start of the operation: 'destroy those in front of you and go fast'.[83]

The choice for counterterrorism instead of COIN also probably had much to do with the fact that France had limited numbers of troops available, and few strategic and matériel reserves in Africa. Budget cuts in recent years have made life difficult for the French Army, and some of the equipment used in Mali was found to be obsolete or inadapted to the climate conditions.[84] Some of the other problems pointed to in the operation included political pressure from Paris to finish as quickly as possible, sometimes without considering the results of engagements on the ground, as well as deficiencies in air transport, logistics, and in the extended supply line.[85] Heat, the corresponding lack of air conditioned facilities, and sickness also posed significant obstacles.[86] The operation was intended to be limited in time, but the full withdrawal had to be suspended in May 2014 after the defeat of the Malian Army at Kidal.[87] The French began to reinforce their contingents in Gao to create what will likely become a permanent base, and in August 2014, consolidated their forces in Africa in a major counterterrorism operation.[88]

Operation Barkhane

France found itself in 2014 with serious threats on several fronts in the Sahel, as well as three active operations: Serval in Mali, Epervier in Chad, and Operation Sangaris in the CAR, which was aimed not at stopping terrorism, but at halting ethnic and religious violence. On 1 August 2014, France shut down Serval, and combined the Serval and Epervier forces into Operation Barkhane. Its headquarters is at N'Djamena, and is composed of 3000–3500 soldiers, 200 armored vehicles, 6 fighter aircraft, 3 drones, and a variety of transport equipment.[89] Barkhane's dual missions are to aid the Sahel countries in their fight against terrorism and to stop terrorist groups from rebuilding their sanctuaries in the region.[90] A number of operations have concentrated on the Salvador Pass in Niger, where French and Nigerien troops have worked to interdict trafficking by terrorist groups in the area.[91]

Barkhane is a 'regionalization' of the response to terrorism in the Sahel. French forces have taken up a central position based on N'Djamena in the east and Gao in the west, which allows them to face the threats from multiple fronts. AQIM remains the primary threat.[92] There are a number of other threats, however, including the instability in southern Libya and the regrouping of jihadist forces there, with spillovers into northern Niger, the continuing problems in Mali, the unrest in the CAR, Al-Shabaab in Somalia, and Boko Haram. The fight against Boko Haram is part of a regional strategy ultimately aimed, in the words of the French Defense Minister, at 'the eradication of jihadist terrorism' in the Sahel.[93]

Barkhane has no time limit, and in December 2014, Le Drian expressly included the fight against Boko Haram in its mandate.[94] This looks to have been the go ahead for Chad, Niger, and Cameroon to put major combat operations against the group in motion. Unlike with operations in northern Niger, however, France has not taken part in combat. France's inaction on the ground is likely due to three factors. First, the French Army is likely stretched very thin in Barkhane, as 3500 soldiers at its maximum is very few to cover such a large region. Second, there appears to be a hierarchy of threats, as France is concentrated much more on dealing directly with the problems of AQIM and affiliated groups in Mali and Niger. Boko Haram appears to be a secondary priority. Third, while there has been a warming of relations between France and Nigeria since early 2014, with some cooperation in counterterrorism operations in the Gulf of Guinea, there is no reason to believe that Nigeria would tolerate the presence of French troops on its soil (*La Tribune*, 28 February 2014). In July 2015, however, France's ambassador to Nigeria indicated that the French government was providing 'intelligence and military support' to the Nigerian Army (*Pulse*, 16 July 2015).

Conclusion

French strategy in Africa is focused on dealing with the threats posed by a number of jihadist terrorist groups and their attempts to destabilize weak African states, as was the case with Mali in 2012 and 2013. France reluctantly intervened in Mali, but restructured its presence after the intervention to be able to respond quickly to other threats in the region. It works closely with its African allies, providing them with equipment and training for their armies, which has shown itself to be a policy with multiple successes and failures.

The interest in the fight against Boko Haram seems fairly new for France, even if the French government has been concerned about the group's activities for some time. The incursions into the territory of its Francophone allies led France to increase its military aid and support the operations of Chad, Niger, and Cameroon. Beyond the worry about the direct attacks on its allies, France is concerned about the potential for the links between terrorist groups in the Sahel. The French government was already concerned in 2014 with signs that Boko Haram was moving out of its traditional area of operations and is particularly worried about the possibility for a link-up with AQIM.[95] Boko Haram's 'pledge of allegiance' to the Islamic State in March 2015 reinforced those fears (*BBC News*, 13 March 2015).[96]

French policy toward Boko Haram will surely turn on the success or failure of the Francophone countries' offensive. It remains to be seen, however, if France would intervene directly in the case of a setback such as in Mali, as its presence in Nigeria likely would not be welcome. French strategy in the Sahel surely has its limits, but for the moment, the compromise between offensive action in certain sectors and support for allies in others is showing some marked successes.

Notes

1. French Presidency, 'Conclusions'.
2. French Presidency, 'Conférence de presse'.
3. Lagneau, 'Boko Haram.'

4. French Foreign Ministry, 'Déclarations de Laurent Fabius'.
5. French Defense Ministry, 'Lancement de l'opération Barkhane'.
6. Earlier, in May 2014, several Nigerian soldiers attempted to murder their commanding officer during operations against Boko Haram. (*BBC News*, 16 September 2014).
7. Pérouse de Montclos, 'Boko Haram', 5–6.
8. French Presidency, 'Conférence de presse'.
9. Caux and Moreno, 'More than 7,000 flee'.
10. Amnesty International, *Des Galons aux épaules*.
11. French Foreign Ministry, 'Cameroun'.
12. French National Assembly, *Rapport d'information*, 143.
13. For many years the treaties were secret, especially regarding the clauses for intervention in internal crises. The Sarkozy government decided to publish them openly after 2008. French Defense Ministry, *Défense et Sécurité Nationale*, 154–5.For the text of some of the current military cooperation treaties see:*Chad*: 'Accord de coopération militaire technique entre le Gouvernement de la République française et le Gouvernement de la République de Tchad, signé à N'Djaména les 6 mars et 19 juin 1976'. Accessed 11 February 2016. www.diplomatie.gouv.fr/fr/dossiers-pays/tchad. *Niger*: 'Accord de coopération technique entre la République française et la République du Niger'. 19 February 1977. Accessed 11 February 2016. www.diplomatie.gouv.fr/fr/dossiers-pays/niger. *Mali*: 'Exclusif – l'accord de défense franco-malien [Texte Intégral]'. (*Malijet*, 19 July 2014). *Cameroon*: 'France-Cameroun : voici les accords de défense'. (*Cameroon Voice*, 21 August 2014).
14. The debate over the military bases in Africa was a particularly fierce one, pitting the Defense Ministry against what was at that point the Cooperation Ministry (absorbed into the Foreign Ministry in 1999). See Foccart, *Tous les Soirs*, 174–5.
15. French National Assembly, *Rapport d'information*, 16.
16. Ibid., 39.
17. Ibid., 53–4.
18. Ibid., 34.
19. French National Assembly, 'Compte-rendu', 3.
20. The depots are in Dakar, Libreville, Djibouti, and Douala.
21. DCSD, 'Les Ecoles Nationales', 1.
22. CICDE, *Renforcement des capacités africaines*, 20.
23. Ibid., 11.
24. Ibid., 25.
25. Bah et al., *African Peace and Security Architecture*, 50–55.
26. CICDE, *Renforcement des capacités africaines*, 19.
27. Gonnet, 'De RECAMP à AMANI Africa', 24.
28. Porte, 'L'assistance militaire', 5.
29. French Defense Ministry, 'BSS'.
30. Magrin, 'Les ressorts de l'intervention tchadienne', 3.
31. French Senate, *Rapport d'information*, 105.
32. Gros et al., 'Serval', 23.
33. Ibid., 23.
34. French National Assembly, 'Compte-rendu', 7.
35. Ibid., 7–8.
36. Ibid., 8.
37. In 2014, Chad had difficulty providing the UN with a reliable organizational chart for the regular army. Ibid., 8.

38. French National Assembly, 'Compte-rendu', 8.
39. Ibid., 5.
40. 'Accord de coopération militaire technique entre le Gouvernement de la République française et le Gouvernement de la République de Tchad'.
41. French National Assembly, 'Compte-rendu', 3.
42. Ibid., 8–10.
43. French National Assembly, *Rapport d'information*, 21.
44. Ibid., 149.
45. Ibid., 23. Chad took part especially in the hard-fought battle at the AQIM stronghold in the Amétataï Valley.
46. Shurkin, *France's War in Mali*, 25.
47. Gros et al., 'Serval', 18.
48. Barrera, *Opération Serval*, 183, 198.
49. Ibid., 242.
50. International Crisis Group, *Niger*, 3, 17, 22–3.
51. Ibid., 1.
52. Ibid., 40.
53. Ibid., 21.
54. Ibid., 46.
55. DCSD, 'La coopération dans le Sahel', 16.
56. French National Assembly, *Rapport d'information*, 142, 229.
57. International Crisis Group, *Niger*, 41–2.
58. French National Assembly, *Rapport fait au nom de la commission des affaires étrangères*, 13.
59. Ibid., 18.
60. Ibid., 13–14.
61. Ibid., 14. It is unusual for French government documents to mention cooperation with other non-African countries, with the exception of the close cooperation between France and the United States in Niger and in Djibouti.
62. Lagneau, 'La Russie va fournir des armes au Cameroun'.
63. Pérouse de Montclos, 'Boko Haram', 9–10.
64. Haenlein, 'Can Chad Tip the Balance'.
65. French National Assembly, *Rapport*, 18.
66. Ibid., 184.
67. European Union External Action Service, 'Common Security and Defence Policy'.
68. D'Evry, 'L'Opération Serval à l'épreuve de doute', 34.
69. French National Assembly, *Rapport*, 178–80.
70. Shurkin, *France's War in Mali*, 1–2.
71. The MUJWA is now part of Mokhtar Belmokhtar's Al-Mourabitoun group, which is allied with AQIM after a December 2015 reconciliation.
72. For a useful discussion of the different groups and the 2012 offensive, see the NATO Report: Assemblée Parlementaire de l'OTAN, *Un arc de*, 3–6.
73. Koepf, 'France and the Fight Against Terrorism in the Sahel', 9–11.
74. Ibid., 13.
75. Gros et al., 3.
76. The *Guépard* system has French brigades continually on alert for overseas deployments. It is a new system, which was not implemented prior to January 2013. General Barrera's 3rd Mechanized Brigade was the first to be sent to Mali alongside Foreign Legion paratroopers and prepositioned forces in French bases. Barrera, *Opération Serval*, 21, 30, 62, 68.
77. Gros et al., 'Serval', 7–9.

78. French National Assembly, *Rapport d'information*, 112.
79. On war aims in Mali, see Gros et al., 'Serval', 3.
80. The most recent (2013) iteration of French COIN doctrine gives much more importance to the offensive than does American COIN doctrine. See CICDE, *Contre-insurrection*.
81. Barrera, *Opération Serval*, 31.
82. French National Assembly, *Rapport d'information*, 34–5.
83. Ibid., 10.
84. Ibid., 99–108. The Caracal helicopter, for example, did not work in the extreme heat conditions of North Mali.
85. D'Evry, 'L'Opération Serval à l'épreuve de doute', 30–3.
86. Barrera, *Opération Serval*, 378.
87. French National Assembly, *Rapport*, 65.
88. Ibid., 39, 49, 65.
89. French Defense Ministry, 'Lancement de l'opération Barkhane'.
90. Ibid.
91. French Defense Ministry, 'Barkhane'.
92. Waddington, 'Understanding Operation Barkhane'.
93. Lagneau, 'Selon M. Le Drian'.
94. French Defense Ministry, 'Déclaration de M. Jean-Yves Le Drian'.
95. French National Assembly, *Rapport d'information*, 122–6.
96. Boko Haram officially changed its name to 'Islamic State's West African Province' in 2015.

Disclosure statement

No potential conflict of interest was reported by the author.

References

Amnesty International. *Des Galons aux épaules. Du sang sur les mains. Les crimes de guerre commis par l'armée nigériane*. AFR 44/1661/2015. Amnesty, 2015.
Assemblée Parlementaire de l'OTAN, Commission de la Défense et de la Sécurité. *Un arc de crise aux portes de l'Europe: un nouveau partenariat stratégique nord/sud pour le Sahel*. Projet de Rapport Spécial, NATO, 10 April 2013.
Bah, Alhaji Sarjoh, Elizabeth Choge-Nyangoro, Solomon Dersso, Brenda Mofya, and Tim Murithi. *The African Peace and Security Architecture: A Handbook*. Addis Ababa: Friedrich-Ebert Stiftung and the African Union, 2014. Accessed 11 February 2016. http://library.fes.de/pdf-files/bueros/aethiopien/10779.pdf.
Barrera, Général Bernard. *Opération Serval: Notes de guerre, Mali 2013*. Paris: Editions du Seuil, 2015.
Caux, Hélène and Benoit Moreno. 2015. 'More than 7,000 flee to western Chad to escape attacks on key town in Nigeria'. *UNHCR*. 9 January.
Centre interarmées de concepts, de doctrines et d'expérimentations (CICDE). *Renforcement des capacités africaines de maintien de la Paix*. Doctrine interarmées, DIA-3.4.7(B), RECAMP (2011), no. 179/DEF/CICDE/NP, 22 September 2011.
Centre interarmées de concepts, de doctrines et d'expérimentations (CICDE). *Contre-insurrection*, Doctrine interarmées, DIA-3.4.4(A)COIN(2013), no. 064/DEF/CICDE/NP (15 April 2013).

D'Evry, Antoine. 'L'Opération Serval à l'épreuve de doute: vrais succès et fausses leçons'. *Focus Stratégique – IFRI – Laboratoire de Recherche sur la Défense* (2015), 1–57.

Direction de la Coopération de Sécurité et Défense (DCSD). 'La coopération dans le Sahel: une approche globale', *Partenaires sécurité et défense: revue de la coopération de sécurité et défense*, no. 275 (2015): 1–20.

Direction de la Coopération de Sécurité et de Défense (DCSD). 'Les Ecoles Nationales à Vocations Régionales', *Partenaires sécurité et défense: revue de la coopération de sécurité et défense*, no. 268 (2012): 8–35.

European Union External Action Service, 'Common Security and Defence Policy: The EUCAP Sahel Mali civilian mission'. January 2015.

Foccart, Jacques. *Tous les Soirs avec de Gaulle: Journal de l'Elysée – I, 1965–1967*. Paris: Fayard/Jeune Afrique, 1997.

French Defense Ministry. 'Barkhane: le Groupement tactique désert "ALTOR" conduit l'opération KOUNAMA'. 5 March 2015. Accessed 11 February 2016. http://www.defense.gouv.fr/operations/sahel/actualites/barkhane-le-groupement-tactique-desert-altor-conduit-l-operation-kounama.

French Defense Ministry. 'BSS: participation du CEMA au "G5 du Sahel"'. 11 April 2014. Accessed 11 February 2016. www.defense.gouv.fr/ema/le-chef-d-etat-major/actualite/bss-participation-du-cema-au-g5-du-sahel.

French Defense Ministry. 'Déclaration de M. Jean-Yves Le Drian, ministre de la Défense, sur l'opération Barkhane dans la sahelienne et sur la politique de défense de la France, à N'Djamena le 31 décembre 2014'. 31 December 2014. Accessed 11 February 2016. http://discours.vie-publique.fr/notices/153000039.html

French Defense Ministry. *Défense et Sécurité Nationale. Le Livre Blanc.* Paris: Odile Jacob, 2008.

French Defense Ministry. 'Lancement de l'opération Barkhane'. 1 August 2014. Accessed 11 February 2016. http://www.defense.gouv.fr/operations/actualites/lancement-de-l-operation-barkhane.

French Foreign Ministry. 'Cameroun – Attaques dans le nord du pays'. 4 August 2015. Accessed 11 February 2016. http://www.diplomatie.gouv.fr/fr/dossiers-pays/cameroun/la-france-et-le-cameroun/evenements/article/cameroun-attaques-dans-le-nord-du-pays-04-08-15.

French Foreign Ministry. 'Déclarations de Laurent Fabius lors de son déplacement au Tchad'. 21 February 2015. Accessed 11 February 2016. http://www.diplomatie.gouv.fr/fr/dossiers-pays/tchad/la-france-et-le-tchad/visites-9039/article/declarations-de-laurent-fabius.

French National Assembly. Commission de la Défense Nationale et des Forces Armées. 'Compte-rendu d'un déplacement au Tchad'. 10 February 2014.

French National Assembly. *Rapport d'information par la Commission de la Défense Nationale et des Forces Armées en conclusion des travaux d'une mission d'information sur l'évolution du dispositif militaire français en Afrique et sur le suivi des opérations en cours*, no. 2114, 9 July 2014.

French National Assembly. *Rapport fait au nom de la commission des affaires étrangères sur le projet de loi, adopté par le Sénat, autorisant l'approbation de l'accord entre le Gouvernement de la République française et le Gouvernement de la République du Cameroun instituant un partenariat de défense*, no. 3308 (5 April 2011).

French Presidency. 'Conclusions du "Sommet de Paris pour la sécurité au Nigeria"'. 17 May 2014. Accessed 10 February 2016. http://www.elysee.fr/declarations/article/conclusions-du-sommet-de-paris-pour-la-securite-au-nigeria/.

French Presidency. 'Conférence de presse du "Sommet de Paris pour la sécurité au Nigeria"'. 17 May 2014. Accessed 11 February 2016. http://www.elysee.fr/conferences-de-presse/article/conference-de-presse-du-sommet-de-paris-pour-la-securite-au-nigeria/

French Senate. *Rapport d'information fait au nom de la Commission des affaires étrangères, de la défense et des forces armées par le groupe de travail 'Sahel'*, no. 720, 3 July 2013.

Gonnet, Général François. 'De RECAMP à AMANI Africa', *Doctrine tactique: revue d'information et de réflexion*, no. 23 (2011): 24–26.

Gros, Philippe, Jean-Jacques Patry, and Nicole Vilboux. 'Serval: Bilan et perspectives', *Fondation pour la recherche stratégique*, Note no. 16/13 (2013).

Haenlein, Cathy. 2015. 'Can Chad Tip the Balance Against Boko Haram?' *RUSI Analysis*. 12 March.

International Crisis Group, *Niger: un autre maillon faible dans le Sahel?* Rapport Afrique no. 208 (19 September 2013).

Koepf, Tobias. 'France and the Fight Against Terrorism in the Sahel: The History of a Difficult Leadership Role.' *Note de l'IFRI* (June 2013): 1–34.

Lagneau, Laurent. 2015. 'Boko Haram: La France va déployer un détachement de liaison et de contact au Cameroun'. *Zone Militaire/OPEX 360*. 17 March.

Lagneau, Laurent. 2015, 'La Russie va fournir des armes au Cameroun pour lutter contre Boko Haram'. *Zone Militaire/OPEX 360*. 17 January.

Lagneau, Laurent. 2014. 'Selon M. Le Drian, l'objectif de l'opération Barkhane est "l'éradication du terrorisme jihadiste"'. *Zone Militaire/OPEX 360*. 22 July.

Magrin, Géraud. 'Les ressorts de l'intervention tchadienne au Mali (2013).' *Echogéo* (2013): 2–13.

Pérouse de Montclos, Marc-Antoine. 'Boko Haram: les enjeux régionaux de l'insurrection'. *Fondation Jean Jaurès*, Note no. 246 (2015): 1–11.

Porte, Lieutenant-Colonel Rémi. 'L'Assistance militaire depuis la seconde moitié du XIXe siècle.' *Doctrine tactique : revue d'information et de réflexion*, no. 23 (2011): 4–5.

Shurkin, Michael. *France's War in Mali: Lessons for an Expeditionary Army*. Santa Monica, CA: RAND Corporation, 2014.

Waddington, Conway. 'Understanding Operation Barkhane'. *African Defense Review* (August 2014).

Al Qaeda in the Islamic Maghreb: Terrorism, insurgency, or organized crime?

Sergei Boeke

ABSTRACT
After incurring significant losses during France's 2013 Operation Serval in Mali, Al Qaeda in the Islamic Maghreb (AQIM) is back. Mokhtar Belmokhtar has rejoined the group, violent attacks are on the increase, and southern Libya offers elements of the group a new safe-haven. This article takes a long view on AQIM, looking at its objectives and ideology, organizational structure, relationship with the local population and revenue model to determine whether they should be labelled as terrorists, insurgents, or ordinary criminals. The article concludes that AQIM generally follows a strategy of terrorism, while some elements and modus operandi could also be indicative of a strategy of insurgency. AQIM's primary commanders have a long-standing relationship with the global Al Qaeda movement, are unlikely to be seduced by the Islamic State, and enjoy significant autonomy in conducting their operations. There is, however, little evidence that supports the view that AQIM is a criminal organization behind a religious façade, and its Salafi–jihadist ideology remains a leading determinant.

Introduction

On 20 November 2015, two gunmen attacked the luxury Radisson Blu hotel in Bamako, Mali, killing 22 people before they were themselves shot by French and Malian Special Forces. The attack was initially claimed by Al Murabitoon, led by Mokhtar Belmokhtar (Khalid Abu Al Abbas), a union of two offshoots from Al Qaeda in the Islamic Maghreb (AQIM). Two weeks later, the 'emir' or commander of AQIM, Abdelmalek Droukdel (Abu Musab Abdel Wadoud) announced that Al Murabitoon had joined AQIM and that the hotel attack was their first joint operation.[1] Then on 15 January 2016, the Splendid hotel and Cappuccino Café in Ouagadougou, Burkina Faso, were hit by a similar attack, killing 30 civilians and wounding more than 56. On the same day, militants attacked a police convoy and kidnapped an elderly Australian couple in the north of the country. AQIM claimed responsibility for the hotel attack and the kidnapping.[2] While these spectacular attacks garnered much international media attention, throughout 2015 neighbouring Mali had already faced a resurgent AQIM. Suicide bombings, rocket attacks, and ambushes inflicted many casualties on local security forces and made the UN Multidimensional Integrated Stabilization Mission in Mali (MINUMSA) one of the most dangerous UN missions ever, with some 60 peacekeepers killed already.

AQIM is not the only armed group responsible for the violence in northern Mali. There is a plethora of armed factions including criminal enterprises, Tuareg separatists, government aligned militias, and several groups that espouse a Salafi–jihadist agenda. In 2012, an armed uprising was started by the 'Mouvement national de libération de l'Azawad' (MNLA), a Tuareg separatist faction, aided by three jihadist groups: AQIM, its offshoot 'Mouvement pour l'unicité et le Jihad en Afrique de l'Ouest' (MUJAO), and Ansar Dine. Once this coalition had forcefully evicted the Malian army and government administration from the north, what started as a secular rebellion was hijacked by the three Salafi–jihadist groups. They would govern the north until January 2013, when their sudden attack on the south provoked a French military intervention. Upon request of the beleaguered government in Bamako, France launched Operation Serval and liberated the north from the jihadists.[3] Since July 2013 the UN has deployed MINUSMA, France has launched a new, regional counterterrorist mission called Operation Barkhane, and the Algiers peace process is attempting to reconcile Tuareg separatists with factions that are aligned with the Malian government and the government itself. While Operation Serval inflicted serious losses on the jihadist groups in 2013, and incidental raids conducted by Barkhane have killed high-level terrorist commanders since, the groups are again becoming more active.[4]

This article will focus on AQIM as the main organization responsible for terrorist attacks in the Sahel and as the 'mother' of several violent offshoots. These include MUJAO and Belmokhtar's Al Murabitoon, which rejoined after a split lasting nearly two years. Ansar Dine and its leader, Iyad ag Ghali (Shayk Abu Fadl), are closely allied to AQIM and are in turn well connected to the newly formed Macina Liberation Front.[5] The exact relationship between the major jihadist groups remains difficult to discern, and the example of an important Malian jihadist, Oumar Ould Hamaha, illustrates how a commander can switch from AQIM to Ansar Dine and finally to MUJAO.[6] It is no coincidence that Belmokhtar has recently rejoined forces with AQIM: both are fiercely loyal to Al Qaeda's leader Ayman Al-Zawahiri and they are facing increasing competition from the Islamic State (IS). In the north, IS has established a firm foothold in Libya, and in the south, in Nigeria, Boko Haram has already pledged its allegiance to Al-Baghdadi. A spokesman for MUJAO announced the group's allegiance to IS in May 2015, but this was quickly denied by other group members.[7] The increase of violence in Mali and beyond, an uptake of media announcements by AQIM commanders, and the budding competition with IS merits a new analysis of AQIM. Taking a long view of AQIM's origins and actions, this article uses a conceptual framework to analyse whether the organization should be categorized as an insurgency, terrorist group, or crime syndicate.

Labels, definitions, and concepts

AQIM has been the focus of significant academic scholarship, although many authors have confined their research to one article, frequently preferring a descriptive analytical approach to a conceptual or theoretical one. Mathieu Guidère has published extensively on AQIM and was one of three experts consulted by the Associated Press to determine the authenticity of several Al Qaeda letters that were discovered in Timbuktu, Mali.[8] Jean-Pierre Filiu, who is an Arabist like Guidère, has equally written quality works on AQIM, rich in primacy sources, before broadening his scope to Al Qaeda in general and the Islamic State.[9] Many authors have researched AQIM's Algerian roots, its relationship with Al Qaeda, and the dichotomy between its focus on the 'near' or 'far enemy', with Jean-Luc Marret notably labelling AQIM a 'glocal' organization.[10] Andrew Lebovich has recently published several works on AQIM and other related Sahel jihadist groups.[11] Nonetheless, the existing body of literature on AQIM is – understandably – strongly embedded in the field of terrorism studies, with consequently neither an argued case for its terrorist label, nor a consideration of other classifications and their potential implications.

From a policy perspective, the decision to label an armed group as terrorists, insurgents, or criminals is an important one. Terrorism is a politically loaded term and is dependent on the subjective opinion of the observer, illustrated by the adage that one man's terrorist is another's freedom fighter. Framing a group as terrorists effectively delegitimizes them, while simultaneously justifying a policy of violence in response. As Philip Herbst argues, '[c]onveying criminality, illegitimacy, and even madness, the application of the term terrorist shuts the door to discussion *about* the stigmatized group or *with* them, while reinforcing the righteousness of the labellers, justifying their agenda's and mobilising their responses'.[12] Conversely, labelling a group as ordinary criminals (notwithstanding that terrorism is also illegal), belittles the underlying grievances, ideologies, and motivations, attributing their actions to solely personal, often material gain. In all cases, the designated label channels a policy reaction that is anchored in the very different fields of counterterrorism, counterinsurgency (COIN), or law enforcement, each centred around its own principles, dogmas, and common practices.

AQIM has been designated a terrorist group by the United Nations Security Council, the United States, and the European Union. Nonetheless, reaching consensus on the definition of terrorism has proven to be extremely difficult; neither academia nor the UN can agree on such a value-laden and subjective term.

Avoiding the debate on definitions, this article will use the revised academic definition of terrorism as formulated by Alex Schmid:

> Terrorism refers on the one hand to a **doctrine** about the presumed effectiveness of a special form or tactic of fear-generating, coercive political violence and, on the other hand, to a conspiratorial **practice** of calculated, demonstrative, direct violent action without legal or moral restraints, targeting mainly civilians and non-combatants, performed for its propagandistic and psychological effects on various audiences and conflict parties.[13]

The concept *insurgency* has provoked less debate, with general recognition that it is a strategy (not a tactic) to achieve political and military control over a population and territory. Traditionally insurgencies have consisted of irregular movements that have sought to mobilize a part of the population to assist in overthrowing the governing authorities.[14] Nonetheless, distinguishing between terrorists and insurgents remains fraught with difficulty, as they often share the same modus operandi.

According to Duyvesteyn and Fumerton, it is essential to regard terrorism and insurgency as two distinct *strategies* of irregular war.[15] The fundamental differences can be divided into three categories. First, the political objectives differ. Terrorism aims to provoke a response through violence to attain a political effect. Insurgents, conversely, intend to force political change through political and military control of a territory and its population. Secondly, the organizational structures differ as a result of the diverging objectives. Terrorists generally act in small and secret conspiracies, while insurgencies need a large and relatively open shadow state structure. Finally, for organizations following a terrorist strategy, active involvement of the population is not critical for success, although public support can shape and constrain both the actions of terrorists and the governments that counter them.[16] Conversely, for an insurgency, control of or support from the population is essential for strategic success.

This article will use Duyvesteyn and Fumerton's three categories to examine AQIM and add a fourth element: the financial revenue model. By their very nature, illegal organizations like terrorist or insurgent groups will revert to illegal activities to fund their operations. It is important to investigate whether these fundraising activities present an intrinsic clash with the group's professed ideology. For example, drugs are officially *haram* (forbidden or sinful) in Islam, and even smoking and alcohol were banned when the jihadists governed northern Mali. If they subsequently traffic these goods, it could imply that material gain trumps religious or ideological motives, moving the classification of the organization into the domain of organized crime. When the gap between preaching and practice is sufficiently large, this can be exploited to undermine the group's legitimacy and credibility.

This distinction between terrorism and insurgency, and even the relevance and usefulness of the exercise, is not without controversy. James Khalil, noting that academic research is stove-piped into these two categories with parallel literatures sharing few insights and sources, argues that it is impossible to arbitrarily impose binary distinctions upon continuous variables such as population support and control of territory.[17] David Kilcullen and John Mackinlay have argued that Al Qaeda should be seen as a global insurgency that uses terrorist tactics, since the global jihad has the objective of reinstating the Caliphate and replacing apostate local regimes.[18] Conceptual confusion is compounded by the complexities of the Sahel. In Mali alone, there are a more than a dozen armed groups, including separatists, militias, and jihadi groups. They have different objectives and oscillate between competition and cooperation, with fighters frequently switching groups. 'Last year alone', a Tuareg explained to Peter Tinti in 2014, 'there are people who have changed from Malian military, to separatist rebel, to jihadist, to French ally, all while being narco-traffickers.'[19]

AQIM's historical roots

The origins of AQIM lie in the crucible of the Algerian civil war. Its current generation of commanders, including the Emir Droukdel and commanders such as Belmokhtar and Djamel Okacha all hark back to the original *insurgency* against the Algerian government. In 1992 a broad Islamist movement was robbed of an impending electoral victory by a military coup that cancelled the elections. Algeria immediately descended into violence that only abated at the end of the decade, costing an estimated 200,000 lives. 'Afghan Algerians', the so-called foreign fighters who had returned from 'jihad' or training camps in Afghanistan, played a central role in the conflict. These trained combatants, many of whom had developed personal bonds with the future Al Qaeda leadership and had been infused with its ideology, formed the nucleus of the 'Groupe Islamique Armé' (GIA). The GIA was initially only one of many groups fighting the government, but by 1994 had become the predominant and most violent faction. Based on Salafi–jihadist ideology, it had a particularly uncompromising stance, symbolized by its motto: no agreement, no truce, no dialogue.[20] Those that the group labelled *takfir* (enemies of Islam), were classified as legitimate targets and therefore deserved to be killed, even if they were Muslim elderly, women, or children. Several notorious fatwas by the preacher Abu Qatada in the Salafist weekly bulletin *Al Ansar* (the 'Partisan'), printed in London, justified GIA massacres.[21]

The GIA specifically targeted foreigners; first in Algeria and later in France. In December 1994 the GIA hijacked Air France 8969 from Algiers to Paris. France was the former colonial oppressor, and it was hated for its support of the military regime in Algiers. The hijackers probably intended to fly the plane into the Eiffel Tower but were diverted to Marseille to refuel, where the plane was stormed by elite French police. In 1995 eight bombs exploded in the Paris underground, and a year later, seven Tibherine monks were abducted and beheaded in Algeria, horrifying the French public. These actions contributed to continued international support for the military regime in its fight against the Islamists, and a soft stance on the mass torture and extrajudicial executions that had become institutionalized as part of its counterterrorism policy.[22] There is a strong body of evidence, including testimonies from military defectors, indicating that the security service, the Département du Renseignement et de la Securité (DRS), infiltrated and manipulated the GIA. Agents provocateurs fostered infighting and purges, and its wanton violence undermined the credibility of the general Islamic opposition among locals and the international community. Even investigations into the Air France hijacking and Tibherine murders point to a duplicitous role of the DRS.[23]

The turning point occurred in early 1998, when hundreds of civilians were massacred in the villages of Rais, Benthalla, and others. Here, too, were worrying signs of military units aiding and abetting mass murder.[24] The magazine *Al Ansar* distanced itself from the GIA, and a large faction split off, founding the 'Groupe Salafiste pour la Prédication et le Combat' (GSPC), vowing only to hit government targets. The last remnants of the GIA used the government's reconciliation programme to defect or were hunted down by the Algerian military. Bin Laden and the newly formed Al Qaeda supported the creation of the GSPC and its Afghan Algerians.[25] While the new group firmly aligned itself with the Salafi–jihadist Al Qaeda ideology, in its first communiqué in September 1998 the group emphasized its objective of toppling the Algerian regime, but in no way mentioned any foreign enemy.[26] On 11 September 2003, the GSPC's emir pledged allegiance to Bin Laden and Mullah Omar in a communiqué.[27] On 11 September 2006, exactly five years after 9/11, Al Qaeda leader Al-Zawahiri announced that the GSPC had joined Al Qaeda and urged them to become 'a bone in the throat of the American and French crusaders'.[28] On 26 January 2007 the GSPC, led by Droukdel, announced that it had rebranded itself 'Al Qaeda in the land of the Islamic Maghreb'.

In the mid-2000s, many GSPC/AQIM fighters travelled to Iraq to join the fight against the 'American occupier'. Al-Zarqawi, the leader of Al Qaeda in Iraq (AQI), and Droukdel formed a close relationship, releasing propaganda statements in each other's support.[29] AQIM adopted several modus operandi of Al Qaeda in Iraq, such as suicide bombings which had hardly been used by the GIA during the Algerian civil war. The ability to hit hardened targets such as UN facilities and well-protected military installations has since been an enduring AQIM capability. Although AQIM was inspired by Al-Zarqawi and copied some of his tactics, Abu Yahya al-Libi, a high-ranking Al Qaeda official, used the example of the GIA to warn Al-Zarqawi that his brutality and wanton cruelty would alienate the local population and lead to his demise.[30] Al-Zarqawi ignored the warning, lost popular support, and was killed, but AQIM commanders had learned the lesson well.

Objectives and ideology

A terrorist strategy aims at political change, without necessarily controlling the population. Violence serves as 'propaganda by the deed' and aims to influence a target audience psychologically. Terrorists want to provoke a response, and it is this response – and not their actions – that fulfils their goals. For an insurgency, the political end goal is to establish some manner of governance of the population. An example is the MNLA which launched the uprising in Mali in January 2012 to establish the independent state of Azawad, but saw their rebellion hijacked by AQIM, MUJAO, and Ansar Dine.

The main driver of Al Qaeda's strategy is its Salafi–jihadist ideology. In a rare and extensive 2008 interview with the *New York Times*, Droukdel laid out AQIM's objectives, ideology, and achievements and explained the rationale behind its attacks. The first question asked was why he had joined Al Qaeda, and he replied that is was essential to join forces in the face of the 'unified oppressors' that were fermenting division among Muslim lands, stealing their riches, and corrupting their populations. As for AQIM's goals, Droukdel added:

> Our general goals are the same goals of Al Qaeda the mother, and you know them. As far as our goals concerning the Islamic Maghreb, they are plenty. But most importantly is to rescue our countries from the tentacles of these criminal regimes that betrayed their religion, and their people.[31]

In the interview, Droukdel reiterated the Al Qaeda policy of not recognizing country borders: 'We are one nation with one religion and one language. Our history is the same but our land is divided, torn apart into states by colonialism.' In comparison to the propaganda of the Islamic State, one word was conspicuously absent during the interview: the Caliphate. For Al Qaeda, the establishment of a Caliphate is but a distant objective, one that must not be hastened.[32]

Essential to Al Qaeda's ideology are the teachings of the Egyptian Sayyid Qutb, notably his book *Milestones* (1964), and the concepts of 'far enemy' and 'near enemy'.[33] Jihad is considered a personal obligation and a violent struggle against the apostate regimes in Muslim countries (the 'near enemy') and against the United States and the West (the 'far enemy'). The dilemma of which to focus on has been central to Al Qaeda and AQIM in the past decade, and priorities have changed over time. In Al-Zawahiri's recent speeches, but also in Droukdel's 2008 interview, the emphasis lies on the near enemy.

Government installations and the military – the near enemy – have been repeatedly struck by AQIM, although attacks are frequently underreported by Western media. In June 2005 the remote army base Lemgheity in the Mauritanian desert was attacked by Belmokhtar's unit, killing 17 soldiers.[34] Since then AQIM has conducted dozens of ambushes, killing scores of soldiers and police officers in Algeria, Tunisia, and Mali. The issue of killing civilians remains a sensitive one, eliciting debate after the multiple suicide bombings in Algiers in 2007. In the *New York Times* interview Droukdel reaffirmed that AQIM specifically aimed to strike at official government targets and Western interests, and that considerable effort went into avoiding Muslim casualties, but that some inevitable 'collateral damage' should not detract from an attack's success. The 2015 hotel attacks in Bamako and Ouagadougou were specifically aimed at locations popular with foreigners, and the purported separation of Muslims from non-Muslims in the Bamako hotel was reminiscent of Belmokhtar's 2013 attack on the In Amenas gas plant, where locals were also separated from foreign employees and spared.[35] The specific targeting of government and security forces, and the purported care to avoid civilian casualties, is a common feature of insurgencies and guerrilla campaigns.

AQIM has threatened the 'far enemy' in countless audio and video messages. While it has attacked Western interests in the Sahel on many occasions, it has not managed to successfully launch an attack on the European mainland, unlike for instance Al Qaeda in the Arabic Peninsula (AQAP), responsible for the Charlie Hebdo attack (Paris, January 2015) or IS (Paris, November 2015). This is not for want of trying, and according to French intelligence several attacks in France have been prevented.[36] The hatred against France has remained a constant factor since the GIA attacks, and Droukdel, Belmokhtar, and Iyad ag Ghali have all specifically mentioned France as a primary target in their many media announcements. The 2007 killing of French tourists in Mauritania, frequent hostage takings, and specific threats have frightened away tourists and even forced the Paris–Dakar race to move to South America. AQIM, however, has not inherited the extensive GIA network that was active in London, Brussels, and Paris in the mid-nineties, nor managed to mobilize elements within the large Maghreb diaspora in France. In general, AQIM's continuous targeting of security forces and the purported attempts to avoid civilian casualties have recently been overshadowed by the hotel attacks, strongly indicating a strategy of terrorism.

Organizational structure and recruitment

The different strategies of terrorism and insurgency result in divergent organizational structures and recruitment efforts. For insurgents, whose aim is to ultimately control a population, some sort of shadow governance structure, with formal lines of hierarchy, is necessary. In parallel, the objective of building up a military force to oust the authorities requires a substantial recruitment effort among the local population. The Taliban in Afghanistan, for instance, clearly display both these elements. Groups following a terrorist strategy, conversely, do not need to mobilize the masses, but use small, secretive groups to terrorize and intimidate. They tend to exhibit selective and small-scale recruitment as a result of the secretive nature they must adopt to avoid state counterterrorist efforts.

The organizational structure of Al Qaeda has changed considerably over the years, and its secretive nature makes it hard to analyse. Under pressure from US drone strikes in Pakistan's tribal areas, Al Qaeda has evolved from a centrally directed organization into a worldwide 'franchiser' of terrorist attacks. Some consider it more a 'network organization' or a 'movement' than a classical organization.[37] The Abbottabad letters, consisting of (only) 17 declassified letters from a treasure trove of documents captured during the Bin Laden raid in May 2011, offer a relatively recent insight into organizational issues. While probably not representative, the letters suggest that AQIM was not as important to Al Qaeda central as the other affiliates. AQIM appeared to have a significant degree of autonomy and generally followed advice given by the strategic leadership.[38] On the other hand, letters found in Timbuktu in 2013 offer the AQIM point of view. In a letter from Droukdel to his commanders, he mentions that on several occasions he had sought advice from Al Qaeda central, but not received any guidance back.[39] Aware of the risks of phone or email interception and localization long before the Snowden revelations, Al Qaeda's strategic leadership had to communicate by letter. Internal communication remains a challenge for AQIM, hampering operationalization of the chosen strategy.

AQIM has adapted and adjusted the GSPC's organizational structure, which in turn was largely based on the GIA. During the height of the Algerian insurgency, the GIA consisted of a nebulous network of armed factions headed by emirs, nominally united by the central leadership, but often autonomous in practice.[40] The GIA had divided Algeria into nine zones, a practice that was continued by the GSPC. Over the past decade, more combat and terrorist operations have shifted from northern Algeria to the large southern expanses of the Sahara, Belmokhtar's fiefdom. Now operations have been divided into two sectors, a central emirate for northern Algeria and Tunisia, and a Sahara emirate for northern Mali, Niger, Mauritania, and Libya led by Djamel Okacha (Yahia Abu El Hamam).[41] The central leadership consists of a 14-member Shura council, presided over by Emir Droukdel and including regional commanders and the heads of the political, military, judicial, and media committees.[42] The current AQIM strategic leadership is based in the mountainous region of Kabylie to the east of Algiers, where the ethnic Berber population is engaged in an ancient struggle with the central government for more autonomy.[43] AQIM's basic fighting unit is formed by a *katiba* (also spelled '*katibat*' or '*katibah*'), the Arabic word for phalanx or battalion, which was widely used during the Algerian war of independence (1954–1962). There is no standard number of fighters per katiba, and its size can vary from two dozen combatants to several hundred.

The limits of AQIM's organizational structure were laid bare during the second half of 2012, when together with Ansar Dine and MUJAO it controlled northern Mali. The expulsion of the Malian army and the conquest of the north was initiated by the Tuareg MNLA, but the alliance of convenience with the jihadist groups quickly broke down. MNLA fighters were violently evicted by the jihadist groups or switched sides. The MNLA had become unpopular through widespread pillage and instances of rape in the towns they occupied, were not supported by the non-Tuareg majority, and lacked the finances of the jihadists.[44] Nonetheless, an elaborately written instruction by Droukdel to his lieutenants indicates that conflict with the MNLA was not desired.[45] According to the letter, the decision to go to war with the MNLA, 'after becoming close and almost completing a deal with them. . . . was a major mistake'. The local commanders were chastised in the letter and reminded that the strategic leadership had still not received clarification on the turn of events.[46]

The problem of command and control – or recalcitrant commanders – led to a second strategic mistake, with disastrous consequences for their Islamic state project. Droukdel, ever mindful of the threat of a military intervention, explicitly instructed his commanders to refrain from provoking the international community, even to the point that it was 'better for you to be silent and pretend to be a domestic movement that has its own causes and concerns. There is no call for you to show that we have an expansionary, jihadi, Qaida or any other sort of project.' The order not to provoke was ignored by Ansar Dine, who launched the January 2013 attack on southern Mali, eliciting the immediate and overwhelming French military response. Belmokhtar was another difficult commander, and he was sharply criticized in an extensive 30-point letter from Droukdel for always doing things his own way.[47] The criticism ranged from agreeing to an 'absurdly' low ransom for hostage Robert Fowler (€700,000) to contacting Al-Zawahiri directly and failing to organize large attacks. This and Belmokhtar's personal rivalry with Abu Zeid, another important commander in the Sahara, undoubtedly contributed to him leaving AQIM in December 2012. Days after Operation Serval was launched, his new group called *Katibat al-Mulathameen* (The Masked Brigade) attacked the Algerian In Amenas gas installation, with Belmokhtar subsequently brazenly claiming he had acted on behalf of Al Qaeda.

AQIM's recruitment efforts have known significant ups and downs during the past decade. Diplomat Robert Fowler offers a candid account of life as an Al Qaeda hostage and describes the background of the fighters in Belmokhtar's *katiba*.[48] The jihadists had varied ethic and social backgrounds, with the unit comprising fighters from all over the Sahel. The mainstay of the leadership cadre was Algerian, with 'sub-Saharan Africans clearly second class in the eyes of AQIM'.[49] According to analysts, this is one of the reasons that MUJAO split away, recruiting more within Songhai and other black African communities.[50] Fowler also noted that many of the warriors were extremely young, some even pre-adolescent. Several years later, during the jihadists' 2012 control of northern Mali, hundreds of child soldiers were recruited.[51] As the governing authority, the jihadists could recruit and press-gang children into service without impediment. The so-called Islamic state of Azawad also attracted many foreign fighters from all over Africa, but in contrast to Syria, only a handful from Europe. The three jihadist groups grew at such a rate, setting up training camps in the north, that according to a French intelligence official, if France had waited much longer with Operational Serval it might not have had the capacity to tackle the groups on its own.[52]

The French intervention caused significant losses among the jihadists, killing around 700, taking 430 prisoners, and destroying some 200 tons of arms and ammunition.[53] Under pressure, AQIM urged especially Tunisians not to travel to Syria but join the fight in the Maghreb: 'The front of the Islamic Maghreb today is in desperate need of the support of the sons of Tunisia, Morocco, Libya and Mauritania to repel the French crusade.'[54] This was to no avail, as the conflict in Syria is a much bigger magnet for Tunisian Salafi–jihadists than AQIM, with now probably at least 5000 Tunisians fighting there.[55] This is significantly more than AQIM's current total strength. Only AQIM's small 'Uqba bin Nafi' *katiba* regularly attacks security forces in southern Tunisia.[56] Nonetheless, three years after Serval, AQIM is again recruiting successfully in northern Mali and beyond. By providing information that can be used to target MINUSMA convoys, a local in Mali can earn around €750. In a country where the minimum wage is less than €50 a month, the temptation to work for or with AQIM can be considerable.[57] AQIM's organizational structure and recruitment efforts transformed considerably during the phase that it controlled northern Mali, and reverted to the status quo ante after Operation Serval. This would not only indicate that AQIM follows a terrorist strategy, but also seems to validate this criterion to distinguish between a terrorist strategy and an insurgent one.

Relationship with the population

According to Duyvesteyn and Fumerton, groups with an insurgent strategy have a fundamentally different interaction with the local population than those with a terrorist strategy. The French pioneer in counterinsurgency doctrine, David Galula, argues that for an insurgency the 'exercise of political power depends on the tacit or explicit agreement of the population or, at worst, on its submissiveness'.[58] Population support, either winning the 'heart and minds' or instigating a system of collective oppression, are therefore vital to an insurgency. Terrorist groups, in part due to their secretive nature, are often alienated and isolated from the broader population. By following a terrorist strategy, through violence aimed at civilians, they actually risk being considered an enemy of the people rather than of the government.[59] To characterize the different levels of interaction with the local population, this section will use three levels of *freedom* that a group has in a certain territory. These are freedom of movement, freedom from interdiction (or safe-haven/sanctuary), and finally freedom to control the population. The last level indicates that an insurgency has achieved its objective.

Concerning freedom of movement, survival in the vast and arid plains of the Sahara is not an individual or group challenge, but a social and cultural undertaking. Many nomads and drivers habitually traverse the desert, and cordial relations with 'locals' are a required minimum to allow for an undisturbed travel or presence. The desert is literally dotted with caches of reserve petrol supplies, water reservoirs, car tyres, or other spare materials, left by transporters as a back-up in case of vehicle breakdowns or emergencies. The locals know the owner of each cache, and it is customary practice not to use anyone else's cache unless in an emergency, under the strict condition of replenishing the goods as quickly as possible.[60] AQIM thus has its own caches distributed throughout the huge Sahel area, acknowledged and left untouched by others, just as AQIM respects other caches. AQIM units equally expend a considerable effort in keeping good relations with any locals that are encountered during their travels.[61] Marriage is another effective method of integrating into local communities, and Belmokhtar married into a noble Berabish tribe near Timbuktu, ensuring good relations with powerful tribes.[62] Coexistence with locals was the preferred strategy of AQIM's mobile *katibas*, enabling them to frequently change camps to foil intelligence services that attempted to locate them. Travelling large distances, their modus operandi resemble the traditional nomadic *rezzou*, swift and brutal raids to destroy the enemy. AQIM's current freedom of movement stretches from Mauritania to Niger, and southern Algeria to Burkina Faso.

Sanctuaries offer reprieve from government pursuit and allow for recovery and replenishment after sustaining losses. The whole of northern Mali was effectively a safe-haven for AQIM up until 2013. Within this vast area, they developed a mountainous redoubt in the Ametetai valley, an area of about 25 square kilometres full of caves, crevices, and valleys in the Ardar des Ifoghas. AQIM chose it because it was the only location that provided natural water sources, and it frequently held its hostages there.[63] The valleys were fortified by defensive positions, including heavy machinegun and mortar positions. During Operation Serval it was methodically cleared by elite French and Chadian troops, killing Abu Zeid and decimating his *katiba*. Now surveilled by drones and continuously at risk of a sudden air strike, it no longer offers a safe-haven. Libya has become the new sanctuary. Already during the last months of Gadhafi's reign in 2011, AQIM dispatched teams to establish jihadist cells in the southern regions. These have grown in importance since, and Libya's south-west has been termed a 'vipers nest' for terrorists by the French Defence Minister Le Drian.[64]

When AQIM governed parts of north Mali, from summer 2012 until Operation Serval, its relationship with the local population changed from mutual acquiescence to control. In a May 2012 audio message, Droukdel emphasized the need to gradually impose Sharia. He affirmed that it would be an error to impose all the rules of Islam in one go, but that 'places of drugs, alcohol and immorality had to be closed immediately'. He also called for his AQIM 'brothers' to ensure security in towns under their control, and that essential services such as health care, water, and electricity had to be provided.[65] The Timbuktu letters, probably dating from July, reinforce his earlier message and suggest making concessions with the enemy or locals. This was vital to avoid divisions between the groups and in society, as '[t]he aim of building these bridges is to make it clear that our Mujehadin are no longer isolated in society, and to integrate with the different factions, including the big tribes and the main rebel movement and tribal chiefs.'[66] This illustrates the difficulty of transitioning from a terrorist strategy to an insurgent one. The letter stresses prudence and moderation, comparing the Islamic project in Azawad to a small baby that must be nurtured and helped to stand on its own two feet (in a particularly hostile environment).

Droukdel was adamant that the implementation of the Sharia must not be hastened. Gradual evolution had to be applied in an environment that was ignorant of religion. 'And our previous experience proved that applying Shariah this way, without taking the environment into consideration will lead to people rejecting the religion, and engender hatred toward the Mujehadin, and will consequently lead to the failure of our experiment.'[67] By criminalizing alcohol, smoking, and the music and dance so central to local culture, and meting out harsh *hudud* punishments, the jihadists alienated large parts of the population. The deeply unpopular destruction of the shrines in Timbuktu, carried out by Ansar Dine, was equally criticized by Droukdel in his letter. In 2013 Operation Serval proved him right, and the French were welcomed as liberators by a euphoric population.[68]

Since Operation Serval, AQIM has reverted to a more distant relationship with the locals. There is widespread insecurity, caused in part by the slow Algiers peace process and inter-ethnic violence, and disillusionment with the government's lack of reform. In some areas in the north, there is apparently even less electricity than during the time the jihadists were in control, provoking nostalgia among some for the occupation by AQIM.[69] In November 2015, 50 masked AQIM fighters, arriving in a dozen pick-up trucks, disrupted two different intercommunal meetings in the Timbuktu region. They read out a letter encouraging reconciliation between communities, threatened those that collaborated with the 'Enemies of Islam', and promised to act against rural criminality. Before they left, the fighters distributed USB sticks containing copies of the letter, the Quran, and a video that featured the beheading of a collaborator.[70]

AQIM's relationship with the population has thus changed significantly over time and differs considerably in the areas where it operates. In the broader Sahel, AQIM has extensive freedom of movement and is relatively isolated from the population, although it does respect local customs in the large desert regions. This points to a strategy of terrorism, but is offset for example by current AQIM intimidation in the Timbuktu area. Here the AQIM *katiba* seeks to control the population, threatening collaborators and offering to provide security from petty crime. This deviates from the concept of secretive, alienated terrorist groups and illustrates the difficulty of conceptualizing AQIM's modus operandi in rigid frameworks.

Criminal revenues as a goal or a means

In the fight against terrorism, violent non-state actors are often accused of involvement in organized crime and the drug trade. This is certainly the case for AQIM, with many governments and analysts arguing that its radical Islamist rhetoric merely serves as a cover for the group's profitable criminal activities.[71] Some of the policy implications of this conclusion are clear: a stronger international effort is needed to disrupt illicit trafficking in West Africa, to 'hit AQIM where it hurts' and deprive it of much needed funds.[72] Mindful of the lack of reliable primary sources concerning AQIM's financial income, this section will investigate AQIM's three main revenue generating activities: smuggling, the drug trade, and kidnapping for ransom.

Northern Mali has traditionally been an international crossroads for trade and commerce, and smuggling has always formed a large part of local livelihood. The northern city of Kidal is almost completely dependent on goods that come from Algeria, and the price differences of subsidized goods are readily exploited by smugglers. A matrix of networks that traditionally transports licit goods, such as petrol, tobacco, and foodstuffs, has diversified into illicit goods such as weapons, narcotics, and human-trafficking. According to Judith Scheele, the official distinction between legal and illegal trans-border trade is largely meaningless and has been replaced by what locals deem morally acceptable and what is not.[73] Most of the economy is informal and thus difficult to quantify, but cigarette smuggling has always constituted a large share of the contraband. This is where Mokhtar Belmokhtar would have earned his notorious moniker 'Mr Marlboro'. The accuracy of his reputation, however, is disputed by Mauritanian journalist Lemine Ould Salem, who has interviewed several government officials and traffickers in the region. These are all adamant that Belmokhtar was never a member of the cigarette smuggling networks. Instead he frequently frustrated their business by intercepting contraband convoys, burning cargos of cigarettes after sternly lecturing that they were '*haram*'.[74]

The drug trade has an enormous impact on the region. It took off around 2004 as European port and airport controls were tightened and South American cartels discovered the soft underbelly of West Africa. For cocaine, the most important route has become 'Highway 10', named after the 10th parallel across the Atlantic Ocean. The drugs are brought in by plane or by boat, pass through failing states like Guinea-Bissau and then transit north through Mali.[75] The drugs are transported not by a single organization, but by a complex web of networks, each forming a small link in the supply chain that stretches from the Andes to Europe.[76] There is little empirical evidence to support allegations of direct AQIM involvement in drug smuggling, but it is plausible to assume that it has on occasion, like many other groups in northern Mali, imposed transit fees or provided security escorts.[77] Many reports credit MUJAO with a larger role in the drug trade, and the city of Gao, as their primary base and recruiting ground, is an important hub on the cocaine route.[78]

More important, however, is the role that the government of Mali has played in allowing the drug trade to flourish. During President Amadou Toumani Toure's rule (2001–2012), Mali's political and security structures had become deeply enmeshed in narco-trafficking, corrupting the state to the highest level. The state lost its legitimacy with the population, social relations within communities – especially between elders and the young – were disrupted, and fraught relations between ethnic groups were further exacerbated. The narco-networks embedded themselves so deeply in society that little changed during the jihadists' occupation of the north, and even Operation Serval has not fundamentally affected the trade.[79]

Kidnapping for ransom is the main source of revenue for AQIM. In early 2003, 32 European tourists were abducted by the GSPC in the Algerian Sahara. Half were freed during an Algerian military operation, while the last group ended up in northern Mali and was reportedly released for a total ransom of €5 million. A precedent was set for terrorist groups to kidnap Westerners for ransom. Since 2003, nearly all of the around 60 hostages have been released, with the notable exceptions of Edwin Dyer and Michel Germaneau, who were executed in 2009 and 2010, and Antoine De Leocour and Vincent Delory, who died during a failed rescue attempt by French special forces in 2011. The ransoms have been subject to considerable inflation with €5 million to €10 million per hostage now the reported going rate. According to an investigation by the *New York Times*, at least $91.5 million had been paid to AQIM (and presumably to its partner in crime, MUJAO) between 2008 and 2014.[80] This has led to a vicious cycle where each release provides the incentive for another hostage-taking.

For AQIM, hostage-taking remains a means to an end. Belmokhtar initially challenged the practice of hostage-taking and requested arbitration from AQIM's legal committee, considering it not part of jihad as the hostages were generally non-combatants and civilians. He also feared that the practice would attract unwanted attention from Western security services. AQIM's legal committee ruled that all actions aimed to defend or extend Islam were legitimate jihad actions (subject to 'the Law of War in Islam'), and that Western citizens were to be regarded as combatants, as they had democratically elected governments that supported 'the War on Terror'.[81] After this decision, Belmokhtar also reverted to the practice, kidnapping Robert Fowler in Niger in 2008. In the terrorism versus organized crime debate, Fowler is convinced that the former label applies to AQIM. His reasoning is worth quoting in full:

> Almost since 9/11, there has been a loud debate among securocrats over whether Al Qaeda and its franchises, like AQIM, are bandits, opportunists, thugs, psychopaths, and restless, underemployed youths flying a flag of Islamic convenience, or, conversely, deeply committed religious zealots engaging, Robin Hood-like, in banditry, kidnapping and trafficking to finance the achievement of their Islamic vision. Many, probably most, have opted for some variation of the convenient first option, and many security services still favour this interpretation, mostly, I suspect, because it makes these movements easy to belittle and should make them much easier to defeat. Whatever the reasoning, based on my experience, I know it to be the wrong answer.[82]

The whole of Fowler's book supports the analysis that AQIM's particular fundamentalist take on Islam affected everything to do with the kidnapping and its resolution. Belmokhtar is described as a revered leader with a palpably commanding presence, principled in the radical interpretation of his faith, but who ensured that his hostages were not mistreated or tortured during their captivity.

Fowler notes how he and his fellow hostage were continually hounded by many zealous members of the *katiba* 'to become slaves of Allah', but that they tenaciously managed to resist converting to Islam. Belmokhtar finally put the issue to rest by saying that a conversion could not be imposed and had to be voluntary.[83]

Governments invariably offer carefully formulated denials that they pay ransoms, but money is frequently paid through or by others. When confronted by the otherwise imminent death of one of their nationals, countries are less principled when it comes to the policy of offering no ransoms or significant concessions. The stance of Algeria, the United Kingdom, and the United States to under no circumstances pay ransoms is a wise one, and has been agreed as desirable state practice in the Global Counter Terrorism Forum (GCTF). It also figured in a separate declaration of the June 2013 G8 in Lough Erne. Here the agreement to 'unequivocally reject the payment of ransoms to terrorists' did not last beyond October when France paid more than €20 million to secure the release of the four hostages taken at Arlit, Niger.[84] For the Sahel hostages, France, Switzerland, and Spain have paid the largest share of the ransoms, and their nationals are not coincidentally kidnapped most frequently. Nonetheless, Fowler rebukes the Anglo-Saxon allies that criticized Canada for paying the ransom that secured his release, presenting several lesser known cases of hypocrisy in Iraq and Afghanistan.[85] If states and companies do manage to resist the temptation to pay large ransoms to secure the release of their nationals, this will impact enormously on AQIM's ability to finance its operations. It would also end the trend of continuing hostage takings in the Sahel.

The available evidence does not support the analysis that AQIM's jihadist rhetoric is merely the façade of a criminal organization that has self-enrichment as its primary objective. Just as Belmokhtar's reputation as a cigarette smuggler is hard to reconcile with local evidence, AQIM's role in the drugs trade seems equally marginal. This stands in stark contrast to the large role that the corrupt Malian government has played in allowing the drug trade to flourish, for instance by facilitating passage and obstructing law-enforcement efforts. This would imply that the counterterrorism strategy of cutting AQIM's drug revenue misses the point and could prove counterproductive. The drug trade probably has a bigger negative influence on Malian society than terrorism, and the international community should avoid approaching the problem through the prism of counterterrorism, where the state is both a victim and a partner in the fight. Only through fighting corruption and fundamentally reforming government institutions and practices can the problem of drugs be addressed.

Conclusion

Despite experiencing serious setbacks over the past decade, AQIM has shown remarkable continuity and resilience. The jihadist galaxy in Mali and the broader Sahel may at first glance appear to be fractured, but personal connections and a shared history grant AQIM considerable influence over other Salafi–jihadist groups. AQIM's current commanding cadre, the 'old guard' harking back to the Algerian GIA and GSPC, is fiercely loyal to Al Qaeda's Al-Zawahiri, and will not be seduced by IS. The reintegration of Belmokhtar into AQIM's ranks will significantly increase operational capacity, and the recent hotel attacks indicate a potential new and deadly tactic targeting civilians and Western interests.

In distinguishing between a strategy of terrorism and one of insurgency, Duyvesteyn and Fumerton's framework offers useful categories to compare the characteristics of each. First, AQIM's objectives and ideology are closely aligned with Al Qaeda, and strongly indicate a strategy of terrorism rather than insurgency. The Caliphate is not an immediate goal, and by targeting the 'far enemy' AQIM aims at provoking Western reactions. Secondly, AQIM's organization displays all the elements of a typical terrorist one: small, mobile, and clandestine units rather than a large shadow organization. When the opportunity unexpectedly arose to govern northern Mali as an 'Islamic state' in 2012, AQIM and its partners were unprepared. Despite warnings by the strategic leadership, local commanders made all the mistakes they were instructed to avoid. Thirdly, as a result of their Sahelistan project, AQIM changed its relationship with the local population from acceptance of customs and loose integration into the local fabric, to a position of governance and responsibility. Ultimately, they alienated the locals, and Operation Serval removed them from power. AQIM has since recovered and reverted to its traditional and effective modus operandi: ambushes, lightning raids, and attacks across the Sahel. In the region of Timbuktu, however, it seems that AQIM is again seeking to control the population. This is more indicative of a strategy of insurgency and illustrates the limits of trying to fit AQIM's modus operandi into a conceptual framework. After all, AQIM's different commanders display strong autonomous traits, impeding management by their strategic leadership and academic conceptualization alike.

Finally, the evidence does not support the accusation that AQIM is a criminal organization with a religious façade. Within the drug trade, AQIM plays but a small role if any at all, while government corruption and complicity are primarily responsible for the flourishing narcotics trade. AQIM's main source of income remains ransoms, and as long as these are paid new hostages will be kidnapped. As for the label insurgent or terrorist, there is no controversy in concluding that AQIM is extremely adept at using terrorist tactics, and that their intent and capacity to do so is unlikely to diminish in the near future.

Notes

1. SITE Intelligence Group, 'AQIM Announces Joining Al Muribatoon'.
2. Weiss, 'AQIM Takes Couple Hostage'.
3. Boeke and Schuurman, 'Operation "Serval"'.
4. UN Security Council, *Report on Situation Mali*.
5. Zenn, 'Sahel's Militant "Melting Pot"'.

6. Ibnein, 'Oumar Ould Hamahada'.
7. Lebovich, 'Hotel Attacks and Realignment'.
8. Guidère, 'Timbuktu Letters: New Insights'.
9. Filiu, *Al-Qaeda in the Islamic Maghreb*.
10. Marret, 'Al-Qaeda in Islamic Maghreb'.
11. Lebovich, 'Hotel Attacks and Realignment'.
12. Herbst, *Talking Terrorism*, 164.
13. Schmid, 'The Definition of Terrorism', 86–7 (emphasis in original).
14. See Galula, *Counter-Insurgency Warfare*.
15. Duyvesteyn and Fumerton, 'Insurgency and Terrorism', 27–41.
16. Schuurman, 'Defeated by Popular Demand'.
17. Khalil, 'Know Your Enemy'.
18. Kilcullen, 'Countering Global Insurgency'.
19. Tinti, *Trafficking and Instability*.
20. Martinez, *Algerian Civil War*, 209.
21. Kepel, *Jihad*, 263–73.
22. Amnesty International, *Algeria*.
23. Baralon, 'Tibhirine'.
24. Yous, *Qui a tué à Benthala?*
25. Mokaddem, 'Les Afghans Algériens', 75–82.
26. Guidère, *Al Qaïda, Conquête du Maghreb*, 63.
27. For the translated text, see Tazaghart, 'AQMI', 212–13.
28. 'Al-Qaeda "Issues France Threat"'.
29. Hunt, 'Islamist Terrorism in Northwestern Africa'.
30. Atiyah, *Letter to Zarqawi*.
31. 'Interview with Abdelmalek Droukdal'.
32. Pankhurst, 'Caliphate and Strategy of al-Qaeda'.
33. Gerges, *The Far Enemy*.
34. Salem, 'Ben Laden du Sahara', 68–72.
35. Lebovich, 'Hotel Attacks and Realignment'.
36. Jauvert, 'Mali: Histoire Secrète'.
37. Zimmerman, *The Al Qaeda Network*.
38. Gartenstein-Ross, 'Al Qaeda in Islamic Maghreb'.
39. Al-Qaida Papers (Letter from AQIM's Shura Council to Masked Brigade's Shura Council).
40. Baud, 'Groupe Islamique Armé (GIA)'.
41. Hagen, 'Al Qaeda in Islamic Maghreb' (presentation).
42. Al-Qaida Papers (Letter from AQIM's Shura Council to Masked Brigade's Shura Council).
43. Perrigueur, 'Les Montagnes de Kabylie'.
44. Lecocq et al., 'Hippoppotamus and Eight Blind Analysts'.
45. Siegel, 'AQIM's Playbook in Mali'.
46. Mali-al-Qaida's Sahara Playbook, Chapter 3, page 3.
47. Al-Qaida Papers (Letter from AQIM's Shura Council to Masked Brigade's Shura Council).
48. Fowler, *A Season in Hell*.
49. Ibid., 134, 148.
50. Lebovich, 'Mergers, MUJAO, and Mokhtar Belmokhtar'.
51. Bacchi, 'France's War in Mali'.
52. Lasserre and Oberlé, *Notre Guerre Secrète*, 43–44.
53. Boeke and Tisseron, 'Mali's Long Road Ahead'.

54. Al-Andulus Media, 'Call to Youth of Islam'.
55. Schmid, *Foreign (Terrorist) Fighter Estimates*.
56. Zelin, Gartenstein-Ross, and Lebovich, 'Al-Qa'ida's Tunisia Strategy'.
57. Chauzal, *Fix the Unfixable*.
58. Galula, *Counterinsurgency Warfare*, 8.
59. Crenshaw, 'The Causes of Terrorism', 393.
60. See Scheele, *Smugglers and Saints*.
61. Fowler, *A Season in Hell*, 134, 148.
62. Salem, *Ben Laden du Sahara*, 56–9.
63. Notin, *Guerre de la France*, 595–8.
64. Rodier, 'Libye'.
65. Duhem, 'Nord-Mali Aqmi'.
66. Mali-al-Qaida's Sahara Playbook, Chapter 1, page 2.
67. Ibid., Chapter 1, page 3.
68. Wing, 'French Intervention in Mali'.
69. Chauzal, 'Snapshot of Mali'.
70. Presentation Chief JMAC (MINUSMA), Lille 7 December 2015.
71. Harmon, *Terror and Insurgency in Sahara-Sahel*, 68.
72. Detzi and Winkleman, 'Hitting Where it Hurts'.
73. Scheele, *Smugglers and Saints*, 122–3.
74. Salem, 'Ben Laden du Sahara', 42–5.
75. UNODC, *Cocaine Trafficking in Western Africa*.
76. Tinti, *Trafficking and Instability*.
77. Lacher, *Organised Crime and Conflict*.
78. Harmon, *Terror and Insurgency in Sahara-Sahel*, 149–51.
79. Tinti, *Trafficking and Instability*.
80. Callimachi, 'Paying Ransoms'.
81. Guidère, 'Timbuktu Letters: New Insights'.
82. Fowler, *A Season in Hell*, 150–1.
83. Ibid., 227–8.
84. Follorou, 'Otages d'Arlit'.
85. Fowler, *A Season in Hell*, 310–11.

Acknowledgements

The author would like to thank Isabelle Duyvesteyn, Bart Schuurman, Grégory Chauzal, and Philippe Prevost for their valuable comments on an earlier draft of this article. The research assistance by Thomas Brzezinski was also much appreciated.

Disclosure statement

No potential conflict of interest was reported by the author.

References

Al-Andalus Media. 'Call to the Youth of Islam: To Those Who Aspire to Hijrah in the Way of God in the Islamic Maghreb in General and Tunisia in Particular'. *Jihadology.net*, 17 March 2013. http://jihadology.net/2013/03/17/al-andalus-media-presents-a-new-statement-from-al-qaidah-in-the-islamic-maghrib-call-to-the-youth-of-islam-aspire-to-hijrah-in-the-way-of-god-in-the-islamic-maghrib-in-general-and-tunisia/.

'Al-Qaeda "Issues France Threat"'. *BBC News*, 14 September 2006. http://news.bbc.co.uk/2/hi/europe/5345202.stm.

Al-Qaida Papers. Associated Press. Accessed 10 February 2016. http://hosted.ap.org/specials/interactives/_international/_pdfs/al-qaida-belmoktar-letter-english.pdf.

Amnesty International. *Algeria: Repression and Violence Must End*. October 1994. Index no. MDE 28/008/1994. https://www.amnesty.org/en/documents/MDE28/008/1994/en/.

Bacchi, Umberto. 'France's War in Mali: Child Soldiers on the Frontline'. *International Business Times*, 16 January 2013. http://www.ibtimes.co.uk/mali-child-soldiers-islamists-france-424816.

Baralon, Marguax le. 'Tibhirine, les Expertises Fragilisent la Version Officielle'. *LaCroix*, 2 July 2015. http://www.la-croix.com/Actualite/France/Tibhirine-les-expertises-fragilisent-la-version-officielle-2015-07-02-1330468.

Baud, Jacques. 'Groupe Islamique Armé (GIA)'. *Global Terror Watch*, 7 June 2012. http://www.globalterrorwatch.ch/?p=699.

Boeke, Sergei, and Bart Schuurman. 'Operation "Serval": A Strategic Analysis of the French Intervention in Mali, 2013–2014'. *The Journal of Strategic Studies* 38, no. 6 (2015): 1–25. doi:10.1080/01402390.2015.1045494.

Boeke, Sergei, and Antonin Tisseron. 'Mali's Long Road Ahead'. *The RUSI Journal* 159, no. 5 (2014): 32–40. doi:10.1080/03071847.2014.969942.

Callimachi, Rukmini. 'Paying Ransoms, Europe Bankrolls Qaeda Terror'. *The New York Times*, 29 July 2014. http://www.nytimes.com/2014/07/30/world/africa/ransoming-citizens-europe-becomes-al-qaedas-patron.html?_r=0.

Chauzal, Grégory. *Fix the Unfixable. Dealing with Full-Blown Crisis and Instability: How to Bring Greater Stability to the Sahel?* CRU Policy Brief. The Hague: Clingendael, 2015.

Chauzal, Grégory. 'A Snapshot of Mali Three Years after the 2012 Crisis'. *Clingendael*, 8 June 2015. http://www.clingendael.nl/publication/commentary-snapshot-mali-three-years-after-2012-crisis.

Crenshaw, Martha. 'The Causes of Terrorism'. *Comparative Politics* 13, no. 4 (1981): 379–399. http://links.jstor.org/sici?sici=0010–4159%28198107%2913%3A4%3C379%3ATCOT%3E2.0.CO%3B2-8.

Detzi, Daniel, and Steven Winkleman. 'Hitting Them Where it Hurts: A Joint Interagency Network to Disrupt Terrorist Financing in West Africa'. *Studies in Conflict & Terrorism* 39, no. 3 (2016): 227–239. doi:10.1080/1057610X.2015.1099994.

Duhem, Vincent. 'Nord-Mali – Aqmi: Abdelmalek Droukdel Appelee à Imposer 'Graduellement' la Charia'. *Jeune Afrique*, 24 May 2012. http://www.jeuneafrique.com/175961/politique/nord-mali-aqmi-abdelmalek-droukdel-appelle-imposer-graduellement-la-charia/.

Duyvesteyn, Isabelle, and Mario Fumerton. 'Insurgency and Terrorism: Is there a difference?' In *The Character of War in the 21st Century*, edited by Caroline Holmqvist-Jonsater and Christopher Coker, 27–41. London: Routledge, 2009.

Filiu, Jean-Pierre. *Al-Qaeda in the Islamic Maghreb: Algerian Challenge or Global Threat?* Washington, DC: Carnegie Endowment for International Peace, 2009. http://carnegieendowment.org/files/al-qaeda_islamic_maghreb.pdf.

Follorou, Jacques. 'Otages d'Arlit: Les Dessous de la Négociation'. *Le Monde*, 30 October 2013. http://www.lemonde.fr/afrique/article/2013/10/30/otages-d-arlit-les-dessous-d-une-libera_3505240_3212.html.

Fowler, Robert R. *A Season in Hell: My 130 Days in the Sahara with Al Qaeda*. Toronto: Harper Collins, 2011.

Galula, David. *Counter-Insurgency Warfare: Theory and Practice.* New York: Frederick A. Praeger, 1964. http://louisville.edu/armyrotc/files/Galula%20David%20-%20Counterinsurgency%20Warfare.pdf.

Gartenstein-Ross, Daveed. 'Al Qaeda in the Islamic Maghreb and Al Qaeda's Senior Leadership'. *Defend Democracy*, 19 January 2013. http://www.defenddemocracy.org/media-hit/al-qaeda-in-the-islamic-maghreb-and-al-qaedas-senior-leadership/.

Gerges, Fawaz. *The Far Enemy: Why Jihad Went Global.* Cambridge: Cambridge University Press, 2005.

Guidère, Mathieu. *Al-Qaïda à la Conquête du Maghreb: Le Terrorisme aux Portes de l'Europe.* Monaco: Éditions du Rocher, 2007.

Guidère, Mathieu. 'The Timbuktu Letters: New Insights about AQIM'. *Res Militaris* 4, no. 1 (2014). http://resmilitaris.net/ressources/10184/89/res_militaris_article_guid_re_new_insights_about_aqim.pdf.

Hagen, Andreas. 'Al Qaeda in the Islamic Magreb'. Presentation in AEI's Critical Threats Project, March 2014. http://www.criticalthreats.org/al-qaeda/hagen-aqim-leaders-and-networks-march-27-2014.

Harmon, Stephen A. *Terror and Insurgency in the Sahara-Sahel Region: Corruption, Contraband, Jihad and the Mali War of 2012–2013.* Farnham: Ashgate, 2014.

Herbst, Philip. *Talking Terrorism: A Dictionary of the Loaded Language of Political Violence.* Westport, CN: Greenwood, 2003.

Hunt, Emily. 'Islamist Terrorism in Northwestern Africa: A "Thorn in the Neck" of the United States?' *Policy Focus*, no. 65, February 2007. http://www.washingtoninstitute.org/uploads/Documents/pubs/PolicyFocus65.pdf.

Ibnein, Abu. 'Oumar Ould Hamahada: A Case Study of the Bridges Between Three Groups'. Geneva Centre for Training and Analysis of Terrorism, Centre's Note (CN) 3, 10 January 2013.

'An Interview with Abdelmalek Droukdal'. *The New York Times*, 1 July 2008. http://www.nytimes.com/2008/07/01/world/africa/01transcript-droukdal.html?_r=0.

Jauvert, Vincent. 'Mali: Histoire Secrète d'Une Guerre Surprise'. *Le Nouvel Observateur*, 10 February 2013. http://globe.blogs.nouvelobs.com/archive/2013/02/08/mali-histoire-secrete-d-une-guerre-surprise.html.

Kepel, Gilles. *Jihad: The Trail of Political Islam.* Translated by Anthony F. Roberts. London: I.B. Tauris, 2002.

Khalil, James. 'Know Your Enemy: On the Futility of Distinguishing Between Terrorists and Insurgents'. *Studies in Conflict & Terrorism* 36, no. 5 (2013): 419–430. doi:10.1080/1057610X.2013.775501.

Kilcullen, David J. 'Countering Global Insurgency'. *Journal of Strategic Studies* 28, no.4 (2005): 597–617. doi:10.1080/01402390500300956.

Lacher, Wolfram. *Organized Crime and Conflict in the Sahel-Sahara Region.* Washington, DC: Carnegie Endowment for International Peace, 2012. http://carnegieendowment.org/files/sahel_sahara.pdf.

Lasserre, Isabelle, and Thierry Oberlé. *Notre Guerre Secrète au Mali: Les Nouvelles Menaces Contre la France.* Paris: Fayard, 2013.

Lebovich, Andrew. 'The Hotel Attacks and Militant Realignment in the Sahara-Sahel Region'. *CTC Sentinel* 9, no. 1 (2016): 22–28. https://www.ctc.usma.edu/posts/the-hotel-attacks-and-militant-realignment-in-the-sahara-sahel-region.

Lebovich, Andrew. 'Of Mergers, MUJAO, and Mokhtar Belmokhtar'. *Al-Wasat,* 23 August 2013. https://thewasat.wordpress.com/2013/08/23/of-mergers-mujao-and-mokhtar-belmokhtar/.

Lecocq, B., G. Mann, B. Whitehouse, D. Badi, L. Pelckmans, N. Belalimat, B. Hall, and W. Lacher. 'One Hippopotamus and Eight Blind Analysts: A Multivocal Analysis of the 2012

Political Crisis in the Divided Republic of Mali.' *Review of African Political Economy* 40, no. 137 (2013): 343–357. doi:10.1080/03056244.2013.799063.

Mali-al-Qaida's Sahara Playbook. Associated Press. Accessed 10 February 2016. http://hosted.ap.org/specials/interactives/_international/_pdfs/al-qaida-manifesto.pdf.

Marret, Jean-Luc. 'Al-Qaeda in Islamic Maghreb: A "Glocal" Organization.' *Studies in Conflict & Terrorism* 31, no. 6 (2008): 541–552. doi:10.1080/10576100802111824.

Martinez, Luis. *The Algerian Civil War, 1990–98*. New York, NY: Columbia University Press, 2000.

Mokaddem, Mohamed. *Les Afghans d'Algérie, de la Djamaâ à El Qaïda*. Algeria: ANEP, 2002.

Notin, Jean-Christophe. *La Guerre de la France au Mali*. Paris: Tallandier, 2014.

Pankhurst, Reza. 'The Caliphate, and the Changing Strategy of the Public Statements of al-Qaeda's Leaders.' *Political Theology* 11, no. 4 (2010): 530–552. doi:10.1558/poth.v11i4.530.

Perrigueur, Elisa. 'Les montagnes de Kabylie, refuge de nombreux djihadistes'. *Le Monde*, 24 September 2014. http://www.lemonde.fr/international/article/2014/09/24/les-montagnes-de-kabylie-refuge-de-nombreux-djihadistes_4492713_3210.html.

Rodier, Alain. 'Libye: Le Nid de Vipères'. *Centre Français de Recherche sur le Renseignement*, Note d'Actualité no. 352 (2014). http://www.cf2r.org/fr/notes-actualite/libye-le-nid-de-viperes.php.

Salem, Lemine Ould M. *Le Ben Laden du Sahara: Sur les Traces du Jihadiste Mokhtar Belmokhtar*. Paris: La Martinière, 2014.

Scheele, Judith. *Smugglers and Saints of the Sahara: Regional Connectivity in the Twientieth Century*. New York, NY: Cambridge University Press, 2015.

Schmid, Alex P. 'The Definition of Terrorism'. In *Handbook of Terrorism Research*, edited by Alex P. Schmid, 39–98. London: Routledge, 2011.

Schmid, Alex P. *Foreign (Terrorist) Fighter Estimates: Conceptual and Data Issues'*. ICCT Policy Brief. The Hague: ICCT, October 2015. http://icct.nl/wp-content/uploads/2015/10/ICCT-Schmid-Foreign-Terrorist-Fighter-Estimates-Conceptual-and-Data-Issues-October20152.pdf.

Schuurman, Bart. 'Defeated by Popular Demand: Public Support and Counterterrorism in Three Western Democracies, 1963–1998.' *Studies in Conflict & Terrorism* 36, no. 2 (2013): 152–175. doi:10.1080/1057610X.2013.747072.

Siegel, Pascale Combelles. 'AQIM's Playbook in Mali'. *Combating Terrorism Center at West Point*, 27 March 2013. https://www.ctc.usma.edu/posts/aqims-playbook-in-mali.

SITE Intelligence Group. 'AQIM leader Announces joining of Al Muribatoon, Radisson Blu as First Joint Act'. *SITE Intelligence Group*, 4 December 2015. https://news.siteintelgroup.com/Jihadist-News/aqim-leader-announces-joining-of-al-murabitoon-radisson-blu-attack-in-bamako-as-first-joint-act.html.

Tazaghart, Atmane. *AQMI: Enquête sur les Héritiers de Ben Laden au Maghreb et en Europe*. Paris: Jean Picollec, 2011.

Tinti, Peter. *Illicit Trafficking and Instability in Mali: Past, Present and Future (Research Paper)*. Geneva: Global Initiative against Transnational Organized Crime, 2014.

United Nations Office on Drugs and Crime. *Cocaine Trafficking in Western Africa*. UNODC. https://www.unodc.org/documents/data-and-analysis/Cocaine-trafficking-Africa-en.pdf.

UN Security Council. *Report of the Secretary-General on the Situation in Mali*, S/2015/1030. 24 December 2015. http://www.securitycouncilreport.org/atf/cf/%7B65BFCF9B-6D27–4E9C-8CD3-CF6E4FF96FF9%7D/s_2015_1030.pdf.

Weiss, Caleb. 'AQIM Takes Australian Couple Hostage in Northern Burkina Faso'. *The Long War Journal*, 16 January 2016. http://www.longwarjournal.org/archives/2016/01/aqim-takes-australian-couple-hostage-in-northern-burkina-faso.php.

Wing, Susanna D. 'French Intervention in Mali: Strategic Alliances, Long-Term Regional Presence?' *Small Wars & Insurgencies* 27, no. 1 (2016): 59–80.

Yous, Nesroulah. *Qui a tué à Bentalha?*. Paris: La Découverte, 2000.

Zelin, Aaron Y., Daveed Gartenstein-Ross, and Andrew Lebovich. 'Al-Qa'ida in the Islamic Maghreb's Tunisia Strategy'. *CTC Sentinel* 6, no. 7 (2013): 21–25. https://www.ctc.usma.edu/posts/al-qaida-in-the-islamic-maghrebs-tunisia-strategy.

Zenn, Jacob. 'The Sahel's Militant 'Melting Pot': Hamadou Kouffa's Macina Liberation Front (FLM)'. *Terrorism Monitor* 13, no. 22 (2015): 3–6. http://www.jamestown.org/programs/tm/single/?tx_ttnews[tt_news]=44593&cHash=8b46b953b2373675d248929a39f8264b#.VrsOA0bwDuT.

Zimmerman, Katherine. *The Al Qaeda Network: A New Framework for Defining the Enemy*. AEI's Critical Threats Project, 2013. http://www.aei.org/wp-content/uploads/2013/09/-the-al-qaeda-network-a-new-framework-for-defining-the-enemy_133443407958.pdf.

Shapeshifter of Somalia: Evolution of the Political Territoriality of Al-Shabaab

Bohumil Doboš

ABSTRACT
The article presents the application of a concept of political territoriality in the case of Al-Shabaab. It first presents territoriality as a human strategy based on control of territory. Hereinafter, the set of criteria for the examination of political territoriality is presented. It concludes that given the development of Al-Shabaab, we can identify three distinct periods connected to the 'organization's relation to territory: 2006–2008 – defiance; 2009–2011 – supremacy; and 2012–present – withdrawal. The issue of the deterritorialization of Al-Shabaab since 2012 is also connected to the need to enhance the strategies used against the group as it is becoming more connected to population and functional identification than territory.

The post-Cold War world is increasingly characterized by the proliferation of non-state actors able not only to deny effective management of some territories by the state power or jeopardize its attempt to govern them, but also to effectively take over many functions that are usually attributed to the state. One of the most important factors connected to this issue is the relation of non-state actors (actors not recognized as states and not seeking recognition either (so-called de facto states[1])) to territory – an issue of political territoriality. In the traditional Westphalian thinking political territoriality as one of the forms of political control was primarily connected to the institution of state. This common wisdom is continually deteriorating as many non-state actors use territorial means of political control to achieve their goals (Al-Shabaab, ISIS, Boko Haram, FARC, etc.). Some authors (e.g. Friedrichs, Korbin, Williams, Cerny) present this issue as a part of the shift of the international system from the state-dominated Westphalian system to a more complicated, overlapping, and glocalized neomedievalism.

This article will deal with the issue of the territorial dimension of Al-Shabaab, a radical movement dominating security considerations in southern Somalia since 2006. Al-Shabaab has come through major transformations loosely following the 2006 Ethiopian invasion, its 2009 retreat, and a subsequent 2011 Kenyan invasion of Somalia. These changes were directly connected to the ability and willingness of Al-Shabaab movement to control territory in the country, which has been uncontrolled and an archetype of state failure since the beginning of the 1990s. The paper aims to answer the question of what has been the development of the territorial dimension of Al-Shabaab since 2006. By understanding this development, we aim to shed light on the differences in the strategies Al-Shabaab used throughout its insurgency campaign and the need for the evolution of strategy to eliminate the group which threatens regional stability. We will also illustrate the relation of Al-'Shabaab's territoriality to the nature of the Somali conflict. The main research question is thus – What was the connection of Al-Shabaab to the territory throughout its development?

The paper is divided into three main parts. The first part deals with the theory of political territoriality and the research design that will be used in our case study. This part focuses on an explanation of the importance of political territoriality as a strategy and the possibilities of uncovering the territorial strategy of non-state actors. The second part briefly describes the history and development of Al-Shabaab. The third part analyses the territorial dimension of Al-'Shabaab's operations from 2006 to June 2015.

Political territoriality

In the first part of the paper we need to establish our understanding of a concept of political territoriality, its importance for grasping the behaviour and structure of non-state actors, and a way in which we can connect the theory of territoriality with practice. First, we present the works of authors who have dealt with the issue of political territoriality as these are taken as a basic theoretical framework for the following research; next, we present the concept that will be used throughout the rest of the paper; finally, the research design is explained.

The classic definition of territoriality comes from the work of R. Sack who defines territoriality as a strategy for influence or more specifically as an 'attempt to affect, influence, or control actions and interactions (of people, things, and relationships) by asserting and attempting to enforce control over a geographic area'.[2] He continues by proposing that territoriality is 'the attempt by an individual or group (x) to influence, affect, or control objects, people, and relationships (y) by delimiting and asserting control over a geographic area. This area is the territory.'[3] Territoriality for Sack is socially and geographically rooted; it is the 'geographic strategy to control people and things by controlling area' and 'primary geographical expression of social power'.[4] 'Territoriality establishes control over an area as a means of controlling access to things and relationships.'[5]

Additionally, Sack sees territoriality as socially constructed – unlike physical distance that is not.[6]

Another author who must be mentioned in this context is H. Vollaard. He has described political territoriality as a 'human activity used to create and mould political relationships through socially constructed territories' that is characterized by physical demarcation, and the establishment of coercive and socializing mechanisms and institutions to maintain the control over the area.[7] Territory is, however, only one possible type of definition of relation between power and space – the other two being function (e.g. policy, occupation) and personal characteristics (e.g. ethnicity, religion, gender).[8] It is important to point out, that the other two relations are less geographically fixed.[9]

An additional definition of territoriality points to the fact that it is the process of using territory for political, social and economic ends.[10] Territoriality and territory are thus powerful ways of defining a group membership and they have a significant advantage over a definition of the group by other signs, especially for the need of collective defence, as the protection of borders is easier, swifter, and more transparent than the control of population through such signs as language or ethnicity.[11] Territoriality has two dimensions: delimitation of boundaries and behaviour within them.[12] From an evolutionary perspective, territoriality is widespread; it is a strong and dominant strategy, and it follows strategic logic calibrated to cost–benefit ratios from human evolutionary past.[13] Moving to the institution of the state, territoriality is usually understood as a major component of state sovereignty and the exercise of power over people. The territoriality of the state, furthermore, traditionally has three layers – power, economy, and culture[14] – and must be understood as a multidimensional phenomenon.

Territoriality is, moreover, an important factor in conflicts. The idea of homeland is usually defined territorially; territoriality has a lot of symbolic associations, and many internal conflicts involve territorial stakes.[15] Territorial understanding of homeland as a largely symbolic place and a core of self-determining myths[16] has serious consequences for the nature of conflicts. Conflict potential increases when a concentrated, territorially defined ethnic group clashes with the state – by nature defined by borders – which fears further separatism in its territory.[17] Additionally, despite the fact that the amount of conflicts over non-territorial issues is larger, territorial conflicts are usually deadly while non-territorial ones are not.[18] This means that we can expect a more intense and violent conflict in the context of territorial non-state actors.

The last issue connected to the understanding of territoriality is the process of deterritorialization in the context of globalization. It is argued that globalization creates a multilayered political map with multiple identities which will increase the importance of the flows and networking as an alternative strategy to territoriality, and thus diminishing the importance of territoriality.[19] S. Korbin even argued that the growth of the importance of cyberspace will lead to the almost complete irrelevance of geography for world politics.[20] Even though the effects of cyberspace on international politics have not been as dramatic as presented, it is important to notice the changes in the nature of the relationships among international actors and the role of boundaries in the international system as a result of the information age and the resultant networking. On the other hand, we may observe that globalization changes territoriality in a different manner. As the territorial stakes of states are diminishing, local identities become more important.[21] Moreover, globalization does not have uniform effects all over the globe; ethno-territorial conflicts are still present despite the fact that in some parts of the world (most notably in the European Union) the importance of borders (their ability to keep different territories separated) and territoriality as a main principle of state power is decreasing.[22] Despite the fact that the territoriality of states in some parts of the world might decrease, it is crucial to understand territorial stakes and strategies of other actors.

The process of change in the importance of territoriality may be well illustrated by the example of many African states. State institutions are limited in the majority of countries on the continent, and many of their functions have been overtaken by non-state actors – both local and foreign based. Also many areas are effectively out of state control and many parts of the land are controlled by alternative actors (e.g. Al-Shabaab, Boko Haram). Somalia as an archetype of a collapsed state is a case in point.

In this paper, we understand political territoriality as a strategy of political control that might be practised by any willing actor, not only the state, and is based on control via borders and demarcation of territory. Territoriality possesses an important function as a defence strategy and is the most effective connection between power and space. Moreover, territorial conflicts tend to be more violent as territory often possesses a large symbolic value. Especially in the African case, political territoriality as a strategy is in many cases pursued by non-state actors challenging the institution of state and in others the importance of networks and flows diminishes the importance of territoriality as a successful strategy on a macro-level while strengthening the local territorial affinity. These different approaches towards territoriality are interconnected and might lead towards emergence of territorial conflicts.

As we have presented above, the ethno-territorial conflicts tend to be the most violent and, as noted by T.D. Gurr, the ethnic conflict has been the commonest type of violent conflict since the end of the 1980s.[23] Understanding the nature of the violent non-state actors in areas like Somalia thus helps us to understand their role in the conflict and select the right strategy to mitigate them. Additionally, territoriality is an important factor in the organizational structure of the insurgent groups. For example, P. Staniland has presented a two-dimensional characterization of the organizational strength of insurgent groups where a horizontal level defines the connection of the leaders inside the insurgency, while vertical ties represent the connection of the insurgency to the local communities – a tie closely connected to the issue of territoriality.[24]

Territorial violent non-state actors are thus characterized by their strategy aiming at delimitation and control of defined territory, strong vertical ties, the ability to perform at least some of the state functions in the defined territory,[25] and the potential to engage in violent conflict with other territorial groups or states seeking control of the same territory. Political territoriality is thus a crucial aspect in understanding the organization and nature of non-state actors and many conflicts.

Finally, we intend to present a research design that will reveal the territorial dimension of our chosen non-state actor, Al-Shabaab. When dealing with the territorial affinity of a concrete non-state actor, we must first distinguish two dimensions of such a relationship: *willingness to act in a territorial fashion* (or willingness to pursue political territoriality) and *ability to control territory* (or the ability to pursue political territoriality). The first set of factors deals with the strategy of the actor, while the other focuses on the success of the actor in pursuing the territorial goals. Willingness to be territorial is manifested by five factors: (1) *rhetoric* – clear delimitation of territory a non-state actor strives to control, primarily local and not global ambitions; (2) *attempt to establish institutions* – non-state actors willing to use territorial strategy must attempt to govern its territory; (3) *local penal code* – localized territorial actors will attempt to adapt a legal code, usually arising from some universal ideas, to the local environment; (4) *control of urban and economic centres* – territorial actors will try to establish effective control over economic and urban centres within their claimed territory; (5) *financing through taxation/without looting* – territorial actors, furthermore, try to finance their operations through taxation of trade and/or population as opposed to the predatory nature of violent non-territorial non-state actors. Control of territory might also be divided into five factors in a similar fashion: (1) *population density* – effective control over territory is established only through local inhabitants; (2) *economic output* – controlled territory must be economically viable to sustain itself or to be able to participate in local and/or global economy; (3) *provision of security* – in order to effectively control the territory, the actor must be able to provide security for the population as well as against external actors; (4) *governance* – the actor must establish at least a basic governmental structure to deal with the issues connected to the control of territory and its population; (5) *infrastructure* – territory without proper infrastructure is hardly controllable – the larger the physical area, the worse the problem.

Researched factors are chosen in accordance with the theory of political territoriality as presented above and with the works of Berg and Kuusk on empirical approaches to sovereignty and Zaidi on territorial control.[26] Berg and Kuusk present a theoretical framework dealing with the issues of sovereignty, and some of the factors that they relate to the issue of internal sovereignty are useful for the examination of political territoriality (most notably governance, provision of security, and population). 'Zaidi's article, despite being written in the 1970s and focused on Western Pakistan, presents insights and a crucial methodological approach to the issue of territorial control that remain relevant today. Furthermore, it is important to point out that not all the criteria are connected to the activity of the actor itself. We can clearly see that issues of infrastructure development, population density, and economic output are not connected to the short-term activities of an actor while provision of security or governance is. Thus not all of the factors might be influenced in the short term by the actions of an actor.

History and development of the shapeshifter

The situation in Somalia has been challenging for most of the time since its independence. Following the fall of the regime of S. Barre at the beginning of the 1990s, however, the state has witnessed a full-fledged collapse, bringing the previous issues to new heights. In the 1990s the country de facto split between Somaliland – a province in the north of the country on the territory of the former British Somalia which was able to retain some reasonable state functions – and the southern part of the country where state institutions ceased to exist altogether. In this period the southern part was marked by infighting between warlords trying to obtain as large a profit as possible from the situation at hand and by an unsuccessful attempt of the international community to provide the state with the ability to conduct the basic functions it is usually supposed to provide.[27] The end of the 1990s was, furthermore, marked by the establishment of the semi-autonomous province of Puntland in the north-eastern part of Somalia, which directly challenged some of the attempts to establish a centralized state government but did not call for sovereignty and international recognition.

Despite this anarchic context, the country was almost untouched by foreign Islamist radicalism during this time. While domestic attempts of Al-Itihaad Al-Islaam (AIAI) to establish the ideology of radical Islam in Somalia had some effect (especially the development that led to the establishment of Al-Shabaab[28],), foreign fighters – especially those connected to Al Qaeda – were unable to make proper use of the anarchic Somali environment despite their success in planning the 1998 bombings of the US embassies in Tanzania and Kenya, led from Somali territory. The reason for this, as Menkhaus and Shapiro noticed, is that an environment free from state interference is also an environment easily accessible to foreign agents because they do not have to deal with issues of state sovereignty. The lack of central government also means the lack of an institution to appeal on the international stage and the lack of strong allies that might protect the 'country's territory. If there is at least a weak state in place, it may attempt to protect its sovereignty by international appeals and thus increase the cost of attacks on its territory. However, not only was Al Qaeda in Somalia an easy target for (mainly US) attacks, but it was also despised by the local population. Somalia as an ethnically homogeneous country with a strong clan structure and traditional legal code (although mixed with important elements of Islamic law) is hardly penetrable by foreign agents that bring non-local and non-traditional views of Islam into the traditional society. A combination of easy targeting of bases and the hostility of locals that cooperated with Al Qaeda only for profit made its effort to put the proper infrastructure in place impossible.[29]

The 1998 attacks in Africa and the 2001 attack in New York City brought Somalia back into the international spotlight. This focus was materialized in two attempts to re-establish the central government. First, the Transitional National Government (TNG) was established in 2000 and then accepted by the international community as the official Somali government until 2002. The TNG was based on the Mogadishu-based Hawiye clan. As expected in a Somali clan-based society, this government was rejected by the other clans, which contributed to the establishment of the Transitional Federal Government (TFG). The TFG was based around the Darood clan, which is mainly situated in semi-autonomous Puntland, and was supported by Ethiopia – a historical enemy of Somalia – and later by the forces of the African Union. However, it remained rather irrelevant as well.[30]

This lack of effective state power in combination with the harsh context of warlord battles created an environment that was prepared for the entrance of new actors willing to govern the country. Despite the presence of many alternative actors that attempted to effectively influence at least part of the life in Somalia – be they clans at a local level,[31] pirates as economic actors in some seashore areas,[32] or Puntland and Somaliland as state-like units (Somaliland as comparably much more effective) – it turned out that Somalia was to witness rule by Islamist groups.

Another important factor leading to the successful introduction of radical Islam to Somalia was, according to S.J. Hansen, the devaluation of alternative ideologies in the Somali environment. In the past, ideas like socialism, democracy, and nationalism were exposed as unfit for the Somali environment, both during the misguided rule of S. Barre as well as during the post-Barre anarchy. Additionally, clanism as a traditional form of societal organization was unable to establish an effective counterweight to the ravaging of Somali warlords. In this context, radical Islamism emerged as a new way to improve living conditions in the country.[33]

By the mid-2000s everything was set for the rise of a domestic Islamic movement, and so the success of the Islamic Court Union (ICU) – an umbrella organization of Islamic movements in the country – was not completely surprising. 'The ICU's attempt to govern the country with a focus on Sharia law, cross-clan identity, and the suppression of warlord violence and other violent illegal activities brought the movement some support from the local population. Furthermore, the ICU was able to mitigate a piracy issue in southern Somalia (not in Puntland, though), and by 2006 the organization virtually controlled southern Somalia and successfully challenged the TFG supported by the African Union troops. This situation was, however, unacceptable to the Ethiopian government which perceived ICU as a direct threat; besides, the organization was also observed with caution by the United States. This sense of threat led to direct Ethiopian involvement in the Somali internal conflict which in December 2006 took the shape of military invasion that was supported by the United States and the African Union.[34]

Al-Shabaab as a radical militant wing of the ICU was at the time a small but effective part of the Union that proved its worth on the battlefield due to the high religious zeal of its members and its ability to operate lethally during the battles with 'ICU's opponents prior to the Ethiopian invasion. The Ethiopian military operation was, however, a game-changer in the dynamics of the development of the Islamist movement in Somalia. First, it is important to point out that despite their effectiveness during the struggle amidst different Somali actors, ICU forces were no match for the regular Ethiopian armed forces and could not succeed in a direct confrontation. Second, the ICU as an umbrella organization contained many internal divisions which were only accentuated by losses on the battlefield. Third, Al-Shabaab as a militant and radically Islamist movement proved to be the most effective part of the ICU to counter the Ethiopian progress. This effectiveness was bound to the evolution of methods used to fight the Ethiopian forces – from conventional battles to the use of asymmetric attacks like suicide-bomb attacks, use of improvised explosive devices, etc. In the end, this 'attrition' war was successful and Al-Shabaab was able to force the Ethiopian forces out of the country, which has hosted only Ugandan and Burundi forces under a limited mandate from the African Union since 2009.[35]

Starting in 2008 Al-Shabaab began to increase its territorial hold, and 2009–2010 was arguably the 'organization's peak period; S.J. Hansen calls it the Golden Age of Al-Shabaab.[36] O.K. Mwangi portrays Al-Shabaab between 2009 and 2011 as the best equipped, financed, and organized group in southern Somalia and which controlled the largest share of territory.[37] During this period Al-Shabaab successfully exploited an increasing sense of Somali nationalism which emerged as a reaction to the foreign invasion and put forward visions of the establishment of an Islamic state in larger Somalia (Somalia, Ogaden, Djibouti, Northern Frontier District in Kenya)[38] – ideas previously propagated by a part of the ICU. Al-Shabaab was able to run a comparatively effective organizational pattern thanks not only to the payment of regular fees to its fighters and compensation to the fallen, but also due to an ability to generate its financing by taxation,[39] with its most important financial centre located in the port city of Kismayo, and to provide the functions other Somali actors were usually not able to offer.

The year 2010, however, fully revealed the internal fragmentation of Al-Shabaab – mainly its division between a Somali nationalist faction led by Aweys (a veteran of Somali Islamist movements and the main propagator of the Greater Somalia vision), Robow and al-Afghani, and its more internationalist faction led by A. Godane. The predominance of 'Godane's faction was manifested in many actions Al-Shabaab undertook during the following years. The first was the pledge of loyalty to Al Qaeda in 2010 followed by its acceptance as a part of Al Qaeda in 2012.[40] The second was 'Godane's ability to persuade the rest of the leadership to conduct the so-called Ramadan offensive near Mogadishu in August–September 2010 which was aimed against the AMISOM forces located in the area; the offensive resulted in heavy Al-Shabaab casualties and can be seen as one of the major factors that contributed to the retreat of Al-Shabaab in southern Somalia.[41] The third, and most visibly, the fragmentation led to the purges executed by Godane which rid the organization of 'his critics and left Al-Shabaab a smaller but more coherent and centralized organization.'[42] However, Godane was himself killed in a drone attack on 1 September 2014.[43]

The shift of focus from Somalia towards more regional/global goals was strengthened by the 2011 Kenyan invasion which sought to support the TFG and destroy Al-Shabaab, primarily by taking over the strategic port of Kismayo. Despite the fact that the takeover of Kismayo did not succeed until 2012 and in the end was not a major blow to Al-'Shabaab's operations and even though Al-Shabaab remains present in the countryside, the development had a major impact on the organization. Al-Shabaab turned fully to hit-and-run tactics, focused on attacks and propaganda against Kenya, started to present itself as the protector of disenfranchised Somali minorities (mainly of the Somali population in Kenya), and lessened its level of territorial dependence (e.g. control of major urban centres, amended financing pattern).[44] Al-Shabaab thus remains present only in a sparsely populated region along the Somali–Kenyan border and in some other remote areas in southern Somalia and presents itself with hit-and-run attacks on AMISOM forces with an occasional overwhelming attack abroad (e.g. 2010 – Kampala bombing; 2013 – Westgate attack; 2015 – Garissa University Massacre).

Political territoriality and the shapeshifter

Following our exposition of the concept of political territoriality and its importance, and our brief examination of the development of Al-Shabaab, we shall now apply the criteria examining the level of utilization of political territoriality presented in the first section to the selected case. By this application we shall reveal the nature of Al-Shabaab throughout its development.

Territorial nature

(1) Rhetoric
As previously mentioned, the ICU originally sought to exploit the sense of Somali nationalism and this principle, in addition to cross-clanism and radical Islamism (which was not so strongly present in the ICU rhetoric), was picked up

by Al-Shabaab to gain support in the context of the Ethiopian invasion. Political goals were defined by population (Somalis) and territory (greater Somalia). A stated goal was the establishment of an Islamic state on the territory that is clearly defined both territorially and by population. A territorial strategy was followed even more strongly after the retreat of the Ethiopian forces in 2009.[45] A major change is visible by 2010–2011[46] with the success of the internationalist faction around Godane which made Al-Shabaab part of Al Qaeda,[47] purged Al-Shabaab of the Somali nationalists that were concentrated around Aweys, and stated the 'organization's goals as focused on global jihad.[48] An important part of the rhetoric was, however, always identification with Islam as opposed to clanism, which was despised by Al-Shabaab.[49] Following the 2011 Kenyan invasion and especially the progress of Kenyan forces in 2012–2013, Al-Shabaab turned its attention to global jihad and the struggle of Somalis, especially in Kenya, and of Muslims in general,[50] turning fully from the territorial definition of political relationship to definition by personal characteristics.[51]

(2) Attempt to establish institutions

Al-Shabaab attempted to establish institutions in the areas under its control and in contrast to other Somali actors (with the exception of Somaliland) was rather successful. The areas under its control were subjected to harsh Islamic law while it attempted to mimic some state functions. Al-Shabaab tried to provide a local government that was based on Islamic law in the context of state collapse.[52] This was evident from 2008 when the first Al-Shabaab based administration was established in southern Somalia.[53] Al-Shabaab attempted to govern its territories until it lost control over the important regions following the 2011 Kenyan invasion (a particularly severe loss is observable in the 2012–2013 period), and given its present inability to establish a permanent hold of key areas its governing attempts are limited.

(3) Local penal code

Al-Shabaab, as opposed to the ICU, strongly accentuated the importance of Islamic law in its governing strategy from its beginning.[54] It continuously tried to uproot traditional Somali habits deemed un-Islamic (e.g. use of the traditional drug khat) and fought against piracy (despite the fact that Al-Shabaab sometimes cooperated in it due to the need to find additional sources of financing).[55] It can be safely argued that the ultimate goal of Al-Shabaab was to establish 'Shari'a law purged of the Somali traditions and unique features related to Somali society.

(4) Control of urban and economic centres

Following the retreat of the Ethiopian forces in 2009, Al-Shabaab actively sought control over important centres in southern Somalia. Arguably, the most important centre Al-Shabaab was able to hold was, in the period 2009–2012, the port of Kismayo which was a centre of Al-'Shabaab's economic activity.[56] Al-Shabaab also attempted to take over the capital of Mogadishu and was active in population centres such as Marka, Baidoa, or in the south of the Muduq region.[57] It may be argued that Al-Shabaab was willing to establish a hold over population and economic centres in an environment without strong presence of foreign actors (2009–2011/12).

(5) Financing through taxation

After Al-Shabaab took control of southern Somalia it was able to generate a reasonable profit from taxation of the trade going mainly through the port of Kismayo and the charcoal trade which dominates the southernmost part of Somalia. Even after the Kenyan invasion, Al-Shabaab was still managing checkpoints in the areas of its operations and is still able, to a certain degree, to profit from the charcoal trade.[58] Furthermore, it was estimated that Al-Shabaab was able to generate about US$1.4 million quarterly from the operation of the port of Kismayo alone.[59] This, however, does not mean that it receives no financing from the sources known from other Islamist organizations – charities, kidnapping, foreign funding, etc. It is estimated that in addition to the charcoal trade, throughout its history Al-Shabaab has been financed from state sources – mainly Eritrea, which used the organization as a proxy against Ethiopia – and many Islamic charities around the world.[60]

Ability to control territory

(1) Population density

Somalia is a relatively sparsely populated country (17 persons per km^2 in 2014[61]) and thus the power projection potential in the region is limited. In the southern part of Somalia, the most densely populated parts are located around the cities of Mogadishu and Marka, near the city of Baidoa, in the southern part of the Muduq region, and around the city of Kismayo.[62] Between 2009 and 2012, Al-Shabaab successfully controlled the area between Kismayo and Mogadishu and was hereby active in the most densely populated Somali region apart from Somaliland. Since the abandonment of Kismayo in 2012, Al-Shabaab has been operating in sparsely populated areas,[63] gaining advantage of hideout over the pursuing AU forces while being unable to fully project its power over its area of operation.

(2) Economic output

Al-Shabaab was in control of the main economic structures located south of Mogadishu between 2009 and 2012 and was battling to gain access to Mogadishu as another important economic hub. Its control over Kismayo and trade and movement in the southern part of the country is clearly a sign of control over important economic structures, while its inability to conquer

Mogadishu is a major pitfall. Currently, Al-Shabaab is, as noted previously, active in the charcoal trade in southern Somalia, while missing control over important economic hubs of southern Somalia.

(3) Provision of security
As noted above, Al-Shabaab was able to provide a degree of security that was unprecedented in the region ever since the collapse of the state. Its application of strict Islamic law brought an improvement over the years of anarchy and lawlessness while bringing new threats of its own (harsh prosecution, etc.). Al-Shabaab was, furthermore, able to protect its territories against other Somali actors but not against foreign agents and their regular armies.

(4) Governance
Al-Shabaab successfully established a local government structure in many parts of its controlled territory. In combination with Islamic law, these local governance structures provided the basis of Al-'Shabaab's claims of effectiveness and legitimacy.[64] During its heyday, Al-Shabaab successfully established many quasi-governmental institutions for the governance of its territory.[65] Even some non-governmental institutions have pointed out that Al-Shabaab was able to provide a level of stability that is unmatched by the central government.[66]

(5) Infrastructure
The general state of infrastructure in Somalia is poor. This on one side limited the ability of Al-'Shabaab's power projection, and on the other side it aided Al-Shabaab in the control of a few important roads with checkpoints thus enabling it to control important trade routes with less effort than would have been the case if a more robust infrastructure were present. Furthermore, in the post-2012 period the inadequate infrastructure has aided Al-'Shabaab's survival due to the inaccessibility of a major portion of southern Somalia. Poor infrastructure thus decreased the power projection ability of Al-Shabaab, while it increased its potential to struggle in the post-Kenyan invasion environment and enabled it to better control economic activity in the region which is, however, limited due to the poor state of land communications.[67]

Clearly, Al-'Shabaab's use of political territoriality as a strategy has changed over time. First, there are some physical constraints that limit the potential of successful use of territory, being an asset in the Somali environment – low population density and weak infrastructure. Al-Shabaab, furthermore, pushes through the radical interpretation of Islamic law which in many provisions contradicts Somali tradition and thus distances Al-Shabaab from the territory it tries to control. However, there are also the factors that offer a picture of Al-Shabaab as a willing territorial actor – attempts to control the land, to govern it, and to control major economic and population hubs in the country.

We can clearly observe that there are two sets of factors that have distinguished different periods of political territoriality of Al-Shabaab. The first are the foreign interventions as the organization is unable to directly combat regular armed forces, and the second is a shift in ideology that might diminish the willingness of Al-Shabaab to operate in a territorial fashion in the future. The use of territory is in Al-'Shabaab's case determined by limited physical factors and the ability to provide security. We can, consequently, distinguish three phases in the development of political territoriality of Al-Shabaab: (1) 2006–2008 – defiance; (2) 2009–2011 – supremacy; (3) 2012–present – withdrawal.

The first phase was characterized by the struggle against Ethiopian forces, which in the end led to the grounding of Al-Shabaab in the southernmost part of Somalia and ultimately to the retreat of Ethiopian forces. In this period, Al-Shabaab was centred on the establishment of an Islamic state in greater Somalia with a focus on Somali nationalism and the radical interpretation of Islam and thus successfully combining a personal and territorial principle of political control in the face of foreign invasion. 'The group's rhetoric was supporting territorial goals, it attempted to control territory, it tried to create governing structures (at least by the end of the Ethiopian incursion), and to some extent it used localized non-predatory means of financing. On the other hand, Al-Shabaab forced through a radical interpretation of 'Shari'a law that was not in accordance with local traditions. Nevertheless, all the factors connected to the ability to control land have to be deemed as low as the 'group's territorial reach was rather limited, yet by the end of the period increasing. The deterritorialized nature of Al-Shabaab in this period was caused by its inability to provide governance and security to larger territories and to extract resources from the land. The nature of the conflict was thus unconventional or semi-conventional with Al Qaeda inspired tactics of hit-and-run operations, or the use of suicide-bombings and improvised explosive devices.

The second phase was characterized by Al-'Shabaab's successful domination of major parts of southern Somalia, its attempts to govern and to control major population and economic hubs, as well as by struggles with other actors in the region. We might observe that Al-Shabaab was then pursuing all the factors related to the willingness to act territorially with the exception of the legal code. Regarding actual territorial control, Al-'Shabaab's territorial power projection was limited by structural issues connected to low population density and poor infrastructure. Still, it was able to provide, in the Somali context, a significant level of governance; it controlled important economic centres of the region and was able to provide a fair level of security. On the other hand, the period was also characterized by the closer connection of Al-Shabaab to the global jihadist movement which was materialized in the successful Al-Shabaab bid to become part of Al Qaeda. This ideological shift from local territorially based Islamism to global jihadism together with the threat Al-Shabaab posed to neighbouring Kenya resulted in the appearance of the third phase – a withdrawal of

Table 1. Development of territoriality.

	2006–2008	2009–2011	2012-present
Willingness to control	Limited/Yes	Yes	No/limited
Rhetoric	Yes	Yes	Limited
Attempt to establish	Limited	Yes	No
Local penal code	No	No	No
Attempt to control	Yes	Yes	No
Financing without looting	Limited	Yes	Limited
Ability to control	**Low**	**Medium/high**	**Low**
Population density	Low	Low	Low
Economic output	Low	High	Medium
Security	Low	Medium	Low
Governance	Low	High	Low
Infrastructure	Low	Low	Low

Al-Shabaab. The nature of the conflict in the second phase was closer to conventional warfare; Al-Shabaab was trying to conquer the land as manifested in its attempts to occupy important demographic and economic centres or to disrupt important centres of opposing the TFG and AU.

The third period is marked by significant losses in the amount of territory Al-Shabaab controls, its shift towards political control through personal characteristics (disenfranchised Somalis,[68] East African Muslims, and the global jihadist movement in general), with the issue of lacking support from ordinary Somalis who turned away from the group as a consequence of its brutal rule and indiscriminate killing following the purge of the nationalistic ,faction,[69] and hit-and-run tactics without any attempt to control important parts of southern Somalia. At this time the group not only lost most of its ability to control territory in southern Somalia for longer periods – it retreated to the so-called Sharqistaan (hardly accessible highland area) and to rural areas in the southern part of the country where it can find support by exploiting local grievances[70] – but also became a deterritorialized entity in its strategy. The nature of the conflict thus reverted back to the situation of the first period. The results are presented in Table 1.

As mentioned earlier, the shift in strategy is mainly connected to the issues of Al-Shabaab's leadership and foreign interventions. Despite the challenging nature of the Somali environment, Al-Shabaab was able to maintain fair territorial presence and to provide some of the basic goods; however, all of this this ended with the more violent tactics of Godane whose actions alienated common Somalis. Furthermore, its inability to provide security against foreign agents proved to be arguably even more damaging. This said, it must be pointed out that the major factor that influenced Al-'Shabaab's ability to control territory was the provision of security against both internal (not only warlords or pirates, but also against Al-'Shabaab's violent acts) and external violent actors and intervening armies. With less focus on violence reflecting the potential rise of the nationalist faction inside the organization, and if Kenyan and later Ethiopian forces had not entered Somalia after 2011, Al-Shabaab might have become a relevant territorial actor with a strong presence in southern Somalia.

This shift in the territorial dimension is important from the point of view of strategic choices in mitigation of the Al-Shabaab threat. As Al-Shabaab increasingly operates in a deterritorialized manner, it is important to notice that a territorially based reaction – boots on the ground – is of limited use with the current military presence. Al-Shabaab fighters operate in hardly accessible areas and do not permanently control any major economic and population hub or any territory in general. On the other hand, Al-Shabaab gains its strength from the use of personal characterization of its political enchantment and thus mitigation strategies should aim more at the diminishing of the popularity of its ideology among the groups it targets – mainly Somalis in Kenya and disenfranchised Somali clans. As Al-Shabaab has shifted into its deterritorialized shape, it is important to understand the strategic implications. However, this must be further examined from the perspective of the military theory and some further research focusing on the issue of strategy to counter the remains of Al-Shabaab would be of great use to effectively restrain this organization.

Conclusion

Territoriality is primarily a human strategy of exclusion (and secondarily of inclusion) based on geography and borders. Political territoriality is a strategy of political control based on the same characteristics. There are also other possible strategies of connecting power and space based on personal characteristics or function that might supplement or substitute territoriality. Political territoriality is a socially constructed strategy based on the evolutionary predominance of the territorial definition of power for the collective defence. In the modern world, it has been mainly connected to the institution of the state and the principle of sovereignty, but the shift in post-Cold War international politics has brought the issue of non-state territoriality back into the spotlight. Somalia stands out as one of the prime examples of the return of the importance of the political territoriality of non-state actors. Since the 'state collapse in the early 1990s, many actors have attempted to control at least parts of the territory of this formal state (now more of a fiction) but, with the exception of Somaliland, have largely failed. The most recent and temporarily successful example in southern Somalia is Al-Shabaab.

In this article we have defined the political territoriality of an actor by two sets of criteria: willingness to control territory (defined by 'the actor's rhetoric, attempt to establish governing institutions, establishment of localized penal code, attempt to control economic and urban centres, and financing without predatory means of collecting funds) and ability to control territory (defined by population density, economic output, provision of security, establishment of governing institution, and level of infrastructure development). Applying such criteria to Al-Shabaab, we were able to characterize three phases of the development of its political territoriality: 2006–2008 – defiance; 2009–2011 – supremacy; and 2012–present – withdrawal. The difference between these three periods is mainly characterized by the effects of foreign interventions and the change in Al-'Shabaab's ideology. It is argued that Al-Shabaab ceased to use political territoriality as a result of the prevalence of the globalist faction led by Godane and the 2011 Kenyan invasion. Contemporary Al-Shabaab has shifted from the position of a territorial actor towards a deterritorialized organization defining itself by its appeal for disenfranchised Somali population, its protection of East African Muslims, and its role in the global jihadist movement. The nature of the Somali conflict has also been affected by this development. In the first phase, Al-Shabaab led a guerrilla – sort of liberation – war against the Ethiopian invaders. The second phase was characterized by more conventional means and attempts to conquer and govern territory. The third phase led to the return to the guerrilla and unconventional warfare. The nature of the conflict in Somalia was thus largely marked by the use of political territoriality by Al-Shabaab and its ability to do so. This in turn leads to the need of a strategic change; the AU occupation of southern Somalia will not eradicate Al-Shabaab by itself as the Kenyan and other African Union forces have already achieved control over important geopolitical features inside southern Somalia or at least diminished the permanent hold of Al-Shabaab over a significant portion of land. On the other hand, the strategy needs to address the new identification of Al-Shabaab with certain parts of population that are not yet repulsed by its brutal and indiscriminate tactics and to diminish its popularity in the segments appealed to by its ideology. This final conclusion is a possible theme for future research in the area of insurgency mitigation.

Notes

1. Riegl, 'Terminologie kvazistátů'.
2. Sack, 'Human Territoriality', 55.
3. Ibid., 56.
4. Sack, *Human Territoriality*, 2–3.
5. Ibid., 20.
6. Sack, 'Human Territoriality', 57.
7. Vollaard, 'The Logic of Political Territoriality', 691.
8. Ibid., 690.
9. Ibid., 693.
10. Agnew, *Globalization and Sovereignty*, 6.
11. Goemans, 'Bounded Communities', 29.
12. Kahler, 'Territoriality and Conflict', 3.
13. Johnson and Toft, 'Grounds for War'.
14. Johnston, 'Out of the "Moribund Backwater"', 684–5.
15. Kahler, 'Territoriality and Conflict', 4, 9, 13.
16. Newman, 'The Resilience of Territorial Conflict', 96.

17. See Toft, *The Geography of Ethnic Violence*.
18. Gartzke, 'Globalization, Economic Development, and Territorial Conflict', 179.
19. Johnston, 'Out of the "Moribund Backwater"', 687, 690.
20. Korbin, 'Back to the Future'.
21. Kahler, 'Territoriality and Conflict', 2.
22. Newman, 'The Resilience of Territorial Conflict', 88.
23. Gurr, 'Peoples Against States'.
24. Staniland, *Networks of Rebellion*, 21–2.
25. As P. Williams points out, in some places the population perceives even the harsh rule of violent non-state actors as desirable in comparison to the lawlessness connected to state failure. See Williams, *Violent Non-State Actors*.
26. Berg and Kuusk, 'What Makes Sovereignty a Relative Concept?'; Zaidi, 'Toward a Measure of the Functional Effectiveness of a State'.
27. Bruton, *Somalia*.
28. Murphy, *Somalia: The New Barbary?*.
29. Menkhaus and Shapiro, 'Non-State Actors and Failed States'.
30. Murphy, *Somalia: The New Barbary?*; Menkhaus, 'The Crisis in Somalia'.
31. Menkhaus, 'Governance without Government in Somalia'.
32. Shortland and Percy, 'Governance, Naval Intervention and Piracy in Somalia'.
33. Hansen, *Al-Shabaab in Somalia*, 4.
34. Ibid., 15–48; Shinn, 'Al-Shabaab's Foreign Threat to Somalia'.
35. Ibid.
36. Hansen, *Al-Shabaab in Somalia*, 73.
37. Mwangi, 'State Collapse', 518.
38. Solomon, 'Somalia's Al-Shabaab', 352–3.
39. Marchal, 'A Tentative Assessment', 390, 394; Thomas, 'Exposing and Exploiting', 414.
40. Hansen, *Al-Shabaab in Somalia*; Thomas, 'Exposing and Exploiting', 413.
41. Hansen, *Al-Shabaab in Somalia*.
42. Menkhaus, 'Al-Shabab's Capabilities Post-Westgate', 5; Solomon, 'Somalia's Al-Shabaab', 357; Hansen, *Al-Shabaab in Somalia*.
43. See: http://www.bbc.com/news/world-africa-29034409.
44. Williams, 'After Westgate'; Mwangi, 'State Collapse', 521; Anderson and McKnight, 'Kenya at War'; Menkhaus, 'Al-Shabab's Capabilities Post-Westgate'.
45. Al-Shabaab even declared war on Israel. See http://archive.adl.org/terrorism/symbols/al_shabaab.html.
46. Al-Shabaab merged with Al Qaeda 'to confront the international crusaders and their aggression against the Muslim people'. See http://archive.adl.org/terrorism/symbols/al_shabaab.html. Also in 2012, Ayman al-Zawahiri – leader of Al Qaeda – announced the merger with Al-Shabaab in the following words: 'Today, I have pleasing glad tidings for the Muslim Ummah that will please the believers and disturb the disbelievers, which is the joining of the Shabaab al-Mujahideen Movement in Somalia to Qaedat al-Jihad, to support the jihadi unity against the Zio-Crusader campaign and their assistants amongst the treacherous agent rulers.' See https://news.siteintelgroup.com/Jihadist-News/zawahiri-announces-joining-of-shabaab-to-al-qaeda.html.
47. On the impact of the merger on the self-presentation of Al-Shabaab, see http://csis.org/files/publication/110715_Wise_AlShabaab_AQAM%20Futures%20Case%20Study_WEB.pdf, p. 7.

48. Thomas, 'Exposing and Exploiting', 416. For the discussion over the changing nature of the Al-Shabaab rhetoric between 2007 and 2010, see Curran, 'Global Ambitions'.
49. Mwangi, 'State Collapse', 522–3.
50. This shift is evident when looking at the predominance of the Kenyan issue in Al-Shabaab press statements since 2012. For a clear picture visit SITE intelligence coverage of Al-Shabaab's statements at https://news.siteintelgroup.com/index.php?option=com_customproperties&lang=en&tagId=21&task=tag&view=search&limitstart=0&limit=100.
51. Another sign of this process appears in the statement presented by Al-Shabaab after the Garissa University massacre. The statement presents passages such as: 'It is a well known fact that the Kenyan government has perpetrated unspeakable atrocities against the Muslims of East Africa. [. . .] Throughout East Africa, the Muslims were stripped of all their dignity and subjected to the most inhuman treatment for failing to succumb to the subjugation of the disbelievers. [. . .] The Muslim blood is inviolable whereas the blood of a Kafir [disbeliever] has no protection except by Eeman [belief] or Aman [covenant of security]. [. . .] For as long as your government persists in its path of oppression, implements repressive policies and continues with the systematic persecution against innocent Muslims, our attacks will also continue.' Full text is available at https://www.washingtonpost.com/world/africa/al-shabab-statement-on-deadly-campus-assault-in-kenya/2015/04/04/4577ce52-dad9-11e4-8103-fa84725dbf9d_story.html.
52. Mwangi, 'State Collapse', 514.
53. Garnstein-Ross, 'The Strategic Challenge', 34–5.
54. Nelson and Sanderson, 'Al Shabaab', 3–6.
55. See Hansen, *Al-Shabaab in Somalia*.
56. See Anderson and McKnight, 'Kenya at War'.
57. See http://www.lib.utexas.edu/maps/africa/txu-pclmaps-oclc-795784383-somalia_2012_population_density.jpg.
58. Anderson and McKnight, 'Kenya at War', 10–11; United Nations Security Council, 'Letter dated 10 October 2014', 43–7.
59. United Nations Security Council, 'Letter dated 10 December 2008', 46.
60. Kambere, 'Financing Al-Shabaab'.
61. According to the World Bank. Available at http://data.worldbank.org/indicator/EN.POP.DNST.
62. See http://www.lib.utexas.edu/maps/africa/txu-pclmaps-oclc-795784383-somalia_2012_population_density.jpg.
63. Map of Al-Shabaab activities in 2014 available at United Nations Security Council, 'Letter dated 10 October 2014', 60.
64. Mwangi, 'State Collapse', 522–3.
65. See: Hansen, *Al-Shabaab in Somalia*, 73–102.
66. McFate, *The Modern Mercenary*, 131.
67. For detailed analysis of the state of infrastructure inside Somalia, see World Bank report at http://www-wds.worldbank.org/external/default/WDSContentServer/WDSP/IB/2013/08/13/000445729_20130813141504/Rendered/PDF/802330WP0Somal0Box0379802B00PUBLIC0.pdf.
68. Menkhaus, 'Al-Shabab's Capabilities Post-Westgate', 6.
69. Bryden, 'The Reinvention of Al-Shabaab', 2.
70. Ibid., 11.

Disclosure statement

No potential conflict of interest was reported by the author.

Funding

This work was supported by the Institute of Political Studies, Faculty of Social Sciences, Charles University in Prague under a Specific Academic Research project, no. 260 230/2015 'Proměny a důsledky politických institucí' ['Changes and impacts of political institutions'].

References

Agnew, John. *Globalization and Sovereignty*. Plymouth: Rowman and Littlefield Publishers, 2009.
Anderson, David M., and Jacob McKnight. 'Kenya at War: Al-Shabaab and Its Enemies in Eastern Africa.' *African Affairs* 454, no. 114 (2014): 1–27.
Berg, Eiki, and Ene Kuusk. 'What Makes Sovereignty a Relative Concept? Empirical Approaches to International Society.' *Political Geography* 29, no. 1 (2010): 40–49.
Bruton, Bronwyn E. *Somalia: A New Approach*. New York, NY: Council on Foreign Relations, 2010.
Bryden, Matt. 'The Reinvention of Al-Shabaab: A Strategy of Choice or Necessity?' February 2014, accessed 13 October 2015. http://csis.org/files/publication/140221_Bryden_ReinventionOfAlShabaab_Web.pdf.
Curran, Cody. 'Global Ambitions: An Analysis of Al-Shabaab's Evolving Rhetoric'. 17 February 2011, accessed 18 September 2015. http://www.criticalthreats.org/somalia/global-ambitions-analysis-al-shabaabs-evolving-rhetoric-february-17-2011.
Garnstein-Ross, Daveed. 'The Strategic Challenge of Somalia's Al-Shabaab: Dimensions of Jihad.' *The Middle East Quarterly* 16, no. 4 (2009): 25–36.
Gartzke, Erik. 'Globalization, Economic Development, and Territorial Conflict.' In *Territoriality and Conflict in an Era of Globalization*, edited by Miles Kahler and Barbara F Walter, 156–186. Cambridge: Cambridge University Press, 2006.
Goemans, Hans. 'Bounded Communities: Territoriality, Territorial Attachment, and Conflict.' In *Territoriality and Conflict in an Era of Globalization*, edited by Miles Kahler and Barbara F Walter, 25–61. Cambridge: Cambridge University Press, 2006.
Gurr, Ted Robert. 'Peoples Against States: Ethnopolitical Conflict and the Changing World System'. *International Studies Quarterly* 38 (1994): 347–377.
Hansen, Stig Jarle. *Al-Shabaab in Somalia: The History and Ideology of a Militant Islamist Group, 2005–12*. London: Hurst and Company, 2013.
Johnson, Dominic D. P. and Monica Duffy Toft. 'Grounds for War: The Evolution of Territorial Conflict.' *International Security* 38, no. 3 (2013/14): 7–38.
Johnston, Ron. 'Out of the "Moribund Backwater": Territory and Territoriality in Political Geography.' *Political Geography* 20, no. 6 (2001): 677–693.
Kahler, Miles. 'Territoriality and Conflict in an Era of Globalization.' In *Territoriality and Conflict in an Era of Globalization*, edited by Miles Kahler and Barbara F Walter, 1–23. Cambridge: Cambridge University Press, 2006.
Kambere, Geoffrey. 'Financing Al-Shabaab: The Vital Port of Kismayo'. August 2012, accessed 25 October 2015. https://globalecco.org/financing-al-shabaab-the-vital-port-of-kismayo.

Korbin, Stephen J. 'Back to the Future: Neomedievalism and the Postmodern Digital World Economy.' *Journal of International Affairs* 51, no. 2 (1998): 367–409.

Marchal, Roland. 'A Tentative Assessment of the Somali Harakat Al-Shabaab.' *Journal of Eastern African Studies* 3, no. 3 (2009): 381–404.

McFate, Sean. *The Modern Mercenary: Private Armies and What They Mean for World Order*. Oxford: Oxford University Press, 2014.

Menkhaus, Ken. 'Al-Shabab's Capabilities Post-Westgate.' *CTC Sentinel* 7, no. 2 (2014): 4–9.

Menkhaus, Ken. 'The Crisis in Somalia: Tragedy in Five Acts.' *African Affairs* 106, no. 424 (2007): 357–390.

Menkhaus, Ken. 'Governance without Government in Somalia: Spoilers, State Building, and the Politics of Coping.' *International Security* 31, no. 3 (2007): 74–106.

Menkhaus, Ken, and Jacob N. Shapiro. 'Non-State Actors and Failed States: Lessons from Al-Qa'ida's Experiences in the Horn of Africa.' In *Ungoverned Space: Alternatives to State Authority in an Era of Softened Sovereignty*, edited by Anne L Clunan and Harold A Trinkunas, 77–94. Stanford, CA: Stanford University Press, 2010.

Murphy, Martin N. *Somalia: The New Barbary?: Piracy and Islam in the Horn of Africa*. New York, NY: Columbia University Press, 2011.

Mwangi, Oscar Gakuo. 'State Collapse, Al Shabaab, Islamism, and Legitimacy in Somalia.' *Politics, Religion, and Ideology* 13, no.4 (2012): 513–527.

Nelson, Rick and Thomas M. Sanderson. 'Al Shabaab'. July 2011, accessed 20 September 2015. http://csis.org/files/publication/110715_Wise_AlShabaab_AQAM%20Futures 20Case%20Study_WEB.pdf.

Newman, David. 'The Resilience of Territorial Conflict in an Era of Globalization.' In *Territoriality and Conflict in an Era of Globalization*, edited by Miles Kahler and Barbara F Walter, 85–110. Cambridge: Cambridge University Press, 2006.

Riegl, Martin. 'Terminologie kvazistátů.' [Typology of quasi-states] *Acta politologica* 2, no. 1 (2010): 57–71.

Sack, Robert D. 'Human Territoriality: A Theory.' *Annals of the Association of American Geographers* 73, no. 1 (1983): 55–74.

Sack, Robert D. *Human Territoriality: Its Theory and History*. Cambridge: Cambridge University Press, 1986.

Shinn, David. 'Al-Shabaab's Foreign Threat to Somalia'. *Foreign Policy Research Institute* (2011), http://www.fpri.org/docs/media/alshabaab.pdf.

Shortland, Anja, and Sarah Percy. 'Governance, Naval Intervention and Piracy in Somalia.' *Peace Economics, Peace Science, and Public Policy* 19, no. 2 (2013): 275–283.

Solomon, Hussein. 'Somalia's Al-Shabaab: Clans vs Islamist Nationalism.' *South African Journal of International Affairs* 21, no. 3 (2014): 351–366.

Staniland, Paul. *Networks of Rebellion: Explaining Insurgent Cohesion and Collapse*. Ithaca, NY and London: Cornell University Press, 2014.

Thomas, Mathew J. 'Exposing and Exploiting Weaknesses in the Merger of Al-Qaeda and Al-Shabaab.' *Small Wars and Insurgencies* 24, no. 3 (2013): 413–435.

Toft, Monica Duffy. *The Geography of Ethnic Violence: Identity, Interests and the Indivisibility of Territory*. Princeton, NJ: Princeton University Press, 2003.

United Nations Security Council. 'Letter dated 10 December 2008 from the Chairman of the Security Council Committee established pursuant to resolution 751 (1992) concerning Somalia addressed to the President of the Security Council'. 10 December 2008, accessed 25 October 2015. http://www.poa-iss.org/CASAUpload/ELibrary/S_2008_769_Monitoring_Dec_2008.pdf.

United Nations Security Council, 'Letter dated 10 October 2014 from the Chair of the Security Council Committee pursuant to resolutions 751 (1992) and 1907 (2009) concerning Somalia and Eritrea addressed to the President of the Security Council'.

13 October 2014, accessed 25 October 2015. http://www.securitycouncilreport.org/atf/cf/%7B65BFCF9B-6D27-4E9C-8CD3-CF6E4FF96FF9%7D/S_2014_726.pdf.

Vollaard, Hans. 'The Logic of Political Territoriality.' *Geopolitics* 14, no. 4 (2009): 687–706.

Williams, Paul D. 'After Westgate: Opportunities and Challenges in the War Against Al-Shabaab.' *International Affairs* 90, no. 4 (2014): 907–923.

Williams, Phil. *Violent Non-State Actors and National and International Security*. Zurich: The International Relations and Security Network, 2008. http://www.isn.ethz.ch/Digital-Library/Publications/Detail/?id=93880

Zaidi, Iqtidar H. 'Toward a Measure of the Functional Effectiveness of a State: The Case of West Pakistan.' *Annals of the Association of American Geographers* 56, no. 1 (1966): 52–67.

Jihadist insurgency and the prospects for peace and security

Richard Burchill

ABSTRACT
Modern jihadist insurgency movements pose a threat to global peace and security. Modern jihadist insurgencies are not necessarily posing new operational challenges, instead it is the ideology and belief systems justifying the use of violence that we need to understand better. The ideology fuelling modern jihadist insurgencies, motivating the fighters, acting as a tool for recruiting and support is the key strength these groups have and the one area we have yet to adequately address. We must work to better understand this ideology and how it is utilised otherwise the threat from violent jihadist movements may continue for a very long time.

Introduction

There is no doubt that the terrorism and violence being carried out in the pursuit of jihadist insurgency poses a significant threat to international peace and security. The threat extends from the local instability being experienced in places like Afghanistan and West Africa, to the assertions of authority and control of territory being exercised by Daesh/Islamic State in Syria and Iraq, to the threats posed by lone extremists carrying out violent attacks around the world. As Professor Peter Neumann, Director of ICSR at King's College stated at the 2015 TRENDS/ICSR conference, jihadist insurgency is an 'Incredibly Important topic that will dominate the next decades of our discourse in security studies'.[1] The research presented in this special issue reinforces the impact jihadist insurgency movements are having on global stability as well as how responses to jihadist insurgency need significant improvement.

To date, attention has primarily focused on how we define jihadist insurgency movements and how this influences operational responses through military and security measures. As Rich and Duyvesteyn have explained, we can spend time defining organised, or semi-organised, violent groups in a variety of ways: insurgents, guerrilla movements, national liberation movements, terrorists, gangs, bandits, etc. But more importantly, they assert, attention should be concentrating on how to stop these groups and bring an end to their violence.[2] In relation to jihadist insurgency, it is not just the military or security operations against these groups that need to be successful to stop the violence. It is also essential to address the ideology and belief systems that drive their actions, something we are only starting to see.[3] This final contribution seeks to reinforce the argument that we need to give greater importance to understanding the ideology of jihadist insurgency to bring an end to the violence.

The need for better understanding the ideology and belief systems of jihadist insurgency is critical. It has been admitted that political and military leaders have failed to understand the belief system of Daesh, how the ideas and views they expressed were receiving support.[4] This has not only hampered the operational capacities of the responses to jihadist insurgencies, it is also imperative to ensuring the threat of jihadist insurgency is eliminated. This is not a simplistic matter of non-Muslims failing to understand Islam, it is a debate and discussion that needs to occur within the Islamic community as well as the wider world. We have to start by examining the objective(s) of jihadist insurgency. This can be summarised as the absolute and complete implementation of Islamic law across the world. Jihadist insurgency movements may still be seeking to control a specific territorial space, but their true objective is the implementation of Islamic law globally. Groups vary in their view on how this is to be achieved and the timeline, but it is this end goal we must be aware of. Tied to this is the strong belief that the conflict, objectives, operations, and life in general must all conform to the times of the Prophet Muhammad. It is believed that these times are the purest for Muslims as, it is claimed, the only law that applied was God made law.

It is the ideology and belief systems justifying the use of violence that we need to understand better. It is the ideology that is fuelling modern jihadist insurgencies, motivating the fighters to fight to the death, acting as a major recruiting and support factor for jihadist insurgency movements, as well as giving rise to the potential of a perpetual threat from violent jihadist, even if military operations are successful. Just because religious-based ideology is not at the centre of politics in the West and elsewhere, this does not mean it is unimportant elsewhere.[5] In particular, with the modern jihadist insurgency movements, religious ideology is perhaps the most important factor we need to address, at the very least we need to understand it more and understand it better.

How to understand the meaning(s) of jihad

When discussing jihadist insurgency today we appear to be presented with two simple positions: (1) the violence of the insurgency movements is inherent in Islamic belief and practice; or (2) jihad has only a peaceful meaning in Islamic belief and practice. In many ways, both views are correct. The difficulty is that both positions have a strong foundation in the doctrine, history, and practice of Islam. The greater jihad (peaceful) is about the individual striving to be true to their faith and do all they can to uphold the faith from a personal perspective. The lesser jihad (violence) is associated with the military/violent action taken to protect the faith from attack, or to further the reach of the religion. The greater jihad is about an individual's adherence to their belief system consisting of the spiritual struggle to understand the faith, how best to uphold the faith, and how to remain loyal to the faith. Islam provides significant details on the obligations for adherents regarding prayer, food, personal hygiene, relationships, etc. These are all integral to being a believer in the faith and they are all part of day-to-day life. The nature and details of these obligations are discussed and debated in the context of wider understandings of the faith and can be found in multiple sources and practices.

The lesser jihad relates to specific action for undertaking war/violence at a communal level. As the lesser jihad concerns when force can be used and how force is to be undertaken, it requires significant explanation and regulation in a more organised fashion, which is what has occurred. The obligations and details of the lesser jihad have been set out in Islamic jurisprudence in great detail. As Islam evolved, significant attention was given to the justifications and conduct of the lesser jihad, essentially the decisions and conduct of war. Commentators went to great lengths to develop the policy basis and jurisprudence for jihad leading to the jihad of violence becoming the most prominent understand of the concept. The extensive discussion which has come about through the years does give the impression that it is the lesser jihad which is central to Islam.[6]

The extensive writings on when and where jihad is possible, how it is to be declared, how the jihad is to be waged, how prisoners are to be treated, and how matters are brought to a conclusion provides a great deal of support for the jihadist insurgency to justify their actions. It further provides examples from the historical development of Islam that can be appealed to, providing support for their actions. The most important aspect in all of this is how the insurgency can claim a divine foundation for their views.[7] In setting out their use of violence, evidence and explanation will be drawn from the Quran, then Sunna, in order to instil the interpretation with a divine source leading to the assertion of direct obligations upon anyone claiming to be a true believer. And it is not just at the macro level of justifying violence that jihadist insurgency movements appeal to the divine foundations, they can further utilise existing doctrines to assert individual obligations to undertaken violence in the name of jihad.[8] It is not possible here to explore this matter in depth; the main point is that while we may attempt to say jihadist insurgents are distorting Islam, they are able to make arguments within the existing doctrines.

Attempting to respond to, and combat, jihadist insurgency without understanding this most basic religious foundation will prevent effective responses. The view that the entire world, or at the very least the Muslim world, must only be guided by divine law as experienced at the time of the Prophet has a long trajectory from Ibn Taymiyyah of the thirteenth century, to Muhammad ibn Abd al-Wahhab of the eighteenth century, to Sayyid Qutb in the twentieth century, to Daesh and others today. These commentators have put great import on returning society to the days of the Prophet as the only option. Adherents to this view do vary in how this is to come about with claims saying it will occur through persuasion or the sword. The appeal to living as the Prophet did has an obvious appeal as it is based on a belief that this is the best way to follow the faith. Support for this position is grounded in the divine sources, making attempts to refute its validity difficult to maintain. However, the jihadist insurgency movements all have their own view as to what it means to live as the Prophet lived, and they are adamant that their view is the only legitimate one to follow. This overlooks the long history of Islamic law where there has been substantial diversity in belief and practice.[9] But jihadist insurgents dismiss any deviation from their own ideological view as being contrary to the true belief. A factor that allows an organisation to discredit others and motivate supporters for it offers the only true way to follow.

Understanding the motivation and appeal of jihad

Rich, in this volume, discusses the global impact of the communist ideology in insurgency.[10] The global communist movement did attract a large number of supporters and to a degree a global following. Neither the movement nor the ideology provided a strong message tapping into the inner belief systems of a wide swathe of individuals. The divine foundations for jihadist insurgency, by contrast, provide a direct line between one's actions, their faith, and the rewards, both in this life and in the afterlife. Not only does this message sit with the individual's decision to fight with the insurgency, it also allows the insurgency movements to directly pressure all adherents to the Islamic faith. By asserting that there exists an obligation in their faith that jihad must be undertaken, the insurgency movement can either positively motivate or negatively guilt individuals into action. We continue to question 'why' an individual would join a jihadist insurgency or act on their behalf. While each individual will have individual reasons, it appears the ideology of jihadist insurgency provides a strong motivation for individuals and the group dynamic of the movements.

As explained above, the foundations for jihad are based on divine sources. It is this appeal to the divine that creates a strong motivation for the individual and collective acts of jihadist insurgencies. Islamic doctrine and historical practice provides extensive detail on not only how jihad is to be conducted but also the rewards one will receive. This positive salvation, which is again divinely guaranteed in the ideology, is something past insurgencies did not possess. People believe in political agendas, but the jihadist movement is about a political agenda that seeks not only to bring about a worldview in today's world, but is directly connected, so it is believed, to the individual's position as a true believer and what this means for their salvation. Any attempt to question the divine rewards that directly result from jihad requires a strong refutation of core doctrine of the faith. As two of the articles here show, the people supporting jihadist insurgency may or may not have a grievance, or feeling like something in their life is missing.[11] Regardless, the message from the jihadist insurgency has resonance because of the depth of the belief system and the actual rewards that can be offered. In some cases, as Lindekilde et al. show, individuals may not be drawn by the ideology of jihadist insurgency, but they are seeking means to give their life a degree of certainty and embeddedness.[12] The data from Bakker and de Bont points to similar issues, along with individuals being directly drawn by the ideological ideas of living wholly under Islamic law.[13] Either way, the ideology of the modern jihadist insurgencies allows for widespread appeal and motivation due to the nature of the messages and the direct historical connections that can be drawn.

Modern jihadist insurgency movements understand this position well. When groups like Daesh and Al Qaeda call for Muslims to join the jihad, they will provide substantial direct references to the Quran. One only needs to flip through copies of Daesh's magazine *Dabiq* to see how they are able to continually provide references to the divine in order to motivate their supporters. To take one example, the San Bernadino situation of December 2015 raised a number of questions about the perpetrators' belief in their faith, in particular the fact that they left their child behind. However, in Issue no. 13 of *Dabiq*, Daesh constructs a narrative that gives these individuals a very strong position in the faith through their actions. It first speaks of Syed Rizwan Farook acting so well by having his wife join him in the attack, and how she excelled by taking up the acts, even though women are not required to undertake violent jihad. The article goes on to say how she has lived up to the faith more than most men. The article then explains that the couple cannot be criticised for leaving their young child behind as this is justified by the divine sources. Regardless of whether or not Daesh's interpretation is correct, the motivational impact is clear. They are saying that the actions of these people are fully in line with the faith and that others need to do more to be more like them.

This takes us into the area of the 'hearts and minds' element in countering insurgency. However, it is the insurgency movements that are proving to be more effective in motivating individuals through an appeal to hearts and minds. The intensity and depth of the hearts and minds appeal is compounded as jihadist insurgencies are appealing to the soul as well. As discussed below, great effort needs to be taken to construct other narratives of understandings of jihad in Islamic thought. More critically, it is essential that the responses to jihadist insurgencies place the matter of hearts and minds at the forefront of efforts. Counterinsurgencies today do not end with a clear military defeat, and there is a transition period of security to bring about peace and prevent further attacks. Even if Iraq and Syria are eventually able to take control of their territory to the extent that the national government (however constituted) is able to exercise effective control, we are unlikely to see an end to the jihadist insurgency being led by Daesh. Followers of the Daesh view, or a reformed view will continue to pursue the ultimate objective of bringing their version of Islamic law to the world. It is possible to draw upon divine sources to justify a suspension of violence or to explain defeats, which also work to further motivate fighters to support the cause. In addition, we have to consider the youth in places like Iraq, Syria, or Libya; all they know is a highly radical and reductionist version of Islam. If their states do not develop quickly and these youths remain marginalised and wanting more, they will easily revert to extremist ideologies. Our responses need to continue with military and security approaches, but these will only be effective with a much better understanding of how the appeal to jihad appeals and motivates. As Edwin Bakker has explained, it is important to 'not only focus on the strategic issue, but also focus on who are these people, what attracts them to join this struggle, to be part of insurgency'.[14] Current approaches to countering jihadist insurgency appear based on rigid secularism, which means overlooking the religious beliefs and how we understand what drives these organisations and the individuals supporting them.

The appeal to jihad allows for disconnected networks with no clear command structure as everyone is agreed on the objective being sought. The motivation of jihad has been clear as it works to assign blame to others, helps to attract followers and enthusiasts, and works to show a triumphant vision of the future that individuals, regardless of their particular circumstances can grasp on to. We also have to keep in mind that the appeal and motivation of jihad is not something that has been artificially constructed. While we can argue and disagree with the divine references used by jihadist insurgencies, their source material is sound. The Quran and Sunnah provide, in many respects, a guide and manual for followers. Of course there exists significant potential in diverse understandings, but we have to admit the fact that extremists like Daesh and others are making use of valid sources. It is how they are using these sources that we need to work on overcoming through alternative narratives.

There is plenty that can be done in articulating alternative narratives that do not undermine the foundations of the faith but yet provide a more realistic interpretation relevant to today's world. Take the Daesh/IS statement on 'These Are Our Creeds and Ways'. In it a range of obligations set out in the Quran and Hadith are presented, but then added to the obligations upon Muslims is the statement, 'we believe in the return of the Righteous Caliphate (*al-khilafa al-rashida*), modelled on the practices of the Prophet' (par. 12). Calls for the return of the Righteous Caliphate are common in jihadist literature, but to present an obligation upon Muslims to bring about the return of the Caliphate is a modification in the religious doctrine.[15] While the Caliphate may not be a widely accepted core obligation, Daesh goes further in attempting to legitimise their justification by adding the phrase 'modelled on the practices of the Prophet'. This of course makes the claim sacred; it puts the statement or claim at the basis of an obligation to which all Muslims must adhere, making any counter-claim difficult. The opposing has to make clear their interpretation does not necessarily follow the practices of the Prophet. Even if the practices claimed by the jihadist insurgency are not easily attributed to the Prophet, the line of argumentation used by jihadist makes it difficult to refute.

Jihadist insurgency as a perpetual struggle

One thing that jihadist insurgencies have in common is the final objective of the movement: the full and complete implementation of Islamic law. The form of the Islamic law to be implemented will vary between movements, but they have a common view of ensuring that all societies are organised, and all individuals live and conduct themselves in the same manner as the Prophet did. This objective is not confined to violent insurgent groups; it is also shared by groups we can consider insurgents but who do not regularly use violence. Insurgency is commonly defined as action taken to overcome existing power structures. The belief in implementing Islamic law in all of society, globally, is a form of insurgency, no matter how it is pursued. Organisations, such as the Muslim Brotherhood, and its affiliated network are an example of this form of modern jihadist insurgency. While these organisations appeal to working within the existing political structures, their objective remains the same as Daesh and others, and their willingness to resort to violence is equally prevalent. The ideological foundation for modern jihadist insurgency has been articulated by Sayyid Qutb who called for a strong 'socio-political role for Islam' as a 'universally positive and rational system of thought, belief, and practice'.[16] As the belief is that Islam is a universal system, the jihadist insurgency ideology starts with the premise that insurgency will not end until the entire world is living under Islamic law. The pursuit of this project, as demonstrated in the prominence of jihadist insurgency in today's world, along with the motivational factors in jihad point to the potential that jihadist insurgency movements will continue in one form or another over the longer term, keeping the world in a perpetual conflict.

According to the positions expressed by jihadist insurgency movements, nothing less than the complete application of Islamic law is acceptable. The positioning on this matter is both offensive – it is an obligation to take Islam to others and we have practice from the Prophet to support this – and defensive

– anything less than the absolute presence of Islamic law is a threat to Islam that must be responded to. The objective of modern jihadist insurgencies is not just about particular local conflicts. The growing rhetoric from the extremists is a clear rejection of the current system for international organisation. Admittedly, the current system is far from ideal, but it is a system in which a wide range of systems, beliefs, and ideas are able to coexist. The alternative being pursued by the jihadist insurgencies does not appear to be a viable alternative, and it does not conform with practice from Islamic states in the development of the international system. Saudi Arabia was created as a state in the existing international system in 1932, the kingdom never claimed to be, or called for, a global Islamic caliphate. At the creation of the United Nations in 1945, states with a majority Islamic population composed 15% of the original members, including Egypt, Saudi Arabia, and Turkey. This is not a majority, of course, but there is no evidence that the Islamic states were calling for Islamic law to be the only law applicable to the international system; instead, they all agreed to be part of a system of diverse societies and states. The response to this evidence will follow a constant theme from the jihadist insurgents: the leaders of these communities were not true or loyal Muslims. Since the creation of the UN, no Islamic state or its political leaders has called for the creation of the Caliphate or demanded that only Islamic law, as in the time of the Prophet, should prevail. The Taliban in Afghanistan is an exception, but they did not fully implement Islamic law and their inability to maintain control is evidence of how the message of Islamic law only will not take hold across society. This is not to reject or discredit the importance of Islam in societies that choose to follow the faith. The point is that it is not possible to return modernist societies to the time of the Prophet and be ruled only by the Quran, locally and globally. Furthermore, we have to consider that while the violence of jihadist insurgency can find justification in Islamic doctrine, the current international system provides that the use of violence as a normal function of politics is wholly unacceptable, a position supported by all Islamic states. Extremists may attempt to argue that this system is illegitimate and cannot bind Muslims, but the reality is that it does. Of course the argument that the world overwhelmingly rejects the ideological objectives of jihadist insurgencies is not going to have much of an impact on the extremists. The perpetual battle is likely to continue regardless of the military success in reclaiming territory from Daesh or degrading the operational capability of any of the jihadist insurgency movements. The ideology will continue to motivate and appeal to those seeking violence as there is a historical narrative that says the Prophet continued and prevailed in his efforts with only small numbers of support.[17]

Final thoughts

The current threat from jihadist insurgency is global in nature and consists of both organised and dispersed forms of violence. Joffé's contribution explains that the current global situation of jihadist insurgency is complex, that it lacks any organisational structure, it only has a common ideology.[18] It is important to understand that we should not be focusing on trying to find a clear organisational structure for jihadist insurgencies, even though this is important. Rather, much more analytical attention needs to focus on the common ideology which is directed at bringing about a complete and absolute implementation of Sharia law, by violence if necessary. To combat modern jihadist insurgencies, we have to continue with the military and security approaches, perhaps using better and more appropriate operational tactics that better address the methods being used, rather than relying on past practices that are appearing out of date. Most importantly, efforts need to be directed at the ideology that is driving these groups, motivating the actors involved, and justifying the constant use of violence. These efforts need to engage with the divine foundations upon which jihadist insurgencies are appealing. Since Islam does not have a clear hierarchical structure in authority, as the Catholic Church does in the form of the Pope, we do not have the ability to direct the discussions through an authoritative body. As we see from Daesh or Al Qaeda, they spend a significant amount of time condemning other Muslims for not being true believers. The majority of Muslims, led by their political leaders, need to speak out emphatically against the understandings and justifications of Islam being used by the insurgents. These political leaders need to reassert and reassure their populations and Islamic populations around the world that while the current global system may not be perfect, it is a system that allows for expressions of Islam and provides security for its adherents. We do need to discuss new understandings and this is essential for bringing an end to the violence jihadist insurgents are using and jeopardising global peace and security.

Notes

1. TRENDS Interview with Professor Peter Neumann. Available at http://trendsinstitution.org/?p=1160.
2. Rich and Duyvesteyn, 'The Study of Insurgency and Counterinsurgency', 2.
3. Byman, 'Understanding Islamic State'.
4. Wood, 'What ISIS Really Wants'.
5. Ibid.
6. Afsaruddin, *Striving in the Path of God*, 270–97.
7. Bonner, *Jihad in History*, 10.
8. For a full discussion, see Coughlin, *Catastrophic Failure*.
9. Khadduri, *War and Peace in the Law of Islam*, 34–5.
10. Rich, 'How Revolutionary Are Jihadist Insurgencies?'.
11. Lindekilde et al. 'Who Goes, Why, and with What Effects'; Bakker and de Bont, 'Belgian and Dutch Jihadist Foreign Fighters'.
12. Lindekilde et al. 'Who Goes, Why, and with What Effects'.
13. Bakker and de Bont, 'Belgian and Dutch Jihadist Foreign Fighters'.
14. Interview with Professor Edwin Bakker, http://trendsinstitution.org/?p=1160.

15. For discussion, see Landau-Tasseron, *A Self-Profile of the Islamic State*.
16. Toth, *Sayyid Qutb*, 5.
17. Whiteside, 'The Islamic State and the Return of Revolutionary Warfare'.
18. Joffee, 'Global Jihad and Foreign Fighters'.

Disclosure statement

No potential conflict of interest was reported by the author.

References

Afsaruddin, Asma. *Striving in the Path of God: Jihad and Martyrdom in Islamic Thought*. Oxford: Oxford University Press, 2013.

Bakker, Edwin and Roel de Bont. 'Belgian and Dutch Jihadist Foreign Fighters (2012–2015): Characteristics, Motivations, and Role in the War in Syria and Iraq.' *Small Wars & Insurgencies* 27, no. 5 (2016).

Bonner, Michael. *Jihad in Islamic History: Doctrines and Practice*. Princeton: Princeton University Press, 2008.

Byman, Daniel. 'Understanding Islamic State: A Review Essay.' *International Security* 40, no. 4 (2016): 127–165.

Coughlin, Stephen. *Catastrophic Failure: Blindfolding America in the Face of Jihad*. Washington, DC: Center for Security Policy Press, 2015.

Joffé, George. 'Global Jihad and Foreign Fighters.' *Small Wars & Insurgencies* 27, no. 5 (2016).

Khadduri, Majid. *Law and Peace in the Law of Islam*. Baltimore, MD: The Johns Hopkin Press, 1955.

Landau-Tasseron, Ella. *A Self-Profile of the Islamic State: The Creedal Document*. MEMRI Inquiry and Analysis No. 1253 (1 June 2016).

Lindekilde, Lasse, Preben Bertelsen, and Michael Stohl. 'Who Goes, Why and with What Effects: The Problems of Foreign Fighters from Europe.' *Small Wars & Insurgencies* 27, no. 5 (2016).

Rich, Paul B. 'How Revolutionary Are Jihadist Insurgencies?' *Small Wars & Insurgencies* 27, no. 5 (2016).

Rich, Paul B., and Isabell Duyvesteyn (eds.). *The Routledge Handbook of Insurgency and Counterinsurgency*. London: Routledge, 2014.

Toth, James. *Sayyid Qutb: The Life and Legacy of a Radical Islamic Intellectual*. Oxford: Oxford University Press, 2013.

Whiteside, Craig. 'The Islamic State and the Return of Revolutionary Warfare.' *Small Wars & Insurgencies* 27, no. 5 (2016).

Wood, Graeme. 'What ISIS Really Wants'. *The Atlantic*, March 2015. http://www.theatlantic.com/magazine/archive/2015/03/what-isis-really-wants/384980/.

Afterword

Paul B. Rich

Since this volume of essays was first published in *Small Wars & Insurgencies* the political and military landscape in the Middle East and North Africa has already undergone some significant change, making a generally dismal situation even more alarming as the major powers, with the apparent exception of Russia, lack either the resolve or the ability to intervene in any decisive way to end long-running conflicts. This is an era considerably distanced from the naïve simplicities of the Bush administration's "war on terror," though it is difficult to make any sort of clear prediction on where it might be heading over the next decade or more. One might almost imagine we are in an insuperably complex set of interlocking narratives like the film *Syriana* (2005), scripted by the imaginative Hollywood director Stephen Gaghan. But the narratives of the film are far outrun by the myriad forces we see throughout the world inhabited by jihadist insurgencies: Gaghan posited that the two central dynamics of Middle Eastern politics are oil and weapons, commodities closely linked and interchangeable.[1] The real world is far more complex, with not all Middle Eastern states having oil to sell.

Jihadist Insurgent Movements examined a series of insurgencies with ideologies derived from a variety of political readings of Islamic texts. At points, the collection asked how far these movements were revolutionary, in the sense that they sought both a radical transformation of various societies as well as the global political system. One obvious comparison was with the earlier Bolshevik revolution in Russia and its relatively brief effort to transform international society into a global dictatorship of the proletariat, a utopian ideal that was effectively side-lined by the rise of Stalin the late 1920s and the lurch towards "socialism in one country." The ISIS ideal of transforming global power politics through an expanding Islamic caliphate clearly had similar revolutionary pretensions, though it also draws on earlier patterns of imperialism in the Islamic world.

The shifting balance of power in relation to contemporary jihadist insurgencies reflects three major forces: the complex range of local insurgencies that aspire to be jihadist; the existing pattern of states through the regions where these movements operate; and the role of external great powers, principally the US, Russia, China, and Western European states such as Britain, France, Italy, and Germany. The relationship between these three forces has been in a constant state of flux, making predictions for the future difficult. For some analysts, it appeared that the rapid early territorial gains of ISIS and the scrapping of the boundary between Iraq and Syria signalled the start of a major process of territorial reconstruction in the Middle East and a redrawing of the maps designed, first, at the Treaty of Versailles in 1919 and consolidated in subsequent treaties in the early 1920s. ISIS attempted to position itself as an indigenous revolutionary movement that the self-proclaimed Caliph Abu Bakir Al-Baghdadi stated in July 2014 would not stop until "we hit the last nail in the coffin of the Sykes Picot conspiracy." The movement thus aligned itself with a revolutionary project to reverse a pattern of western imperial domination of the Middle East anchored in the geopolitical construction of divisive Arab states following the collapse of the Ottoman empire and one that had never been successful challenged by the secular Pan Arab movement championed by President Nasser of Egypt in the late 1950s and early 1960s.

The boundaries that were drawn up in the early 1920s were never intended, however, to be final, but only to mark spheres of influence.[2] They became increasingly rigid due to the rise of nationalist movements before and after World War Two, rather like the colonial boundaries in Sub Saharan Africa. The Arab states that have emerged in the Middle East had proved quite durable, coming into existence in cases like Iraq and Syria before World War Two and developing strong state structures under long periods of dictatorial rule. The fact that ISIS has been able to tear up at least one boundary does not necessarily mean that an entire geopolitical reconstruction will take place, only that the state structures of Iraq and Syria failed to maintain full control of their sovereign territory in the context of invasion and civil war.[3] So far, this war has not emerged on quite such a regional scale as the Thirty Years War in Europe between 1618–1648, though given the devastation and social breakdown in such states as Libya, Syria, Iraq, Yemen, and Somalia, any diplomatic resolution is likely to involve some sort of territorial reconstruction, though we appear to be a long way from any new Peace of Westphalia. A long-term peace will still depend, to a considerable extent, on the third of the major forces working through the Islamic world, the great powers: if this leads to any sort of major great power pact, it is safe to assume that neither Syria nor Iraq will survive in their old territorial forms with boundaries being at least adjusted and even one or two new states emerging, such as a Kurdish state – though this is likely to be fiercely opposed by Turkey short of some wider diplomatic package.

It is hard to see the great powers falling out over the areas dominated by jihadist insurgencies, despite the lure of oil. If they do fall apart, it is far more likely to be due to conventional inter-state threats – such as the prospect of Iran gaining nuclear weapons – than over how to deal with Iraq, Syria, Libya, Yemen, Somalia, or the crises in West Africa. To this extent, the region does not present the same sort of global security threat as North East Asia with a nuclear

North Korea or the South China Sea faced with the threat of Chinese sub-imperial expansion, despite some suggestions to the contrary.[4] Indeed, it is precisely because Syria has not presented any sort of direct security threat that the US has been inhibited, under the Obama administration, from making any direct intervention. However the emergence of a pro-Putin US president gives cautious grounds for optimism that a super-power deal may be reached to end the long-running conflict.

Nevertheless, this is a period, as John Bew has remarked, in which the "pre-prepared script runs out".[5] The multiple conflicts throughout the Middle East, North and West Africa as well as further afield have led to selective interventions by the great powers. This selectivity has ensured that the optimism of the post-Cold War era centred on the idea of a new international order has, once and for all, ended: there has, instead, been a return to a rather more Hobbesian age of great power politics that some International Relations idealists liked to imagine had been banished for good in an emerging international society regulated by norms of international law and justice. The great powers will continue to intervene in a largely self-interested way that perpetuate some previous interventions that did so much to forge some of the original jihadist insurgencies: Soviet intervention into Afghanistan in 1979, followed by the US-led allied invasion of Iraq in 2003, the NATO intervention to secure the overthrow of the Qaddafi regime in Libya in 2011, and the more recent Russian intervention on behalf of the Baathist regime in Syria that began in September 2015.

The Syrian civil war has intensified with a relentless savagery and the Assad regime in Damascus has been buttressed by Russian troops and airpower, some of which have come from a Soviet-era aircraft carrier in the Mediterranean. The numbers of opposition activists killed in the conflict range from 301,000 to 470,000 while over 6 million people have been displaced and 4.8 million living as refugees outside the country, many in neighbouring states such as Lebanon and Jordan as well as Western Europe. The refugee crisis is one of major regional proportions given the way it has put immense pressure on many of the surrounding states. Left untackled, the issue threatens to spin out of control if state structures buckle, leading to a further rapid expansion of jihadist insurgent movements and accompanying terrorism.

Elsewhere conflicts continue in North and West Africa, the Horn of Africa, and Yemen as well as parts of South and South East Asia.[6] None appear to overturn the volume's general assessments: jihadist insurgent movements remain significant forces in global politics, though ones prone to fissiparous cleavages given that they often emerge from various other movements already in existence. They display a propensity to impose ideological blueprints on recalcitrant populations, often derived from a garbled interpretation of religious belief such as those movements observing a strict Salafism in the Middle East such as ISIS or the former Al Nusra Front in Syria, now renamed Jabhat al-Sham as it seeks to break its former links with Al Qaeda.[7]

Jihadist insurgencies, as some of the chapters in this collection stressed, are also distinctive in the way that they have largely gone against the trend of ethnic nationalism, such a dominant feature in the politics of the developing world in the decades after 1945. The insurgencies can be undermined, to some degree by external pressure, though doing so risks, as Daniel Byman has warned, encouraging a trend towards international terrorism.[8] This is a theme that some of the chapters in the volume examined in relation to the long-running threat of terrorist attacks in European. It is one that has been made worse by the huge number of refugees fleeing the Syrian Civil War, some of whom may become radicalized and turn to jihadism, especially those who find themselves marginalized on the peripheries of cities such as the squalid *banlieues* outside Paris.

These issues may come to be viewed rather differently in the next few years as political leaderships in the west undergo significant transformation in the wake of the British Brexit and Donald Trump's election as the United States president. ISIS has come under strong pressure in Syria and Iraq and is now facing the prospect of complete military defeat.

In Syria, the dynamic of the original 2011 revolutionary movement that emerged to overthrow the Assad regime appears all but spent as the Russian military intervention seems set to turn the country into a client state. Further afield, the ISIS enclave around Sirte in Libya has come under growing pressure from the forces of the government in Tripoli, though the country remains fragmented into different warring factions that threaten to spill over into neighbouring states, such as the brief ISIS incursion into the southern Tunisian town of Ben Guerdane in early March 2016, killing 53 people, 33 ISIS insurgents, 7 civilians, and 11 members of the Tunisian security forces.[9]

In Nigeria, the insurgency waged by Boko Haram continues, with over 60 attacks mounted between August and November of 2016 alone. Despite a commitment in mid-2014 by the Nigerian president Muhammadu Buhari to "crush" the movement, the Nigerian army has made slow progress, throwing doubt on claims that the Nigerian government and military really control over 95% of Nigerian territory.[10] Certainly, the area described as an "Islamic State" by the leader of Boko Haram, Shehau, has been largely retaken, forming in effect a kind of early version of a wider scale military defeat of Islamic State in Iraq and Syria. But Boko Haram remains a major strategic threat to the stability of Africa's most populous country even if it abandons guerrilla warfare in favour of terrorist attacks.[11]

Elsewhere, in Somalia, a long-standing civil war that has its origins in moves to overthrow President Siad Barre in the late 1980s, has been continuing for decades. The current civil war is not on quite the same scale as in 2005–2007, when conflict raged in the South and Ethiopian troops intervened to seize control of most of the South from the Islamic Courts Union (ICU). This propelled the surviving factions of the ICU to form the more overtly jihadist insurgent movement Harakat Al-Shabaab, which has been fighting both the Somali government, formed in 2012, as the first permanent central government since the start of the civil war, and the African Union force AMISOM, sent to restore order to the country. The youthful nature of the movement is captured in the meaning of the group's label: Al-Shabaab means "movement of striving youth" and can be compared to other jihadist movements based on marginalized youth such as Boko Haram in West Africa, though Al-Shabaab appears not to have the same bitter hatred for educated elites.

Somalia is one of the most fragile states in the world while Al-Shabaab has emerged as a serious security threat in the East Africa region. Its first leader, Ahmed Abdi Godane, was killed in a US airstrike and the group is now led by Sheikh Ahmed Omar; the movement pledged allegiance to Al Qaeda and promotes a political ideology heavily based on a Salafist interpretation of Islam. The movement has favoured high profile terrorist attacks such as the Westgate Shopping Mall in Nairobi in 2013 or the more recent strike at Mandera in North East Kenya in October 2016 that killed six Christians.[12] The insurgency has successfully resisted the Somali government in Mogadishu, which launched Operation Indian Ocean to clean up the remaining pockets of guerrilla resistance and secure what Doboš in this volume has described as the "deterritorialization" of Al-Shabaab. Nevertheless, the sheer longevity of the Somali civil war has to some degree traumatised sections of the population rather like the brutal civil war in Algeria in the 1990s. The country is unlikely to emerge as a major centre of new jihadist insurgency in the next few years, compared to some other societies where jihadism has the potential to galvanise large and alienated younger populations not so familiar with long periods of insurgent war.

One potentially dangerous new war zone is Yemen where a bitter civil war, raging since early 2015, has been exacerbated by the external intervention of regional rivals Saudi Arabia and Iran. The conflict has its roots in the overthrow of the authoritarian president Ali Abdullah Sallah in 2011, which failed to lead to any sort of effective political transition: a problem shared by several other states in the Middle East and North Africa where weak civil society structures lead to a political vacuum at the centre following the overthrow of long-standing strongman regimes. The institutions of the state in these instances become severely weakened or even collapse as examples of what used to be termed "failed" states; this leads centripetal forces to take over, resulting in rising political factionalism, warlordism and, in the case of Yemen, full-scale civil war in one of the poorest states in the region. By August of 2016, the eighteen-month civil war had killed an estimated 10,000 people, small by the standards of the Syrian civil war, but one made more intractable by its sectarian nature. The predominantly Sunni regime of President Abd-Rabbu Mansour Hadi has been supported by a regional alliance led by Saudi Arabia against a rebel group of Shi'a-leaning Houthis (they come from a Shi'a sect known as Zayidism) backed by the Iranians.

Since the chapters in this collection were written it has become increasingly clear that the civil war in Yemen has the potential, unless brought under control, to escalate into a major regional war between Saudi Arabia and Iran. It demonstrates the capacity of modern insurgent conflicts to escalate rapidly if the rival parties become proxies for rival powers in a region already beset by distrust and rivalry. It also reflects the highly uneven nature of war reporting and media interest in zones of conflict around the world. The Yemeni civil war has the potential to drag on for years with relatively little international attention, rather like the Great Lakes conflict in Central Africa. There is little great power interest in bringing the conflict to an end, given that Yemen has no major oil resources and lacks the strategic position of Iraq and Syria. There is no major exodus of Yemeni refugees to Europe and the country appears too remote to represent any sort of major strategic threat no matter who is in power, unless the conflict spills over into regions where the west does have significant interests such as the Gulf States and Oman.[13] The example provides a good insight into the media roots of modern international terrorism: if a conflict devastating a society is not enough to gain international attention, then more drastic forms of global attention-seeking may be required like support for a movement or movements already categorized as representing terrorist threats to the west and its security, and core values: like the old *Ultrabrite* toothpaste advert "it gets you noticed."

The operation of global media is crucial to the way that Jihadist insurgencies expand and develop. Outside the Middle East, "Al Qaeda" and "ISIS" are, to a considerable degree, brand labels since there is considerable doubt over how much actual support the rival movements can really deliver to movements at the local level in terms of money, weapons, recruits, and organizational support. The brand labels can be taken up and later dropped by rival insurgent leadership anxious to prove themselves to their youthful followers and dangerous to the global media. This rivalry becomes an important dynamic in the expansion of terrorism in regions such as West Africa. Jason Burke has described how rivalry between Al Qaeda and ISIS acts as an incentive for newer groups to establish themselves as rival to older groups, in a pattern all to reminiscent from the sociology of teenage gangs. A new faction calling itself the Islamic State in the Western Sahara has emerged, for instance, in the West African state of Burkina Faso, partly in response to an ongoing insurgency in neighbouring Mali by Al Qaeda in the Maghreb (AQIM), a movement broadly aligned with Al Qaeda – though security consultants tend to down-play its longer-term threat to the region given the pressure that ISIS is now under in Iraq and Syria.[14]

What, after all, does it **mean** for a movement to "align" itself with a larger "parent" body? We are rather a long way from the thesis, so prominent in terrorism studies in the late 1970s and 1980s, that international terrorism was, in some way, a grand conspiracy fomented by the KGB, despite the momentary appeal of the American author Claire Sterling's two books. *The Terror Network* (1981) and *The Time of the Assassins* (1984).[15] There is little evidence to suggest, either, that there is a global terrorist jihad or some form of closely linked "insurgent archipelago," though theories of this kind have pandered to populist rhetoric on the right in both Europe and the United States.[16] Jihadist insurgent movements remain both complex and decentralized: they pose a security threat at both the local and regional levels. Some of the larger and more developed cells can serve as potential reservoirs for recruits to underground terrorist cells in the west. In addition, many of these cells can make use of social media to recruit followers from abroad, either as potential new recruits willing to travel to war zones or to engage in home-grown terrorist attacks which may be only on the small scale such as knifings or shootings of selected targets.

It is thus impossible to speak of any "wave" of Jihadist terrorism being even remotely "spent," given that processes of social and political marginalization continue and jihadist ideologies still offer a promise of identity and hope to groups of alienated and disaffected Islamic youth scattered around the world. The future patterns of radicalization will depend, however, not only on internal factors within the Islamic world but external political processes in the west as well as Russia and the way that "counter terrorism" policies are managed.

Here the election of Donald Trump must inevitably give cause for concern, though populist politicians in the US have traditionally exhibited unstable ideological attachments that lead to a significant incongruity between words and deeds. But Trump has certainly made various strands of "racist" discourse politically more acceptable on both sides of the Atlantic even before he has entered the White House, while attacks on the "political correctness" of metropolitan liberal elites makes the liberal agenda of "deradicalization" of marginalized Islamic youth somewhat harder to achieve. So far, the United States has been largely isolated from the huge numbers of refugees fleeing to Western Europe from the Syrian civil war and from further desolate economies in Eritrea, Afghanistan, and parts of West Africa. It remains an open question how far these new immigrant communities can be satisfactorily "absorbed" into the societies of Western Europe: even if many find jobs, this is not an automatic guarantee against future radicalization given that Jihadist appeals can often have as much impact on relatively affluent or well-off youth as those without jobs. Prisons too will certainly serve as major recruiting grounds and, if terrorist attacks such as those in France continue, there is the prospect of increasingly repressive government policies emerging in the future in Western Europe in efforts to control or at least contain future jihadist-style movements.

Notes

1. The film can be criticized for replacing the older cinematic orientalism of fantasy concerning the Arab world and the Middle East centred on mysterious sheikhs, camels, intrigue, and the dark winding streets of Baghdad with a newer orientalism of complexity that effectively subjugates the viewer with myriad narratives that are hard fully to understand. This is an outlook that has dangerous implications given that Donald Trump initially called for a complete shutdown on all Muslim immigration to the US "until our representatives can figure out what is going on," *The Atlantic*, December 7 2015.
2. Robin Wright, "How the Curse of Sykes-Picot still haunts the Middle East," *New Yorker*, April 30 2016.
3. Marc Grossman and Simon Henderson, *Lessons from Versailles for Todays Middle East*, Yale Global Online, 22 October 2014. www.yaleglobal.yale.edu. Accessed 4 December 2016.
4. See for instance, Nader Hashemi, "Why Syria Matters," *The Cairo Review of Global Affairs*, Spring 2014. www.thecairoreview.com. Accessed 5 December 2016.

5. John Bew, "The Syrian Civil War and the return of great power politics," *New Statesman*, 15 December 2015.
6. Jihadist terrorism has been partly examined in the recent *Small Wars & Insurgencies* special issue 28–01 2017 entitled "Countering insurgencies, terrorism and violent extremism in South Asia," edited by Shanthie De Souza.
7. Martin Chulov, "Al-Nusra Front cuts ties with AL Qaeda and renames itself," *The Guardian*, 28 July 2016.
8. Daniel Byman, "Fighting salafi-Jihadist Insurgencies: How much does Religion Really Matter?" *Studies in Conflict and Terrorism*, 36, 5, 2013.
9. Ewan MacAskill, "International Libya Force readied as dozens killed in Tunisia," *The Guardian*, 7 March 2016.
10. Jason Burke, "Nigerian clashes cast doubt on claim that Boko Haram is on its knees," *The Guardian*, 20 November 2016.
11. Jacob Zenn, "Nigeria: Boko Haram is not 'defeated' but Buhari's strategy is working," *African Arguments*, 5 January 2016. www.allafrica.com. Accessed 1 December 2016.
12. *Daily Telegraph*, 6 October 2016.
13. Said Bourrich, "Why do some wars like the Syrian Civil War get more attention than others, such as the Yemeni civil war?" *Quora*, October 2 2016, www.quora.com. Accessed 2 December 2016.
14. Jason Burke, "ISIS and al-Qaida turf wars in Africa may push fragile states to breaking point," *The Guardian*, 6 October 2016.
15. Those involved in prosecuting Palestinian terrorists in the 1970s captured by the police tended to see the Soviet Union as being only peripherally involved in what one Italian magistrate told Loretta Napoleoni was a "chain of terrorist Do-it Yourselfs across the Middle East" that the Palestinian were left to manage. Loretta Nepoleoni, *Terror Inc: Tracing the Money Behind Global Terrorism*. Harmondsworth: Penguin Books, 2004, 72. The concept of "do it yourself" terrorism can be, to some extent, reapplied to some modern jihadist insurgent movements who are initially supported by seed money from the parent terror organization such as Al Qaeda or ISIS and then left to fend for themselves.
16. John Mackinlay, *The Insurgent Archipelago*. London: Hurst 2009.

Index

Note: Page number in **bold** type refer to figures
Page numbers in *italic* type refer to tables
Page numbers followed by 'n' refer to notes

Abbas, Mallam 164
Abbasid Caliphate 52
Abbottabad letters 193–4
Adji-Kosseï base 173
al Adl, Saif 19
al Adnani, Abu Mohammed 36
Afghan Algerians 190, 191
Afghan-Soviet War 9–10, 16, 19, 73, 242
al-Afghani, I. 216
African Peace and Security Architecture 173
African Standby Force (ASF) 173
African Union (AU) 102, 216
African Union Mission in Somalia (AMISOM) 217
Afuwa, Husseini 165
Ag Ghali, Lyad 187
AIAI (Al-Itihaad Al-Islaam) 214
Aideed, M.F. 6
Air France hijacking 190
Al Jihad movement (Egypt) 58
Al Qaeda (AQ): Abbottabad letters 193–4; affiliates 6–7, 77; al Zarqawi 59–61; leadership in Afghanistan 61; merger with ISIL 66; political–religious ideology 58; rivalry with IS 245; worldwide franchiser 77, 193, 245
Al Qaeda in the Arabic Peninsula (AQAP) 77, 193
Al Qaeda in Iraq (AQI) 24, 58, 60, 61, 77
Al Qaeda in the Islamic Maghreb (AQIM): and Boko Haram 180; criminal revenues 198–201; historical roots 190–1; hotel attacks (2015) 186, 192–3; kidnapping 200, 201, 202; Libya 99–100; Niger 175; objectives and ideology 191–3; Operation Serval 178; organizational structure 193–6; organized crime 200–1, 202; overview 186–8; recruitment 195–6; relationship with the population 196–8; smuggling 199; Timbuktu letters 194, 197
Al-Shabaab: and Al Qaeda 217, 221, 225n46, 225n47; deterritorialized operative manner 223, 224, 244; economic output of Somalia 219–20; Ethiopian invasion 216; global jihad 218, 226n50, 226n51; ideology 224; internal fragmentation 216, 217, 222; rhetoric 217–18, 226n48; security threat 244; sharia law 218; Somalin infrastructure 220–3, 226n67; taxation 219; territoriality **222**, 223; urban and economic centres 218–19
Algerian civil war 190
Algerian Salafist Group for Preaching and Combat 159
Algerian war for independence 82, 86n37
American Soldier, The (Stouffer) 140–1
Ametetai valley 197
AMISOM (African Union Mission in Somalia) 217
Amnesty International (AI) 154, 171
Anbar Awakening 62, 63, 65
Anbar province 37, 44n101
Anbar Sunni protest movement 35
Ansar al-Shar'ia 77–8
Ansar al-Sharia Libya 98
Ansar al-Sharia – Derna 98
Ansar Dine 178, 187, 198
apocalyptic vision 84, 119, 125n66

INDEX

AQAP (Al Qaeda in the Arabic Peninsula) 77, 193
AQI (Al Qaeda in Iraq) 24, 58, 60, 61, 77
AQIM *see* Al Qaeda in the Islamic Maghreb (AQIM)
Arab Counter Revolution 7
Arab nationalism 58
Arab Spring: media-savvy democratic movements 7; regimes' brutal response 11–12; social movements 78, 86n22; Tunisia 59; West misreading 12
Arab Winter 59
archaeological sites destruction 50, 52, 198
Armstrong, D. 53
Asbat al-Ansar (League of Partisans) 59
ASF (African Standby Force) 173
al-Assad, Bashar 12, 118
al-Assad, Hafiz 19
assassination campaigns 21, 22, 40
Ataturk, Kemal 51
ATPs (Awaiting Trial Prisoners) 154
Atran, S. 141
AU (African Union) 102, 216
Awaiting Trial Prisoners (ATPs) 154
Awakening movement 17, 20–1, 24–5, **26**, 42n32
Aweys, H.D. 216
Azzam, Abdullah 73, 74, 76

Baathist regimes 56
Baathist state 11
al Baghdadi, Abu Bakr 36, 54, 241
al Baghdadi, Abu Omar 24, 36, 37, 119, 158–9, 162n34
Bakker, E. 113, 116, 235; and de Bont, R. 234; and Grol, P. 118; Grol, P. and Weggemans, D. 114, 118
Balandier, G. 11
band of brothers 140–1
Bandura, A. 141
Baqubah 25, 29–30, *29*, **29**
Baqubah Sahwa movement 30
al-Barnawi, Khalid 165–6
Barre, President 214, 215, 243
Barrera, General 178
Bataillons d'Intervention Rapide (BIR) 176
Battar Brigade 99
Belmokhtar, Mokhtar 159, 186, 187, 195, 199–201
Ben Ali, Zimine 59
Benghazi moment 91
Berg, E., and Kuusk, E. 213
Bertelsen, P. 132
Bew, J. 242

bin Laden, Iman 62
bin Laden, Osama 7, 58, 60, 76
BIR (*Bataillons d'Intervention Rapide*) 176
Black Hawk Down 6
Boeke, S. 5
Boko Haram: African / Arab jihadist groups 162n37; allegiance to IS 158, 180; AQIM links 180; atrocities committed 154, 156, 171, 243; coexistence with infidels 157, 162n29; criminality / violating sharia 155; doctrine 159; doves 164–5; financial sources 156, 161n27; hawks 165–7; local sect to regional threat 151–7; marriage customs 151, 160n5, 160n6; mercenaries 154–5; nickname 151, 160n3; opportunists 167; overview 150–1; prison breakouts / radicalization / convictions 153–4, 161n11; security forces abuse 152, 155–7; women's involvement 158, *see also* French counterterrorism
Bolshevik revolution 53, 240
Bremer, P. 57
Buduma of Lake Chad Islands 155
Buhari, Muhammadu 157, 171, 243
Burke, J. 245
Byman, D. 243

caliphates: caliph as a prince 8; deliberate construction 79; Gwoza 158, 162n32; Islamic State creation (2014) 54; past 52; re-emergence of idea 58, 62, 236
Cameroon military aid 176, 182n61
Cameroonian Army 176–7
Cappuccino Café 186
Castroite revolution 11, 18
Chad, Lake 157, 171
Chadian Army 169, 170, 171, 174–5
charismatic figures 119
Che Guevara 11
Chechen fighters 64
Chechen guerrilla tactics 64
Church and state separation 8
cigarette smuggling 199
Civilian Joint Task Force (CJTF) 154, 161n16
clanism 215
Cold War 16
collective defence and group membership 211
communist ideology 233
communist movement 54
Community of Defenders of Black Muslims 159

250

INDEX

Conflict Records Research Centre (CRRC) 36, 44n96
Context group 118, 125n125
conventional warfare 222
Coolsaet, R. 115, 116
Corymbe (anti-piracy operation) 176
counterinsurgency doctrine 196, 234–5
Cromwell, Oliver 55
CRRA (Conflict Records Research Centre) 36, 44n96
cyberspace 211–12

Dabiq (IS magazine) 234
Daesh *see* Islamic State (IS)
Dan Fodio, Usman 155
Daoud, Mahamat 166
Darood clan 215
Dawa 63, 138
Dawn coalition 94
de Bont, R., and Bakker, E. 234
death penalty for terrorists 171
Déby, Idriss President 170–1
Defence of the Muslim Lands, The (Azzam) 73
Degauque, Muriel 111
della Porta, D. 139
Democratic Unionist Party 55
Département du Renseignement et de la Securité (DRS) 191
Derrida, J. 83
Diani, M. 139
Diem regime 16, 21, 22, 62
Diffa state of emergency declaration 156
Dobos, B. 244
Dodge, T. 57, 62
Droukdel, Abdelmalek 186, 190, 191, 192, 195, 198
DRS (Département du Renseignement et de la Securité) 191
drug trafficking 189, 199–200, 201
Duyvesteyn, I.: and Fumerton, M. 189, 196, 202; and Rich, P.B. 231

Ecomog militia 155
Egypt: Mubarak government 76; Muslim Brotherhood 59
Eljarh, M. 99
embassy bombings 58, 76
Enlightenment values 82
eschatological visions 84, 119, 125n66
ethnic nationalism 242–3
ethno-territorial conflicts 212
EU Maritime Force (EUNAVFOR Med) 102
Eurojust 112

European Union Training Mission (EUTM-Mali) 177
extrajudicial executions 156, 191

Fabius, Laurent 169
failed states 244
Falk, R. 92
Fall, B. 16, 23
Fanon, F. 84
far enemy 74, 75, 78, 188, 192, 193
Faraj, Muhammad 73
FARC (Fuerzas Armadas Revolucionarias de Colombia) 111
Farook, Syed Rizwan 234
fi sahat al-jihad (field of jihad) 6
Filiu, J.-P. 7, 188
Fishman, B. 92
Foi, Bugi 164
foreign fighter syndrome 80–3
foreign fighters: action preparedness 137–9; age 113–14, **113**; Algeria 81, 86n36; case studies 132, 134–5, 136, 138, 145; definition 131; faith 114, 119, 125n66; geographical origin 112–13, **113**; life embeddedness 133–5, 137, 143, 145; marital status 116, **116**; numbers 81, 123n1, 123n2, 123n4; overview 109–12, 130–2; peer pressure 83, 119; phenomenon 111–17; pull factors 118–19; push factors 117–18; radicalization in jail 143, 145; recruitment 135–7; research 110, 123n5, 132–3; roles 120–2; sex 114, **114**, 124n32; social affiliation 116–17; social dynamics 119–20; socioeconomic background and education 115, **115**, 117; Syria and Iraq 81, 86n35; threat of those that return 141–3, **141**; who stays behind and why 139–41, 144; women 122
Fowler, Robert (hostage) 195, 200–1
framing theory 136
France: anti-piracy operation 176; bilateral military cooperation 172, 174, 181n13; military assistance to Chadian Army 174–5; as primary target of AQIM 193; strategy in Africa 180
Freedom Summer (1964) 139
French counterterrorism: Africa 172–3; Cameroonian Army 176–7; Chadian Army 174–5; Elysée summit 168, 170; Malian Army 177–8; Nigeria 169–72; Nigerian Army 175–6; Operation Barkhane 179–80; overview 168–9; RECAMP program 173; Sahel 178–80

French military bases in Africa 172–3, 181n14
French National Assembly 175
Fromson, J., and Simon, S. 51
Fuerzas Armadas Revolucionarias de Colombia (FARC) 111
Fumerton, M., and Duyvesteyn, I. 189, 196, 202

Gaddafi, Colonel 54, 89, 242
Gaghan, S. 240
Galtimari Commission 152, 153
Galula, D. 17, 196
gang warfare theorists 19
Garma 25, 27–8, *28*, **28**
Gartenstein-Ross, D. 34
GCTF (Global Counter Terrorism Forum) 201
General National Congress (GNC) 94, 95, 97
Gerges, F.A. 90
al-Ghawi, Khalifa 97
GIA *(Groupe Islamique Armée)* 178, 190, 191, 193
Gillier, Vice-Admiral 176
Giwa military barracks 154
Global Counter Terrorism Forum (GCTF) 201
Global Islamic Resistance Call, The (al-Suri) 74, 85n9
global jihad: foreign fighter syndrome 80–3; ideology 73–5; initial challenge 75–7; overview 72–3; strategic alternative 77–8; third way 78–80
GNC (General National Congress) 94, 95, 97
Godane, A. 216, 217, 218, 224, 244
Governance in the Middle East and North Africa (Kadhim *et al.*) 90
Great Lakes conflict in Central Africa 245
greater powers 9–10, 241, 242
grey zone 74, 80
Grol, P.: and Bakker, E. 118; Bakker, E. and Weggemans, D. 114, 118
group identification 137
group membership and collective defence 211
group polarization 137, 138
group think 119, 138
Groupe Islamique Armée (GIA) 178, 190, 191, 193
GSPC *(Groupe Salafiste pour la Prédication et le Combat)* 159, 191, 194

Guépard rapid reaction force 173, 178, 182n76
guerrilla insurgencies 9, 10–13
guerrilla movements 6, 8
guerrilla warfare 6, 63–4
Guidère, M. 188
Gurr, T.D. 212

Haddad, F. 55
al Hadi, Abd 32, 43n84
Hadi, Abd-Rabbu Mansour President 244
al Hadithi, Samir Safwat 27
Haftar, General 93, 95, 96, 101, 105n23
Hamaha, Oumar Ould 187
Hansen, S.J. 215, 216
Harakat al-Shabaab 243–4
Hassan, Abubakar 164
Hausa fish traders 155
Hawiye clan 215
Hegghammer, T. 49, 68n8, 119
Hegira uprising 58
Herbst, P. 188
Hirst, P. 53
al-Hisbah agents 121
Ho Chi Minh regime 22
Hoffman, B. 66
Holder vs. Humanitarian Law Project 2–3
Hollande, François President 168, 172
homeland as symbolic place 211
homoerotic idealism 83
hostages converting them to Islam 201
House Homeland Security Committee 81
House of Representatives (HoR) 94, 95, 96, 105n28
al-Hukayma, Muhammed 66
Husayn, Sharif 58
El-Hussain, Omar Abdel Hamid 145–6
Hussein, Saddam 56–7

Ibn Khaldun 17, 18, 37–9
Ibn Taymiyyah, Ahmad 158
ICU (Islamic Court Union) 215, 216, 217, 243
ideological warfare 16
IGC (Iraqi Governing Council) 62
illicit goods 199
Ingram, H. 35
Inspire (Al Qaeda publication) 21–2
insurgency: meaning 189; political goal of governance 192
insurgent leaders' writings 10
Integrity and Reform Commission 93
international actors 212
International Brigades 111
international order (Westphalian) 52

INDEX

international terrorism as KGB conspiracy 245, 247n15
Iran: foreign policy 2; Islamic Revolution 73, 85n4; Sunni attitudes towards 82
Iraq: American invasion 82, 242; foreign fighters 81, 86n35; sectarian war 11, 12; sectarianism 56; Shi'ite-dominated coalition 61; Sunni provinces 16
Iraqi Body Count database 24, 25–6
Iraqi Governing Council (IGC) 62
Iraqi Security Forces (ISF) 63, 65
ISCI (Islamic Supreme Council of Iraq) 63
ISIS (Islamic State of Iraq and the Levant) see Islamic State (IS)
Islam: forced conversion to 201; recruits' knowledge of 9; Salafist interpretation 8; socio-political role for 236
Islam For Dummies 9, 13n7
Islamic Court Union (ICU) 215, 216, 217, 243
Islamic jurisprudence 232
Islamic law: absolute and complete implementation 231, 233, 236, 238; Al-Shabaab 218; criminality of jihadist groups 155; divinely inspired obligations 2, 73, 85n5, 138, 233; gradual imposition strategy 197, 198; Taliban 237; understanding of 3, 9
Islamic Revolution Iran 73, 85n4
Islamic state of Azawad 195
Islamic State (IS): and Al Qaeda (AQ) 66, 245; foreign fighters 64, 66; founding 11, 16, 40n5; in Libya 98–9; political goals 17; pseudo-state 16, 41n7; religious ideology 2, 3, 23, 231, 235–6; revolutionary warfare 17–18; status in international law 51; terror group 17, 41n10; weaponry 64–5
Islamic State in West Africa 158
Islamic State in the Western Sahara 245
Islamic Supreme Council of Iraq (ISCI) 63
Islamic youth deradicalization 246
Islamic Youth Shura Council (IYSC) 99
Islamist Shura Council of Benghazi 98
al-Issawi, Rafi 63
Issoufou, Mahamadou 175, 176
Al-Itihaad Al-Islaam (AIAI) 214
IYSC (Islamic Youth Shura Council) 99

Jabhat al-Nusra 6
Jabhat al-Sham 242
al Janabi, Ahmad Muzahim 33
al Janabi, Sabah al Azab 32, 33
Jaysh Rijal at-Tariqa an-Naqshbandiyya (JRTN) 79

al-jihad fi sabil Allah (striving in the way of God) 1
jihad meanings 1, 3, 8, 19, 232–3
jihadist insurgency defining 8–10, 231
jiziya (canonical taxes) 79, 86n26
Joffés, G. 237–8
Join the Caravan (Azzam) 73
Joint Task Force (JTF) 152
Jones, J. 141
JRTN (*Jaysh Rijal at-Tariqa an-Naqshbandiyya*) 79
JTF (Joint Task Force) 152
Jurf ah Sakhr 25, 27, **27**, *28*, 32–4, 39, 42n57

Kadhim, A.K., *et al.* 90
Kaplan, J. 73
al Karamah (Dignity) campaign 24, 32
katiba (fighting unit) 194
Katibat al-Mulathameen (The Masked Brigade) 195
Kato da Gora (the men with clubs) 154
Kelman, H.G. 141
Kennedy, P. 67
KGB conspiracy, international terrorism 245, 247n15
Khalaf, R. 51
Khalil, J. 189–90
al-Khansaa brigade 122
Khomeini, Ayatollah 57
kidnapping 200, 202
Kilcullen, D. 190
Kismayo (port) 219
Korbin, S. 211
Kuperman, A. 91–2
Kurds 60
Kuusk, E., and Berg, E. 213

Landsturm 67
LAS (League of Arab States) 91
Le Drian, J.-Y. 179, 197
League of Arab States (LAS) 91
League of Nations Mandate 56–7
Lebovich, A. 188
Lee, D. 35, 36, 43n92
Leninist vanguard parties 52–3
Libya: and AQIM 197; armed conflict 90, 104n5; external actors 100–2, 105n49; Islamic groups 76; national elections 92–3, 94; NATO intervention 90–2, 103, 104n12, 242; overview 89–90; partition (2014–15) 92–5; post-intervention plan 92, 103, 104n20; rival parliaments 94–5; second civil war 89, 103; US involvement 91, 104n10; violence against citizens 91–2; warring parties 96–100

253

INDEX

Libya Islamic Fighting Groups (LIFG) 98
Libya Shield Force 97
Libyan Ministry of Defence 97
life embeddedness 133–5, 137, 143, 145
life psychology 133
LIFG (Libya Islamic Fighting Groups) 98
Lord's Resistance Army 157

McAdam, D. 35, 139
McCuen, J. 17–18
Mackinlay, J. 190
Mahamat, Brahim Seid General 170
Maitatsine Islamic sect 157
al-Majmaai, Shaykh Houssam Ulwan 30
Maktab al-Khidma 74
Mali: and AQIM 197, 198, 202; *coups d'état* 177; European Union Training Mission (EUTM-Mali) 177; government drug trade corruption 199–200
Malian Army 177–8
al Maliki, Nuri 57, 62–3
Maliki, Prime Minister 21, 42n32
Management of Savagery, The (Naji) 66–7
Mao, Chairman 16, 19, 40
Mardini, R. 29–30
Mark, David Colonel 156
Marret, J.-L. 188
marriage customs: AQIM 197; Boko Haram 151, 160n5, 160n6
Marshall, A. 7
martyrdom cult 74–5
Marxism–Leninism utopian ideology 53
Marxist movements 11
al-Mawdudi, Abu al-Ala 57
Mayer, A. 52
media: Arab Spring 7; power and importance 67, 245; social media audience 52
MENA (Middle East and North Africa) 90, 104n1
Menkhaus, K., and Shapiro, J.N. 214
mental health, jihadists 116
Metz, S. 10, 18
Middle East: overthrow of states 50; Western imperial thinking 12
Middle East and North Africa (MENA) 90, 104n1
migrant crisis 102, 170, 242, 243, 246
Milestones (Qutb) 192
military strategies 5–6, 202
Misrata brigades 97
MJTF (Multilateral Joint Task Force) 170, 171
MNLA (Mouvement national de libération de l'Azawad) 187, 194

Mogadishu 10, 219–20
Mosul 25, 30–2, **31**, 42n59, 43n78
Mouvement national de libération de l'Azawad (MNLA) 187, 194
Mouvement pour l'unicité et le Jihad en Afrique de l'Ouest (MUJAO) 187, 195, 199
Movement for Oneness and Jihad in West Africa (MUJWA) 178, 182n71
Mozambique 8
Muduq region 219
al Muhajir, Abu Hamza 24, 36
Mujahideen Shura Council 23
mujahidin movements 75
MUJAO (Mouvement pour l'unicité et le Jihad en Afrique de l'Ouest) 187, 195, 199
MUJWA (Movement for Oneness and Jihad in West Africa) 178, 182n71
multiculturalism (British) 83
Multilateral Joint Task Force (MJTF) 170, 171
Al-Muntada Trust Fund 159, 162n38
Muqadimmah, The (Ibn Khaldun) 18
al Murabitoon 186, 187
Muslim Brotherhood 2–3, 58, 59, 93, 97, 100
Muslim chiliasm 84
Muslim minority communities 82–3
Muslim World League (WML) 58
Mustapha, Jimoh 166
Mwangi, O.K. 216
myth-making (modern) 52

Nada, Ahmad 30
Naji, Abu Bakr 66–7, 80
Napoleoni, L. 60
Nasser, Gamel Abdel 54
national liberationist Marist movements 11
near enemy 188, 192
Neglected Duty, The (Faraj) 73
Neumann, P. 230
New Middle East, The (Gerges) 90
Niger: *coups d'état* 175; Salvador Pass 179; travel ban 157
Nigeria: emergency rule (2013) 154; Presidential Committee 153; security forces abuses 155–7
Nigerian Army 169, 171–2, 175–6, 243
NigeriaWatch database 156
Nijmeijer, Tanja 111
Ninewa, Wilayat 31
non-state actors 209, 213
al Nusra Front 79, 242

INDEX

al-Obaydh, Abdulfattah 78
al-Obeidi, Hameed Khaleel 30
OIC (Organization of Islamic Cooperation) 58
oil sales 79
Okacha, Djamel 194
Omar, Sheikh Ahmed 244
Operation Anaconda 61
Operation Barkhane 169, 179–80
Operation Dawn 97
Operation Dignity 94, 95, 96
Operation Epervier 173
Operation Indian Ocean 244
Operation Serval 169, 178–9, 195, 197, 200, 202
Operation Snake's Sting 95
Orange Order in Northern Ireland 55
Organization of Islamic Cooperation (OIC) 58
organized crime 189, 200–1, 202
Ottoman empire 12

Palestinian issue 82
Palmyra ruins 52
Papal Zouaves 111
Paris underground bombing (1995) 190
party legitimacy and taxes 23
peace and security prospects: counterinsurgency 234–5; greater powers role 241, 242; jihad motivation and appeal 233–6; jihad understanding the meanings 232–3; overview 230–1; perpetual struggle 236–7; Western political transformation 243
peer pressure 83, 119
People's Revolutionary Party 22
Petraeus, General 62
piracy, Somalia 218
political defining moments, global 6, 243
political isolation law 93, 94
political outreach techniques 34
political power objective 2
political process model 35
political territoriality 211, 223
political vacuum 244
post-intervention plan for Libya 92, 103, 104n20
Powell, Colin 60
Powell, V. 55
prison radicalization 143, 145, 153
psychological problems (jihadists) 116
psychological weapons 36

Puntland 214, 215
Puritan radicals 55
Putnam, R.D. 139

Qaddafi, Muammar 54, 89, 242
Qutb, Sayyid 57, 66, 192, 236

racist discourse of Trump 246
radicalizing milieus 136, 144
Radisson Blu hotel 186, 192–3
Ramadi 65
ransom payments 201
Rapoport, D. 72, 73, 85n4
RECAMP program 173
recruitment: AQIM 193; foreign fighters 135–7; religious / ideological knowledge 9, 83; to war zones or home-grown attacks 246, *see also* foreign fighters
Red River Delta 23
refugee crisis 102, 170, 242, 243, 246
regional jihadist terrorist movements 50–1
religious beliefs: and guerrilla insurgencies 10–13; hold on followers 234; local and communal identities 10; and politics 8; role in insurgencies 1, 11, 13n12, 234; and secularism 235
religious ideology: Islamic State 23; politicised sacred texts 9
Republican Medina Division 25
revolutionary jihadist insurgencies: containment policy 63–7; Islamic State and Iraq 56–9; Islamic State rise of 59–63; manufactured medievalism 52, 237; national liberation and sectarianism 54–6; overview 49–54; regional movements 50–1
revolutionary warfare: assassination campaigns 21, 22, 40; Awakening deaths 34; campaign against traitors 22–4; coercion, co-option, and carrots 36–9; demise 16, 40n4; discussion 34–6; hypothesis 19–21; Islamic State (IS) 17–18, 26–7, **32**, 39; overview 15–17; Salafist-jihadism 18–19; Sunni resistance 24–5, *34*; Vietnamese communists and IS (comparing) 21–3
revolutionary warfare theory 17
rhetoric 217–18, 226n48, 237
Rich, P.B. 233; and Duyvesteyn, I. 231
righteous war narrative 51
Robow, M. 216

255

INDEX

Rosenthal, J. 97
Russia, Bolshevik revolution 53, 240

Sack, R. 210–11
al Sada, Muktada 63
al-Sadr, Baqir 57
al-Sadr, Sadiq 57
safe houses 120
Sageman, M. 83, 113, 114, 116
Sahel countries 174
Sahwa: Al Qaeda in Iraq (AQI) 77; attacks **33, 35**; deaths 26; repentance offer to 36–7, *see also* Awakening movement
Salafi-jihadism 16, 73, 74, 192
Salafism 74, 85n6
Salafist Group for Preaching and Combat 99–100
Salem, Lemine Ould 199
Sallah, Ali Abdullah President 244
Salvador Pass 179
San Bernadino situation 234
Saudi Arabia: international system 237; Wahhabism 9
Sayigh, Y. 92, 104n21
Scheele, J. 199
Schmid, A. 189
sectarianism: active / passive 55–6, 60; definition 55; MENA 54–5
secularism 235
Security Council Resolutions 51, 67, 91
Shapiro, J.N., and Menkhaus, K. 214
sharia law: absolute and complete implementation 231, 233, 236, 238; Al-Shabaab 218; criminality of jihadist groups 155; divinely inspired obligations 2, 73, 85n5, 138, 233; gradual imposition strategy 197, 198; Taliban 237; understanding of 3, 9
Sharia4Belgium 112, 116, 118, 119–20
Shariff, Ali Modu 155
Sharqistaan 222
Shekau, Abubakar 152, 158, 159, 162n32, 166, 170, 243
Sherif, Ali Modu 152
Shi'ism 57
Shi'ite revolutionary ideology 49
Shura Council of Benghazi Revolutionaries 98
Simon, S., and Fromson, J. 51
Sinn Fein 55
smuggling 199
social media 52
Social Movement Theory 35, 36, 135, 136

social movements: global appeal 77; seeking to resemble 84; study of 136, 137
soldiers harvest campaign 65
Somali nationalism 217
Somalia: civil war 243; clan structures 215; as a collapsed state 212, 223; economic output 219–20; Ethiopian invasion 216, 221; infrastructure 220–3, 226n67; Kenyan invasion 218, 224; overview 209–10; piracy 218; political territoriality 210–14; population density 219, *see also* Al-Shabaab
Somaliland 214
sovereign states (Westphalian) 50, 209
Soviet Commissariat of Foreign Affairs 53
Soviet state identity 53
Spain, Napoleonic invasion 10, 13n10
Spanish civil war 82
Splendid hotel 186, 192–3
Staniland, P. 212
state-controlled economy 56
statehood crisis 11
Sterling, C. 245
Stevens, Christopher Ambassador 78
Stouffer, S.A., *et al.* 140–1
suicide attacks 75, 121, 131, 158, 171
Sunni jihadism 75
Sunni protest camp at Hawija 63
al Suri, Abu Musab 19, 20, 27, 74, 76
Sykes Picot conspiracy 241
Syria: al-Assad regime brutality 118; Baathist regime 12; demonstrations 59; foreign fighters 81, 86n35; guerrilla movements 6; mobilisation of the people 67; refugee crisis 243, 246; revolutionary movement (2011) 243; Russian intervention 242
Syriana (2005) 240, 246n1

Taber, R. 19
Tablighi Jamaat (Society for Spreading Faith) 159
takfir concept 20, 190
Talebans of Nigeria 151, 158
Taliban in Afghanistan 19, 193, 237
Tawhid wal Jihad 19–20
al Tawid al Yihad 60
taxes 23, 79, 86n26
territoriality 210–11, 223
Terror Network, The (Sterling) 245
terrorism, definition 189
Terrorism Act (2013) 153, 161n9
terrorism *vs.* organized crime 200–1, 202

INDEX

TFG (Transitional Federal Government) 215, 216, 217
theocratic doctrine 57
Tibherine monks, beheading 190
Tikrit 65
Timbuktu letters, of AQIM 194, 197
Timbuktu shrines 198
Time of the Assassins, The (Sterling) 245
TNG (Transitional National Government) 215
Toure, Amadou Toumani President 199
Tozy, Mohamed 83
training camps 19
Transitional Federal Government (TFG) 215, 216, 217
Transitional National Government (TNG) 215
travel ban 157, 162n28
Treaty of Brest Litovsk (1918) 53
Treaty of Paris (1955) 22
Treaty of Versailles (1919) 241
Treaty of Vienna (1815) 7
tribal outreach officer 37–9, 44n100
Trotsky, L. 53
Trump, Donald 246
Tuareg separatist 175, 177, 178, 187, 194
Tunisia: demonstrations 59; dignity revolution 11–12; multi-party regime 7
Turaki, Malam Kabiru 153
Tzu, Sun 67

Umaru, Mallam Sanni 152, 159
ummah 50, 76
Ummayad Caliphate 52
UN (United Nations) 237; High Commissioner for Refugees 170; Multidimensional Integrated Stabilization Mission in Mali (MINUMSA) 187; Support Mission in Libya (UNSMIL) 95
United Arab Republic in Egypt 58
United Nations (UN) 237
USS *Cole* 58, 76

Van Ostaeyen, P. 114
Van San, M. 117–18
Versailles Peace Settlement (1919) 12–13
Viet Cong assassination campaign 21, 22
Vietnam, Diem government 21
Vietnamese People's Revolutionary Party 16
violence as religious obligation 3, 232, 233
Violence Without Moral Restraint (Kelman) 141
Vollaard, H. 211
von Clausewitz, C. 67

Waffen-SS 111
Wahhabism (Saudi Arabia) 9
war crimes 171–2
War of the Flea, The (Taber) 19
weaponry: availability in Iraq 59; Islamic State (IS) 64–5; supply 5, 79
Weenink, A. 116
Weggemans, D., Bakker, E. and Grol, P. 114, 118
Wehrey, F. 99
Westphalian model of international order 50, 52, 209
Whiteside, C. 53
WML (Muslim World League) 58
World Islamic Front against Jews and Crusaders 58

Yemen war zone 244–5
Yusuf, Abib 167
Yusuf, Mohammed 151, 152, 155, 156, 158, 164–5

Zaidi, I.H. 213–14
al Zarqawi, Abu Musab: death 24; failures 16; indoctrination of members 20, 42n29; key role in Al Qaeda 59–61, 77; relationship with Droukdel 191; sectarian strategy 61; training camp 19
Zawahiri, Ayman 66, 76, 77
Zeidan, Ali 93, 105n24